MACROECONOMICS
THEORY AND POLICY

SECOND EDITION

MACROECONOMICS
THEORY AND POLICY

SECOND EDITION

Fred R. Glahe

University of Colorado

HARCOURT BRACE JOVANOVICH, INC.

New York   Chicago   San Francisco   Atlanta

To my parents

ISBN: 0-15-551266-8

Library of Congress Catalog Card Number: 76-39626

Printed in the United States of America

Preface

Like the first edition, the second edition of *Macroeconomics: Theory and Policy* provides a rigorous but mathematically simple treatment of macroeconomic theory, measurement, and policy. We have retained the essential character of the first edition and continue to emphasize graphic exposition.

A comparison between this book and a macroeconomics textbook of twenty years ago would reveal differences due primarily to the impact of one person: Milton Friedman, the 1976 Nobel laureate in economics. Friedman's contributions to monetary theory, consumption theory, international finance, economic history, and macroeconomic theory have produced what may well be a counterrevolution in economic thought. Without doubt, he is the most influential economist of the third quarter of the twentieth century. In this textbook we provide a systematic and coherent integration of Friedman's contributions to macroeconomic theory and policy within the traditional *IS-LM* framework; we also present the contrasting views of economists who disagree with all or part of the Friedman paradigm.

The most significant change in coverage in this edition is the addition of Chapter 15, "International Trade and Finance." This chapter emphasizes international finance and examines the economic problem of maintaining equilibrium in the balance of payments without sacrificing full employment or price stability. To accomplish this, we explore the rudiments of international exchange markets and the balance of payments. We extend the *IS-LM* model to incorporate international trade and finance. The extension used, which is unique to this book, explicitly incorporates variable domestic and foreign price levels within a manageable framework.

In addition to the construction and application of an open macroeconomic model, we have made the following changes in the second edition.

1. By presenting capital and investment theory (Chapter 5) before consumption theory (Chapter 6) in this edition, we are able to introduce the concept of present value before the intertemporal theories of consumption.

2. We have expanded Chapter 5 to include a discussion of the present value criterion of investment decision making and an explanation of the superiority of this criterion to the internal rate criterion.

3. Chapter 6 now includes an examination of the life-cycle hypothesis and its relationship to the permanent income hypothesis. To explain this relationship, we employ the fundamental Fisherian two-period consumption optimization theory.

4. Chapter 8, "The Supply of Money," now includes an examination of the various definitions of money and the recent institutional changes that have made these definitions critical. The graphic derivation of the money supply function has been improved and clarified.

5. The discussion of the Phillips curve has been greatly expanded, and we now use the natural rate of unemployment hypothesis to explain the joint occurrence of high unemployment and inflation.

6. The discussion of the current U.S. inflation in Chapter 13 ("The Monetarist Interpretation of History") has been updated and expanded. In this chapter we also critically examine Peter Temin's challenge to the Friedman-Schwartz interpretation of the great depression.

7. Chapter 16 ("Macroeconomic Policy") is essentially new. The views and recommendations contained there follow directly from the theory and empirical evidence presented in the preceding chapters. Thus students will not be left with the impression that there are no answers to current economic problems.

In addition to these major changes, there have been many minor additions and deletions. Throughout this edition we have kept the exposition as readable and accessible as possible.

In the preparation of the second edition I have benefited from the comments and suggestions of many of my colleagues at the University of Colorado—especially Barry Poulson, Robert McNown, and Larry Singell. I am also indebted to Richard Lipsey of Queens University, Kingston, Ontario, Canada, and to James Buchanan of Virginia Polytechnic Institute and State University, for their comments. I wish to thank the reviewers of the second edition: George H. Blackford of the State University of New York at Buffalo, Harold C. Cochrane of Colorado State University, and Yash Mehra of Illinois State University. I also wish to thank Deborah Boswell, who so ably typed the revisions and additions for this edition. As always, I am grateful to my wife, Nancy, for providing an environment conducive to the writing of this book.

Fred R. Glahe

Contents

1 Measuring Macroeconomic Activity

1-1 Introduction

Macroeconomics is the branch of economics that seeks to answer such questions as: What determines the level of unemployment? How is the general price level determined, and what is the relative importance of the various factors that influence it? What determines the level of macroeconomic activity and its growth or decay over time?

In contrast to macroeconomics, *microeconomics*, the other main branch of economics, seeks to answer such questions as: How is the purchasing behavior of an individual influenced by the price of a commodity? How does a firm determine the quantities of resources to buy and the way they are to be combined to produce goods and services? What determines the pattern of distribution of the goods and services that the economy produces?

Whereas microeconomics can be studied without any reference to macroeconomics, the converse is not true; consequently we must employ certain tools and theories of microeconomic analysis in this book. Except for a rudimentary knowledge of supply and demand analysis, no knowledge of microeconomics is assumed. When specific microeconomic tools and theories are introduced, they are explained prior to their use.

Macroeconomic analysis is concerned with why macroeconomic activity is at a given level and how this level can be raised or lowered. It is evident that prior to any understanding or control of this activity we must be able to measure it. The branch of macroeconomics that is concerned with measuring macroeconomic activity is called *national income accounting*. In this chapter we examine the conceptual framework on which national income accounting is based and define certain fundamental macroeconomic variables are used extensively in this book.[1]

1-2   Stocks and Flows

In this book we will be dealing with two kinds of variables: *stock* variables and *flow* variables. Stock variables are measured *at a given instant in time,* whereas flow variables are measured *over a period of time.* For example, consider a barrel of cider. When the barrel is full, say, at 12 noon on July 4, 1976, it contains 33 gallons of cider. This quantity is the *stock* of cider at this instant in time. Now suppose that the barrel is tapped and one 12-ounce glass is poured every 30 seconds. The *flow* of cider is 24 ounces per minute, or 11.25 gallons per hour. Note that the flow variable has a time dimension (gallons per hour), whereas the stock variable does not—it merely exists. In this particular example, with a flow of 11.25 gallons per hour, the stock of cider at 1 P.M. on July 4, 1976 will have declined to $33 - 11.25 = 21.75$ gallons.

Now consider the following example, in which a continuous flow is produced by a stock that does not diminish but remains constant. Suppose that on January 1 you deposit $100,000 in a savings account in a bank that pays an annual interest rate of 5% on such accounts. Your deposit, which is a stock, will pay in interest $0.05 \times \$100,000 = \$5,000$ per year. This payment of interest has a time dimension and must therefore be a flow variable. However, in contrast with our previous example, as long as the bank continues to pay 5% and you make no withdrawals from the initial deposit, the flow of $5,000 per year will continue indefinitely. If you leave all or a portion of the interest payment in the account and make no withdrawals, then the stock and flow variables will grow simultaneously.

In this example, if your entire stock of wealth were the $100,000 and you did not work, then the $5,000 per year would be your personal income. If the rate of interest remained at 5%, you would be able to consume $5,000 of goods and services per year permanently.

1-3   National Income

One of the most widely used measures of macroeconomic activity is the *gross national product* (GNP), which is defined as *the market value of all final goods and services produced by a nation's economy during the course of a year.* Because the

---

[1] We do not attempt to explain all the details and complexities involved in the actual measurement of these variables. To do so adequately would require the equivalent of a small book. The following references are suggested: J. P. Powelson, *Economic Accounting* (New York: McGraw-Hill, 1955), Chapters 14–20; U.S. Department of Commerce, *National Income: A Supplement to the Survey of Current Business* (Washington, D.C.: U.S. Government Printing Office, 1954); and U.S. Department of Commerce, *U.S. Income and Output: A Supplement to the Survey of Current Business* (Washington, D.C.: U.S. Government Printing Office, 1958).

GNP is measured in dollars of goods and services per year, it is a flow variable. The goods produced can be subdivided into *consumer goods* and *producer goods.* Consumer goods include those products that are usually purchased by households (examples are bread, milk, and shoes). Producer goods, or as we shall more often refer to them, *capital goods,* include those products that are usually purchased by business firms (examples are machinery, warehouses, and factories). Clearly many goods could serve as either consumer goods or capital goods. For example, if a firm purchases a camera to photograph its products, then the camera is a capital good; if a household purchases a camera to photograph its members, then it is a consumer good. Hence the ultimate purchaser determines whether a good is a consumer good or a capital good.

In our definition of gross national product the word *final* is critical, because without it we might end up with an exaggerated measure of real production due to *double counting.* For example, when we buy a newspaper its market value should obviously be added to the national product figures. But what about the newsprint and ink purchased by the newspaper publisher? Should they be included in the gross national product as well? No, because newsprint and ink production are already included in the production of the newspaper. Adding their value to the GNP would result in their being counted twice. The ink and newsprint are examples of *intermediate goods.* Only final goods and services, which are composed of intermediate goods and services, are included in the gross national product.

Production of the final goods and services that constitute the GNP occurs when three primary factor inputs—*land, labor,* and *capital*—are employed by business firms. If we assume that the quantity of land is constant and that departures from the labor force are exactly matched by arrivals, then the only factor of production subject to change is the capital stock. The capital stock can change because as capital is used in the production process it undergoes wear and tear, and unless it is replaced as it wears out, the stock will gradually decline. Now if the stock of capital is allowed to decline, then the economy's maximum attainable GNP in any given year will similarly decline. To prevent this decline in output and to maintain a constant GNP potential, the portion of the capital stock that is consumed in the production process must be replaced. Some of the goods produced by the economy are capital goods, and if the quantity of capital goods produced is equal to the quantity of capital consumed, the capital stock will remain constant.

It is evident that if an economy wishes to maintain a constant standard of living as its minimum goal, then the total annual output of its goods and services cannot be entirely devoted to the satisfaction of individual or social wants. Some of the economy's total output must be used for capital replacement, and hence the maximum amount of goods and services that can be consumed will be less than the GNP. This measure of the maximum amount of goods and services available for consumption is called the *net national product* (NNP) and is obtained by subtracting the value of the capital consumed in the production process K_c from the GNP, or symbolically,

$$NNP = GNP - K_c \qquad (1\text{-}1)$$

Personal income is defined by economists as an individual's maximum continuous command over goods and services. *National income,* which is the sum of all personal incomes, must therefore be equal to *a nation's maximum continuous command over goods and services.* This definition of national income is equivalent to our definition of net national product, so that

$$Y \equiv NNP \qquad (1\text{-}2)$$

where Y is national income.[2]

National income can be measured via two different approaches, which in the absence of errors and omissions yield identical results. The first approach measures the sum of all income payments to the factors of production for the use of their services, whereas the second measures the amount of expenditures on all final goods and services that comprise the net national product. These two approaches are equivalent, because the former measures the left-hand side of identity (1-2) and the latter measures the right-hand side.

Income-received Approach

Using the income-received approach, we define national income as

$$Y = Y_w + Y_r + Y_i + Y_{\pi r} + Y_{\pi d} \qquad (1\text{-}3)$$

where Y_w = income paid to individuals in the form of wages, salaries, commissions, bonuses, and other forms of employee earnings before deductions for taxes

Y_r = net income from rentals and royalties

Y_i = interest income

$Y_{\pi r}, Y_{\pi d}$ = business profits (retained and disbursed, respectively) of corporations, partnerships, and proprietorships before taxes

Disposable income is a concept very close to national income, and as we shall learn in Chapter 3 it plays an important role in the determination of aggregate demand. *Disposable income is the maximum purchasing power of households out of current receipts,* and it is symbolically defined as

$$Y_d = Y - Y_{\pi r} - T_x + T_r \qquad (1\text{-}4)$$

where Y_d = disposable income

T_x = taxes

T_r = transfer payments

For simplicity we assume throughout this book that all taxes are *direct taxes* and that there are no *indirect taxes.* Direct taxes can be either *income taxes* or *poll taxes;* examples of indirect taxes are the sales tax and the excise tax. The amount

[2] In the national income accounting procedures of the U.S. Department of Commerce a narrower definition of national income is employed, with the result that the accounting measure of national income is slightly less than NNP. For our purposes identity (1–2) is conceptually correct.

of revenue raised by an income tax depends on the level of income. Because we will be constructing a theory of income determination, the amount of revenue so raised will be determined within the model; therefore an income tax is called an *endogenous* tax. The poll or head tax raises a fixed level of revenue (for a given population size) independent of the level of income; therefore, it is called an *exogenous* tax.

A *transfer payment* is a payment of money to an individual by the government or a business firm for which there is no corresponding service or good exchanged in the accounting period. Examples of transfer payments are veterans' benefits, social security payments, medicare, aid to dependent children, the school lunch program, and charitable gifts donated by firms. Transfer payments can be considered negative taxes. Therefore, if we define *net taxes T* to be equal to taxes *minus* transfers, then equation (1-4) can be expressed as

$$Y_d = Y - Y_{\pi r} - T \qquad (1\text{-}5)$$

Throughout this book, when we refer to "taxes" we mean *net taxes* (unless otherwise specified), which are represented by the symbol *T*.

In our definition of disposable income we use the term "receipts" rather than "earnings" because, as should now be clear, the amount of income received (disposable income) is not necessarily equal to the amount of income earned, due to the presence of retained business profits, taxes, and transfers.

Equation (1-5) may be rewritten

$$Y = Y_d + Y_{\pi r} + T \qquad (1\text{-}6)$$

and because the disposable income of households can either be spent on consumer goods and services or saved, equation (1-6) can be expressed as

$$Y = C + S + Y_{\pi r} + T \qquad (1\text{-}7)$$

where C = consumption expenditures of households
S = savings of households

Expenditure Approach

If we measure national income by calculating the total value of expenditures on the final goods and services that comprise the NNP, then we use the definition

$$Y = C + I + G + (Ex - Im) \qquad (1\text{-}8)$$

where C = household expenditures on consumer goods and services
I = net investment
G = government purchase of goods and services
$(Ex - Im)$ = exports *minus* imports, or net exports

With the exception of expenditures on consumer goods and services, which we have already mentioned, we now examine each of the broad categories of expenditures specified in equation (1-8).

We have previously explained that if the level of income is to remain constant, then a portion of the gross national product must be used for capital replacement. In this situation the level of gross investment I_g (that is, the economy's total expenditure on capital goods) is equal to K_c, and hence the level of net investment, defined as

$$I = I_g - K_c \qquad\qquad (1\text{-}9)$$

must be zero. This need not be the case. If the level of gross investment exceeds the quantity of capital consumed in the production process, then net investment will be positive, the capital stock of the economy will grow, and this in turn will cause the flow of national income to grow. Alternatively, if $I_g = 0$, then the capital that has been consumed is not being replaced and we have a negative net investment equal to K_c. In this situation the capital stock will decline over time.

Investment (gross and net) includes the purchase of *business structures,* such as manufacturing plants, warehouses, and stores, and *producer's durable equipment,* such as lathes, milling machines, typewriters, and trucks. The category of investment also includes expenditures on all *residential structures,* including both owner-occupied and rental housing.

One form of capital good that does not immediately suggest itself is *inventory.* A firm must have sufficient inventories of intermediate goods (if it is a producer) or of final goods (if it is a retailer) to conduct its business efficiently. Hence inventories are one part of the firm's capital stock. If the economy were static, then inventories of intermediate and final goods would remain fixed from year to year and we would not be concerned about their impact on national income. However, because we do not have a static economy and in the past firms have erroneously estimated their actual inventory needs, the stocks of inventories often change drastically from one year to the next. The stock of inventory goods is a part of the economy's stock of capital, so that changes in the inventory stock are equivalent to net investment flows. When the stock of inventories increases, positive net investment is occurring; when the stock of inventories decreases, negative net investment is occurring. Hence the *change* in the level of inventories of either intermediate or final goods during the course of a year is included in the calculation of that year's level of net investment.

The federal, state, and local governments of the United States are major purchasers of the final goods and services produced by business firms. The government also makes direct purchases of resources; these are primarily the labor services supplied by government employees. There has long been a debate over whether government purchases should be divided between those for consumption purposes and those for investment purposes. Many argue, for example, that the purchase of a school building should not be treated in the same way as the purchase of the electricity needed to light the school building. Instead of trying to categorize all government purchases as either consumption or investment, the standard practice in national income accounts is to have only one category of goods and services that is simply called *government.* Not all government expenditures are included in this category, however. Because they are not part of production, government transfer payments such as federal old-age benefits, medicare, and veterans' benefits are excluded.

To varying degrees all economies are *open* economies; that is, they engage in international trade. The object of computing national income is to measure economic activity, so that it is logical to include the market value of all exported goods and services in the national income. Even exported goods that are intermediate goods in the production process in some other country are final goods in the exporting country and should be included in that country's national income. For the same reason we must be certain *not* to include the market value of imported final goods and services in the national income. The market value of imported intermediate goods (for example, foreign-manufactured transistors in domestically produced electronic equipment) must be subtracted from the sale price of the good containing them. If we do not do this, then the market price of the good will give us an inflated measure of the economic activity. In our example, if the full market price of the electronic equipment is used, the national income figures will falsely imply that the imported transistors were produced domestically. To prevent this we could subtract the cost of the transistors from the final market price of the product in which they are used. In actual practice, however, we do not subtract the imported component directly from domestic goods and services. Instead, we deduct the total value of all imported goods and services from the total value of all exported goods and services. The effect is the same, but this indirect method is computationally easier.

Throughout this book we assume that retained business profits are zero; that is, $Y_{\pi r} = 0$. This assumption does not significantly distort any of the conclusions we shall reach regarding macroeconomic theory or policy. Also, in Chapters 1–14 we will concern ourselves with the construction and analysis of a macroeconomic model of a closed economy and will not take up the problems associated with international trade and finance until Chapter 15. Hence in Chapters 2–14 we will assume that Ex − Im = 0. Incorporating this assumption into equation (1-8) and the assumption that retained business profits are zero into equation (1-7), we obtain the following definitions of national income, which will be employed intensively throughout this book:

$$Y = C + S + T \qquad\qquad (1\text{-}10)$$

$$Y = C + I + G \qquad\qquad (1\text{-}11)$$

1-4   Popular Misconceptions About National Income Accounts

Probably the most popular misconception about national income accounts is that they were devised to measure social welfare. It is true, of course, that some relation exists between the GNP and social welfare, but this relation is not exact nor is it intended to be. National income accounts were actually devised to measure changes in the level of economic activity, not in the quality of life. A typical measure can clarify this point. As incomes rise, the number of automobiles per capita also rises. But the automobile pollutes the air over our major cities, and in the absence of antismog devices air pollution and respiratory diseases will rise. The increase in disease raises the income of hospitals, physicians, nurses, drug companies, mortuaries, and others, and this is duly recorded as an increase in the GNP. Such increases in the GNP can hardly be equated with rising social welfare.[3]

Another popular misconception is that the total production of goods and services is recorded in national income accounts. Where activities such as gambling and prostitution are illegal, their market value is excluded from these accounts. This may seem inconsistent when we realize that the market value of these activities in the state of Nevada, where they are legal, is recorded by the national income accountant. By adopting the arbitrary rule of excluding all illegal transactions, the national income accountant is freed from having to decide what is of social value.

Many economic activities do not have market valuations, and their values must be imputed. One example of such an imputation is the value of the food and fuel produced and consumed on a farm. Another is the service performed by financial intermediaries such as banks. However, the total of these inferred values is quite small compared to the total value of the nonmarket activities that are excluded. For example, if you have a garage tune the engine of your car, then the cost of parts and labor is entered in the national income accounts. But if you tune your engine at home, only the cost of the parts you purchased is entered in these accounts. The labor services you rendered to yourself are ignored. If a member of the household takes care of the home, washes clothing, and prepares meals, these services are not included in national income. But if a maid and a butler are hired, their services are included. Theoretically, it would be possible to assign values to these as well as other economic activities and to add them to the national accounts, but for practical purposes a line must be drawn somewhere. Where this line has been drawn in the income accounts is not as important as the fact that it has been drawn, so that the accounts can be maintained consistently from one year to the next. After all, it is not the measured value of the GNP in any year that particularly interests us; it is the change in the GNP that reflects changing economic activity. This is especially true when our main concern is to prevent high unemployment levels or rising prices. Consistency in the national accounts facilitates our measurement of this change.

1-5   Measuring Income and Product Over Time

One of the first things you learn in mathematics is that you cannot add apples and oranges. We applied this rule to our analysis of national product and income when

---

[3] For a discussion and critique of one attempt to obtain a measure of economic welfare (MEW) see Kenneth Stewart, "National Income Accounting and Economic Welfare: The Concepts of GNP and MEW," *Review of the Federal Reserve Bank of St. Louis* (April 1974), 18–24.

we defined national product in terms of the market value of all final goods and services. We are not able to sum such items as automobiles, magazines, and toothpaste; to obtain some measure of production we must sum their market values (price *times* quantity) in dollars.

This method permits us to compute the national income, but it raises two additional problems, which can be classified as the price-level problem and the quality problem.

The Price-level Problem

If the prices of goods and services remain constant from one year to the next and if all other conditions remain equal, changes in the dollar value of the GNP over time accurately reflect the underlying changes in production. For example, if the GNP in 1946 was $209.6 billion and in 1975 was $1,499 billion and prices remained constant, then we could conclude that economic activity in this 29-year period increased more than seven times. But suppose that instead of prices remaining constant, inflation occurred and the price of most goods and services rose. To compare the 1946 market value of the GNP with the 1975 market value would then clearly result in an exaggeration of the real change in economic activity. This bias can be removed if we have an appropriate price index that can be used to "deflate" (that is, adjust) the GNP figures measured in prices existing at the time when the GNP was computed. The price index used to "deflate" GNP figures in the United States is called the *implicit price deflator for the GNP,* and it is prepared by the Bureau of Economic Analysis, U.S. Department of Commerce. It is called an *implicit* deflator because it is not computed directly. Each subcomponent of a component of the GNP (for example, the single-dwelling residence subcomponent of the gross investment component) is first measured in prices that are prevailing or current during the time period in which the economic activity occurred. These data are then deflated by the appropriate price index for that subcomponent, and the resulting figures are said to measure, with respect to the base period of the price index, the volume of output in the subcomponent in real or constant dollars. After all subcomponents of a particular component have been deflated, they are summed to give the value of the GNP component in constant dollars. Next, all components are summed to give the GNP in constant dollars. By dividing GNP in current dollars by GNP in constant dollars and then multiplying this amount by 100, we implicitly derive the GNP price deflator. This can be mathematically stated as

$$IPD_t = \frac{GNP_t}{RGNP_t} \times 100 \tag{1-12}$$

where IPD_t = implicit GNP price deflator for year t
   GNP_t = GNP in dollars that were current in year t
   $RGNP_t$ = real GNP in year t, measured in terms of base-year dollars

The GNP figures for the United States during 1946–75 appear in Table 1-1. The second column of the table lists GNP in prices that prevailed during the year in

TABLE 1-1   GNP Statistics

Year	GNP in Billions of Current Dollars	RGNP in Billions of Constant 1972 Dollars	Implicit GNP Price Deflator (1972 = 100)
1946	209.6	475.7	44.06
1947	232.8	468.3	49.70
1948	259.1	487.7	53.13
1949	258.0	490.7	52.59
1950	286.2	533.5	53.64
1951	330.2	576.5	57.27
1952	347.2	598.5	58.00
1953	366.1	621.8	58.88
1954	366.3	613.7	59.69
1955	399.3	654.8	60.98
1956	420.7	668.8	62.90
1957	442.8	680.9	65.02
1958	448.9	679.5	66.06
1959	486.5	720.4	67.52
1960	506.0	736.8	68.67
1961	523.3	755.3	69.28
1962	563.8	799.1	70.55
1963	594.7	830.7	71.59
1964	635.7	874.4	72.71
1965	688.1	925.9	74.32
1966	753.0	981.0	76.76
1967	796.3	1,007.7	79.02
1968	868.5	1,051.8	82.57
1969	935.5	1,078.8	86.72
1970	982.4	1,075.3	91.36
1971	1,063.4	1,107.5	96.02
1972	1,171.1	1,171.1	100.00
1973	1,306.3	1,233.4	105.92
1974	1,406.9	1,210.7	116.20
1975	1,499.0	1,186.4	126.35

SOURCE   *Economic Report of the President*, 1976 (Washington, D.C.: U.S. Goverment Printing Office), pp. 171, 172, and 174.

which the production of goods and services occurred. The third column lists the values of GNP in constant 1972 dollars, obtained in the manner just described. Dividing the second column (GNP) by the third column (RGNP) gives us the value of the implicit GNP price deflator, in the fourth column. For example, the 1960 GNP measured in 1960 dollars is $506 billion; the same GNP measured in dollars of 1972 purchasing power is $736.8 billion. Hence the implicit deflator is $(GNP_{1960} \div RGNP_{1960})100 = (506 \div 736.8)100 = 68.67$.

The implicit GNP price deflator is the best overall measure of aggregate price change that we possess.[4] An examination of Table 1-1 reveals that the general trend of prices in the United States has been upward over the last 29 years. A comparison of RGNP figures from different time periods can provide a fairly accurate estimate of changes in economic activity. Once again, consider the 1946 and the 1975 GNP figures of $209.6 billion and $1,499 billion, respectively. Consulting Table 1-1, we see that these figures are measured in current, or nominal, dollars; therefore, our earlier estimate of a sevenfold increase in production is biased upward. We can, however, compare output in constant 1972 dollars, and this comparison shows that real GNP has increased only about 2.5 times instead of 7.2 times. To avoid this type of confusion, all economic variables in this book, unless we explicitly state otherwise, are considered to be given in real terms.

The Quality Problem

Over long periods of time the quality of some products, such as aspirin or table salt, does not change; it remains constant. Hence, if 100 five-grain aspirin tablets cost $0.50 in 1930 and the same amount sells for $1.00 today, we can conclude that the doubling in price is a purely inflationary phenomenon unrelated to any change in the product. However, few products or services in our economy have not undergone major quality changes over the years.

In January 1930, a fully equipped Ford sedan sold for $600 in Detroit (bumpers and spare tire extra). Today, a fully equipped Ford sedan sells for over $5000. If we were simply to compare the prices of these two cars, ignoring quality change, we would erroneously conclude that the price of automobiles increased approximately eight times. Obviously, we cannot ignore the quality differences in these two products, because much of the increase in the price of the current model over the 1930 model can be explained as the result of an increase in quality. The new Ford is a vast improvement over the 1930 car, featuring, for example, power steering, power windows, power disc brakes, air conditioning, and V-8 engine. The Bureau of Labor Statistics, which computes the wholesale price index of automobiles, attempts to take into consideration the quality changes in automobiles each year. When certain safety features, such as head restraints, collapsible steering columns, and shoulder harnesses, were required by federal law, the price of automobiles increased. But because part of this increase was attributable to quality changes (the added safety features), the wholesale price index of automobiles was raised proportionately less than the price of the automobiles themselves. The actual

---

[4] Other price indexes, such as the consumer price index and the wholesale price index, are also used to measure price change, but they are not as well suited to measuring the general level of prices as the GNP deflator. For an excellent introduction to price indexes and their limitations see William H. Wallace, *Measuring Price Changes: A Study of the Price Indexes* (Richmond, Virginia: Federal Reserve Bank of Richmond, 1970).

computations involved in adjusting for quality changes can become quite complicated.[5]

With regard to the services side of national product, little or no attempt is made to adjust for quality changes. If we consider the quality changes in haircutting over the last quarter century or compare the Boston Symphony of 1946 with that Symphony today, it is probably justifiable to ignore any potential change in quality. With regard to medical services, however, this is clearly wrong. We all complain about the high cost of this service, but is it justifiable to compare the $2 office call of 1939 with the $14 office call today and say that the price has risen seven times? Who would prefer to be treated by the 1939 physician, given the advances that have been made in medical science? Nonetheless, quality changes of this nature are usually ignored because it is difficult to make adjustments for them.

1-6   Concluding Remarks

In this chapter we have emphasized the conceptual framework on which the national income and product accounts are based. We defined *gross national product* as the total output of all final goods and services in a given period of time and *national income* as the maximum annual continuous command over goods and services. National income and gross national product were shown to differ by an amount equal to capital replacement. For simplicity, we assumed that retained business profits and international trade do not exist; this enabled us to define national income as $Y = C + I + G$, or $Y = C + S + T$. Although no attempt was made to explain all the details and complexities involved in actually computing national income statistics, some of the major problems presented by these computations and their treatment in national income accounting were discussed. Of particular importance was the method of "deflating" national income statistics measured in current dollars to obtain time-series data in constant, or real, dollars.

[5] For example, see Zvi Griliches, "Hedonistic Price Indexes for Automobiles: An Econometric Analysis of Quality Change," *Government Price Statistics Hearings,* U.S. Congress, Joint Economic Committee, January 24, 1961 (Washington, D.C.: U.S. Government Printing Office, 1961), pp. 173–96. Reprinted in *Readings in Economic Statistics and Econometrics,* Arnold Zellner, ed. (New York: Little, Brown, 1968), pp. 103–30.

2 Aggregate Supply

2-1 Introduction

One of the main objectives of this book is to construct a macroeconomic model that can be used to determine the equilibrium levels of national income and prices. This model employs the economist's two most powerful but simplest tools—demand curves and supply curves. The particular curves we will use are those of aggregate demand and aggregate supply. The *aggregate demand curve* depicts the quantity of national income, or net national product, that would be *purchased* at each general price level. The *aggregate supply curve* depicts the quantity of national income that would be *produced* at each general price level. In this chapter we construct two basic aggregate supply curve models, which will be used extensively throughout this book.

2-2 The Aggregate Production Function

The level of national income that an economy can produce depends on the quality and quantity of its *factors of production* (land, labor, and capital) and on its level of technology. The relationship between the factors of production and technology, on the one hand, and national income, on the other, is called the *aggregate production function,* which is written

$$Y = Y(K, N, L, T) \qquad (2\text{-}1)$$

where Y = national income
$\qquad K$ = tangible capital
$\qquad N$ = human capital, or more simply, labor
$\qquad L$ = land
$\qquad T$ = technology

Equation (2-1) simply says that income is a function of technology and the factors of production: land, labor, and capital.

In Chapters 2–16 we will be concerned primarily with short-run macroeconomic problems, for which it is reasonable to assume that capital, land, and technology are fixed. The employment of labor is assumed to be variable, and hence labor is the *variable factor of production in our model*.[1] Given these simplifying assumptions, the aggregate production function can be expressed as

$$Y = Y(N) \qquad (2\text{-}2)$$

Because land, capital, and technology are all fixed, the level of national income is a function only of the quantity of labor employed. As the employment of labor increases, the level of national income increases as well.

The aggregate production function in equation (2-2) is depicted graphically in Figure 2-1. The shape of the aggregate production curve is concave from below, indicating that as more and more workers are combined with the fixed factors of production, the additional, or marginal, worker adds a smaller and smaller amount to the quantity of national income produced. In other words, this production function assumes *diminishing marginal returns to labor* at all levels of employment.

Figure 2-1 tells us that if the level of employment of labor is N_0, then the level of national income produced will be Y_0. However, because we do not know the level

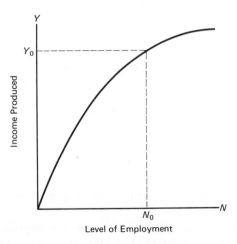

FIGURE 2-1   *The Aggregate Production Function*

[1] In Chapter 17 we will study economic growth and construct models in which labor, capital, and technology are all variable factors of production.

of employment, our immediate task is to construct a theory that determines employment.

2-3   The Aggregate Supply of Labor

To construct a theory of the aggregate supply of labor, we must first construct its microeconomic counterpart, which is based on the behavior of the individual. The individual is faced with the problem of deciding how much of the total available time in a given period (a day, week, month, or longer period) should be devoted to work and how much should be devoted to leisure. We assume that division of an individual's time between work and leisure will be influenced by the real wage he or she is offered. The *real wage* is defined as the money, or *nominal*, wage divided by the price level, or symbolically

$$\omega = \frac{W}{P} \tag{2-3}$$

where ω = real wage
$\quad W$ = money, or nominal, wage
$\quad P$ = price level

In addition we assume that the individual behaves rationally, which in economic theory simply means that he or she seeks to maximize personal welfare. As individuals maximize their welfare, they trade off leisure for work, and the extent of this tradeoff depends on the real wages they are offered.

The modern theory of consumer behavior provides us with the tools for analyzing individual choice. The horizontal axis in Figure 2-2 measures, from left to right, the number of hours per day spent in leisure, the maximum number being 24. Because all time is spent on either leisure or work, 24 hours *minus* leisure time must equal working time. Hence the number of hours spent working can be measured from right to left below the leisure time scale, as we have done in Figure 2-2. The vertical axis in the figure measures the daily real earnings of the individual in constant dollars. Suppose that the price level remains constant in our analysis and that it is equal to unity; then the daily real earnings simply equal the hourly nominal wage multiplied by the number of hours worked. In equation form, this can be expressed as

$$E = H \cdot \frac{W}{P} = H \cdot \frac{W}{1.0} = H \cdot W \tag{2-4}$$

where E = daily earnings in constant dollars
$\quad H$ = number of hours worked per day

Equation (2-4) expresses a linear relationship between earnings and hours worked for a given hourly wage. Therefore, this equation can be depicted in Figure 2-2 by a series of straight lines, all originating at the right end of the horizontal

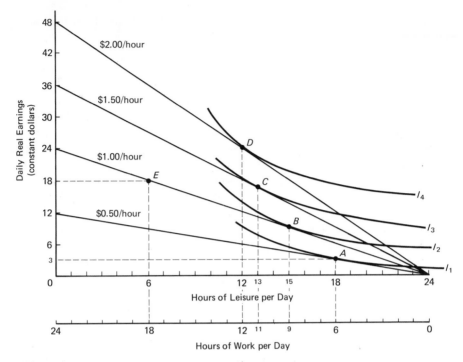

FIGURE 2-2   *Indifference Curve Analysis of Individual Behavior Toward Leisure and Work*

scales and intersecting the vertical axis at various points. For example, if the hourly wage is $1.00, then the straight line depicting equation (2-4) originates from the horizontal axis where zero hours are worked per day, because $E = (0)(1.0) = 0$, and intersects the vertical axis at a daily earnings of $24, because $E = 24 \times 1.0 = \$24$. For any number of hours worked between these two extremes, the daily earnings received can be read from this line. (If, say, 18 hours are worked per day and the hourly wage is $1.00, we would be at point E on the $1.00 per hour line in Figure 2-2 and the daily earnings would be $18.) As the hourly wage rises, the lines depicting equation (2-4) intersect higher points on the vertical axis, but the horizontal axis intercept remains at 24 hours of leisure per day. The hourly wage determines the slope of the straight lines, and these lines, referred to in the theory of consumer choice as *constraint lines*, geometrically represent the wage constraint under which an individual maximizes utility.

A hypothetical individual's set of *indifference curves* I_1, I_2, I_3, and I_4 are also shown in Figure 2-2. A given indifference curve depicts the various combinations of earnings and leisure that will maintain our hypothetical individual at the same level of utility; therefore, our individual is indifferent to a choice between any of these combinations. It is assumed that for a given number of hours worked per day the individual will always prefer more daily earnings to less. As more hours are worked, the individual can remain at the same level of indifference only if he or she is compensated with more daily earnings. Hence the indifference curves are negatively sloped. They are also normally assumed to be concave when viewed from above. In addition to these characteristics, (1) indifference curves cannot intersect, and (2) an indifference curve passes through every point in the earnings–leisure space (that is, there are an infinite number of indifference curves).

Any combination of earnings and work designated by a point on indifference curve I_4 will be preferred over any point on I_3, and thus I_4 represents a higher level of utility than I_3. By the same reasoning, I_4 and I_3 are preferred over I_2, and I_4, I_3, and I_2 are preferred over I_1. This can be stated symbolically as

$$I_4 > I_3 > I_2 > I_1 \tag{2-5}$$

Obviously, an individual is maximizing utility when he or she is on the highest attainable indifference curve. For a given real hourly wage, this maximization will occur at the point where an indifference curve is tangent to the corresponding wage constraint line. For example, when the hourly wage is $0.50, the highest possible indifference curve that can be reached is I_1, which is just tangent to the $0.50 per hour wage constraint line at point A in Figure 2-2. Faced with working for this hourly wage, our hypothetical individual chooses to work 6 hours per day and earn $3.00. Now suppose that the hourly wage rises to $1.00 per hour. Our individual is rational, so he or she moves to point B, where I_2 is just tangent to the $1.00 per hour wage constraint line, and begins working 9 hours and earning $9.00 per day. The utility-maximizing choices of the individual when offered hourly wages of $1.50 and $2.00 are designated by the respective points C and D in Figure 2-2. By varying the hourly wage rate in this fashion, we can determine the daily number of hours our individual will supply at any real hourly wage.

In Figure 2-3 the information on individual behavior derived in Figure 2-2 is presented in a slightly different manner to give us a *supply of labor curve*. The real

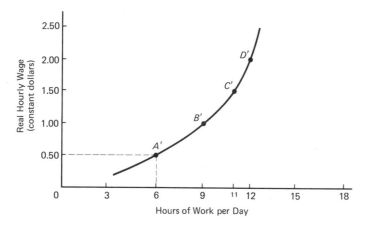

FIGURE 2-3   *An Individual's Supply of Labor*

wage per hour is plotted on the vertical axis, and the hours of work supplied per day, which now increase from left to right, are plotted on the horizontal axis. In Figure 2-2, if the hourly wage is $0.50, then the individual chooses to be at point A, working 6 hours per day. Point A' in Figure 2-3 corresponds to point A in Figure 2-2, with the difference that the vertical axis in Figure 2-3 measures the real *hourly* wage rather than *total* real earnings. In a similar manner, points B', C', and D' in Figure 2-3 correspond to points B, C, and D in Figure 2-2. The curve drawn through points A', B', C', and D' in Figure 2-3 is the individual's supply of labor curve, which we observe slopes upward to the right.[2] By changing the time span under consideration, an individual supply of labor curve for a week, month, year, or longer period can be derived similarly.

To derive an *aggregate supply of labor curve,* we simply sum the quantity of labor supplied by all individuals in an economy at a given real wage. By varying the wage offered we obtain a series of points that plot the curve for the aggregate supply of labor S_N. Such a curve is illustrated in Figure 2-4, where the vertical axis, as before, measures the real wage and the horizontal axis measures the number of units of labor supplied. The aggregate supply of labor curve has the same basic shape as the individual curve, but because the former represents the summed behavior of

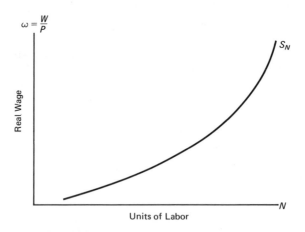

FIGURE 2-4   *The Aggregate Supply of Labor*

[2] Using a diagram similar to Figure 2-2, it can be shown that if the hourly wage rate rises high enough, the supply of labor may decrease and we may have a *backward-bending* supply curve. This means that if the individual's income grows sufficiently large, then he or she will choose to allocate further wage increases to the "purchase" of more leisure. We will not spend time analyzing this situation, because it does not seem to occur to any great extent in the developed nations. It may, however, be a very real phenomenon in the less-developed nations, and students from such nations should be alert to this culturally biased assumption as well as to others that no doubt appear in this book. An additional point worth mentioning at this time is that in many instances in economics the results obtained from theoretical analyses are ambiguous and the final answers depend on empirical research. We will reencounter this problem several times in the remainder of this book.

many individuals, its slope at any given wage is much shallower than that for the individual curve.

2-4   The Aggregate Demand for Labor

The theory of the aggregate demand for labor is also based on microeconomic analysis. The microeconomic unit that demands labor is the business firm. In this chapter we assume that the firm operates under the conditions of perfect competition and, for our present purpose, that it is so small that its behavior can have no effect on the price of the factors of production it buys or on the price of the product it sells. In other words, the business firm is what economists call a *price taker.*

Because we are interested in the firm's demand for labor and in what determines this demand in the short run, we also assume here that all factor inputs with the exception of labor are held constant. Stated another way, we assume that the only variable input available to the firm is labor. The firm can hire as many units of labor as it desires at the market-determined nominal wage of $10 per unit. Similarly, because we have assumed perfect competition, the firm can sell as many units of production as it wishes at the market-determined price of $21 per unit.

If a firm is to survive in perfect competition, then it must *maximize profits,* because the pressure of competition eliminates all profits in excess of the minimum amount required to maintain the firm's operations. It is obvious that a firm is not maximizing profits if its profits can be increased by hiring an additional worker. Hence a perfectly competitive firm will continue to hire additional workers up to the point where the marginal worker no longer increases profits. The manner in which the firm in our example determines its optimal level of employment is quite simple: As long as an additional worker contributes more to the revenue that the firm receives from the additional output he or she produces than the worker contributes to the costs of the firm, it will be in the interest of the firm to hire that worker. The change in the revenue received by the firm when it hires an additional worker is called the *value of the marginal product* VMP, which is simply the *marginal product of labor* MP_N multiplied by the price per unit P for which the product sells, or

$$VMP = MP_N \cdot P \tag{2-6}$$

Because the perfectly competitive firm can hire as many workers as it desires at the going money wage, the *cost of the marginal product* CMP is a constant equal to the money wage. As long as VMP $>$ CMP, a firm can increase its profits by hiring more workers. The firm will continue to hire workers up to the point where

$$VMP = CMP = W \tag{2-7}$$

Data for a typical perfectly competitive firm are given in Table 2-1. Column (1)

TABLE 2-1   The Profit-maximizing Employment Behavior of a Perfectly Competitive Firm

(1)	(2)	(3)	(4)	(5) $(3) \times (4)$	(6) Nominal Wage per $=$ Unit of Labor $W = CMP$ Nominal Cost of Marginal Product
Units of Labor N	Units of Total Product TP	Units of Marginal Product MP_N	Product Price per Unit P	Value of Marginal Product VMP	
0	0	—	$2	$ 0	$10
1	20	20	2	40	10
2	38	18	2	36	10
3	53	15	2	30	10
4	63	10	2	20	10
5	68	5	2	10	10
6	70	2	2	4	10

specifies the units of labor N that are combined with the fixed factors of production. Column (2) lists the total number of units of output, or the *total product* TP, that can be obtained with various quantities of labor. Column (3) gives the marginal product of labor MP_N; that is, the additional output that will be produced by an increment of labor. (Note that the figures in this column continually decline, indicating that we have *diminishing marginal returns* to labor.) In column (4) we have the price per unit for which the product sells P, which because we are in perfect competition, remains constant at $2. Multiplying the marginal product by the product price gives us the value of the marginal product VMP, in column (5). The wage per unit of labor is a constant that is equal to the cost of the marginal product CMP, as indicated in column (6).

We can readily see from the data in Table 2-1 that the value of the marginal product is greatest when only one worker is employed. However, the firm is obviously not maximizing profits at this level of operation, because hiring an additional worker would increase the firm's revenue by $36 and add only $10 to the firm's operation costs. Hence, the firm in Table 2-1 would continue to hire until it employed five workers, because at that level of employment the VMP of the fifth worker would exactly equal the CMP. At this point we may well ask why the firm would bother to hire the fifth worker when the impact of his or her employment on the firm's revenue and cost are equal. Why not stop at four workers? This conclusion would be valid if we could hire only whole units of labor. However, if we allow for the assumption that fractional units of labor can be employed, then as long as the firm hires less than 5 units, profits can be increased by hiring fractionally more than 4 units. The firm's profits will be maximized as it approaches employment of 5 units.[3]

The results of our calculations in Table 2-1 are graphed in Figure 2-5, where MP_N and VMP are both given on the vertical axis and the units of labor employed appear on the horizontal axis. Given a nominal wage of $10, the firm will hire 5 units of

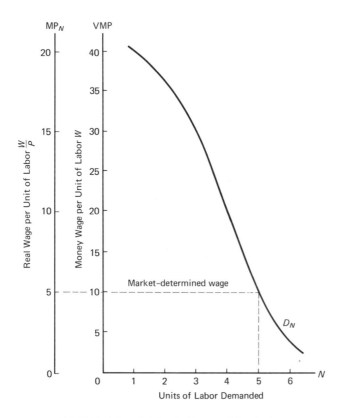

FIGURE 2-5   A Firm's Demand for Labor

[3] This can easily be proved if we use the optimizing techniques of differential calculus. Given the production function

$$TP = f(N) \qquad (2\text{-}7a)$$

if the supply of labor is infinitely elastic at money wage W and if the price of the firm's product is constant at P, then the firm's profits π can be expressed as

$$\pi = P \cdot TP - W \cdot N \qquad (2\text{-}7b)$$

Differentiating (2-7b) with respect to N and setting this equal to zero, we obtain

$$\frac{d\pi}{dN} = P\frac{dTP}{dN} - W = 0 \qquad (2\text{-}7c)$$

Since $dTP/dN = MP_N$, we obtain the result

$$P \cdot MP_N = VMP = W = CMP \qquad (2\text{-}7d)$$

labor to maximize profits. If the money wage rises to $20, then the firm will reduce its employment to 4 units. If we know the value of the money wage, then the curve drawn in Figure 2-5 indicates the number of units of labor the firm will demand. This curve is therefore the firm's demand for labor curve, and it is consequently labeled D_N.

If the worker chose to be paid not in money but in units of product, then the firm would pay the worker 5 units of product if the money wage were $10, because $W/P = 10/2 = 5$. Because the worker is being paid in units of product, we can call this the real wage. As the real wages of workers rise, fewer workers will be hired. This conclusion is shown in Figure 2-5, where MP_N corresponding to VMP appears on the vertical axis. Thus a profit-maximizing firm will hire workers up to the point where their wage in terms of the product they produce (their real wage) exactly equals the marginal product of the last worker hired. This can be easily proved by rearranging equation (2-7) to obtain

$$MP_N = \frac{VMP}{P} = \frac{W}{P} = \omega \qquad (2-8)$$

where ω = the real wage. Hence the firm's demand for labor is actually a function of the real wage of labor, and if the marginal product of labor diminishes as additional workers are hired, then the demand for labor curve will have a negative slope, as illustrated in Figure 2-5.

The aggregate demand for labor, like the aggregate supply of labor, is obtained by simply summing the total number of units of labor demanded by all firms in the economy at various real wages. Figure 2-6 illustrates the curve for the aggregate demand for labor D_N as a function of the real wage. Like the firm's demand curve, the aggregate demand curve is negatively sloped. Because it represents the summed behavior of many firms, its slope at a given real wage is much shallower than that for the individual curve.

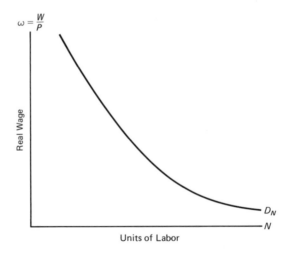

FIGURE 2-6   *The Aggregate Demand for Labor*

2-5   The Aggregate Supply Curve

The *aggregate supply curve* depicts the quantity of national income that would be produced at different price levels. In this section we derive two different aggregate supply curves. The first is based on the assumption that perfect competition exists in *all* markets. This implies that the money or nominal wage paid to workers is perfectly flexible upward or downward, because their decision to work or not to work is based solely on the real wage they are offered. The second supply curve is based on the assumption that perfect competition exists in all markets *except* the labor market. In this market we assume that the money wage paid to workers is perfectly flexible upward but absolutely rigid downward. In other words, workers will not or cannot accept any reduction in money wages irrespective of the price level and therefore irrespective of their real wage.

Flexible Wages: Perfect Competition in All Markets

The perfectly competitive aggregate supply model is based on the following system of equations:

$$Y = Y(N) \tag{2-2}$$

$$\omega = \frac{W}{P} \tag{2-3}$$

$$S_N = S_N(\omega) \tag{2-9}$$

$$D_N = D_N(\omega) \tag{2-10}$$

$$D_N = S_N = N_{FE} \tag{2-11}$$

where FE = full-employment level

We have already discussed equations (2-2) and (2-3). Equations (2-9) and (2-10) simply state in functional notation the conclusions we reached in Sections 2-3 and 2-4, namely, that the aggregate supply of labor and the aggregate demand for labor are functions of the real wage. Equation (2-11) specifies that the labor market is always in equilibrium and that this equilibrium level is the *full-employment* level, because every worker who desires employment at the market-determined real wage is employed.[4]

Figure 2-7 is a graphic derivation of the aggregate supply curve based on the preceding system of equations. In Figure 2-7(a) the aggregate supply of labor and demand for labor curves are drawn somewhat differently from those in Figures 2-4 and 2-6, because the axes have been reversed. Labor employment is now on the vertical axis, and real wages appear on the horizontal axis. As we can see, the demand for labor is equal to the supply of labor at the equilibrium real wage ω_e. At this real wage every worker who desires employment is employed and full employment exists.

---

[4] In Chapter 12 we will modify this definition of full employment and adopt an alternative one that allows for frictional unemployment.

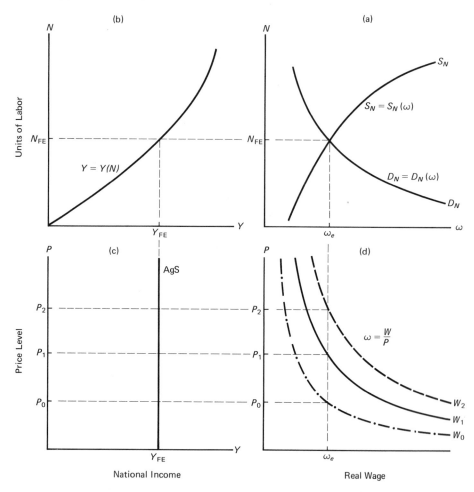

FIGURE 2-7   *The Aggregate Supply Curve: Perfect Competition in All Markets*

Figure 2-7(b) is the aggregate production curve we encountered in Figure 2-1, but once again the axes have been reversed. Because the level of employment is N_{FE}, the level of output will be the full-employment level of output Y_{FE} shown in Figure 2-7(b).

Both the level of employment and the level of output in this model are determined fully by the real variables encompassed in Figures 2-7(a) and 2-7(b), so that the aggregate supply curve AgS derived in Figure 2-7(c) is perfectly price inelastic at the full-employment level of output.[5] In other words, no matter what the price level, the level of real output does not change. But if the level of production is independent of the price level, then what is the function of the price level in this model? The answer is that the price level determines the nominal wage W. The curves in Figure 2-7(d) show the inverse relationship between the price level and the real wage for a constant nominal wage, as specified by equation (2-3). For a given nominal wage W_1, for example, the curve labeled W_1 in Figure 2-7(d) tells us the value of the corresponding real wage at any price level. When prices are high, the real wage corresponding to a given nominal wage is low; conversely when prices are low, the real wage is high. Because this model of aggregate supply specifies that labor market equilibrium *always* exists, it follows that the real wage is always equal to the equilibrium wage ω_e. Therefore when the price level is P_1, the nominal wage must be W_1, as shown in Figure 2-7(d). Now suppose that the price level rises to P_2. Because the real wage cannot change, the nominal wage must rise to W_2. This rise in the money wage is possible because we are assuming that the money wage is flexible upward or downward. It is depicted graphically in Figure 2-7(d) by the nominal (money) wage curve W_2, which gives us a real wage ω_e at price level P_2. Finally, we assume that the price level falls. A falling price level and a constant real wage mean that the nominal wage must fall; such a decline is possible in this aggregate supply model because we have perfect competition in the labor market. If the price level were to fall to P_0, then the nominal wage would have to fall to W_0 for the real wage to remain at ω_e, as shown in Figure 2-7(d).

Downwardly Rigid Wages: Imperfect Competition in the Labor Market

The second aggregate supply model we will examine assumes that workers will accept increases in their nominal wage but will never accept any reduction in the prevailing nominal wage. This assumption is an extreme formulation of a generally observed economic phenomenon that occurs in recessions. In a recession there is a downward pressure on prices. For the labor market to remain in equilibrium, it follows that there must be reductions in the nominal wage for the real wage to remain constant. It has been suggested, however, that workers seem to prefer unemployment to any reduction in their nominal wage. The traditional view in explaining this phenomenon can be based on one or all of the following arguments:

1. Federal and state minimum wage legislation, which in recent years has been broadened to cover almost all of the labor force, establishes a floor below which money wages cannot legally fall.
2. The rapid increase of trade unionism in the twentieth century has produced conditions under which labor contracts establish the nominal wage for considerable periods of time into the future. Hence when the price level begins to fall in a recession, it is legally impossible for firms to reduce their nominal wage.
3. Closely allied to the second argument is the argument that the institutional nature of trade unions creates a situation in which union officials are extremely reluctant to relinquish hard-won nominal wage increases.
4. Individual workers suffer from what economists call *money illusion;* they do not assess their wages in real terms but in money terms. If the price level falls, labor market equilibrium necessitates a proportional decline in nominal

---

[5] For a review of the concept of elasticity and its graphic representation when a curve is either perfectly elastic or perfectly inelastic, see Appendix B.

wages. However, because workers suffer from money illusion, they think that a decrease in their nominal wage is also a decrease in their real wage, and they resist this reduction.

The modern view is based on the information workers use to determine the nominal wage at which they will sell their labor services.[6] The information available to the worker is classified as (1) data on past prices and nominal wages, and (2) data on current prices and nominal wages. The worker uses the first set of data to formulate expectations of future prices and wages. If prices and wages have been stable in the past, then the worker will expect them to remain so in the future. Given these expectations, the worker will be unwilling to sell his or her labor today for less than it was worth yesterday. The second set of data tells the worker that other workers who are still employed are making about the same nominal wage today that they were yesterday. Because the worker feels that the quality of his or her labor services today is as good as it was yesterday, he or she will refuse any reduction in the money wage. In such cases the worker will prefer to be laid off to have the time to search for a comparable job. The opportunity cost of this job-search process is equal to the earnings the unemployed worker would have received at the lower nominal wage. These forgone earnings can be thought of as the cost that the worker must incur to obtain information concerning job opportunities. A worker who is correct in assuming that the prior nominal wage is equal to the current equilibrium nominal wage will be able to find another job in a reasonable length of time. On the other hand, if the worker's judgment is in error and the prevailing equilibrium nominal wage is below the prior nominal wage, the worker will remain unemployed. During this period of unemployment, the worker is in effect "purchasing" information with the forgone earnings he or she could have been receiving at the lower nominal wage. Eventually, enough information will be "purchased" for the worker to revise his or her expectations and accept a job at a lower nominal wage. The time the worker takes to revise these expectations depends on the amount by which the equilibrium nominal wage declines. As the decline increases, the time required to purchase sufficient "information" increases, producing the observed downward rigidity in money wages.

We can express the model that incorporates this behavior pattern in terms of the following system of equations:

$$Y = Y(N) \tag{2-2}$$

$$\omega = \frac{W}{P} \tag{2-3}$$

$$S_N = S_N(\omega) \tag{2-9}$$

$$D_N = D_N = (\omega) \tag{2-10}$$

$$N = N_{FE} = S_N = D_N \quad \text{if } \omega = \omega_e \tag{2-12}$$

$$N = D_N < N_{FE} \quad \text{if } \omega > \omega_e \tag{2-13}$$

[6] For example, see Armen A. Alchian, "Information Costs, Pricing, and Resource Unemployment" in Edmund S. Phelps et al., *Microeconomic Foundations of Employment and Inflation Theory* (New York: W.W. Norton, 1970), pp. 27–52.

With the exception of equations (2-12) and (2-13), the equations in this system are identical with those used in the perfectly competitive model of aggregate supply. Equation (2-12) says that as long as the real wage is equal to the equilibrium real wage, full employment exists. Hence if we have upwardly flexible nominal wages, then a rise in the price level is accompanied by a proportional increase in the nominal wage but the real wage remains constant at ω_e. Equation (2-13) is based on the assumption that a decline in prices is not accompanied by *any* reduction in the *prevailing* nominal wage, so that the real wage rises and exceeds the equilibrium real wage ω_e. When this happens, the quantity of labor employed N is determined by the demand for labor D_N.

The effect that these assumptions of imperfect competition in the labor market have on the aggregate supply curve is illustrated in Figure 2-8. Suppose that initially

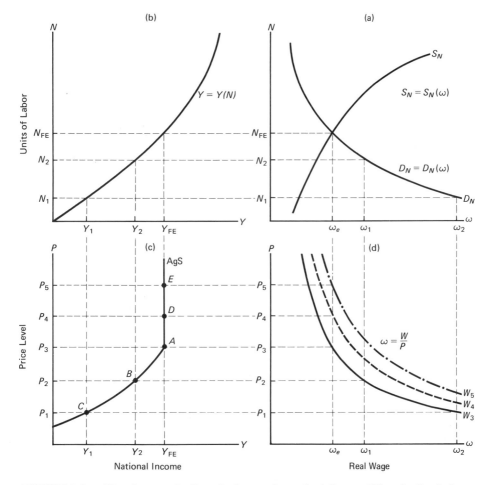

FIGURE 2-8　*The Aggregate Supply Curve: Imperfect Competition in the Labor Market (Downwardly Rigid Nominal Wages)*

the labor market is in equilibrium and that we therefore have full employment. The real wage is ω_e, and if the price level is P_3, then the nominal wage is W_3, as shown in Figures 2-8(a) and 2-8(d). With output at the full-employment level Y_{FE} and the price level at P_3, we are at point A in Figures 2-8(c).

Now suppose that the price level falls to P_2. By assumption our nominal wage remains fixed at W_3; therefore, the real wage rises to ω_1, as shown in Figure 2-8(d). When the real wage becomes greater than ω_e, we know from equation (2-13) that the quantity of labor demanded will be determined by the labor demand curve D_N. Hence the quantity of labor demanded will be N_2, which is less than N_{FE}. With employment at N_2, the level of output falls to Y_2, and we are now at point B in Figure 2-8(c). If the price level were to fall once more, to P_1, then employment and output would fall to N_1 and Y_1, respectively. We would then be at point C in Figure 2-8(c). Drawing a curve through points A, B, and C in Figure 2-8(c) gives us the portion of the aggregate supply curve that exists when prices fall below the prevailing full-employment price level.

Now we will derive the aggregate supply curve for the case of rising prices. If the price level rises from P_3 to P_4, then the nominal wage will rise from W_3 to W_4, because we are assuming that workers will accept increases in their money wages and that the labor market will remain in equilibrium at the real wage ω_e. Output remains at Y_{FE}, so that we are at point D in Figure 2-8(c). Should the level rise to P_5, by the same line of reasoning we will be at point E in Figure 2-8(c). Drawing a straight line through points A, D, and E in Figure 2-8(c) gives us the portion of the aggregate supply that exists when prices rise above the prevailing full-employment price level.

An inspection of the imperfectly competitive aggregate supply curve that we have derived in Figure 2-8(c) reveals that, like the perfectly competitive aggregate supply curve, it is perfectly price inelastic when prices rise above the prevailing full-employment price level. However, when there is imperfect competition and prices decline below the prevailing full-employment price level, the aggregate supply curve becomes price elastic. This characteristic of price elasticity for the aggregate supply curve for a downwardly rigid nominal wage will prove quite useful in subsequent analyses.

One more characteristic of the imperfectly competitive aggregate supply curve should be mentioned. In our discussion of the full-employment price level we have consistently designated it the "prevailing" full-employment price level. This was done for a purpose. When the price level rises above the current full-employment price level, the nominal wage also rises, full employment is maintained, and the new and higher price level becomes the *prevailing* full-employment price level. The new nominal wage is then the minimum acceptable nominal wage.

This characteristic is graphed in Figure 2-9, where the aggregate supply curve represented by the solid line is the same curve that we derived in Figure 2-8. The initial prevailing full-employment price level is P_3. As long as the price level is less than or equal to P_3, we will be on the segment of the aggregate supply curve designated by points A, B, and C. But suppose that the price level rises to P_4. because nominal wages are flexible upward, they will rise from W_3 to W_4, as shown

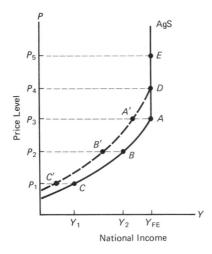

FIGURE 2-9   *The Aggregate Supply Curve's Ratchet Effect*

in Figure 2-8(d), and W_4 becomes the minimum acceptable nominal wage. If prices then decline again to P_3, we cannot return to point A because the nominal wage cannot decrease to W_3. Instead, we must move to point A' in Figure 2-9. Should the price level fall even further, to P_2, we will arrive at B' rather than B. The price-inelastic portion of the imperfectly competitive aggregate supply curve possesses what economists call a "ratchet effect": we can move up the vertical portion of the curve, but we cannot move down again.

2-6   Concluding Remarks

In this chapter we have constructed theories to explain the aggregate demand for labor and the aggregate supply of labor. Both theories were based on a microeconomic approach and, with assumptions about the degree of nominal wage flexibility in the labor market, were used to derive two theoretically different aggregate supply curves. Assuming perfect nominal wage flexibility, we derived an aggregate supply curve that is perfectly price inelastic at the full-employment level of output. The second aggregate supply curve, based on the assumption that nominal wages were perfectly rigid downward but perfectly flexible upward, was perfectly price inelastic above the prevailing full-employment price level but price elastic below that level.

In the real world neither of these aggregate supply curves holds true. In the short run money wages are inflexible downward and the imperfectly competitive model best approximates reality; in the long run the perfectly competitive model is more nearly correct. We shall use both of these models throughout the remainder of this book, and our choice of which one to use will depend on the context and purpose of our analysis.

3 The Simple Theory of Aggregate Demand

3-1 Introduction

Because the levels of national income, employment, and price are determined by the interaction of aggregate supply and aggregate demand, our immediate task is to construct a model of aggregate demand. Once this is accomplished, we can use this model in conjunction with the models of aggregate supply derived in Chapter 2 to analyze various macroeconomic problems and controversies.

Because the model of aggregate demand that we will eventually construct is too complex for us to use yet, we first employ a very simple model to explain certain macroeconomic concepts and later construct the more sophisticated model. This approach allows us, as we proceed, to examine some of the traditional analyses that have been conducted with the simple model of aggregate demand and to discover some of the weaknesses inherent in this model.

3-2 The Simple Model

We begin by assuming we have an economy in which there is no international trade, no retained corporate earnings, no business transfers, and no government and hence no taxation or government transfers. Given this set of assumptions, it follows from the discussion of national income accounting in Chapter 1 that national income is defined as

$$Y = C + I \tag{3-1}$$

where Y = real national income
C = real consumption
I = real net investment

It also follows from our assumptions that because we have no taxation, real disposable income Y_d equals national income; therefore we can rewrite equation (3-1)

$$Y_d = Y = C + \bar{I} \tag{3-2}$$

The distinguishing characteristic that separates the simple model of aggregate demand from the sophisticated model is the assumption we make concerning the level of net investment. In the simple model we assume that net investment is *exogenous*; that is, its level is determined outside the model and is a given factor. In the more sophisticated model net investment is *endogenous*; its level is determined within the model and is an unknown for which we must solve. To signify that the level of net investment is exogenous we use the symbol $\bar{I}$, as shown in equation (3-2).

Equation (3-2) clearly indicates that if net investment is exogenous and known, then the determination of consumption permits us to compute the level of aggregate demand easily. An inspection of Figure 3-1, a scatter diagram of consumption time-series data plotted against concurrent levels of disposable income, leads us to

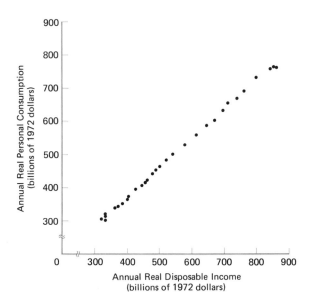

FIGURE 3-1   *Consumption and Disposable Income Data for the United States: 1946–1972*

SOURCE Economic Report of the President, 1976 *(Washington, D.C.: U.S. Government Printing Office)*, p. 191.

the hypothesis that consumption is a function of disposable income.[1] At this point in the construction of our model of aggregate demand it is not necessary to examine the exact functional relationship between consumption and income (we will save this for Chapter 6). Here we simply assume that consumption is a linear function of disposable income; that is

$$C = a + bY_d \tag{3-3}$$

where $0 < b < 1$

Equation (3-3) is called a *consumption function*, where a is the vertical intercept of the function and b is its slope, which for the equation given is constant for all values of disposable income.[2] The slope of the consumption function is called the *marginal propensity to consume* MPC, and it specifies the fraction of each additional dollar of disposable income received that will be spent on consumption. We can express this symbolically as

$$\text{MPC} = \frac{\Delta C}{\Delta Y_d} \tag{3-4}$$

Figure 3-2 is a graph of the consumption function specified by equation (3-3) for the special case where $a > 0$ and $0 < b < 1.0$. Point a on the graph is the vertical intercept, and point b, the slope of the line, is equal to the tangent of the angle θ, which is the angle that the line forms with the horizontal. Another term, which will be quite useful to us in Chapter 6, is the *average propensity to consume* APC, which is simply the ratio of consumption to disposable income and is symbolically defined as

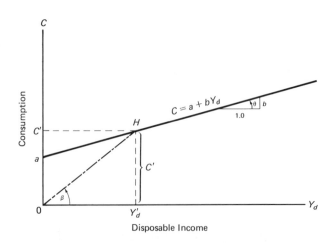

FIGURE 3-2   A Linear Consumption Function

[1] Readers who are unfamiliar with the scatter diagram, the difference between cross-sectional and time-series data, and linear least-squares regression should read Appendix A at this time.

[2] Readers who are unfamiliar with or "rusty" in the geometric interpretation of slope and its relationship to differential calculus should read Appendix B at this time.

$$\text{APC} = \frac{C}{Y_d} \tag{3-5}$$

The APC can also be simply defined geometrically with the use of Figure 3-2. Consider point H on the graph of the consumption function. The level of disposable income at this point is Y_d', and the corresponding level of consumption is C' by equation (3-5) the APC at point H must be C'/Y_d'. Now consider the dashed line drawn in Figure 3-2 from the origin to point H. Lines such as these are called *rays*. The slope of this ray is equal to the tangent of the angle β in Figure 3-2 and is therefore equal to C'/Y_d'. Hence the slope of the ray to point H is the APC at point H. By inspection we can see that $\tan \beta > \tan \theta$, and hence APC $>$ MPC. It is obvious that as we move to the right along the graph of the consumption function, the slopes of the respective APC rays diminish. Thus we can conclude that for consumption functions of the type illustrated in Figure 3-2, the APC declines as income rises but will always exceed the MPC.

Equations (3-2) and (3-3) together form a system of two equations in two unknowns. Using this system, it is possible to solve for the level of consumption and aggregate demand. Substituting the right-hand side of equation (3-3) into equation (3-2), we obtain

$$Y = a + bY_d + \bar{I} \tag{3-6}$$

and because $Y = Y_d$, we can rearrange equation (3-6) so that

$$Y(1 - b) = a + \bar{I} \tag{3-7}$$

Solving for the level of aggregate demand, we obtain[3]

$$Y = \frac{1}{1 - b}(a + \bar{I}) \tag{3-8}$$

To solve for the level of consumption, we merely substitute equation (3-8) into equation (3-3) and rearrange to obtain

$$C = a + \frac{b}{1 - b}(a + \bar{I}) \tag{3-9}$$

A numerical example would be helpful at this point. Suppose that the following conditions are given:

$$\bar{I} = \$10 \text{ billion} \tag{3-10}$$

$$C = 5 + 0.8Y_d \tag{3-11}$$

where all magnitudes are calculated in constant dollars. Substituting this information into equation (3-8), we obtain

$$Y = \frac{1}{1 - 0.8}(5 + 10) = \$75 \text{ billion} \tag{3-12}$$

---

[3] This solution holds if and only if $b \neq 1$; otherwise we would be required to divide by zero, an undefined operation.

which is the level of aggregate demand consistent with conditions (3-10) and (3-11). The level of consumption at this level of national income is

$$C = 5 + 0.8(75) = \$65 \text{ billion} \tag{3-13}$$

An alternative approach to solving for the level of aggregate demand becomes apparent if we recall that savings are equal to the difference between disposable income and consumption, or

$$S = Y_d - C \tag{3-14}$$

where S represents savings. Substituting the right-hand side of equation (3-3) for C in equation (3-14), we obtain

$$\begin{aligned} S &= Y_d - a - bY_d \\ &= -a + (1 - b)Y_d \end{aligned} \tag{3-15}$$

Equation (3-15) is called a *savings function*; its slope $1 - b$, which is called the *marginal propensity to save* MPS, specifies the fraction that will be saved out of each additional dollar of disposable income received. We can express this concept symbolically as

$$MPS = \frac{\Delta S}{\Delta Y_d} \tag{3-16}$$

The MPS is always equal to unity minus the MPC. Digressing for a moment, we can prove this statement if we take the definition of disposable income

$$Y_d = C + S \tag{3-17}$$

and assume a change in disposable income ΔY_d. Because any change in disposable income results in a change in consumption ΔC and a change in savings ΔS, the new level of disposable income is defined as

$$Y_d + \Delta Y_d = C + \Delta C + S + \Delta S \tag{3-18}$$

Subtracting equation (3-17) from equation (3-18) gives us

$$\Delta Y_d = \Delta C + \Delta S \tag{3-19}$$

Finally, dividing both sides of equation (3-19) by ΔY_d, we obtain

$$1 = \frac{\Delta C}{\Delta Y_d} + \frac{\Delta S}{\Delta Y_d} \tag{3-20}$$

The first term on the right-hand side of equation (3-20) is the MPC defined in (3-4), and the second term is the MPS defined in (3-16). Hence the statement that the MPS is always equal to unity *minus* the MPC is true by definition.

Returning now to our alternative approach to the solution of aggregate demand, we know that according to our assumptions

$$Y = Y_d = C + S \tag{3-21}$$

If we equate equations (3-1) and (3-21), then we obtain

$$C + I = Y = C + S \tag{3-22}$$

which, when C is subtracted from both sides, reduces to

$$I = S \tag{3-23}$$

Equation (3-23) is the statement of a condition of equality that must prevail when we are solving for aggregate demand. Conversely, we can use this requirement of equality to solve for aggregate demand. If net investment is exogenous, then substituting the right-hand side of equation (3-15) into equation (3-23) gives us

$$\bar{I} = -a + (1 - b)Y_d \tag{3-24}$$

Rearranging (3-24), we then obtain

$$Y_d = \frac{1}{1 - b}(a + \bar{I}) \tag{3-25}$$

Because $Y_d = Y$ in this model, equation (3-25) is identical to equation (3-8).

Equation (3-23) is quite important for two reasons. First, it points out the fundamental accounting relationship that the total income received but not consumed is always equal to net investment. Second, for any given level of net investment, there is *only one* level of national income that will produce an equivalent level of savings. The seeming paradox of these two statements can be resolved if we introduce the concepts of *actual*[4] savings S_a and *actual investment* I_a and then contrast them with *desired savings* S_d and *desired investment* I_d. The first statement considers that the relationship between savings and investment is simply an accounting identity; that is, it is a condition of equality that always exists simply by definition. Hence, at any instant in time it necessarily follows that

$$I_a = S_a \tag{3-26}$$

The second statement refers to a condition in which savers and investors are simultaneously satisfied with their levels of saving and investing and do not wish to alter these levels. When this condition prevails, then

$$I_d = S_d \tag{3-27}$$

By definition the condition described by equation (3-26) must always prevail, but the condition specified by equation (3-27) need not. If an inequality exists between desired savings and desired investment, then aggregate demand will change.

To demonstrate what we mean by these statements, let us assume that households behave in such a manner that actual savings are always equal to desired savings and that all undesired investment occurs during inventory changes. For example, suppose that we have a situation in which

$$S_a = S_d > I_d \tag{3-28}$$

---

[4] In economic literature the terms *realized* or *ex post* are often used in place of "actual," and the terms *planned* or *ex ante* are often used in place of "desired."

That is, desired savings are equal to actual savings but are greater than desired investment. This can occur in very short-run situations, because households may not purchase all the output in excess of the amount retained in business inventories. Business inventories then increase to a greater than desired level, and because inventory change is one form of net investment, a condition of undesired net investment results. Producers soon note this buildup of inventories, and they curtail production and wait for sales to deplete inventories until the desired inventory level is achieved again. As production is reduced, income falls and so does the actual level of savings resulting from the savings function. Aggregate demand declines until the level of desired savings is equal to the level of desired net investment. If the opposite condition prevails (that is, $S_d < I_d$), then an insufficiency of producers' inventories exists and income increases as production speeds up. Thus goods are being added to inventories faster than they can be sold, and inventories reach their desired level. Savings rise as income rises, until the point where $S_d = I_d$ is reached.

In the context of the simple model we will be examining here and in Chapter 4, the condition $S_d = I_d$ represents a situation in which no forces endogenous to the model exist to alter aggregate demand. Hence the level of aggregate demand that prevails when desired savings are equal to desired investment is called the *equilibrium level* of aggregate demand.

3-3   A Graphic Solution

The algebraic and numerical analysis we have examined thus far can also be described graphically. In this section we first present a graphic method for determining the equilibrium level of aggregate demand. We then examine this simple theory of aggregate demand in conjunction with the two theories of aggregate supply developed in Chapter 2.

Aggregate Demand

Figure 3-3 illustrates the linear consumption function of the numerical example specified in equation (3-11). This graph has a vertical intercept of $5 billion and a slope, or MPC, of 0.8. Also drawn in Figure 3-3 is a ray that intersects the horizontal axis at a 45° angle. Any point on this ray is equidistant from either axis. Thus the point where the consumption function intersects the 45° ray (point *B*) indicates the level of disposable income that generates an equivalent level of consumption, or zero savings. Now since

$$Y_d = Y = C + \bar{I} \tag{3-2}$$

and the level of investment is a constant, if we shift the consumption function vertically upward $10 billion at every level of income, the resulting curve will give us the sum of consumption and investment at every income level. This curve is

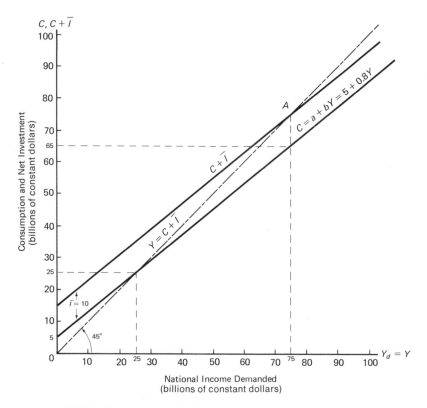

FIGURE 3-3   *Graphic Solution of Aggregate Demand*

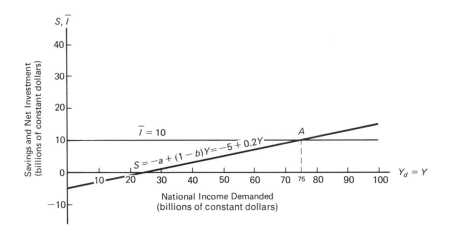

FIGURE 3-4   *Alternative Solution of Aggregate Demand*

labeled $C + \bar{I}$, and it intersects the 45° ray at point A in Figure 3-3. Because every point on the ray is equidistant from both axes, it follows that at point A the condition $Y = C + \bar{I}$ prevails, and we have the graphic solution to the equilibrium level of aggregate demand. According to Figure 3-3, the equilibrium level of aggregate demand is $75 billion and the corresponding level of consumption is $65 billion. Both of these results are in exact agreement with our previous numerical solutions.

The alternative approach to determining the equilibrium level of aggregate demand also has a graphic solution. This is illustrated in Figure 3-4, where the savings function corresponding to the consumption function of our numerical example is drawn. The savings function has a vertical intercept of −$5 billion and a slope, or MPS, of $1 - 0.8 = 0.2$. As we just learned, the equilibrium level of aggregate demand occurs when $I_d = S_d$. The savings function in Figure 3-4 is a function of desired savings; therefore when $S = \bar{I}$ the level of income sufficient to generate S is the equilibrium level of aggregate demand. Graphically we find this solution by drawing a horizontal line that intersects the vertical axis at the level of exogenous net investment $\bar{I}$, which in this example is $10 billion. The level of income corresponding to the point of intersection between the net investment line and the savings function is the equilibrium level of aggregate demand. The savings function intersects the net investment line at point A in Figure 3-4, and the corresponding level of national income is $75 billion—the same result we obtained in our numerical solution.

Aggregate Demand and Supply

The two aggregate supply models developed in Chapter 2 can now be combined with our simplified analysis of aggregate demand. First we will consider the interaction of aggregate demand with the downwardly rigid wage aggregate supply model. The aggregate demand curve AgD in Figure 3-5 is representative of the

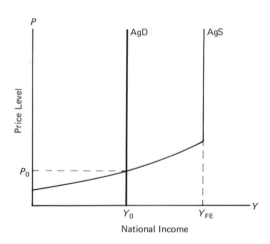

FIGURE 3-5   *Aggregate Demand and the Downwardly Rigid Wage Aggregate Supply*

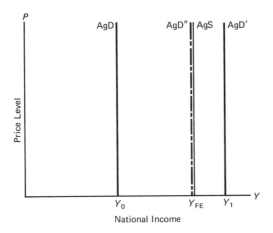

FIGURE 3-6 *Aggregate Demand and the Perfectly Flexible Wage Aggregate Supply*

aggregate demand curves that our simple theory produces. We can clearly see that the simplified theory of aggregate demand produces an aggregate demand curve that is perfectly price inelastic. This occurs because all the factors that influence the determination of aggregate demand are real. The price level has nothing to do with the level of aggregate demand. The aggregate demand curve is shown intersecting the aggregate supply curve in Figure 3-5 at a less than full-employment level of income Y_0. This is the equilibrium level of national income,[5] and the equilibrium price level is P_0. Three characteristics of the simplified model of aggregate demand are worth mentioning at this point. First, the equilibrium level of aggregate demand is also the equilibrium level of national income. Second, the equilibrium price level is determined solely by the aggregate supply curve, given the level of aggregate demand. Both of these characteristics are due to the perfect price inelasticity of the aggregate demand curve. Third, if a condition of less than full employment exists, there are no forces endogenous to the model that can produce full employment.

A perfectly flexible wage aggregate supply curve AgS is shown in Figure 3-6. Also shown are three aggregate demand curves AgD, AgD', and AgD", representing, respectively, a level of aggregate demand less than, greater than, or equal to the full-employment level. If aggregate demand is equal to AgD or AgD', then there is no equilibrium level of income and price. In the former case, the price level asymptotically approaches zero due to continuous excess aggregate supply; in the latter case, the price level approaches infinity due to continuous excess demand. If the level of aggregate demand is equal to the full-employment level of aggregate supply, we have an equilibrium level of income but *no* determinate equilibrium price level, because any price level will be consistent with AgD = AgS. This is a

---

[5] In Chapters 3 and 4 we refer to the intersection of the AgD curve in the AgS curve's price-elastic portion as one of equilibrium. Strictly speaking, this is not correct, as we shall see in Chapter 11. It is, however, sufficiently accurate for our purposes at this time.

completely unsatisfactory conclusion for any economy that uses money to effect the exchange of commodities. Clearly, the conclusions reached here concerning cases in which aggregate demand is equal to or greater than the full-employment level of aggregate supply apply to the downwardly rigid wage example in Figure 3-5 as well.

The preceding analysis clearly illustrates the inadequacies and shortcomings of the simple model of aggregate demand. The simple model is compatible *only* with a downwardly rigid wage aggregate supply model—and then only when aggregate demand is less than the full-employment level. We must study several more chapters of theoretical analysis before we will be able to specify a model that is free from these deficiencies. However, it should be obvious at this point that the sophisticated theory must have a price-elastic aggregate demand curve.

3-4   Changes in Investment

At the beginning of this chapter we assumed that the level of investment was exogenous. We continue to maintain this assumption here, but we now permit exogenous changes that can alter the level of investment. For example, suppose that a change in the level of net investment results from the discovery of a large oil field. As entrepreneurs seek to exploit this discovery, the level of net investment rises from $\bar{I}$ to $\bar{I}'$ and is permanently maintained at this level from one period to the next. This permanent change in net investment $\bar{I}' - \bar{I} = \Delta\bar{I}$ initially creates a condition of *disequilibrium*, because $I_d > I_a = S_a = S_d$. Both producers' and sellers' inventories fall below the desired level as households maintain their level of consumption. To return inventories to their desired level, manufacturers increase production, income rises, and the level of savings increases until $I_d = I_a = S_a = S_d$. Hence, when productive resources are not utilized, an increase in investment results in an increase in both income and savings.

The only model of aggregate supply that is appropriate to this analysis at the present time is the downwardly rigid wage model, because it permits a determinate level of income at less than full employment.

Algebraically, the new equilibrium level of aggregate demand and income Y' can be obtained by solving

$$Y' = C + \bar{I}' = C + \bar{I} + \Delta\bar{I} \tag{3-29}$$

This is easily done by substituting the consumption function of equation (3-3) into (3-29) to obtain

$$Y' = a + bY' + \bar{I} + \Delta\bar{I} \tag{3-30}$$

Then solving for Y' we obtain

$$Y' = \frac{1}{1-b}(a + \bar{I} + \Delta\bar{I}) \tag{3-31}$$

which is the new equilibrium level of demand and income. Note that equation (3-31) is merely equation (3-8) with the added term $\Delta \bar{I}$.

Now suppose that we take the numerical example we have been using through-out this chapter and allow net investment to increase from $10 billion to $15 billion. The change in net investment $\Delta \bar{I}$ is $5 billion, and the new level of aggregate demand and income can then be easily found. According to equation (3-31), the new level of income is

$$Y' = \frac{1}{1 - 0.8}(5 + 10 + 5) = \$100 \qquad (3\text{-}32)$$

The graphic solution to this problem is shown in Figure 3-7. The new level of aggregate demand corresponds to the intersection of the $C + \bar{I} + \Delta \bar{I}$ curve with the 45° ray at point B in Figure 3-7. The new level of income corresponds to the intersection of the new aggregate demand curve AgD' and the aggregate supply

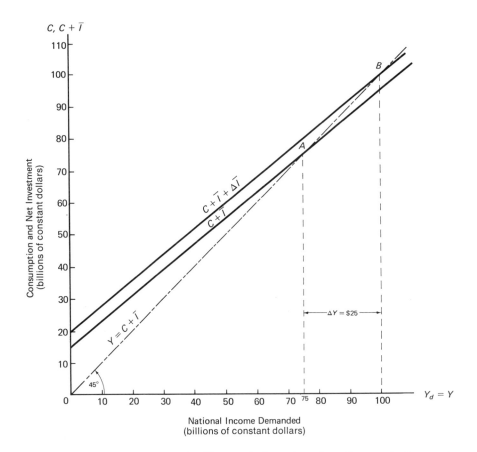

FIGURE 3-7   *The Effect of a Change in Investment on Aggregate Demand*

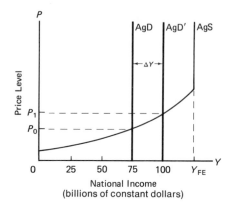

FIGURE 3-8 *The Effect of a Change in Investment on the Equilibrium Level of Income*

curve in Figure 3-8. Because the aggregate demand curve is perfectly price inelastic, the new equilibrium level of aggregate demand is equal to the new equilibrium level of income. The change in income

$$\Delta Y = Y' - Y = 100 - 75 = \$25 \text{ billion} \tag{3-33}$$

is of more than passing interest, because for every $1 of additional net investment, $5 of additional income were created. We now examine how this occurs and what determines the magnitude of the resulting increase in income.

3-5   The Multiplier

Subtracting equation (3-8) from equation (3-31), we obtain

$$Y' - Y = \frac{1}{1 - b}(a + \bar{I} + \Delta \bar{I}) - \frac{1}{1 - b}(a + \bar{I})$$

$$\Delta Y = \frac{1}{1 - b}\Delta \bar{I} \tag{3-34}$$

Equation (3-34) gives us the change in income that results from a change in exogenous investment. The only factor that influences the change in income for a given $\Delta \bar{I}$ is b, the marginal propensity to consume. As the MPC approaches unity, the resulting change in income becomes greater.

Dividing both sides of equation (3-34) by $\Delta \bar{I}$, we obtain the ratio

$$\frac{\Delta Y}{\Delta \bar{I}} = \frac{1}{1 - b} = \mu_I \tag{3-35}$$

which is the number of times an additional dollar of net investment will increase income. This number is independent of any initial values of $\bar{I}$ or Y and is also independent of the magnitude of $\Delta \bar{I}$. In our simple model, this number depends exclusively on the slope of the consumption function and can therefore be computed prior to any change in investment. Once this number is computed, if we multiply it by $\Delta \bar{I}$, we obtain the corresponding change in income. For this reason the ratio, denoted μ_I, is referred to as the *investment multiplier*.

We have just seen that an increase in the level of investment creates an increase in the level of aggregate demand that is some multiple of the change in investment and also that (in our simple model) this multiple is a function of only the MPC. These results may seem strange at first, but a closer analysis will show that they are reasonable, given the assumption of our model.

To understand the economic workings of the multiplier, it is necessary to assume that changes from one level of income to another do not occur instantaneously but require a certain time period to be achieved. Let us assume that this time period is broken down into many subperiods of one week in length and, further, that income received in one week is expended on consumption goods and additions to savings during the following week. Using our numerical example, the equilibrium level of aggregate demand Y_0 corresponding to a level of intended net investment of $10 billion is $75 billion. This is shown in Figure 3-9 by the horizontal line intersecting the vertical axis at $75 billion. When net investment undergoes a permanent rise from $10 billion to $15 billion, the immediate effect in the first period is to raise income from $75 billion to $80 billion.[6] Because aggregate supply is less than the

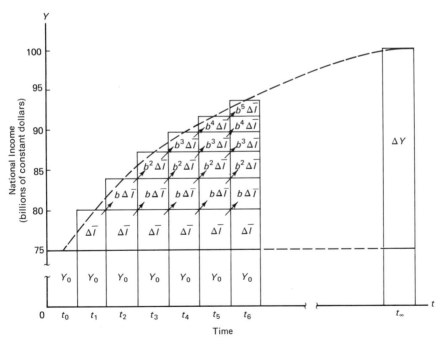

FIGURE 3-9   *The Continuous Injection Multiplier*

[6] For simplicity we assume that the production of the additional investment goods can be accomplished in one week.

full-employment level, income rises to \$80 billion at the end of the first week, giving households an additional \$5 billion of income to spend on consumer goods during the next week. However, due to our assumption about their behavior, households will spend only $b(5) = 0.8(5) = \$4.0$ billion of that newly generated income on consumption in the next week. Hence, total expenditures in the second week are $Y_0 + \Delta \bar{I} + b(\Delta \bar{I})$. Income in the second week rises by the increased amount resulting from expenditures on consumer goods during that week $b\Delta \bar{I}$, in addition to the continued increase in investment expenditures $\Delta \bar{I}$. Hence, the level of income at the end of the second week Y_2 is

$$Y_2 = Y_0 + \Delta \bar{I} + b\Delta \bar{I} = \$84 \tag{3-36}$$

At the beginning of the third week, total expenditures increase again as the additional income earned from producing the additional consumption goods $b\Delta \bar{I}$ and the continuing additional investment $\Delta \bar{I}$ are used by households for consumption and saving. Thus households spend

$$b(b\Delta \bar{I}) + b\Delta \bar{I} = b^2 \Delta \bar{I} + b\Delta \bar{I} \tag{3-37}$$

on consumption in the third week. Adding this expenditure to the continuing investment increase $\Delta \bar{I}$ and the original level of expenditure, we find that the new level of income at the end of the third week Y_3 is

$$Y_3 = Y_0 + \Delta \bar{I} + b\Delta \bar{I} + b^2 \Delta \bar{I} \tag{3-38}$$

We can now deduce that the level of income at the end of n weeks will be

$$Y_n = Y_0 + \Delta \bar{I} + b\Delta \bar{I} + b^2 \Delta \bar{I} + \cdots + b^{n-1}\Delta \bar{I} \tag{3-39}$$

To find the sum of this series, we multiply both sides of equation (3-39) by b to obtain

$$bY_n = bY_0 + b\Delta \bar{I} + b^2 \Delta \bar{I} + b^3 \Delta \bar{I} + \cdots + b^{n-1}\Delta \bar{I} + b^n \Delta \bar{I} \tag{3-40}$$

Then, subtracting (3-40) from (3-39) gives us

$$(1 - b)Y_n = Y_0(1 - b) + \Delta \bar{I}(1 - b^n) \tag{3-41}$$

and solving for Y_n, we obtain

$$Y_n = Y_0 + \Delta \bar{I}\left(\frac{1 - b^n}{1 - b}\right) \tag{3-42}$$

If we assume that

$$0 < b < 1 \tag{3-43}$$

we can now conclude that b^n becomes very small as n becomes very large, so that as $n \to \infty$, the equilibrium level of aggregate demand approaches

$$Y_n = Y_0 + \left(\frac{1}{1-b}\right)\Delta\bar{I} \tag{3-44}$$

Subtracting Y_0 from both sides of (3-44) and dividing both sides by $\Delta\bar{I}$, we obtain

$$\frac{Y_n - Y_0}{\Delta\bar{I}} = \frac{\Delta Y}{\Delta\bar{I}} = \frac{1}{1-b} = \mu_I \tag{3-45}$$

which is the same as the result in (3-35). Thus we have shown that the mysterious behavior of the multiplier has a rational economic explanation—namely, induced secondary consumption expenditure.

The multiplier we have just discussed is usually referred to as the *continuous injection multiplier,* because the level of investment is maintained at $\bar{I} + \Delta\bar{I}$ in each subsequent period. The net result of this continuous injection at the end of n periods is a permanent change of income.

Another multiplier yields the same mathematical solution but has an entirely different economic interpretation. This multiplier is called the *single injection multiplier,* which means that the level of exogenous investment increases to $\bar{I} + \Delta\bar{I}$ in the first period but returns to its old level $\bar{I}$ in the next period and remains at $\bar{I}$ thereafter. Figure 3-10 is a graphic representation of this multiplier constructed from the data in our previous examples, except that $\Delta\bar{I}$ exists only in the first period.

As a result of the single injection of $5 billion, income at the end of the first period reaches a peak of $80 billion. Therefore, the change in income at the end of the first period ΔY_1 is $5 billion. Because investment returns to its original level of $10 billion in the second period, where it remains thereafter, the change in income in the second period is entirely the result of households spending $b\Delta Y_1$ of their

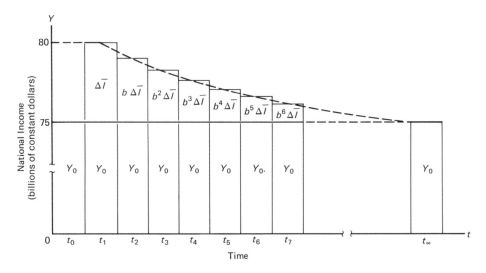

FIGURE 3-10   *The Single Injection Multiplier*

increased income on consumption goods, so that

$$\Delta Y_2 = b\Delta Y_1 = b\Delta\bar{I} \qquad (3\text{-}46)$$

Applying the same line of reasoning, we conclude that the change in income in the third period is

$$\Delta Y_3 = b\Delta Y_2 = b(b\Delta Y_1) = b^2\Delta\bar{I} \qquad (3\text{-}47)$$

If we let $\Sigma\Delta Y$ represent the sum of the changes in income over n periods, then by induction we can write

$$\Sigma\Delta Y = \Delta Y_1 + \Delta Y_2 + \Delta Y_3 + \cdots + \Delta Y_n$$
$$= \Delta\bar{I} + b\Delta\bar{I} + b^2\Delta\bar{I} + \cdots + b^{n-1}\Delta\bar{I} \qquad (3\text{-}48)$$

Solving for the sum of (3-48) in the same manner, we obtain

$$\Sigma\Delta Y = \Delta\bar{I}\left(\frac{1}{1-b}\right) \qquad (3\text{-}49)$$

Dividing both sides of (3-49) by $\Delta\bar{I}$ then gives us

$$\frac{\Sigma\Delta Y}{\Delta\bar{I}} = \frac{1}{1-b} \qquad (3\text{-}50)$$

which, except for the sigma notation, is mathematically the same as (3-45) but has an entirely different economic interpretation. As Figure 3-10 illustrates, $\Sigma\Delta Y$ measures the total change in income over time, where the equilibrium level of income returns to its initial value. In contrast, ΔY of the continuous injection multiplier measures the permanent change in the level of income that prevails at the end of a period of time.

Throughout the remainder of this book, when we refer to "the multiplier" we mean the continuous injection multiplier, unless we expressly state otherwise.

3-6   Concluding Remarks

In this chapter we constructed a simple model of aggregate demand. We learned that the feature that simplifies this model is *not* the fact that it contains only a few variables and ignores the government sector, but the fact that investment is regarded as exogenous. Algebraic and graphic techniques that allow us to solve for the equilibrium level of aggregate demand were discussed, and the resulting aggregate demand curve was shown to be perfectly price inelastic. We saw that the equilibrium level of income is determined jointly by the aggregate demand and supply curves. With a perfectly price-inelastic aggregate demand curve, we learned that this creates certain problems. With a flexible wage aggregate supply curve, the simple model of aggregate demand does not give us an equilibrium level of income unless aggregate demand is equal to the full-employment level—and at this level of aggregate demand there is no determinate price level. These same problems occurred when we examined the downwardly rigid wage aggregate supply curve, *except* for levels of aggregate demand less than the full-employment level. Because determinate levels of both income and price can be achieved for these levels of aggregate demand, we concluded that the simple model of aggregate demand is only suited to the less than full-employment situation in which wages are rigid downward. Finally, we examined the impact on the income level of a change in the level of exogenous net investment. The level of income was shown to rise by a multiple of the increase in net investment. This factor of multiplication, the *investment multiplier,* was in turn shown to depend solely on the value of the marginal propensity to consume.

4 Government and the Simple Theory of Aggregate Demand

4-1 Introduction

At the conclusion of Chapter 3 we left our theory of aggregate demand in a rather unsatisfactory condition. The interaction of the simple theory of aggregate demand with the perfectly flexible wage aggregate supply model did not necessarily yield an equilibrium level of income, and if an equilibrium was achieved, the price level was indeterminate. Combining our theory of aggregate demand with the downwardly rigid wage aggregate supply model was an improvement in that an equilibrium level of income and price existed if the level of aggregate demand was less than the full-employment level of aggregate supply. This solution is only somewhat more satisfactory, however, because an equilibrium level of income less than the full-employment level is socially undesirable. In this chapter we add the role of government to our simple theory of aggregate demand and learn how *fiscal policy*—regulation of the level of government expenditure and taxation—can be used to achieve full employment.

4-2 The Simple Model Incorporating Government

In Chapter 3 we defined aggregate demand as the sum of the demand from all sectors of an economy composed only of household and business sectors. In this

48

chapter we broaden our analysis to include the demand of the government sector. Therefore, by definition, aggregate demand becomes

$$Y = C + I + G \tag{4-1}$$

where all values are again measured in constant dollars (that is, money value deflated by the general price level P). Retaining our previous assumptions from Chapter 3

$$C = a + bY_d \tag{4-2}$$

$$I = \bar{I} \tag{4-3}$$

and incorporating the assumptions

$$G = \bar{G} \tag{4-4}$$

$$T = \bar{T} \tag{4-5}$$

where $\bar{G}$ and $\bar{T}$ are exogenously determined values of government expenditure and net taxation, respectively, we can then express equation (4-1) as

$$Y = a + bY_d + \bar{I} + \bar{G} \tag{4-6}$$

Equation (4-6) contains two unknowns Y and Y_d and thus is not solvable. However, if we recall that

$$Y_d = Y - T \tag{4-7}$$

then equation (4-6) can be written

$$Y = a + b(Y - \bar{T}) + \bar{I} + \bar{G} \tag{4-8}$$

We now have one equation containing one unknown. Solving for the unknown Y, we obtain

$$Y = \frac{1}{1 - b}(a - b\bar{T} + \bar{I} + \bar{G}) \tag{4-9}$$

an equation that specifies the equilibrium level of aggregate demand.

An alternative method for expressing the conditions of equilibrium of aggregate demand can be easily derived. Starting with equation (4-1)

$$Y = C + I + G$$

recall that

$$C = Y_d - S \tag{4-10}$$

Substituting the right-hand side of equation (4-7) into (4-10) gives us

$$C = Y - T - S \tag{4-11}$$

Substituting the right-hand side of equation (4-11) into (4-1), we then obtain

$$Y = Y - T - S + I + G \tag{4-12}$$

Canceling the Ys and rearranging terms, we finally obtain

$$S + T = I + G \tag{4-13}$$

an identity stating that savings *plus* taxes must always be equal to investment *plus* government spending. However, this constitutes an equilibrium level of aggregate demand only when desired savings and taxes are equal to desired investment and government expenditures. If an inequality exists in this sense, then the level of aggregate demand will adjust itself until equality is achieved.

For a numerical example, let us assume that

$$C = 5 + 0.8Y_d$$

$$\bar{I} = \$10 \text{ billion}$$

$$\bar{G} = \$20 \text{ billion} \tag{4-14}$$

$$\bar{T} = \$20 \text{ billion}$$

where all values are measured in constant dollars.

Note that government expenditure is equal to government revenue in this example, or in other words, the government has a *balanced budget*. Substituting these assumptions into equation (4-9), we obtain a level of aggregate demand

$$Y = \frac{1}{1 - 0.8}[5 - 0.8(20) + 10 + 20]$$

$$= \$95 \text{ billion} \tag{4-15}$$

In the numerical example given in Chapter 3, where the consumption function and the level of exogenous investment were identical to those in this example, the level of aggregate demand was $75 billion. Expanding the simple model to include the government sector has increased the level of aggregate demand by $20 billion. If we can determine how the government sector influences the level of aggregate demand, then we will be in a position to employ fiscal policy to obtain full employment.

The impact of changes in government fiscal policy on aggregate demand can be analyzed in the same way that we analyzed changes in the level of investment in Chapter 3. Starting with equation (4-9), let government spending increase by ΔG. This increases aggregate demand by some amount ΔY, so that the new level of aggregate demand becomes

$$Y + \Delta Y = \frac{1}{1 - b}(a - b\bar{T} + \bar{I} + \bar{G} + \Delta G) \tag{4-16}$$

If we subtract equation (4-9) from equation (4-16), we obtain

$$\Delta Y = \frac{1}{1 - b}\Delta G \tag{4-17}$$

and, by rearranging terms, we obtain the government spending multiplier

$$\mu_G = \frac{\Delta Y}{\Delta G} = \frac{1}{1-b} \tag{4-18}$$

As we can see, the government spending multiplier is identical to the investment multiplier we derived in Chapter 3.

However, this result is not the same for the tax multiplier. If we start once again with equation (4-9), given a change in the level of taxes, the new level of aggregate demand becomes

$$Y + \Delta Y = \frac{1}{1-b}[a - b(\bar{T} + \Delta\bar{T}) + I + G] \tag{4-19}$$

Subtracting equation (4-9) from equation (4-16), as before, gives us

$$\Delta Y = \frac{1}{1-b}(-b\Delta T) = \frac{-b\Delta T}{1-b} \tag{4-20}$$

Rearranging terms, we obtain the tax multiplier

$$\mu_T = -\frac{b}{1-b} \tag{4-21}$$

which for a tax increase produces, as we might expect, a decline in aggregate demand. Note that the absolute value of the tax multiplier is less than the government expenditure multiplier, so that an increase in government spending matched by an equal increase in taxation results in an overall increase in aggregate demand. This can easily be proved. Suppose that a balanced budget increase in government spending occurs, so that

$$\Delta G = \Delta T = \Delta E \tag{4-22}$$

where ΔE represents the equal change in expenditure and revenue. The increase in aggregate demand resulting from the increased government expenditure is then

$$\Delta Y_G = \frac{\Delta E}{1-b} \tag{4-23}$$

and the decrease in aggregate demand resulting from the increase in taxation is

$$\Delta Y_T = \frac{-b\Delta E}{1-b} \tag{4-24}$$

Summing the increase and decrease in aggregate demand, we determine that the resulting change in demand is

$$\Delta Y = \Delta Y_G + \Delta Y_T = \Delta E\left(\frac{1}{1-b} - \frac{b}{1-b}\right) = \Delta E \tag{4-25}$$

Dividing both sides of (4-25) by ΔE, we then obtain

$$\mu_{BB} = \frac{\Delta Y}{\Delta E} = 1 \tag{4-26}$$

where μ_{BB} is the *balanced budget multiplier* and is equal to unity.

If government spending rises by $10 billion and this amount is matched by an equal increase in taxes, the net result is an increase in aggregate demand of $(10)(1) = \$10$ billion. We obtain this result because every $1 increase in government expenditure increases aggregate demand by $1/(1 - b)$ dollars, whereas a $1 increase in taxes reduces aggregate demand by $-b/(1 - b)$ dollars. Because there is an equal increase in taxes for each $1 increase in government expenditure, the net effect of both on aggregate demand is

$$\frac{1}{1 - b} + \frac{-b}{1 - b} = \frac{1 - b}{1 - b} = 1.0$$

Hence, a $10 billion increase in expenditure and taxation will increase aggregate demand by $10 billion.

Now suppose that government expenditure increases by $10 billion but that taxes do not increase. In this case the change in aggregate demand is

$$\Delta Y = \frac{10}{1 - b} = 10\mu_G \tag{4-27}$$

The numerical value of ΔY is therefore a function of the marginal propensity to consume b. As b approaches unity, the value of the multiplier and the resulting value of ΔY both increase. In our numerical example, $b = 0.8$, $\mu_G = 5$, and therefore the change in aggregate demand ΔY is $5(10) = \$50$ billion.

Initially, we assumed that taxes were independent of the level of income. We now make the somewhat more realistic assumption that taxes are a *linear function* of the level of income. This means that our model's system of equations is now

$$Y = C + I + G \tag{4-1}$$

$$C = a + bY_d \tag{4-2}$$

$$I = \bar{I} \tag{4-3}$$

$$G = \bar{G} \tag{4-4}$$

$$Y_d = Y - T \tag{4-7}$$

$$T = h + tY \tag{4-28}$$

In equation (4-28) t is the *marginal rate of taxation* and h is a constant. The *income tax function* of equation (4-28) is illustrated by the solid line in Figure 4-1. As we can see, this function in analogous to the consumption function illustrated in Figure 3-2. The vertical intercept is determined by the constant h, and the slope of the function is determined by the marginal rate of taxation t. The *average rate of taxation* at any given level of income will be equal to the slope of the ray drawn to the corresponding point on the tax function at that level of income. In Figure 4-1, for example, if the level of income is Y_0, then the corresponding point on the tax function is A, and the average rate of taxation is given by the tangent of the angle β.

A change in income taxation can be generated by a change in the marginal rate of taxation, a change in the vertical intercept, or some combination of these two

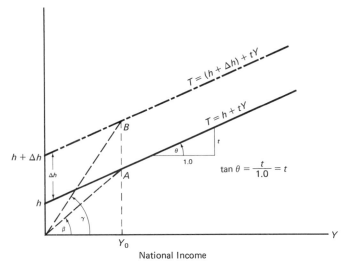

FIGURE 4-1   *The Income Tax Function*

parameters. Suppose that the vertical intercept increases from h to $h + \Delta h$ and that the marginal rate of taxation remains constant. The tax function then shifts upward, as indicated by the dashed line in Figure 4-1. The average rate of taxation at income level Y_0 then becomes equal to the slope of the ray from the origin to point B on the new tax function. Because $\tan \gamma$ is greater than $\tan \beta$, we can conclude that a tax increase that raises the vertical intercept also raises the average rate of taxation at any given income level. If we had chosen to illustrate the effect of increasing the marginal rate of taxation while holding the vertical intercept constant, we would have reached the same conclusion.

A tax function of the type illustrated in Figure 4-1 (that is, one with a positive intercept) is said to be *regressive*, because as the level of income rises, the parameters of the tax function being held constant, the average rate of taxation decreases. If the value of the vertical intercept h is negative, then the function is said to be *progressive*, because the average rate of taxation rises as income rises. In addition, this function provides transfers in excess of taxes to households below a certain minimum income level, so that their net tax T is negative. If the tax function passes through the origin (that is, $h = 0$), then it is neither progressive nor regressive; rather it is a *proportional* tax. In the remainder of this chapter we employ the tax function that has a positive intercept to illustrate more clearly certain aspects of mathematical and graphic analysis, but keep in mind that this need not be the case.

It is extremely difficult to determine the exact nature of aggregate tax function of the United States; this is due both to the complexities of U.S. tax laws and to the fact that these taxes are imposed at federal, state, and local levels. One recent study concludes that the U.S. tax system is essentially proportional for most households.[1] However, this study is based on the assumption that consumers bear the brunt of corporate income and property taxes in the form of higher prices. When this occurs, the very rich pay tax rates that are only slightly higher than the tax rate for the average household. If this assumption is incorrect (that is, if the owners of capital do bear the major portion of corporate income and property taxes), then the tax rate is progressive in the upper-income brackets.[1]

To compute the level of aggregate demand when taxes are a function of income, we substitute equations (4-2), (4-3), and (4-4) into equation (4-1) to obtain

$$Y = a + bY_d + \bar{I} + \bar{G} \tag{4-29}$$

Equation (4-7) can now be written

$$Y_d = Y - (h + tY) \tag{4-30}$$

and we can substitute equation (4-30) into equation (4-29), which gives us

$$Y = a + b[Y - (h + tY)] + \bar{I} + \bar{G} \tag{4-31}$$

Finally, solving equation (4-31) for Y, we obtain

$$Y = \frac{1}{1 - b + bt}(a - bh + \bar{I} + \bar{G}) \tag{4-32}$$

which is the equilibrium level of aggregate demand.

For a numerical example, let us assume that

$$\begin{aligned}
C &= 5 + 0.8Y_d \\
\bar{G} &= 20 \\
\bar{I} &= 10 \\
T &= 10 + 0.1Y
\end{aligned} \tag{4-33}$$

where, as before, all magnitudes are measured in dollars of constant purchasing power, or real dollars. Substituting the appropriate values from (4-33) into equation (4-32), we obtain

$$Y = \frac{1}{1 - 0.8 + (0.8)(0.1)}[5 - 0.8(10) + 10 + 20] \tag{4-34}$$

$$= \$96.4 \text{ billion}$$

The level of taxation is then

$$T = h + tY = 10 + 0.1(96.4) = \$19.64 \text{ billion} \tag{4-35}$$

and we note that a deficit of $0.36 billion exists in the government budget.

Using the procedures outlined in equations (4-16), (4-17), and (4-18), new

---

[1] Joseph A. Pechman and Benjamin Okner, *Who Bears the Tax Burden?* (Washington, D.C.: Brookings Institution, 1974).

investment and government expenditure multipliers can easily be derived; these are

$$\mu'_G = \mu'_I = \frac{1}{1 - b + bt} \tag{4-36}$$

The primes indicate that these multipliers differ from the multipliers that we derived previously. In comparison with these earlier multipliers, we can see that

$$\frac{1}{1 - b + bt} < \frac{1}{1 - b} \tag{4-37}$$

for positive values of t. Therefore the impact of changes in investment or government spending on aggregate demand will be smaller when an income tax system exists. The practical significance of this factor is that the equilibrium level of income is less sensitive to fluctuations in the level of investment, so that the effect of either an increase or a decrease in business activity on income is automatically diminished. This characteristic, sometimes referred to as *built-in stability*, results because as investment declines there is a corresponding decline in income; taxes, which are a function of income, then automatically fall, increasing disposable income at any given income level and causing a multiplier effect to operate in the opposite direction to the investment multiplier. The overall effect is a smaller decline in income. On the other hand, increases in government expenditure have a smaller impact on aggregate demand, a factor that is sometimes undesirable because it reduces the effect of fiscal policy.

Finally, let us examine the form of the tax multiplier that is used in conjunction with the income tax. Here we consider two possible tax multipliers. The simpler of the two indicates the impact of a change in the average rate of taxation caused by a change in the constant term from h to $h + \Delta h$, holding the marginal rate of taxation constant. Starting with equation (4-32), a change in h produces a change in the equilibrium level of aggregate demand that can be expressed as

$$Y + \Delta Y = \frac{1}{1 - b + bt}(a - bh - b\Delta h + \bar{I} + \bar{G}) \tag{4-38}$$

Subtracting equation (4-32) from (4-38), we obtain

$$\Delta Y = \frac{-b\Delta h}{1 - b + bt} \tag{4-39}$$

which after rearranging terms yields a new tax multiplier

$$\mu_{Th} = \frac{\Delta Y}{\Delta h} = \frac{-b}{1 - b + bt} \tag{4-40}$$

This tax multiplier has a smaller value than the tax multiplier in (4-21), because if $\Delta h > 0$, for example, then as income falls the income-associated portion of the total income tax automatically declines and somewhat offsets the increase in the average rate of taxation.

The second income tax multiplier we consider here is used to measure the effect of a change in the marginal rate of taxation. This income tax multiplier is given by[2]

$$\mu_{Tt} = \frac{-bY}{1 - b + bt} \tag{4-41}$$

The most interesting characteristic of this multiplier is that its value depends on the value of income prevailing at the time the change in the marginal rate of taxation occurs. No other multiplier that we will derive in this book possesses this characteristic. Economically, this means that a given change in t will have a small effect on income when income is low and a large effect on income when it is high.

The following conclusions can be drawn from the preceding analysis:

1. Changes in the level of government spending and taxation affect the level of aggregate demand.
2. Balanced budget increases (decreases) are not neutral; they increase (decrease) aggregate demand.
3. A greater increase (decrease) in aggregate demand can be achieved if increases (decreases) in government expenditure are *not* matched by equal changes in government taxation.
4. A tax that is a function of income reduces the impact on the economy of changes in investment and government spending.

4-3   Graphic Analysis

The foregoing mathematical analysis can be easily described graphically. The graphic solution to the numerical example in Chapter 3 is repeated in Figures 4-2 and 4-3. Recall that in this example

[2] To derive equation (4-41), we rewrite equation (4-32)

$$Y = (a - bh + \bar{I} + \bar{G})(1 - b + bt)^{-1} \tag{4-41a}$$

Then taking the derivative of Y with respect to t, we obtain

$$\frac{dY}{dt} = -b(a - bh + \bar{I} + \bar{G})(1 - b + bt)^{-2} \tag{4-41b}$$

which can be rewritten

$$\frac{dY}{dt} = \frac{-b(a - bh + \bar{I} + \bar{G})}{(1 - b + bt)(1 - b + bt)} \tag{4-41c}$$

Recalling that

$$Y = \frac{a - bh + \bar{I} + \bar{G}}{1 - b + bt} \tag{4-41d}$$

the income tax rate multiplier can be written

$$\mu_{Tt} = \frac{dY}{dt} = \frac{-bY}{1 - b + bt} \tag{4-41e}$$

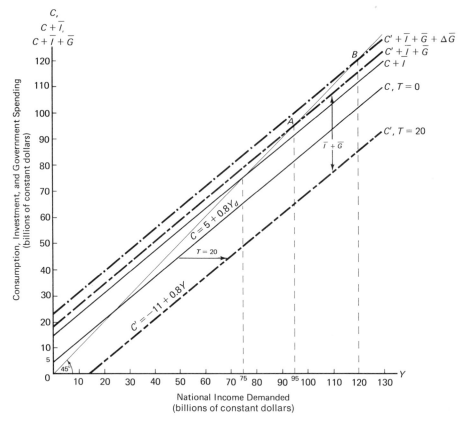

FIGURE 4-2   *Determination of Aggregate Demand with Government Spending and Exogenous Taxes*

$$C = 5 + 0.8Y_d$$

$$\bar{I} = \$10 \text{ billion}$$

$$\bar{G} = 0$$

$$\bar{T} = 0$$

The equilibrium level of aggregate demand is $75 billion, as indicated by the solid lines in Figures 4-2 and 4-3, which are simply reproductions of the functions graphed in Figures 3-3 and 3-4.

When the government sector is added and government expenditure and taxes are assumed to be exogenous, the assumptions of the numerical example then become

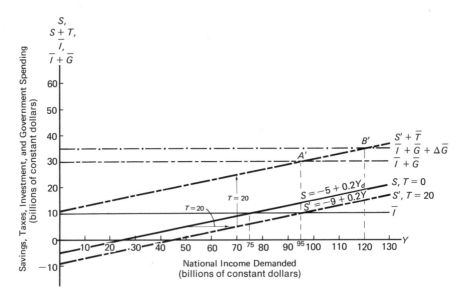

FIGURE 4-3   *Alternative Determination of Aggregate Demand with Government Spending and Exogenous Taxes*

$$C = 5 + 0.8Y_d$$

$$\bar{I} = \$10 \text{ billion}$$

$$\bar{G} = \bar{T} = \$20 \text{ billion}$$

The fact that our model now includes taxation means that disposable income is no longer equal to national income but is instead equal to national income *minus* taxes, or

$$Y_d = Y - T \tag{4-7}$$

This is important, because the consumption function expressed in the preceding numerical example cannot be illustrated as a function of national income. It is therefore necessary to transform this consumption function into a relationship between consumption and national income, so that it can be graphed with national income on the horizontal axis. To accomplish this we substitute equation (4-7) into equation (4-2). Then, setting $T = \bar{T}$, we obtain

$$C' = a + b(Y - \bar{T}) = a - b\bar{T} + bY \tag{4-42}$$

where the prime indicates the transformed consumption function. The slope of the adjusted consumption function remains unchanged, but its intercept declines by $b\bar{T}$, causing the entire function to shift downward by this amount. The adjusted function does not shift downward by an amount equal to the entire tax, because only a portion of the tax revenue is derived from reductions in consumption; the remainder results from reductions in saving.

In our numerical example, this gives us the equation

$$C' = 5 - (0.8)(20) + 0.8Y$$
$$= -11 + 0.8Y \tag{4-43}$$

Note that this consumption function exists only for $\overline{T} = \$20$ billion. If the level of taxation changes, then the consumption function, which is expressed as a function of national income, also changes. The relationship between consumption and disposable income, however, does *not* change, because consumption is a specific function of disposable income rather than of national income.

In a similar manner we can easily derive the relationship between savings and national income, obtaining

$$S' = -a - (1 - b)\overline{T} + (1 - b)Y \tag{4-44}$$

or in terms of our numerical example

$$S' = -9 + 0.2Y \tag{4-45}$$

Equations (4-43) and (4-45) are graphed in Figures 4-2 and 4-3, respectively. As we can clearly see, the graphic implication of introducing an exogenous tax is to shift the zero tax consumption and savings functions to the right by an amount equal to the tax and downward by $b\overline{T}$ and $(1 - b)\overline{T}$, respectively. To obtain the graphic solution given in Figure 4-2, we vertically add the consumption curve in equation (4-43) to the exogenously determined levels of net investment and government expenditure to derive the new curve $C' + \overline{I} + \overline{G}$. This simply accounts for our second and third sources of demand G and I, which must be added to C' to yield total demand. The new curve intersects the 45° ray at point A, and hence the corresponding level of national income, $95 billion, is the equilibrium level of aggregate demand and income. The alternative graphic solution appears in Figure 4-3. By adding taxes vertically to the savings curve given by equation (4-45), we derive the new curve $S' + \overline{T}$. Similarly, by adding $\overline{G}$ vertically to the $\overline{I}$ curve, we obtain the $\overline{I} + \overline{G}$ curve. The level of income corresponding to the point where the $S' + \overline{T}$ curve intersects the $\overline{I} + \overline{G}$ curve is the equilibrium level of aggregate demand. This intersection occurs at point A' in Figure 4-3, where the corresponding level of income is $95 billion.

The effect of a $5 billion increase in government spending, if taxes remain constant, can be easily determined from Figures 4-2 and 4-3. First, however, let us compute the changes in aggregate demand and income that result.

The government spending multiplier in equation (4-18) gives us a multiplier here of

$$\mu_G = \frac{1}{1 - b} = \frac{1}{1 - 0.8} = 5.0 \tag{4-46}$$

Thus the change in aggregate demand ΔY is $\mu_G \cdot \Delta \overline{G} = (5)(5) = \$25$ billion, and the new level of aggregate demand and income is therefore $120 billion.

In Figures 4-2 and 4-3 the new level of aggregate demand is found simply by adding $\bar{I}$, $\bar{G}$, and $\Delta\bar{G}$ to the adjusted consumption function C' or by equating $S' + \bar{T}$ with $\bar{I} + \bar{G} + \Delta\bar{G}$. The new level of aggregate demand is the one that corresponds to points B and B' in Figures 4-2 and 4-3, respectively. It is equal to $120 billion, just as we calculated algebraically.

When an income tax exists, the graphic solution is basically the same as it is when an exogenous tax prevails. The only major difference is that the equation used to draw the relationship between consumption or savings and income is slightly more complicated. Suppose that the assumptions contained in the preceding income tax numerical example

$$C = 5 + 0.8Y_d$$

$$\bar{I} = \$10 \text{ billion}$$

$$\bar{G} = \$20 \text{ billion}$$

prevail and that the tax function is

$$T = 10 + 0.1Y$$

With the income tax specified by equation (4-28), the adjusted consumption function can be generally expressed as

$$C' = a + b[Y - (h + tY)]$$
$$= a - bh + (b - bt)Y \tag{4-47}$$

and the adjusted savings function can be expressed as

$$S' = -a + (1 - b)[Y - (h + tY)]$$
$$= -a - (1 - b)h + (1 - b)(Y - tY) \tag{4-48}$$

In terms of the specific assumptions of our numerical example, we then obtain

$$C' = 5 - (0.8)(10) + [(0.8) - (0.8)(0.1)]Y$$
$$= -3 + 0.72Y \tag{4-49}$$

and

$$S' = -5 - (1 - 0.8)(10) + (1 - 0.8)(Y - 0.1Y)$$
$$= -7 + 0.18Y \tag{4-50}$$

These adjusted consumption and savings curves are shown in Figures 4-4 and 4-5 with the consumption and savings curves C and S that would exist if there were no taxes. We can see that as in our previous graphic analysis, the adjusted consumption and savings curves lie to the right of the zero tax curves.[3] However, in the case

---

[3] This conclusion is valid only if $h > 0$. If $h < 0$, then the vertical intercepts of the adjusted consumption and savings functions will lie above the intercepts of the unadjusted functions and the adjusted functions will intersect the unadjusted functions.

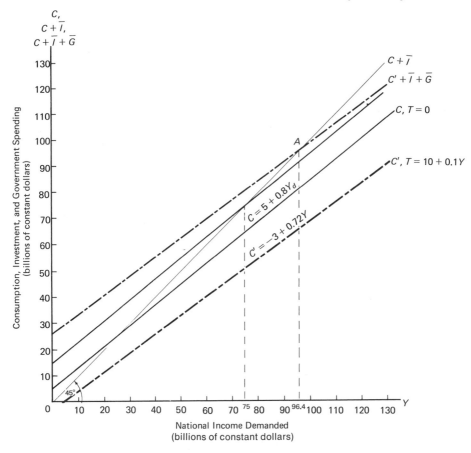

FIGURE 4-4   *Determination of Aggregate Demand with Government Spending and Income Taxes*

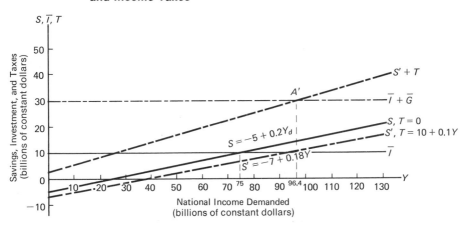

FIGURE 4-5   *Alternative Determination of Aggregate Demand with Government Spending and Income Taxes*

of the exogenous tax the horizontal displacement of the adjusted curves is a constant amount, whereas in the case of the income tax the displacement increases as the level of income rises. This is because taxes are a constant in the case of the exogenous tax, so that the MPC and MPS remain unchanged in the adjusted functions; however, in the case of the income tax the MPC and MPS decline, because the taxes are a function of income. This decline in the MPC and MPS reduces the slope of the adjusted functions, and hence the horizontal distance separating them from the unadjusted functions increases as income increases.

Once the adjusted consumption and savings curves are drawn, the graphic solution to the equilibrium level of aggregate demand is almost identical with the solution graphed in Figures 4-2 and 4-3. To the adjusted consumption curve C' in Figure 4-4, we simply add vertically the exogenously determined levels of investment and government spending. The level of income corresponding to the point where the combined curve $C' + \bar{I} + \bar{G}$ intersects the 45° ray is the equilibrium level. This is point A in Figure 4-4, where the level of income is \$96.4 billion. The graphic solution via the alternative method illustrated in Figure 4-5 is somewhat more complicated, because the level of taxation varies with income, so that the amount of tax added to the adjusted savings function to obtain the $S' + T$ curve is not a constant. However, this problem can be easily overcome by summing equation (4-50) and the income tax equation $T = 10 + 0.1Y$ to obtain

$$S' + T = (-7 + 0.18Y) + (10 + 0.1Y)$$
$$= 3 + 0.28Y \tag{4-51}$$

The adjusted savings function *plus* the tax function can now be drawn in Figure 4-5. The level of income corresponding to the point where the $S' + T$ curve intersects the $\bar{I} + \bar{G}$ curve is the equilibrium level of aggregate demand. This is point A' in Figure 4-5, where the corresponding level of income is \$96.4 billion.

Changes in the equilibrium level of aggregate demand that result from changes in the level of government spending and net investment are easily handled in Figures 4-2, 4-3, 4-4, and 4-5 by shifting either the $C' + \bar{I} + \bar{G}$ curve or the $\bar{I} + \bar{G}$ curve. If there is a change in taxation, however, the process becomes more complicated, because the consumption and savings functions must once again be adjusted due to the change in the level of disposable income corresponding to a given level of national income.

4-4   The Full-employment Surplus

In Section 4-2 we pointed out that an income tax is a built-in automatic stabilizer in an economy. During recessions, as income falls, government revenue also declines; if government expenditures remain fixed, then the expansionary effects of the automatic budget deficit offset the decline in private aggregate demand. If the budget was initially in balance at full employment, the observed deficit in the recession is due to the economy's influence on the budget, *not* the budget's influence on the economy. In other words, a deficit does not necessarily imply that the government is consciously pursuing an expansionist policy to offset the recession; instead, the government may simply be pursuing a passive policy. To overcome this ambiguity, economists have devised the concept of the *full-employment surplus*. This is an estimate of the amount by which government tax revenue would exceed government expenditure *if* the economy were at full employment. In the actual computation of the full-employment surplus, the economy is assumed to be operating at full employment when an unemployment rate of 4% prevails for all civilian workers in the labor force.[4]

For simplicity, we assume that taxes are proportional to income; that is

$$T = tY \qquad (4\text{-}52)$$

where the marginal rate of taxation t is also the average rate of taxation. For a given marginal rate of taxation at the full-employment level of income, the full-employment level of taxes is

$$T_{FE} = tY_{FE} \qquad (4\text{-}53)$$

Now suppose that a given level of government expenditure $\bar{G}$ has been budgeted. Then the surplus in tax revenue at full-employment will be $T_{FE} - \bar{G}$. If

$$T_{FE} - \bar{G} > 0 \qquad (4\text{-}54)$$

then a *positive full-employment surplus* exists. If

$$T_{FE} - \bar{G} < 0 \qquad (4\text{-}55)$$

then a *negative full-employment surplus,* or a *full-employment deficit,* exists. Obviously, when tax revenues at full-employment are equal to government expenditures, the full-employment surplus is zero.

The implications of the concept of the full-employment surplus for fiscal policy are illustrated in Figure 4-6. Initially, the marginal rate of taxation is t_0 and the budgeted level of government spending is $\bar{G}_0$. The tax function $T = t_0 Y$ and the level of government expenditure are represented by the solid lines in Figure 4-6. At full employment Y_{FE}, tax revenues equal government expenditures and the full-employment surplus is zero. But suppose that instead of being at Y_{FE}, the economy is in a recession and the level of income is Y_0; then $\bar{G}_0 > T$, and a deficit automatically occurs. This result has important implications for fiscal policy, because the casual observer may interpret the deficit as an indicator of expansionary, counterrecessionary action on the part of government, when it is simply the

---

[4] The selection of the 4% rate occurred in the early 1960s, when this figure was a good estimate of the full-employment rate of unemployment. This is no longer the situation, for reasons that we will examine in more detail in Chapter 12. However, to maintain consistency in the time-series data, the 4% rate has been retained. Moreover, changes in the full-employment surplus computed on this consistent basis are not sensitive to the choice of the unemployment rate, and hence they can be used to indicate changes in the direction of fiscal policy.

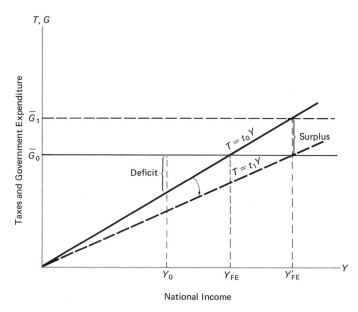

FIGURE 4-6   *The Full-employment Surplus*

result of built-in economic stabilizers. Rather than being expansionary, the govern-ment budget is actually neutral. To have a truly expansionary fiscal policy, government expenditures must be increased or the marginal rate of taxation must be reduced. Of course, these actions would increase the deficit at Y_0, and an unsophisticated analysis of the budget might lead us to conclude that it is too expansionary. The concept of the full-employment surplus helps us to avoid these pitfalls.

This concept and its simple analysis also have policy implications for a growing economy. Suppose that the employment level is Y_{FE}, given our initial set of conditions and a balanced budget. If the productive capacity of the economy grows, then the full-employment level of income will increase from Y_{FE} to Y'_{FE}. If government expenditure and the rate of taxation remain constant at $\overline{G}_0$ and t_0, respectively, then the positive full-employment surplus shown in Figure 4-6 will automatically emerge. As the economy grows, there will be a corresponding growth in the full-employment surplus. This ever-increasing budget surplus has the opposite effect on a growing economy that an increasing deficit has on a declining economy; that is, an increasing surplus is contractionary and restrains the rate of economic growth. For this reason, economists refer to this phenomenon as *fiscal drag.* To eliminate fiscal drag, government expenditures must increase or the marginal rate of taxation must decline over time. These two possibilities appear in Figure 4-6 as the dashed lines representing the higher level of government expenditure $\overline{G}_1$ and the new tax function $T = t_1 Y$. If either of these two changes (or some combination of the two) occurs, then the full-employment surplus at Y'_{FE} will be zero.

Figure 4-7 shows the estimated U.S. government full-employment surplus ex-

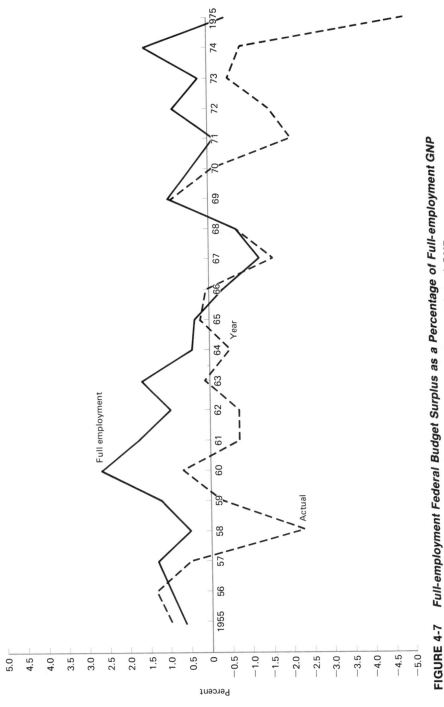

**FIGURE 4-7   Full-employment Federal Budget Surplus as a Percentage of Full-employment GNP
and Actual Federal Budget Surplus as a Percentage of Actual GNP**

SOURCE Council of Economic Advisors, unpublished documents.

pressed as a percentage of full-employment GNP. For the purposes of comparison, the actual federal budget surplus as a percentage of actual GNP is also graphed in this figure. The economy is operating at or near a 4% rate of unemployment when the two curves coincide. As we can see, the late 1950s and the early 1960s were characterized by high full-employment surpluses, while during the same period the actual federal budget was operating for the most part with deficits. The resulting fiscal drag was believed by some economists to be the cause of the slow economic growth and the high unemployment levels in this period. The tax cut of 1964 was originally proposed in 1961 on the grounds that the economy was actually operating at less than full employment and that the deficit resulting from a tax cut would disappear quickly as the economy expanded. The fact that consumption expenditures rose rapidly between the beginning of 1964 and the middle of 1965 led many economists to deduce that the policy conclusions of the Keynesian multiplier theory examined in Chapters 3 and 4 were essentially correct. As we shall see in more detail in subsequent chapters, other economists have argued that the increase in consumer expenditures was the result not of the tax cut but of an expansion of the money supply that began in 1961.

4-5   Concluding Remarks

In Chapter 3 we discovered that there were no "built-in" forces in the simple theory of income determination that could automatically produce a full-employment level of income. In this chapter, we have learned how an exogenous force—government fiscal policy—can increase or decrease the level of aggregate demand and hence be used to attain full employment. If aggregate demand is less than aggregate supply, then a fiscal policy of increased expenditure, decreased taxation, or a combination of these two factors will increase aggregate demand and restore full employment. Should aggregate demand exceed aggregate supply, a contractionary fiscal policy can be imposed to realign aggregate demand with aggregate supply and to stop the inflation created by the excess demand. If government revenue is collected by means of an income tax, the economy possesses automatic built-in stabilizers that act as shock absorbers in periods of recession or inflation. Because these stabilizers automatically generate budget deficits or surpluses, the true impact of the budget on fiscal policy during recession or inflation cannot be measured by the actual surplus or deficit in the budget. To measure the expansionary or contractionary effect of the government's budget, we use the full-employment surplus, which is an estimate of the amount by which tax revenues would exceed or be less than government expenditures if full employment prevailed.

The shortcomings of our simple model of income determination that were pointed out in Chapter 3 still persist after the model has been expanded to include the government sector. These shortcomings are present in the simple model because its aggregate demand curve is perfectly price inelastic. In Chapters 5–10, we will expand the theory of aggregate demand to derive a price-elastic aggregate demand curve. We will then use this more sophisticated theory of aggregate demand in conjunction with our two models of aggregate supply to explore various problems in macroeconomic theory and policy.

5 Capital and Investment

5-1 Introduction

In our simple model of aggregate demand we treated net investment as if it were exogenous to the model. In our more sophisticated model we consider investment to be *endogenous*, or determined within the framework of the model. Before we can develop this model, however, we must understand what motivates the firm to purchase capital goods and what determines the rate at which these goods are acquired.

5-2 Behavior of the Firm

A basic assumption of microeconomics is that the primary objective of the firm is to maximize profits. We have already invoked this assumption in Chapter 2 to derive the firm's demand for labor function. We will use it again to derive the firm's demand for capital goods function. In addition, we will assume that the firm has perfect knowledge and that no uncertainty surrounds the investment decision.

Given that the firm operates to maximize profits over some planning horizon, which particular capital goods out of the almost infinite number available does the firm acquire? The simple answer is that the firm purchases only those capital goods that maximize its profits. But why do some capital goods contribute to profit maximization while others do not? The answer to this question can be found in the following example. Suppose that a firm has $40,000 in cash and only two available investment opportunities. The first capital good costs $20,000, will last exactly one year, will have zero scrap value at the end of one year, and will yield revenue of $22,000 in excess of operating costs. The second capital good has the same characteristics as the first, except that its revenue yield will be $21,000 in excess of operating costs. Both forms of investment have positive rates of return. The percentage rate of return on the first investment is

$$\left(\frac{\$22,000}{\$20,000} - 1\right) \cdot 100 = 10\% \tag{5-1}$$

and the percentage rate of return on the second investment is

$$\left(\frac{\$21,000}{\$20,000} - 1\right) \cdot 100 = 5\% \tag{5-2}$$

From the firm's point of view, the first investment opportunity is preferable to the second; however, this is not equivalent to saying that the second investment should be forgone or even that the first investment should be undertaken. Before this decision can be made, a third alternative for the use of the firm's money should be considered: the firm can purchase one-year bonds. If the interest rate on these bonds is greater than 10%, then the firm can maximize profits by buying only bonds; that is, the firm can make a financial investment without making a real investment. With a rate of return on one-year bonds of 6%, for example, the first investment project will be undertaken, because it has a yield of 10%. The second investment, which has a yield of less than 6%, would be rejected and the firm would use its remaining funds to purchase one-year bonds yielding 6%. Finally, if the one-year bond rate is below 5%, then both investments will be undertaken. This simple example points out that a firm maximizes profits by undertaking only those investment projects that have a higher rate of return than the market rate of interest.

The rate of return on the firm's real investment is called the *internal rate of return,* and the rate of return on the firm's purchase of financial assets is called the *external rate of return.* The difference between the firm's internal and external rates of return is called the firm's *net internal rate of return.* The profit-maximizing firm therefore attempts to undertake all investment projects with a positive net internal rate of return. In the preceding example, the internal rates of return i_I on the first and second investment projects are 10% and 5%, respectively. With an external rate of return i_E of 6%, for example, the net internal rate of return i_N on the first project is

$$i_{N_1} = i_{I_1} - i_{E_1} = 10 - 6 = 4\% \tag{5-3}$$

and the net internal rate of return on the second project is

$$i_{N_2} = i_{I_2} - i_{E_2} = 5 - 6 = -1\% \tag{5-4}$$

Because the net internal rate of return is positive on the first project and negative on the second project, the first will be undertaken and the second will be rejected.

For simplicity of exposition, we have assumed here that the firm had funds available to purchase both capital goods. However, this assumption is not essential to our argument. If financial markets were perfect and there were no administrative costs involved in borrowing, the firm would be able to either borrow or lend at the market rate of interest. Now, suppose that the firm has no money with which to make either investment and that the market rate of interest is 6%. If the firm borrows $20,000 at 6%, then at the end of one year it will have to pay back ($20,000)(1.06) = $21,200. The first investment yields $22,000 in excess of operating costs in one year; therefore, the firm can borrow $20,000 at 6% for one year, repay principal *plus* interest of $21,200 at the end of the year, and earn a profit of $22,000 − $21,200 = $800. If the second investment is undertaken, it will yield $21,000 in revenue in excess of operating costs, but the repayment of the $20,000 loan and the $1,200 in interest will result in a net *loss* on this project of $21,200 − $21,000 = $200. The $800 profit on the first project represents a net internal rate of return of 4%, whereas the loss of $200 on the second project signifies a net internal rate of return of −1%. Thus we have demonstrated that given our set of assumptions, it makes no difference in the investment decision-making process whether the firm uses its own funds or borrows.

In this section, we have greatly simplified the investment decision problem to highlight the implications of the profit-maximizing assumption for the behavior of the firm. Perhaps our most drastic departure from reality has been the assumption that the typical capital good has a life of only one year, when in reality the average capital good is much more durable. This assumption is necessary only to simplify the mathematics involved; it does not significantly distort our conclusions about the basic behavior of the firm. However, before we can progress further in our study of capital and investment theory, we must drop this assumption and learn a few mathematical tools that enable us to handle capital goods with life spans of many years.

5-3   The Mathematics of Investment

If we placed $100 in a savings account in a bank that paid 6% interest compounded annually, our account would grow in one year according to the formula

$$R_1 = (1 + i)P_v \tag{5-5}$$

where R_1 = the amount in the account or the return on the deposit at the end of one year

i = annual interest rate

P_v = original value of the deposit, or the *present value* of the account when it is opened

In this example, the return in one year would be

$$R_1 = (1 + 0.06)(\$100) = \$106$$

To consider another example, suppose that someone owes you $106, but payment is not due for one year. What would be the value of this IOU today? Obviously, even if the payment in the future is absolutely certain, no one would give you $106 for the IOU, because they could deposit $100 in the bank and receive the same return of $106 in one year. In fact, as long as you ask any price above $100 for the IOU, you will not sell it. At a price of $100, potential buyers would be indifferent to a choice between buying your IOU and placing $100 in a savings account. Thus the value of the IOU today, its *present value*, is $100. We can solve for the present value directly if we rewrite equation (5-5) so that it reads

$$P_v = \frac{R_1}{1 + i} \qquad (5\text{-}6)$$

which gives ($106) ÷ (1.06) = $100 as the present value of the IOU. It should be apparent that equation (5-6) can be used to obtain the present value of any return one year hence at any annual rate of interest.

This relatively simple concept of the present value of a future payment or return is crucial to an understanding of the theory of investment. To realize why this is so, we recall the simple investment decision example given in the preceding section. There we learned that a firm will undertake all investment projects whose internal rate of return exceeds the external rate of return. The rate of interest that equates the present value of an investment to its purchase cost P_c is the firm's internal rate of return i_I on that project. For example, consider the first investment project in the preceding section. Its return in excess of operating costs is $22,000, and its purchase cost is $20,000. Taking equation (5-6) and solving for the value of i_I that will give us $P_v = P_c = $20,000$, we obtain

$$i_I = \frac{R_1}{P_v} - 1 = \frac{R_1}{P_c} - 1 = \frac{\$\,22{,}000}{\$\,20{,}000} - 1 = 0.10 \qquad (5\text{-}7)$$

which in percentage terms is 10%. Not surprisingly, we observe that this is exactly the same internal rate of return we computed in equation (5-1). If we use equation (5-7) to compute i_I for the second investment project, we find that the result is 5%.

Thus far in our analysis of the investment behavior of firms, we have been dealing with simple examples of investment projects that have a life of only one year. Before we begin to analyze more realistic investment projects with lives greatly in excess of one year, we must develop our mathematical tools somewhat further. Let us return to our savings account example and suppose that we left the original deposit in the bank for two years. Then the value of the account at the end of two years would be

$$R_2 = R_1(1 + i) = P_v(1 + i)(1 + i) = P_v(1 + i)^2 \qquad (5\text{-}8)$$

where R_2 represents the return on the original deposit in two years. The present value of this return two years hence is therefore

$$P_v = \frac{R_2}{(1 + i)^2} \qquad (5\text{-}9)$$

Generalizing, we can express the present value of any single payment or receipt n years in the future as

$$P_v = \frac{R_n}{(1 + i)^n} \qquad (5\text{-}10)$$

where R_n is the value of a receipt or payment n years hence.

Now suppose that we maintain n savings accounts in various banks throughout the country and that we plan to withdraw one deposit *plus* the accrued interest from a different bank at the end of each year, beginning with the first year. It is obvious that the total present value of all these savings accounts is given by

$$P_v = \frac{R_1}{1 + i} + \frac{R_2}{(1 + i)^2} + \frac{R_3}{(1 + i)^3} + \cdots + \frac{R_n}{(1 + i)^n} \qquad (5\text{-}11)$$

where P_v now represents the present value of the stream of payments $R_1, R_2, \ldots, R_n$.

In addition to giving us the present value of a stream of payments resulting from the sequential closing of n savings accounts, equation (5-11) can also be used to compute the present value of a capital good with a life of n years. This is accomplished simply by interpreting the stream of payments in equation (5-11) as the stream of revenue in excess of operating costs that the capital good yields throughout its life. Thus for an investment project that has a purchase cost of P_c and an expected annual yield in excess of operating costs of $R_1, R_2, \ldots, R_n$ for n years, the rate of interest in equation (5-11) that will give us $P_v = P_c$ is the project's internal rate of return i_I. Unfortunately, the calculations required to solve equation (5-11) for i_I are quite tedious, but we can simplify this problem by making a few assumptions.

First, we assume that all annual returns in excess of operating costs are equal; that is

$$R_1 = R_2 = R_3 = \cdots = R_n = R \qquad (5\text{-}12)$$

Equation (5-11) can now be rewritten

$$P_v = R[(1 + i)^{-1} + (1 + i)^{-2} + \cdots + (1 + i)^{-n}] \qquad (5\text{-}13)$$

Equation (5-13) is a geometric series, and its sum can be determined first by multiplying both sides of the equation *by* $(1 + i)$ to obtain

$$P_v(1 + i) = R[1 + (1 + i)^{-1} + (1 + i)^{-2} + \cdots + (1 + i)^{-(n-1)}] \qquad (5\text{-}14)$$

Then subtracting (5-1) from (5-14) and canceling terms gives us

$$iP_v = R[1 - (1 + i)^{-n}] \qquad (5\text{-}15)$$

or

$$P_v = \frac{R}{i}[1 - (1 + i)^{-n}] \qquad (5\text{-}16)$$

Equation (5-16) can be used to determine the rate of interest i that will give a present value of the income stream R equal to the purchase cost of the capital good P_c. By definition, this rate of interest will be the firm's internal rate of return i_I on the investment. For example, suppose that a capital good with a life of 10 years yields an annual net revenue of $300 and costs $2,200. What is this investment's internal rate of return? If we rewrite equation (5-16)

$$P_v = P_c = \$2,200 = \frac{\$300}{i_I}[1 - (1 + i_I)^{-10}] \tag{5-17}$$

then we see that it contains only one unknown i_I, so that it is possible to solve for i_I. Because (5-17) is a high-order equation, the required value of i_I cannot be easily determined directly, but it can be found by the method of iteration. This simply means that we select a value of i_I, substitute it into the right-hand side of equation (5-17), and calculate the value for this term. If the computed value of the right-hand side is equal to the value of P_c on the left-hand side of equation (5-17), then we have determined the correct value of i_I; if it is not, then another value of i_I must be selected. This process is repeated by trial and error until the (approximately) correct value of i_I is determined. Now suppose that we select the value 0.05 for i_I. Then substituting this value into the right-hand term of equation (5-17), we obtain

$$\frac{\$300}{0.05}[1 - (1.05)^{-10}] = \$6,000\,(1 - 0.614) = \$2,320$$

Because $2, 320 > $2, 200, we must select a higher value of i_I and repeat the calculation. Suppose that this time we let $i_I = 0.06$. We then obtain

$$\frac{\$300}{0.06}[1 - (1.06)^{-10}] = \$5,000\,(1 - 0.56) = \$2,200$$

Thus the firm's internal rate of return on this project must be 6%.

If we wish, we can simplify our analysis even further by assuming that the life of the capital good is infinite. In this case equation (5-16) approaches in the limit

$$P_v = \frac{R}{i} \tag{5-18}$$

as $n \to \infty$. For a capital good with an infinite life, the internal rate of return can easily be found by letting $P_c = P_v$ and solving equation (5-18) for i_I, or

$$i_I = \frac{R}{P_c} \tag{5-19}$$

For example, suppose that the capital good in the preceding example has an infinite life. Its internal rate of return would then be

$$i_I = \frac{\$300}{\$2,200} = 0.136$$

or 13.6%. Observe that by lengthening the life of the capital good from 10 years to infinity we more than double its internal rate of return. Now suppose that the price of the capital good rises from $2,200 to $3,000. The internal rate of return will then fall from 13.6% to 10%. This downward movement of the internal rate of return as the purchase price of capital goods increases will play a critical role in our examination (in Section 5-5) of the factors that determine the level of net investment.

Equation (5-18) can also be used to determine the present value of a bond that does not have a maturity date. Bonds without maturity dates, normally called *consols*, stipulate that the owner will receive a constant return in so many dollars every year. When consols are initially sold, usually by governments, P_c must equal P_v. This equality is determined by the market rate of interest. For example, if $R = \$100$ and $i = 5\%$, then the consols would be offered on the bond market for

$$P_c = P_v = \frac{\$100}{0.05} = \$2,000$$

Once the consols are sold, the initial buyers may decide to resell them at a later date, but the price at which these bonds can be resold will be $2,000 only by coincidence. For example, suppose that one week after this consol is sold, the rate of interest rises to 6%. A newly issued consol that promises to pay $100 per annum in perpetuity sells for $100 ÷ 0.06 = $ 1,666. A person who wishes to purchase a consol paying $100 per annum will not pay more than $1,666 for it, so that the maximum market price that will be paid for last week's $2,000 consol is $1,666. The person who purchased a consol last week and sells it this week therefore incurs a loss of $ 2,000 −$ 1,666 = $334, which is referred to as a *capital loss*. On the other hand, if the rate of interest falls to 4% instead of rising to 6%, then a newly issued consol will sell for $100 ÷ 0.04 = $2,500. In this example, a person who wishes to buy a consol paying $100 per annum after the interest rate decreases will pay as much as $2,500 for it. Thus the person who paid $2,000 for such a consol the previous week will be able to sell it for $2,500 and will reap a *capital gain* of $500. These simple examples explain the often repeated but little understood rule that *bond prices and interest rates vary inversely; when interest rates fall, bond prices rise, and vice versa.*

5-4   The Marginal Efficiency of Capital and Optimal Capital Stock

Thus far we have learned that a firm that maximizes profits and operates under conditions of certainty in perfect financial markets will undertake all investments whose internal rate of return exceeds the external rate of return, where the external rate of return is defined as the market rate of interest.

As the firm invests, its stock of capital increases. Because the firm will clearly undertake the most profitable capital projects first, the internal rate of return on the marginal unit of capital will decline because of diminishing returns. As a result of its assumed profit-maximizing behavior, the firm will undertake all investment projects up to the point where the internal rate of return on the marginal unit of

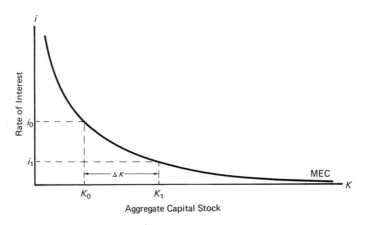

FIGURE 5-1   *The Marginal Efficiency of Capital*

capital is equal to the market rate of interest. When this occurs, the firm has the exact quantity of capital it desires and its stock is said to be *optimal*.

The relationship between the quantity of capital desired by the firm and the rate of interest therefore becomes the firm's demand for capital. By summing the demand for capital of all firms in the economy at alternative rates of interest, we can construct a curve for the aggregate demand for capital. The curve illustrated in Figure 5-1 specifies the internal rate of return on the marginal unit of capital to the economy's capital stock, which is called the *marginal efficiency of capital* or *MEC*. This curve is drawn under the assumption that the economy's labor supply, natural resources, level of technology, and expectations of future business activity all remain constant.

If the market rate of interest is i_0 and the stock of capital is K_0, we can see from Figure 5-1 that the desired stock of capital will be equal to the actual stock of capital; thus we can say that the stock of capital is optimal. When the stock of capital is optimal, the capital stock is not growing and net investment is zero. If the rate of interest now falls from i_0 to i_1, then the desired capital stock K_1 will initially exceed the actual capital stock K_0 by ΔK and the existing stock will no longer be optimal. Because the internal rate of return on the marginal unit of capital exceeds the market rate of interest i_1 when the capital stock is K_0, firms will undertake new investment projects, net investment will be positive, and the capital stock will grow. In Section 5-5 we will examine what determines the rate at which net investment occurs as the capital stock grows from one optimal level to the next.

The MEC curve in Figure 5-1 is drawn in such a way that at very low rates of interest the optimal capital stock becomes almost infinite. To understand why this is true, consider the investment project of creating new agricultural land on the U.S. continental shelf along the Gulf of Mexico. This could be accomplished by filling the shelf with low-grade soil and topping the fill with dredgings from Mississippi River silt deposits. This "created" land would be as productive as the best land now in existence and would therefore have a positive net revenue. An average acre of farm land in Iowa during 1976 sold for about $900. Using equation (5-18) and assuming a 5% interest rate, we find that the long-run annual net return expected on this land is

$$R = iP_v = (0.05)(\$900) = \$45 \text{ per acre} \tag{5-20}$$

If we assume that our continental shelf land will yield the same net revenue and if we know the cost of creating this land, then we can calculate the rate of interest that will equate present value with purchase cost. Martin Bailey[1] estimates that if the first 50 miles along the 1,500-mile coast of the Gulf of Mexico were filled in, 48 million acres would be created at a cost of $19,600,000 million. The net revenue per year on this acreage would be $(\$45)(48,000,000) = \$2,160$ million. If we equate purchase cost P_c with present value P_v and solve for the internal rate of return i_I, then equation (5-19) gives us

$$i_I = \frac{R}{P_c} = \frac{\$2,160}{\$19,600,000} = 0.0001102 \tag{5-21}$$

or an interest rate of about 0.011%. Thus if the market rate of interest falls below 0.011%, this vast investment project will become profitable. Of course, these figures are only rough estimates intended to suggest the orders of magnitude involved. The only crucial part of our argument here is that the investment opportunity must be a long-lived one, such as land creation, and must have a positive annual net revenue. This type of investment always contains some positive market rate of interest that makes the project economically feasible. Thus when drawing an MEC curve, it is not unreasonable to show that it is asymptotic to the horizontal axis.

5-5   The Marginal Efficiency of Investment

As we demonstrated in Section 5-4, the curve for the marginal efficiency of capital is the curve for the economy's demand for capital. Now assume that an economy has the MEC curve shown in Figure 5-2. In addition, assume that the market rate of interest is 5% and that the stock of capital is optimal at a level of $50 billion. Because the actual stock of capital is equal to the desired stock, it is not growing and net investment is zero. This means that gross investment I_G is equal to capital consumption K_c. Now suppose that the market rate of interest falls from 5% to 3%. An inspection of Figure 5-2 reveals that the desired stock of capital is now $175 billion but that initially the actual capital stock remains at $50 billion—a less than optimal level. This means that $125 billion of net investment is required to raise the capital stock to its new profit-maximizing level. The questions we intend to answer in this section are:

1. What determines the rate at which this net investment occurs?
2. How long will it take for the capital stock to return to an optimal level?

[1] Martin J. Bailey, National Income and the Price Level, 2nd ed. (New York: McGraw-Hill, 1971), p. 143.

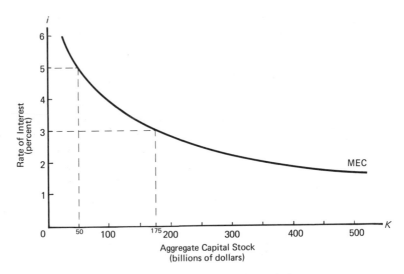

FIGURE 5-2   A Hypothetical MEC Curve

If the capital goods industry had an unlimited production capacity, the answers to these two questions would be very simple. Net investment would occur at the rate of $125 billion per time period, and only one time period would be required to reach a new optimal capital stock. However, these answers are incorrect, because their underlying assumption that the capital goods industry has an unlimited productive capacity is false. The capital goods industry, like all other industries, experiences rising costs as production increases. The typical supply curve of the capital goods industry is similar to the one in Figure 5-3. Throughout a rather wide band of output the supply of capital curve is horizontal, indicating constant returns

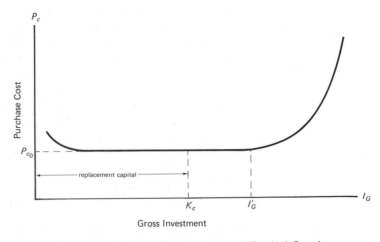

FIGURE 5-3   The Supply Curve of Capital Goods

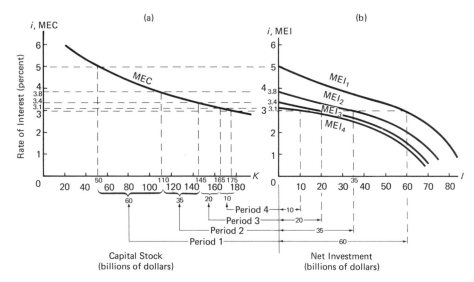

FIGURE 5-4   *The Relationship Between the Marginal Efficiency of Investment and the Marginal Efficiency of Capital*

to the variable factors of production. At either quite low or quite high levels of output, marginal costs increase and the supply curve bends upward. When the stock of capital is optimal, the capital goods industry produces the exact amount of capital required to replace the capital goods that have worn out during the period. This is the quantity of capital production K_c shown in Figure 5-3. If the capital goods industry is asked to supply capital for net investment, it can do so at the constant cost of P_{c_0} only up to the level of output I'_G. Thereafter, marginal costs begin to rise, increasing the purchase cost of capital. As we learned in Section 5-3, an increase in the purchase cost of capital causes a decline in the internal rate of return on investment in addition to the decline that results from an increasing capital stock. Hence the internal rate of return on investment begins to fall at a faster rate than the marginal efficiency of capital, thereby limiting the amount of net investment that will occur within a given time period. Because the actual amount of net investment per period is likely to be much less than the desired increase in the capital stock, the capital stock will require several time periods to grow to its new optimal level.

Figure 5-4 illustrates the process of capital growth that occurs when the rate of interest falls from 5% to 3% and the optimal capital stock subsequently rises from $50 billion to $175 billion. Figure 5-4(a) is simply a reproduction of the relevant portion of Figure 5-2, showing that the immediate effect of a drop in the rate of interest from 5% to 3% is an incentive for firms to increase their aggregate capital stock by $125 billion.

Figure 5-4(b) shows the relationship between the internal rate of return and *additions* to the capital stock. This relationship is called the *marginal efficiency of investment, or MEI.* For every level of capital stock there is an associated MEI curve. When the market rate of interest is 5% in time period 0 in Figure 5-4, the stock of capital is optimal and net investment is zero. Therefore the MEI curve associated with this capital stock MEI_1 must intersect the vertical axis in Figure 5-4(b) at 5%. When the interest rate falls from 5% to 3%, the desired capital stock exceeds the actual capital stock and net investment occurs. As firms acquire net investment in time period 1, initial units of capital are purchased at the constant price of P_{c_0}, as shown in Figure 5-3. Thus a decline in the internal rate of return on net investment occurs at the same rate as that in the capital stock, and the MEI curve MEI_1 is initially convex from below. Fairly soon, however, marginal costs in the capital goods industry begin to rise and the supply curve of capital goods bends upward at an increasing rate. When this happens, the internal rate of return on net investment declines at a faster rate than that of the capital stock, and MEI_1 becomes concave from below, as shown in Figure 5-4(b). As soon as the internal rate of return on additions to the capital stock reaches the market interest rate of 3%, net investment in period 1 ceases. As we can see in Figure 5-4(b), the amount of net investment in period 1 amounts to $60 billion. This means that the capital stock at the beginning of period 2 is $110 billion and that the MEC of the marginal unit of capital is 3.8%, as shown in Figure 5-4(a). The MEI curve for time period 2 MEI_2 intersects the vertical axis of Figure 5-4(b) at 3.8%, as it must, and thus lies below and to the left of MEI_1. We are now able to derive the vertical intercept of MEI_2 by determining to what value the interest rate would have to rise at the end of the first time period for the new existing capital stock be optimal. Figure 5-4(a) tells us that a capital stock of $110 billion is optimal if the rate of interest is 3.8%. Therefore MEI_2 must indicate $I = 0$ at this rate of interest. The MEI_2 curve achieves a 3% rate of return when net investment is $35 billion, and hence the capital stock in time period 2 grows from $110 billion to $145 billion. The process of capital stock adjustment to the new optimal stock requires two additional periods (illustrated in Figure 5-4), after which net investment returns to zero.

This example demonstrates that the MEI curve—the relationship between the rate of interest and the level of net investment—is shown to be the *demand for net investment curve*. Due to rising costs in the capital goods industry, a desired increase in the capital stock is likely to occur over several time periods, during which the MEI curve shifts downward and to the left.[2]

5-6   Investment and Shifts in the MEC Curve

We have just shown that the marginal efficiency of investment is the demand for net investment that relates the level of net investment to the interest rate. This

---

[2] The convex portion of the MEI curves in Figure 5-4(b) becomes a decreasingly smaller part of the total curves as the capital stock grows, because we implicitly assume that the capacity of the capital goods industry remains constant. This means that as the capital stock grows, there is an accompanying growth in the level of capital replacement required in each time period and the difference between K_c and I'_G diminishes. If we were to relax this assumption and allow for growth in the capital goods industry, this would not necessarily occur.

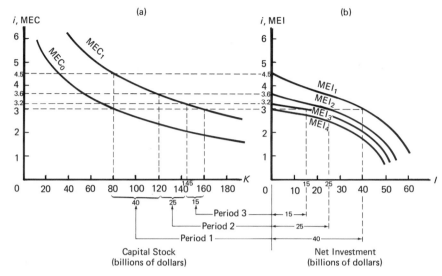

FIGURE 5-5   *The Capital Stock Adjustment Process Resulting from a Shift in the Marginal Efficiency of Capital*

emphasis on the role of the interest rate in developing the concept of the MEI curve does not imply that the rate of interest is the only variable that affects investment. This is no more true than that the price of a good is the only factor that determines the quantity of the good that is demanded. Anything that causes the MEC curve to shift also affects the level of net investment by causing a shift in the MEI curve. Recall from Section 5-4, that the MEC curve is defined given the assumptions that the economy's labor supply, natural resources, level of technology, and expectations of future business activity are all constant. A change in any of these factors would clearly produce a shift in the MEC curve, which in turn would shift the MEI curve and alter the level of net investment.

The effect of a shift in the MEC curve on the level of investment is shown in Figure 5-5. Initially, we assume that the marginal efficiency of capital is MEC_0, the market rate of interest is 3%, and the capital stock is $80 billion. Under these conditions, the marginal efficiency of capital is also 3%, the stock of capital is optimal, and net investment is therefore zero. Now suppose that there is an increase in income caused by a technological change. This increases expectations on the part of business that the return on capital will be higher in the future, and the MEC curve shifts to the right from MEC_0 to MEC_1. At the market interest rate of 3% (which is assumed to remain constant throughout this example), the desired capital stock becomes $160 billion [see Figure 5-5(a)]. The existing capital stock is now less than optimal, and net investment occurs.

The marginal efficiency of investment curve in the first time period is MEI_1, as shown in Figure 5-5(b). This curve intersects the vertical axis at 4.5%, because at this interest rate MEC_1 indicates that the initial capital stock of $80 billion is optimal and net investment is therefore zero. However, the prevailing interest rate is 3%, so that net investment during the first time period is $40 billion, as indicated by MEI_1 in Figure 5-5(b). The capital stock grows from $80 billion to $120 billion, as shown in Figure 5-5(a). In period 2, net investment equals $25 billion and the capital stock increases to $145 billion. In the final period of adjustment, net investment is $15 billion, the capital stock reaches its optimal level, and net investment ceases. That net investment is zero in period 4 is shown by the curve MEI_4 intersecting the vertical axis in Figure 5-5(b) at the market interest rate of 3%.

This rather simple example shows that factors in addition to the rate of interest can play important roles in affecting the level of net investment.

5-7   An Alternative Investment Criterion

In the preceding sections we examined the internal rate of return criterion for investment decision making. An alternative approach for determining whether an investment project should be undertaken is the *net present value criterion.*

The net present value NP_v of an investment project is the present value of the project's returns in excess of operating costs *minus* the cost of the project. Mathematically this can be expressed as

$$NP_v = P_v - P_c = R_1(1 + i)^{-1} + \cdots + R_n(1 + i)^{-n} - P_c \qquad (5-22)$$

where i is the market rate of interest. If $NP_v > 0$, then the present value of the project's returns in excess of operating costs exceeds the cost of the project; therefore, the economic profits earned by the firm on this project will be positive. On the other hand, if $NP_v < 0$, then the present value of the project's returns will not be sufficient to pay for the cost of the project and profits will be negative. Because we assume that the firm seeks to maximize economic profits, only projects with $NP_v > 0$ should be undertaken.

When $NP_v = 0$, the market rate of interest will be equal to the internal rate of return on the investment, because

$$NP_v = P_v - P_c = 0 \qquad (5-23)$$

and therefore

$$P_c = P_v = R_1(1 + i)^{-1} + \cdots + R_n(1 + i)^{-n} \qquad (5-24)$$

In Section 5-3 we defined the internal rate of return as the rate of interest equating $P_v = P_c$, which occurs, as shown in equation (5-23), when $NP_v = 0$.

If the firm is considering many investment projects, then the NP_v of each project is computed using the prevailing market interest rate. These projects are then ranked in descending order according to their NP_v values to indicate the desirability of the various projects. When this ranking process is applied to various interest rates, the number of projects with $NP_v > 0$ will increase as the interest rate decreases. Hence, the firm's investment expenditures will be inversely related to

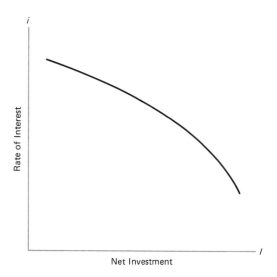

FIGURE 5-6   *The Aggregate Investment Function*

the market interest rate. A summation of the investment expenditures of all firms at various interest rates yields an aggregate investment function with a shape similar to the one shown in Figure 5-6.

The general conclusion that there is an inverse relation between investment and the interest rate, just shown via the net present value criterion, is identical to the conclusion obtained from the internal rate of return criterion. We now examine why one of these criteria is said to be superior to the other.

5-8   Superiority of the Net Present Value Criterion

Suppose that a firm has two potential investment projects—Projects I and II—with identical purchase costs of $18,500, which yield revenues in excess of operating costs for five years, as shown in Table 5-1. Furthermore, assume that the firm can

**TABLE 5-1   Revenues in Excess of Operating
Costs for Investment Projects I and II**

	Project I $P_c = \$18,500$	Project II $P_c = \$18,500$
n = 1	− $1,000	$750
2	4,500	3,500
3	7,500	6,000
4	9,000	7,500
5	3,000	3,500

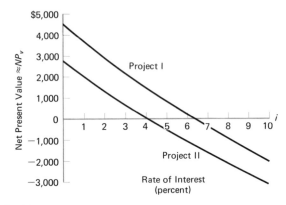

FIGURE 5-7   *The Net Present Value of Projects I and II*

undertake either project, but not both. The net present value NP_v of each of these projects is graphed in Figure 5-7 for interest rates from 0–10%. As we have already shown, the interest rate at which $NP_v = 0$ is the internal rate of return for the investment project. The internal rates of return for Projects I and II are 6.38% and 4.13%, respectively, and are indicated by the horizontal intercepts of the NP_v curves in Figure 5-7.

Now, according to the NP_v criterion, the project whose NP_v is greater at the going market interest rate is the preferred project and will be undertaken if $NP_v > 0$. For investment Projects I and II, the NP_v of Project I always exceeds the NP_v of Project II for all rates of interest, as shown in Figure 5-7. Thus according to the NP_v criterion, Project I will always be preferred to Project II. If the internal rate of return criterion is used, Project I will be preferred to Project II, again because their respective internal rates of return are 6.38% and 4.13%. Hence for investment projects whose revenue streams in excess of operating costs produce NP_v curves similar to those shown in Figure 5-7 (that is, not intersecting at positive net present values), either investment decision criterion can be used.

However, all investment projects do not produce NP_v curves similar to the ones graphed in Figure 5-7. Suppose that a firm is considering two potential projects—Projects III and IV—that have the same purchase cost and life as Projects I and II but have entirely different revenue streams, as shown in Table 5-2. The NP_v curves for these projects are graphed in Figure 5-8. The NP_v curves for Projects III and IV, in contrast to those of Projects I and II, intersect at positive net present values. This intersection occurs because the revenue stream of Project III is heavily weighted in the fifth year and the revenue stream of Project IV is heavily weighted in the first year. This means that at high interest rates the $20,000 that Project III earns in the fifth year is much more discounted when its present value is calculated than the $15,000 first-year earnings of Project IV. When interest rates are low, the increase in the present value of the $20,000 exceeds that of the $15,000. Hence at interest rates below 5.4% the present value of Project III is greater than the present value

TABLE 5-2   Revenues in Excess of Operating Costs for Investment Projects III and IV

	Project III $P_c = \$18,500$	Project IV $P_c = \$18,500$
n = 1	$1,000	$15,000
2	1,000	3,000
3	1,200	1,500
4	1,400	1,500
5	20,000	500

of Project IV, whereas if $i > 5.4$, the reverse is true.

The internal rates of return on Projects III and IV are 6.50% and 8.91%, respectively, as indicated by the horizontal intercepts of their NP_v curves in Figure 5-8. Now, according to the internal rate of return criterion, Project IV is *always* preferred to Project III. However, according to the NP_v criterion, Project III is preferred if the market rate of interest is less than 5.4% and Project IV is preferred if the rate is greater than 5.4%. In situations such as the one illustrated in our example, the investment decision criteria can yield conflicting results. Which criterion should be followed in such cases? We can easily answer this question by looking at the problem from a different perspective.

The reason the firm invests is to earn profits. Because the firm also seeks to maximize profits, it should rank investments according to profitability. However, profits are earned over time and differ from accounting period to accounting period. To be evaluated, these streams of profits must be measured at the same point in time. This can be done in the following manner. Suppose that the firm has

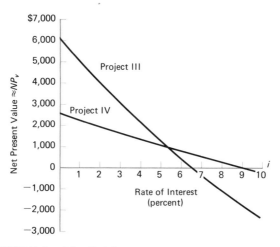

FIGURE 5-8   *The Net Present Value of Projects III and IV*

$18,500. With this money the firm can undertake Project III or Project IV, or it can deposit the $18,500 in a bank account, where it will earn the market rate of interest. If the market rate of interest is 6%, then the bank account will be worth $ 18,500 (1.06)^5 = \$24,757$ in five years. If either Project III or IV is undertaken, it will yield the revenue *minus* operating cost streams given in Table 5-2. Obviously, the money obtained from these returns, rather than remaining idle, will be placed in a bank account where it will earn 6% interest. Assuming that the returns are earned at the *end* of each accounting period, the value of the returns from Project III at the end of the fifth year will be

$$1,000(1.06)^4 + 1,000(1.06)^3 + 1,200(1.06)^2 + 1,400(1.06) + 20,000 = \$25,282$$

and those from Project IV will be

$$15,000(1.06)^4 + 3,000(1.06)^3 + 1,500(1.06)^2 + 1,000(1.06) + 500 = \$25,756$$

Subtracting the value of the $18,500 bank account at the end of the fifth year from each of these profit calculations gives us the amount by which the firm's accumulated profits from either Project III or Project will be greater than the amount in the bank account after five years. Performing these calculations, we can see that Project III yields $529 more than the bank account and Project IV yields $999 in excess of the bank account. Project IV will therefore be preferred to Project III. The internal rates of return being 8.91% on Project IV and 6.5% on Project III, the internal rate of return criterion will dictate the same investment decision as the NP_v criterion, because at 6% the NP_v for Project IV is $746 whereas the NP_v for Project III is $395.

Now suppose that the market rate of interest is 3%. If $18,500 is placed in a bank account, it will be worth $18,500 (1.03)^5 = \$21,447$ in five years. The returns from Project III at the end of the fifth year will be

$$1,000(1.03)^4 + 1,000(1.03)^3 + 1,200(1.03)^2 + 1,400(1.03) + 20,000 = \$24,933$$

and those from Project IV will be

$$15,000(1.03)^4 + 3,000(1.03)^3 + 1,500(1.03)^2 + 1,000(1.03) + 500 = \$23,282$$

Subtracting $21,477 from each of the preceding calculations gives us the amount by which the firm's accumulated profits will be improved if either Project III or Project IV is undertaken. Project III produces $3,486 more than the bank account, and Project IV produces $1,835 in excess of the bank account. Project III is therefore preferred to Project IV in this situation. This is the same result we would reach if we applied the NP_v criterion, because the NP_v of Project III at a 3% interest rate is $3,007 whereas the NP_v of Project IV is $1,583. However, if we use the internal rate of return criterion, we will reach the opposite conclusion. Hence a firm that wishes to maximize the future value or, equivalently, the present value of its profit stream will always apply the NP_v criterion.

5-9   The Accelerator

Suppose that net investment is partially a function of the change in output and sales or, more precisely, income. We can express this conclusion mathematically as

$$I_t = \alpha(Y_{t-1} - Y_{t-2}) \qquad (5\text{-}25)$$

Equation (5-25) states that net investment in period t is proportional to the change in income between periods $t - 2$ and $t - 1$. Theories of investment such as this that are based on income changes are called *accelerator theories*.

One of the drawbacks of the accelerator model described by equation (5-25) is that it assumes all investment is a function of a change in income ΔY. It would be more reasonable to assume that only a component of net investment is a function of ΔY. A component that is closely related to change in income (as empirical research has proved) is net inventory investment.

We now construct a dynamic model of income determination based on the accelerator theory of investment. Although this theory is quite simple and has several shortcomings, nevertheless it forms the basis for many sophisticated models of income determination. Suppose that we are dealing with a simplified economy in which there is no government sector. The national income can therefore be defined as

$$Y = C + \bar{I} + \Delta J \qquad (5\text{-}26)$$

where $\bar{I}$ is net investment *minus* inventory investment and ΔJ is the change in inventory stock, or the net inventory investment. We assume that all investment except inventory investment is exogenous. We also assume that consumption in time period t is proportional to income in the previous period, or

$$C_t = kY_{t-1} \qquad (5\text{-}27)$$

Finally, we assume that the desired stock of inventories J is proportional to the income in the previous time period. Thus

$$J_t = jY_{t-1} \qquad (5\text{-}28)$$

where j is the factor of proportionality.

From the preceding definition of J_t, it follows that

$$J_{t-1} = jY_{t-2} \qquad (5\text{-}29)$$

Therefore, net inventory investment in period t will be

$$\Delta J_t = J_t - J_{t-1} = j(Y_{t-1} - Y_{t-2}) \qquad (5\text{-}30)$$

Income in period t can now be defined by

$$Y_t = kY_{t-1} + j(Y_{t-1} - Y_{t-2}) + \bar{I} \tag{5-31}$$

Equation (5-31) is an example of an entire set of equations called *second-order difference equations*.[3] Their direct solution is beyond the scope of this book, but we can still determine the characteristics of equation (5-31) by analyzing it accounting period by accounting period using various assumed values for the parameters k and j.

Suppose that we are initially in a state of equilibrium and that income remains constant from one year to the next, so that $\Delta J = 0$. If $k = 0.5$, $j = 0.8$ and $\bar{I} = \$110$, then the equilibrium level of national income in period $t - 1$ will be

$$Y_{t-1} = 0.5(Y_{t-2}) + 0.8(0) + 110 \tag{5-32}$$

Because $Y_{t-2} = Y_{t-1}$

$$Y_{t-1} = \frac{1}{0.5}(\$110) = \$220 \tag{5-33}$$

Now suppose that for some reason external to our model, net noninventory investment falls to \$100 in period t, where it remains for the remainder of our analysis. By assuming constant noninventory investment, we can greatly simplify the following analysis without altering the basic concept of how the accelerator theory interacts with the multiplier theory to produce fluctuations in income.[4]

Income in period t now becomes

$$Y_t = 0.5(\$220) + 0.8(\$220 - \$220) + \$100 = \$210 \tag{5-34}$$

The decline of income in period t activates the operation of the accelerator, because $\Delta Y < 0$. Income in period $t + 1$ will therefore be

$$Y_{t+1} = 0.5(\$210) + 0.8(\$210 - \$220) + \$100$$
$$= \$105 - \$8 + \$100 = \$197 \tag{5-35}$$

and in $t + 2$ it will be

$$Y_{t+2} = 0.5(\$197) + 0.8(-\$13) + \$100 = \$188.1 \tag{5-36}$$

These calculations are performed through the $(t + 14)$th time period in Table 5-3. An examination of this table reveals that the oscillations introduced to the level of national income by the decline of noninventory investment tend to dampen out and that by period $t + n$ a new equilibrium level of national income of \$200 is reached. This oscillation in national income is graphed in line A in Figure 5-9.

The damped oscillatory behavior in this model does not occur simply by chance but is the direct result of the values chosen for the parameters k and j. Suppose

---

[3] For a simple yet thorough treatment of difference equations, see W.J. Baumol, *Economic Dynamics: An Introduction*, 3rd ed. (New York: Macmillan, 1970).

[4] One of the first economists to study this interaction was P.A. Samuelson in his famous article, "Interactions Between the Multiplier Analysis and the Principle of Acceleration," *Review of Economics and Statistics* **21** (May 1939), 75–78.

TABLE 5-3 An Example of Multiplier and Accelerator Interaction with Damped Oscillations

$$k = 0.5, \quad j = 0.8$$

Time Period	C	ΔJ	Ī	Y	ΔY
$t - 2$	110	0.0	110	220.00	
$t - 1$	110	0.0	110	220.00	0
t	110	0.0	100	210.00	−10.00
$t + 1$	105	− 8.0	100	197.00	−13.00
$t + 2$	98.5	−10.4	100	188.10	− 8.9
$t + 3$	94.05	− 7.12	100	186.93	− 1.17
$t + 4$	93.46	− 0.94	100	192.53	+ 5.60
$t + 5$	96.26	+ 4.48	100	200.74	+ 8.21
$t + 6$	100.37	+ 6.57	100	206.94	+ 6.20
$t + 7$	103.47	+ 4.96	100	208.43	+ 1.49
$t + 8$	104.22	+ 1.19	100	205.41	− 3.03
$t + 9$	102.70	− 2.42	100	100.28	− 5.12
$t + 10$	100.14	− 4.10	100	196.04	− 4.24
$t + 11$	98.02	− 3.39	100	194.63	− 1.41
$t + 12$	97.31	− 1.13	100	196.18	+ 1.55
$t + 13$	98.09	+ 1.24	100	199.34	+ 3.15
$t + 14$	99.67	+ 2.52	100	202.19	+ 2.85
.					
.					
$t + n$	100	0	100	200	0

that the original conditions prevail but that our choice of parameter values is $k = 0.5, j = 1.2$. The resulting effect on national income is calculated in Table 5-4. An inspection of this table reveals that oscillations in income also occur in this example but that here they are not damped and the model is explosive. This is visually apparent in Figure 5-9, where curve B is drawn through the points plotted from the data given in Table 5-4. The economic process traced by curve B is said to be *dynamically unstable,* whereas the process traced by curve A is said to be *dynamically stable.*

Now consider the dynamic economic process that occurs when $k = 0.5$ and $j = 0.05$. The time path of national income is computed in Table 5-5 for the original initial conditions and disturbance. In this example there are no oscillations, but the disturbance is damped; that is, each successive level of income asymptotically approaches the new equilibrium. This is illustrated in Figure 5-9 (p. 89) by curve C.

The last example we consider is the case in which no oscillations are present but the model explodes. If we assume that $k = 0.5$ and $j = 3.0$, then from the time path of income computed in Table 5-6 it is readily apparent that the model explodes. Each successive change in income becomes absolutely larger than the previous change. This exploding economic process is traced by curve D in Figure 5-9.

TABLE 5-4 An Example of Multiplier and Accelerator Interaction with Explosive Oscillations

$k = 0.5, \quad j = 1.2$

Time Period	C	ΔJ	$\bar{I}$	Y	ΔY
t − 2	110.0	0	110	220.0	
t − 1	110.0	0	110	220.0	0
t	110.0	0	100	210.0	−10
t + 1	105.0	−12	100	193.0	−17
t + 2	96.5	−20.4	100	176.1	−16.9
t + 3	88.05	−20.28	100	167.77	− 8.33
t + 4	83.88	−10.0	100	173.89	+ 6.12
t + 5	86.94	+ 7.34	100	194.29	+20.40
t + 6	97.14	+24.48	100	221.62	+27.33
t + 7	110.81	+32.80	100	243.61	+21.99
t + 8	121.81	+26.39	100	248.19	+ 4.58
t + 9	124.10	+ 5.50	100	229.60	−18.60
t + 10	114.8	−22.32	100	192.48	−37.12
t + 11	96.24	−44.54	100	151.70	−40.78
t + 12	75.85	−48.94	100	126.92	−24.79
t + 13	63.46	−29.74	100	133.71	+ 6.80
t + 14	66.86	+ 8.16	100	175.02	+41.3
t + 15	87.51	+49.56	100	237.07	+62.05
t + 16	118.54	+74.46	100	293.00	+55.93
t + 17	146.50	+67.12	100	313.62	

TABLE 5-5 An Example of Multiplier and Accelerator Interaction with no Oscillations, but Damped

$k = 0.5, \quad j = 0.05$

Time Period	C	ΔJ	$\bar{I}$	Y	ΔY
t − 2	110	0	110	220.00	
t − 1	110	0	110	220.00	0
t	110	0	100	210.00	−10.0
t + 1	105	−0.5	100	204.50	− 5.5
t + 2	102.25	−0.275	100	201.98	− 2.52
t + 3	100.99	−0.13	100	200.86	− 1.12
t + 4	100.43	−0.06	100	200.37	− 0.49
t + 5	100.18	−0.02	100	200.16	− 0.21
t + 6	100.08	−0.01	100	200.09	− 0.05
.					
.					
.					
t + n	100	0	100	200	0

The exact values of the parameters k and j that will yield the preceding results can be computed using difference equation analysis. For our purposes here, it is sufficient to present the solution to this problem when $0 < k < 1$ and $0 < j < 4.0$. Figure 5-10 is divided into four zones A, B, C, and D, corresponding to the four general cases illustrated by curves A, B, C, and D in Figure 5-9. The coordinates of points lying within any of these zones yield values of the parameters k and j that will

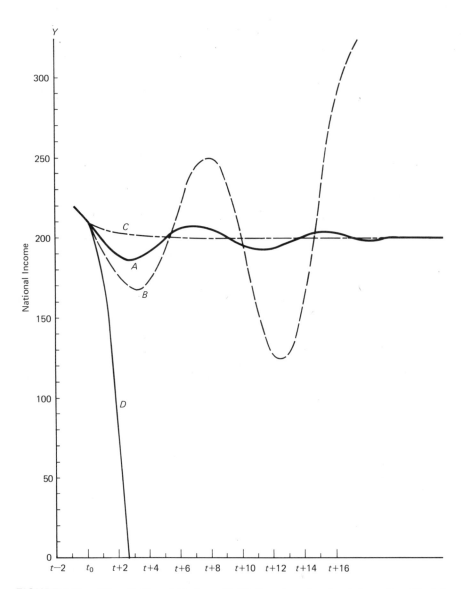

FIGURE 5-9   Time Paths of Various Multiplier–Accelerator Interaction Models

**TABLE 5-6   An Example of Multiplier and Accelerator Interaction
with no Oscillations, but Exploding**
$$k = 0.5, \quad j = 3.0$$

Time Period	C	ΔJ	Ī	Y	ΔY
t − 2	110	0	110	220.0	0
t − 1	110	0	110	220.0	0
t	110	0	100	210.0	− 10.0
t + 1	105	− 30.0	100	175.0	− 35.0
t + 2	87.5	−105.0	100	82.5	− 92.5
t + 3	41.25	−277.5	100	−136.25	−218.75

generate an economic process similar to the corresponding curve. For example, the coordinates of point *b* in Figure 5-10 give us the parameter values *k* = 0.5 and *j* = 1.2. When these parameter values are substituted in our accelerator model, the result is a time path of income that is explosive *and* oscillating, as shown by curve *B* in Figure 5-9.

The model we have examined in this section is clearly only one simple model chosen from a whole set of multiplier–accelerator models. More complicated and, correspondingly, more realistic models usually lack the explosive characteristics of the model developed here.

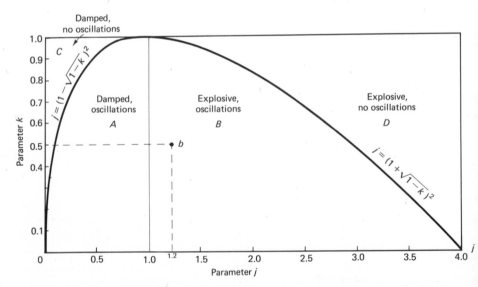

**FIGURE 5-10   *Values of the Parameters* k *and* j *that Yield Alternative Time
Paths of Income***

5-10   Results of Empirical Research

The body of literature that is concerned with empirical investigations of the determinants of investment is large and diverse. In addition, the method of approach and the techniques used in this research are on a level of complexity that is beyond the scope of this book. Fortunately, however, Michael Evans[5] has examined and summarized the results from the most recent work in this area. After his examination of the empirical research, Evans reaches the following conclusions concerning investment in the manufacturing industries:

1. The interest rate is an important factor in determining the level of investment. A 25% change in the long-term interest rate (say, from a rate of 5% to a rate of 4%) will cause a change in the level of net investment of 5–10% over a two-year period after an initial lag of about one year.
2. A 1% change in output will result in an increase in net investment of 1.5–2% over a two-year period.
3. In some manufacturing industries, a change of 1% in the cash flow received by firms will change net investment by 0.25–0.5%. In other manufacturing industries and in all nonmanufacturing industries, the effect on investment is zero.
4. Inventory investment is a function of sales, the stock of inventory, and the change in unfilled orders. Other variables, such as interest rate and cash flow, are of no apparent importance.

The preceding conclusions reached by Michael Evans say nothing about the MEC curve, but they can be interpreted in light of the theory developed in this chapter. The first conclusion can be considered to describe the movement along the MEC curve as the rate of interest changes and produces a change in net investment. The remaining three conclusions can be collectively interpreted as a description of a shift in the MEC curve resulting from changing business expectations that produces observed changes in net investment.

5-11   Concluding Remarks

In this chapter we have developed a theory of capital and investment. To do this, we developed a few simple mathematical tools to compute the internal rate of return. Here we showed that a profit-maximizing firm undertakes all investment projects whose internal rates of return exceed the market rate of interest. It therefore follows that the aggregate behavior of a business firm should be to maintain a stock of capital whose internal rate of return at the margin will exactly equal the rate of interest. The relationship between the aggregate capital stock's rate of return and the stock of capital is called the *marginal efficiency of capital* (MEC). Equating MEC with the market rate of interest gives us the economy's demand for capital function.

[5] Michael K. Evans, *Macroeconomic Activity: Theory, Forecasting, and Control* (New York: Harper & Row, 1969), pp. 133–42 and 220.

When the actual stock of capital is equal to the desired stock, the stock is said to be *optimal*. When the actual stock is less than the desired stock, positive net investment results. The relationship between the internal rate of return and the level of investment is defined as the *marginal efficiency of investment* (MEI). Due to the limited capacity of the capital goods industry, the purchase price of investment eventually begins to rise as output is increased, and this causes the MEI curve to decline more rapidly than the MEC curve. This leads us to conclude that the growth of the capital stock to the desired optimal stock will be extended over several time periods. Changes in the optimal capital stock can result from a shift in or a movement along the MEC curve.

In this chapter we also learned that in some situations the internal rate of return criterion results in ranking investment projects in some other order than the descending order of desirability. An alternative criterion, the *net present value criterion,* was shown to be superior to the internal rate of return criterion because the former always ranks investment projects optimally. Despite this shortcoming, however, the internal rate of return approach is quite useful, because it provides insight into the stock-flow relationship that exists between the stock of capital and the flow of investment. For this reason we shall retain the terminology developed in our discussion of the marginal efficiency of capital and the marginal efficiency of investment throughout the remainder of this book.

The *accelerator theory of investment* was also developed in this chapter, and a simple dynamic model incorporating this theory was examined. The peculiar properties of this model result from the interaction of the accelerator with the multiplier and from the simplified assumptions on which the model is based.

An examination of the most recent empirical investigations of the investment behavior of firms supports the basic theoretical framework developed in this chapter.

6 Consumption

6-1   Introduction

In Chapter 3 we assumed on the basis of very limited empirical evidence that the consumption function is linear and not proportional to disposable income. In this chapter we explore the shortcomings of this assumption and the major alternative hypotheses that have been formulated since the mid-1940s.

6-2   The Absolute Income Hypothesis

Even before the publication of John Maynard Keynes's *The General Theory of Employment, Interest, and Money,* some economists had argued that consumption and income were functionally related. However, Keynes was the first to stress the importance of this relationship and to make it one of the central parts of macroeconomic theory. Keynes hypothesized that the properties of the consumption function are determined by the following principles:

1. The propensity to consume is a fairly stable function, so that as a rule, the amount of aggregate consumption mainly depends on the amount of aggregate income.
2. Men are disposed, as a rule and on the average, to increase their consumption as their income increases, but not by as much as the increase in their income.

3. A higher absolute level of income will tend, as a rule, to widen the gap between income and consumption. For the satisfaction of the immediate primary needs of a man and his family is usually a stronger motive than the motives towards accumulation, which only acquire effective sway when a margin of comfort has been attained. The reasons will lead, as a rule, to a greater *proportion* of income being saved as real income increases.

4. A rising income will often be accompanied by increased saving, and a falling income by decreased saving, on a greater scale at first than subsequently.[1]

The first statement is important because it means that the level of consumption, which is the single largest component of aggregate demand, can be accurately predicted. The second statement says that the marginal propensity to consume will be less than unity. The third states that the average propensity to consume will diminish as disposable income increases, or in other words, that increases in consumption will be less than proportional to increases in income. Finally, the fourth implies that the marginal propensity to consume will be less in the short run (for example, during a recession or a boom) than it will be in the long run. Early disciples of Keynes placed primary emphasis on the first three points, and the resulting theory of consumption later became known as the *absolute income hypothesis,* so named because the theory explicitly assumes that consumption is a function of either a household's or a nation's absolute income. A simple linear consumption function incorporating these Keynesian assumptions is illustrated in Figure 6-1. The specification of this consumption function is the same one we have used throughout this book. The consumption function is linear; the MPC is therefore constant, but it is less than the APC, because the intercept is a positive term. In addition, the APC diminishes as disposable income increases.

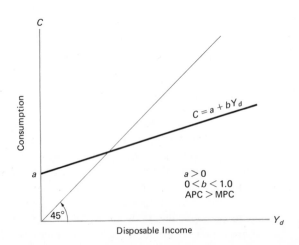

FIGURE 6-1   *The Nonproportional Consumption Function*

[1] John Maynard Keynes, *The General Theory of Employment, Interest, and Money* (New York: Harcourt Brace Jovanovich, 1936), pp. 96, 97.

A consumption function that is hypothesized to possess the properties of the absolute income hypothesis obviously lends itself to empirical investigation, and contemporaries of Keynes lost little time testing his theories. The results of these early empirical investigations strongly supported the absolute income hypothesis. This early research was based on two kinds of data: (1) the aggregate time-series data that had recently become available, and (2) the cross-sectional household budget studies that had been collected since the early nineteenth century.

Figure 6-2 illustrates the essential nature of studies that employed aggregate time-series data during the 1929–1939 period. Real disposable income is plotted against real consumption, and a linear regression line is fitted to the data by the method of least squares. For this particular set of data, the consumption function is estimated to be

$$C = 24.97 + 0.77Y_d \qquad (6-1)$$

where all units are measured in billions of dollars. Equation (6-1) is of the general form $C = a + bY_d$ and is in accord with the absolute income hypothesis. Specifi-

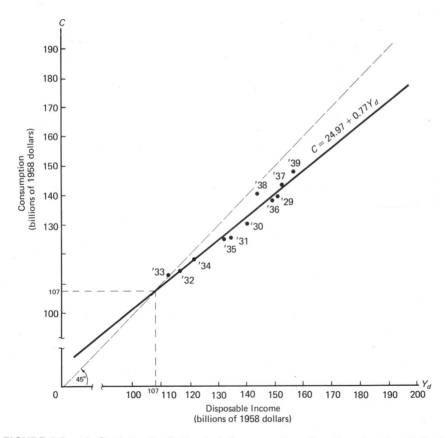

FIGURE 6-2   *A Statistically Estimated Consumption Function for the United States: 1929–1939*

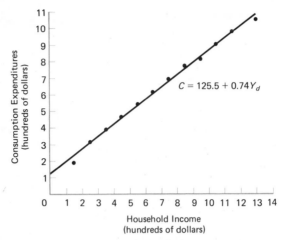

FIGURE 6-3   *Cross-sectional Consumption Function for Normal Families in 1901*

SOURCE Dorothy S. Brady, "Family Saving, 1888 to 1950," in *A Study of Saving in the United States,* Vol. 3, by Raymond W. Goldsmith, D.S. Brady, and Horst Mendershausen (Princeton, N.J.: Princeton University Press, 1956), p. 182.

cally, the MPC is positive, less than unity, and less than the APC, and consumption is not proportional to income because equation (6-1) has a nonzero intercept.

Cross-sectional budget studies also produced results that were not inconsistent with the absolute income hypothesis. The consumption expenditures and savings of families in 1901 are plotted in Figure 6-3. For this set of data, the least-squares linear estimate is given by

$$C = 125.5 + 0.74Y_d \tag{6-2}$$

This cross-sectional consumption function is also in accord with the absolute income hypothesis.

It is hardly surprising that economists in the early 1940s, armed with seemingly conclusive empirical studies such as these, were certain that Keynes's conjectures were correct. Unfortunately, their great expectations were soon to be proved false by two events.

The U.S. government employed many economists during World War II. One of their tasks was to plan for the eventual demobilization that would follow the war, and this involved predicting the behavior of consumption expenditures during the immediate postwar period. It was correctly believed that demobilization would produce a short-run decline in disposable income, but it was incorrectly assumed that this decline would be accompanied by a reduction in consumption expenditures. Actually, the exact opposite occurred. In constant 1958 dollars, disposable income fell from $229.7 billion in 1945 to $227.0 billion in 1946 to $206.3 billion in 1947; however, consumption rose from $183.0 billion in 1945 to $203.5 billion in 1946 to $206.3 billion in 1947. Clearly, in this instance the absolute income hypothesis did not produce good predictions, and economists started to rethink the absolute income consumption theory.

The second major event that made economists seriously question the validity of the absolute income hypothesis was the work of Simon Kuznets. In the early 1940s, Kuznets began to release the initial results of his monumental study of U.S national income accounts.[2] In extending data on aggregate disposable income and savings back to 1869, Kuznets discovered that the percentage of disposable income consumed had remained constant despite a large growth in income. Algebraically, this function can be easily and simply written

$$C = bY_d \qquad\qquad (6\text{-}3)$$

In other words, Kuznets found that the long-run aggregate consumption function is proportional to disposable income and therefore that the long-run APC remains constant and is equal to the MPC.

6-3   The Relative Income Hypothesis

We have just learned that the validity of the absolute income hypothesis was seriously challenged within ten years after the publication of Keynes's *General Theory*. Research on consumption behavior revealed cases in which the absolute income hypothesis produced erroneous predictions. This same research also indicated that consumption behavior was more complicated than had originally been presumed. It became obvious to economists that any satisfactory theory of consumption would have to take into account and explain three empirical discoveries:

1. Cross-sectional studies reveal a nonproportional consumption function—that is, a decreasing APC as Y_d increases—and APC $>$ MPC.
2. Long-run aggregate consumption is proportional to income, so that APC = MPC.
3. Aggregate data ranging over the expansion and contraction phases of the business cycle reveal a short-run aggregate consumption function that is nonproportional with APC $>$ MPC. Such data and the resulting consumption function appear in Figure 6-2, where the 1929–1939 time period encompasses the great depression.

One of the earliest attempts to derive a theory of consumption in accord with these empirical discoveries was James Duesenberry's two-part *relative income hypothesis*.[3] The first part of this hypothesis does not assume that a household's consumption is a function of its absolute income. Instead, the household's position in the income distribution of all households is considered, to determine the relative income of the household. If the absolute income of each household increases by the same percentage, then the household's relative position in the distribution

---

[2] Simon Kuznets, *Uses of National Income in Peace and War* (New York: National Bureau of Economic Research, 1942) and *National Product Since 1869* (New York: National Bureau of Economic Research, 1946).

[3] James Duesenberry, *Income, Saving, and the Theory of Consumer Behavior* (Cambridge, Mass.: Harvard University Press, 1949).

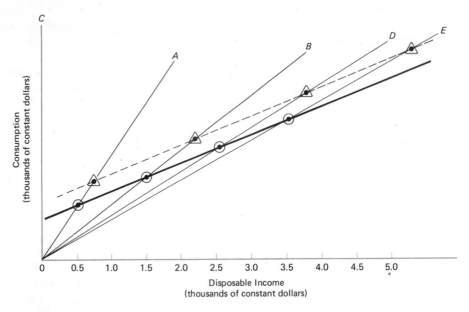

FIGURE 6-4   *Consumption Function Under the Relative Income Hypothesis*

remains the same. The household's relative income therefore remains constant, although its absolute income has increased. Duesenberry argued that if a household's relative income remains constant as its absolute income increases, then the household will continue to spend the same fraction of its additional income on consumption that it did prior to the increase. In other words, the household's APC remains constant. Perhaps this concept can best be explained graphically. In Figure 6-4 the solid cross-sectional consumption function passes through circled points that give average disposable income and consumption in four income brackets. The APC of each of these income–consumption points is given by the slope of the ray drawn from the origin through the point. Now suppose that the absolute income of all households increases by 50%, so that the household with an average income of $500 now has an average income of $750, the household with an average income of $1,500 now has an average income of $2,250, and so forth. According to the relative income hypothesis, there is no change in the relative incomes of all households: each household will consume the same fraction of its absolute income that it did before the increase. Thus the income–consumption point in Figure 6-4 for the household now earning $750 must lie on the ray that passes through the income–consumption point corresponding to an income of $500. This is the point inside the triangle on ray 0A in Figure 6-4. Similarly, the income–consumption data points corresponding to the other income levels can be located on their respective rays. These points are also shown inside triangles in Figure 6-4, where the new cross-sectional consumption function is the dashed line that passes through these four points.

The results obtained via the relative income hypothesis are quite different from the results obtained via the absolute income hypothesis. According to the latter hypothesis, we would simply remain on the original consumption function and the APC for each household would decline. Using the former hypothesis, we find that the entire function shifts upward as each household's APC remains constant.

Now we can examine how the relative income hypothesis explains the long-run proportionality of the aggregate consumption function. Suppose that the household with an initial income of $2,500 represents the national average income. If economic growth amounts to 50% and if the income distribution remains constant (a fairly close approximation to what has happened in the United States during the last 100 years), the household whose income of $2,500 is equal to the national average remains the average household when its income increases by 50% to $3,750. In Figure 6-4 we can see that the initial and the final income–consumption points of the average household lie on ray 0D. Because the APC of the average household remains constant over time, it necessarily follows that the aggregate long-run consumption function will also exhibit a constant APC. This must be true because if we multiply the number of households by the income and consumption of the average household, we obtain the aggregate national income and consumption. Even if economic growth is accompanied by a growing population, the ratio of consumption to income APC will remain constant if the income distribution remains constant.

Thus far, we have been able to use the relative income hypothesis to reconcile the nonproportionality of the cross-sectional household consumption studies with the long-run proportionality of the aggregate national income data. We must now explain the nonproportionality of the short-run aggregate data over the course of the business cycle. To do this, Duesenberry invoked the second part of his relative income hypothesis, stating that it is much easier for households to adjust to rising incomes than to falling incomes. As the household's absolute income rises, its standard of living also rises, and this higher standard soon becomes the *expected* standard of living. Thus as a household's income begins to decline in a recession, its attempt to maintain this higher standard of living results in a less rapid decline in consumption than in income. This can result from a reduction in the desired level of savings to the extent that consumption can be maintained at or near the previously obtained level. In other words, if absolute income declines by 10%, for example, households will reduce consumption by less than 10%, the aggregate APC will rise, the MPC will fall, and an inequality between APC and MPC will result. Moreover, the APC and MPC will not return to their long-run equality, according to Duesenberry, until the highest previously obtained income level is reached once again. Because consumption does not decline in proportion to the decline in national income, the aggregate consumption function that is observed over a period when national income is declining will have a smaller MPC than the MPC of a consumption function that has a continuously rising income. An aggregate consumption function derived from data collected during the great depression, as is given in equation (6-1), will have a slope of approximately 0.77; however, the MPC of the long-run aggregate consumption function derived from Kuznets's data will be about 0.89. The relative income hypothesis states that this difference between the long-run MPC and the short-run MPC results from the fact that the peak real disposable income of 1929 was not surpassed until 1939.

This characteristic of Duesenberry's relative income hypothesis, sometimes referred to as the "*ratchet effect*," is illustrated in Figure 6-5. Beginning with a disposable income of zero, we assume a steady, uninterrupted growth in income up to Y_{d_1}. As this growth in disposable income occurs, consumption is proportional to income, as is shown by the long-run aggregate consumption function C_{LR} in Figure 6-5. Now suppose that a recession occurs when Y_{d_1} is reached and that disposable income falls to Y_{d_0}. Due to the ratchet effect, consumption does not fall back along C_{LR}, but instead falls back along the short-run consumption function C_{SR}. Consumption will therefore be C_0' rather than C_0. Since $C_0' > C_0$ at Y_{d_0}, the APC will be higher than it was when disposable income was Y_{d_1} and the MPC will be lower. As the economy recovers from the recession and disposable income begins to rise again, consumption occurs along C_{SR} until the previous peak level of disposable income Y_{d_1}, is reached. At this point consumption once again moves out along C_{LR}.

We have now seen how the relative income hypothesis can be used to resolve many of the questions raised by the empirical analysis of cross-sectional budget studies and aggregate time-series data. Unfortunately, the relative income hypothesis itself is not without certain shortcomings. First, this hypothesis states that an increase in the aggregate level of full-employment income always produces a proportional increase in consumption, whether this increase is large or small. This appears in Figure 6-5 as the full-employment, growth-path consumption function C_{LR}, which is drawn in proportion to disposable income. Empirical evidence

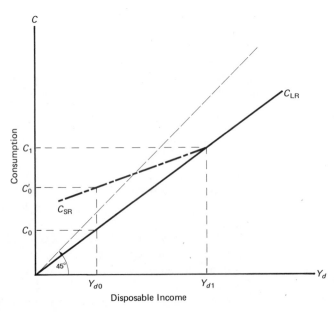

FIGURE 6-5   *Long-run and Short-run Aggregate Consumption Functions with Duesenberry's Ratchet Effect*

suggests, however, that exceptionally large and unexpected increases in national income initially produce less than proportional increases in consumption. Second, the relative income hypothesis considers consumer behavior to be irreversible; that is, if a decline in disposable income should prevail for a long period of time, the theory states that consumption will continue to be determined by the short-run consumption function and that households will continue to dissave forever. This is clearly impossible, and it is more reasonable to assume that households will eventually return to C_{LR}. Third, according to the relative income hypothesis, a recession must always be accompanied by a decline in consumption. However, there have been instances, such as the 1948–1949 recession, when disposable income fell and consumption rose. Despite these flaws, the relative income hypothesis was a major advance over the absolute income hypothesis.

6-4   Optimal Consumption Over Time

Both the absolute income hypothesis and the relative income hypothesis assume that the consumption–saving decision is based on current income or on some previously obtained level of income. Another, perhaps more fruitful approach is to consider an individual consumer. If we assume that an individual attempts to maximize utility over his or her lifetime rather than over a single period, then the individual's utility function is

$$U = U(C_0, \ldots, C_t, \ldots, C_T) \tag{6-4}$$

where total lifetime utility depends on consumption in every period up to the time of death in period T. If we assume that the present value of total lifetime consumption cannot exceed the present value of lifetime income,[4] or that

$$Y + Y_1(1 + i)^{-1} + Y_2(1 + i)^{-2} + \cdots + Y_T(1 + i)^{-T}$$
$$= C_0 + C_1(1 + i)^{-1} + C_2(1 + i)^{-2} + C_T(1 + i)^{-T} \tag{6-5}$$

then in effect equation (6-5) is the budget constraint under which the individual seeks to maximize utility. This equation implies that an individual's consumption in a given period can, within the limits of the constraint, exceed income in that same period either by borrowing against future income or by spending saved income and interest from prior time periods.

To understand the implications of equations (6-4) and (6-5) more fully, we examine the two-period case, in which the individual's income is Y_0 in period 0 and Y_1 in period 1. The individual seeks to maximize

$$U = U(C_0, C_1) \tag{6-6}$$

subject to the constraint

$$C_0 + C_1(1 + i)^{-1} = Y_0 + Y_1(1 + i)^{-1} \tag{6-7}$$

---

[4] When an individual inherits wealth, it is assumed that he or she bequeathes an equal amount.

If $Y_0 > C_0$, in the initial time period, the resulting savings can then be lent at an interest rate of i. Thus the amount of money available for consumption in period 1 will be

$$(Y_0 - C_0)(1 + i) + Y_1$$

If $C_0 = 0$, then the maximun attainable consumption in period 1 will be $Y_0(1 + i)$ + Y_1. Similarly, the maximum consumption in period 0 if $C_1 = 0$ will be equal to $Y_0 + Y_1(1 + i)^{-1}$. In case of consumption maximization in period 1, all the income in period 0 will be lent at an interest rate of i, whereas maximum consumption in period 0 will be obtained by borrowing an amount of money whose present value is equal to future income Y_1. The money values of these two extreme conditions appear on the vertical and horizontal axes of Figure 6-6. All possible money values of consumption lie on the straight line that connects these two points on the axes. Thus if the dollar value of consumption in period 0 is Y_0, then the dollar value of consumption in period 1 must be Y_1. This is indicated in Figure 6-6 by the fact that the point on the consumption constraint line corresponding to Y_0 simultaneously corresponds to Y_1. If consumption in period 0 exceeds Y_0, this result can occur only if enough of Y_1 is borrowed so that consumption in period 1 is less than Y_1. This case is also illustrated in Figure 6-6. If consumption in period 0 is less than Y_0, then the opposite effect will occur. Thus the consumption-constraint line in Figure 6-6 gives all the consumption possibilities in periods 0 and 1, and its position[5] is determined by Y_0, Y_1, and i.

Now if we assume that we know the individual's utility function—that is, equation (6-6)—then we can construct indifference curves U_0, U_1, and U_2 as shown in Figure 6-7. These indifference curves are similar to the ones we used in Chapter 2: a given curve represents all the possible combinations of C_0 and C_1 such that total utility U remains constant. As before, greater utility is associated with the indifference curves that are further from the origin. The consumption-constraint line in Figure 6-6 is also reproduced in Figure 6-7. The indifference curve U_0 intersects the consumption-constraint line at points A and B, and respective consumption bundles of (C_0', C_1') and (C_0'', C_1'') yield a utility of U_0. However, points A and B do not yield the maximum utility. This is determined by the point of tangency C between U_1 and the consumption-constraint line. Consumption bundles C_0^* and C_1^* produce a maximum utility of U_1 given the constraint imposed by Y_0, Y_1, and i. Any

---

[5] The slope of the consumption constraint line is determined solely by the interest rate i. PROOF: Dividing the distance from the origin to the vertical intercept by the distance from the origin to the horizontal intercept gives us the slope of the consumption constraint, or

$$-\frac{Y_1 + Y_0(1 + i)}{Y_0 + Y_1(1 + i)^{-1}} = -\frac{Y_1(1 + i) + Y_0(1 + i)^2}{Y_0(1 + i) + Y_1}$$

$$= -\frac{[Y_1 + Y_0(1 + i)]}{Y_1 + Y_0(1 + i)} \times (1 + i)$$

$$= -(1 + i)$$

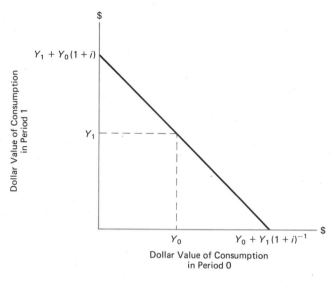

FIGURE 6-6   *The Consumption Constraint*

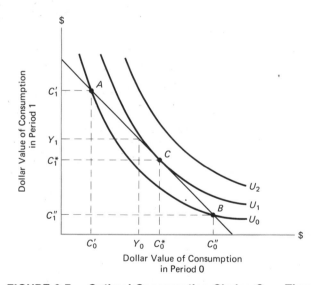

FIGURE 6-7   *Optimal Consumption Choice Over Time*

point on U_2 is preferred to point C, but because the indifference curve in this case lies to the right of the consumption-constraint line, the points on U_2 are unobtainable. Figure 6-7 shows that utility maximization for the individual represented is

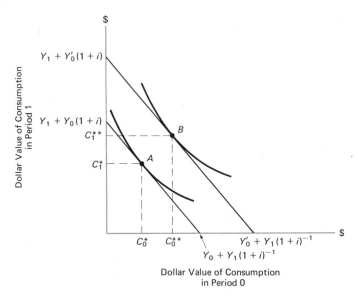

FIGURE 6-8   *The Effect of an Increase in Income in Period 0 on Consumption Choice*

obtained by having a consumption level in period 0 that is in excess of Y_0. This can be accomplished by borrowing $Y_0 - C_0^*$ from the income in period 1. This in turn will cause the consumption in period 1 to be less than Y_1 by an amount that is equal to $(Y_0 - C_0^*)(1 + i)$.

We are now in a position to analyze the effect of an increase in income in one time period on consumption in different time periods. Suppose that income in period 0 increases from Y_0 to Y_0'. This will produce a horizontal displacement to the right of the consumption-constraint line by an amount that is equal to $Y_0' - Y_0$. The new consumption-constraint line will be parallel to the original line, as shown in Figure 6-8. Prior to the increase in income in period 0, utility maximization occurs at point *A*. If we make the reasonable assumption that consumption itself is a *normal good*—that is, that the quantity of the good purchased increases as income increases—then the new position of utility maximization must lie above and to the right of point *A*. This conclusion is represented by the position of the new utility maximization point *B*, in Figure 6-8, which indicates that an increase in income in one period produces an increase in consumption not only in that period but in other periods as well. If the increase in income is *unanticipated*, then only consumption in the period of income increase and all subsequent periods will be affected; if the increase in income is *anticipated*, then consumption in all periods will be affected. Another conclusion we can draw from this analysis is that consumption in a given period increases by a smaller amount than income in that period, because point *B* lies above point *A*. Thus we have established the microeconomic theoretical basis for the assumption that the marginal propensity to consume will be less than unity.

Several theories of the consumption function are based on the theoretical analysis of consumer behavior over time that we just examined. All these theories are variations of the same fundamental relationship

$$C_t = f(P_v Y_t), \qquad \frac{\Delta C_t}{\Delta P_v Y_t} > 0 \qquad\qquad (6\text{-}8)$$

which states that an individual's consumption in period t is a function of the present value of both present and future income $P_v Y_t$ and that if $P_v Y_t$ increases, then consumption in period t also increases.

We now present a somewhat detailed examination of two consumption theories that are based on the concepts we have been exploring in this section.

6-5   The Life-cycle Hypothesis

One consumption theory that is based on equation (6-8) is the *life-cycle hypothesis* of R.E. Brumberg, Albert Ando, and Franco Modigliani.[6] This theory begins with the empirical fact that the average individual's income is lower at the beginning and the end of life than it is during the middle years. The income stream of the average individual appears in Figure 6-9, where t_0 is the time at which the individual begins to earn income and T is the time of death. The life-cycle hypothesis argues that maximization of the average individual's utility produces a stream of consumption that is constant or slightly rising over time, represented by the positively sloped straight line in Figure 6-9. It is assumed that the individual maximizes utility subject to the constraint of equation (6-5); that is, the present value of the consumption stream cannot exceed the present value of the income stream.[7]

Given the objective of a constant or slightly rising consumption stream and an income stream that rises and then falls, the individual will normally be a net borrower when young, a net saver in the middle years to repay earlier debts and prepare for retirement, and finally a net dissaver during retirement. This life cycle of consumption is shown in its entirety in Figure 6-9.

The concept of life-cycle consumption can explain the nonproportionality between consumption and income that is observed in cross-sectional consumption studies of the type represented by Figure 6-3. Suppose that we select a random sample of households from the population and then rank them according to their income. Those households with higher than average incomes will tend to contain a disproportionate number of middle-aged income earners, precisely because this segment of the population tends to earn higher than average incomes. Conversely,

---

[6] Franco Modigliani and R.E. Brumberg, "Utility Analysis and the Consumption Function: An Interpretation of Cross-section Data," in K.K. Kurihara (ed.), *Post-Keynesian Economics* (New Brunswick, N.J.: Rutgers University Press, 1954); and Albert Ando and Franco Modigliani, "The 'Life-cycle' Hypothesis of Saving: Aggregate Implications and Tests," *American Economic Review* (March 1963), 55–84.

[7] If the individual wishes to leave a bequest, the present value of consumption will be less than the present value of income.

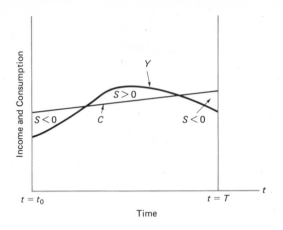

FIGURE 6-9   *Income and Consumption Over the Life Cycle*

those households with incomes that are less than the average will tend to contain a disproportionate number of either young or old income earners, because this portion of the population tends to earn lower than average incomes. According to the life-cycle hypothesis, the APC of middle-aged (high-income) individuals will be lower than the APC of either young or old (low-income) individuals, so that the APC of households will decline as income rises. In other words, the life-cycle hypothesis predicts that cross-sectional budget studies will be characterized by a nonproportional relationship between consumption and income with APC > MPC. Thus the life-cycle hypothesis can be used to explain the empirical data illustrated in Figure 6-3.

To extend this theory still further, we can assume that if an individual's present value of income increases and the interest rate remains constant, then the individual's consumption will increase proportionately in the present period and in future periods. We can therefore write that consumption in period t will be

$$C_t^i = \lambda^i P_v Y_t^i, \qquad 0 < \lambda < 1 \tag{6-9}$$

where the superscript i indicates that this relationship exists for the ith individual. Now if both the income distribution and the age distribution of the population remain fairly constant over time, then the aggregate consumption function can be expressed as

$$C_t = \lambda P_v Y_t \tag{6-10}$$

Equation (6-10) is of little use, however, unless we can measure the present value of expected future income. Ando and Modigliani define $P_v Y_t$ at time t_0 as

$$P_v Y_0 = A_0 + L Y_0 + \sum_{t=1}^{T} \frac{L Y_t}{(1 + i)^t} \tag{6-11}$$

where A_0 = market value (present value) of all nonlabor assets at time t_0

$\quad\quad LY_0$ = labor income in time period t_0

$$\sum_{t=1}^{T} \frac{LY_t}{(1 + i)^t} = \text{present value of future labor income}$$

The first two terms on the right-hand side of equation (6-11) can be directly measured. The last term cannot be measured, because it is based entirely on expectations; however, we can simplify this term if we assume that individuals earn an expected average labor income LY_0^e in time period t_0 that can be expressed as

$$LY_0^e = \frac{1}{T - 1} \sum_{t=1}^{T} \frac{LY_t}{(1 + i)^t} \tag{6-12}$$

where $T - 1$ = the life expectancy of the population.

Equation (6-11) can now be rewritten

$$P_v Y_t = A_0 + LY_0 + (T - 1)LY_0^e \tag{6-13}$$

and our only remaining hurdle is estimating LY_0^e. Ando and Modigliani assume that expected average labor income is proportional to current labor income, or

$$LY_0^e = \beta LY_0 \tag{6-14}$$

Thus equation (6-13) can be written

$$P_v Y_t = A_0 + LY_0 + (T - 1)\beta LY_0 \tag{6-15}$$

and the consumption function given by equation (6-10) can be written

$$C_t = \lambda[A_0 + LY_0 + (T - 1)\beta LY_0]$$
$$= \lambda A_0 + \lambda[1 + \beta(T - 1)]LY_0 \tag{6-16}$$

Ando and Modigliani used U.S. data to estimate the parameters λ and β in equation (6-16). They found

$$C_t = 0.06A_t + 0.7LY_t \tag{6-17}$$

In the short run, the quantity of nonlabor assets remains constant, and $0.06A_t$ can be considered a constant term. Then as labor income rises and falls during the business cycle, we obtain the nonproportional aggregate consumption function labeled SR in Figure 6-10. Thus the life-cycle hypothesis is consistent with the empirical observation that the marginal propensity to consume of the aggregate consumption function is less than the average propensity to consume during the business cycle.

Nonlabor assets will grow in the long run, causing the consumption function in Figure 6-10 to shift upward. Over time, this shift *may* in turn trace a series of points on a long-run aggregate consumption function passing through the origin. This result is illustrated by the *LR* curve in Figure 6-10. A long-run consumption function with the characteristic APC = MPC is not inherent to the life-cycle hypothesis but depends on the behavior of specific economic variables. To discover what these variables are, we divide both sides of equation (6-17) by national income Y_t to obtain

$$\frac{C_t}{Y_t} = 0.06\frac{A_t}{t} + 0.7\frac{LY_t}{Y_t} \qquad (6\text{-}18)$$

The term on the left-hand side of equation (6-18) is a measure of APC. For this to remain fairly constant over long periods of time, the ratio of assets to national income A_t/Y_t and the ratio of labor income to national income LY_t/Y_t must either remain approximately constant or move in counteractive directions. Estimates of the values of these ratios from 1890 to the present reveal that there has been a slight upward trend in the ratio of labor income to national income and a counteractive downward trend in the ratio of assets to national income. Thus the life-cycle hypothesis does offer an explanation for the long-run proportionality observed between consumption and income.

Like any theory, the life-cycle hypothesis has certain shortcomings. First, it assumes the young and old to be dissavers when they are actually net savers, which reduces the ability of this hypothesis to explain the nonproportionality of cross-sectional budget studies. Second, the assumptions used to estimate expected future income yield a consumption function, such as the one given by equation (6-17), which places great importance on any change in current labor income. Thus the life-cycle hypothesis treats income changes that are clearly temporary as if they are permanent changes. This contradicts the fundamental concept of the hypothesis and can lead to erroneous policy prescriptions. In the next section we examine

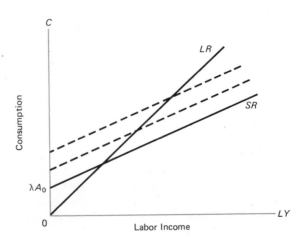

FIGURE 6-10   *Life-cycle Aggregate Consumption in the Short Run and the Long Run*

a consumption theory that is closely related to the life-cycle hypothesis but that does not exhibit this particular shortcoming.

6-6   The Permanent Income Hypothesis

Milton Friedman, like Brumberg, Ando, and Modigliani, bases his theory[8] of consumption behavior on the theory of rational consumer behavior over time that we examined in Section 6-4. Unlike Brumberg, Ando, and Modigliani, however, Friedman does not impose the constraint given by equation (6-5). Instead, Friedman assumes that households attach as much importance to the consumption of their heirs as they do to their own consumption.

The life-cycle hypothesis and the formal statement of Friedman's theory both begin with the equation

$$C = \lambda P_v Y \qquad\qquad (6\text{-}9)$$

where $P_v Y$ is the present value of all future income streams, or the value of the stock of human wealth *plus* nonhuman wealth. *Human wealth*, or as it is sometimes called, *human capital*, is the income derived from selling the household's labor services. Nonhuman wealth comprises tangible assets, such as money, bonds, equities, and real estate, and consumer durables, such as automobiles, television sets, and refrigerators. Because consumer durables are part of a household's stock of wealth, their purchase *cannot* be treated as consumption; rather it is regarded as a form of saving. The imputed value of the flow of services provided by these durable goods is what Friedman considers consumption.

In our examination of the life-cycle hypothesis we learned that one of its major drawbacks is its measurement of the present value of wealth. Friedman avoids this pitfall by rewriting equation (6-9)

$$C = kiP_v Y \qquad\qquad (6\text{-}19)$$

where k = a factor of proportionality
i = the rate of interest

Now if we assume that the stock of total wealth is maintained intact (that is, passed on to heirs), $iP_v Y$ is the value of the permanent flow of income Y_p that this stock of wealth will provide. Equation (6-19) can therefore be written

$$C_p = kY_p \qquad\qquad (6\text{-}20)$$

where permanent consumption C_p is the planned or anticipated consumption from permanent income. This formulation of the consumption function in terms of permanent income, rather than total wealth, gives Friedman's theory its name: the *permanent income hypothesis.*

---

[8] Milton Friedman, *A Theory of the Consumption Function* (Princeton, N.J.: Princeton University Press for the National Bureau of Economic Research, 1957).

Like total wealth, permanent income and consumption cannot be directly measured but must be defined in terms of measurable concepts. Therefore, Friedman constructs the definitions

$$Y_m = Y_p + Y_{tr} \tag{6-21}$$

$$C_m = C_p + C_{tr} \tag{6-22}$$

Measured income Y_m is the sum of permanent income and transitory income Y_{tr}. *Transitory income* is unplanned or unanticipated income and can be positive *or* negative. Similarly, *measured consumption* C_m is the sum of permanent or planned consumption and transitory consumption C_{tr}. *Transitory consumption* is unanticipated consumption.

Until this point in our explanation of the permanent income hypothesis we have examined a series of definitions that can be neither supported nor contradicted by empirical data. Friedman now makes a series of assumptions regarding the statistical relationships that exist between permanent and transitory consumption, permanent and transitory income, and transitory consumption and income. First, Friedman assumes that

$$R_{Y_{tr}, Y_p} = 0 \tag{6-23}$$

that is, that there is no correlation between Y_{tr} and Y_p, where R is the symbol for the correlation coefficient.[9] This assumption implies that if we take a random sample from a homogeneous population of households whose permanent incomes are normally distributed and separate these households into measured income brackets, then the average measured income bracket will have an average transitory income $\overline{Y}_{tr}$ that is equal to zero. Thus for the average measured income bracket

$$\overline{Y}_m = \overline{Y}_p \tag{6-24}$$

We obtain this important result because for every household that has a permanent income below the sample's average permanent income but appears in the average measured income bracket due to a positive transitory income component, there is a corresponding household that has a permanent income above the average permanent income but appears in the average measured income bracket due to a negative transitory component. The cancellation of the positive and negative transitory incomes of households in the average measured income bracket follows from our assumption that income is normally distributed for similar households (farmers, for example). In a normal distribution the number of households below the average permanent income that may experience good fortune and be temporarily pulled up into the average measured income bracket is exactly matched by the number of households above the average permanent income that may experience misfortune and be temporarily pulled down into the average measured income bracket. Thus Y_{tr} is canceled out in the average measured income bracket.

[9] Students who are unfamiliar with the concept of the correlation coefficient should read Appendix A.

Assumption (6-23) can also be employed to explain why cross-sectional budget studies show that APC > MPC. This follows from the fact that among measured income brackets that are higher than the average bracket, there are more households that are fortunate and have positive transitory incomes that push them into the higher income bracket than there are households that are unlucky and drop down into this bracket with negative transitory incomes. This happens simply because as we move into higher measured income brackets in a normally distributed sample, the absolute number of potential households with a chance of receiving a positive Y_{tr} exceeds the absolute number of households with a chance of receiving a negative Y_{tr}. As we move into higher and higher measured income brackets above the average income bracket, this phenomenon becomes increasingly significant and Y_{tr} is positively correlated with Y_m. In other words, as we move into higher measured income brackets above the average measured income bracket $\overline{Y}_m$, Y_{tr} becomes increasingly larger. Using the same line of reasoning, as we move into lower measured income brackets below the average measured income bracket, Y_{tr} becomes increasingly smaller; that is, Y_{tr} becomes more negative, since $Y_{tr} = 0$ for the average measured income bracket.

Next, Friedman assumes that

$$R_{C_{tr}, C_p} = 0 \qquad (6\text{-}25)$$

that is, that there is no correlation between transitory consumption and permanent consumption. Finally, Friedman assumes that there is no correlation between C_{tr} and Y_{tr}, or that

$$R_{C_{tr}, Y_{tr}} = 0 \qquad (6\text{-}26)$$

Friedman's last two assumptions imply that when we separate our random sample from the population of similar households into measured income brackets, positive transitory consumption in each bracket will be canceled by negative transitory consumption, so that

$$C_m = C_p \qquad (6\text{-}27)$$

in each bracket.

We now have enough information to construct the cross-sectional permanent income consumption function and to show that although APC = MPC for this function, the corresponding measured income consumption function has an APC > MPC in accordance with empirical budget study results. In addition, we can now determine the average permanent income of any measured income bracket.

Let us assume that we conduct a budget study of a group of similar households and that the resulting data are given in Table 6-1. Average measured income $\overline{Y}_m$ is $5,000, and average measured consumption $\overline{C}_m$ is $4,300. From equations (6-24) and (6-27) we know that these values are also equal to average permanent income $\overline{Y}_p$ and average permanent consumption $\overline{C}_p$, respectively.

The permanent income consumption function can now be estimated. To learn how this is accomplished, consider Figure 6-11 and recall that $C_p = kY_p$. The consumption function is linear and must pass through the origin. Because two

TABLE 6-1   Hypothetical Cross-sectional Data from a Sample of Similar Households

(1) Measured Disposable Income	(2) Measured Income Y_m	(3) Measured Consumption C_m	(4) Permanent Consumption $C_p = C_m$	(5) Permanent Income Y_p	(6) Transitory Income Y_{tr}
$ 0–2,000	$1,000	$1,500	$1,500	$1,745	– $745
2,000–4,000	3,000	2,900	2,900	3,370	– 370
4,000–6,000	5,000 $= \bar{Y}_m$	4,300 $= \bar{C}_m$	4,300 $= \bar{C}_p$	5,000 $= \bar{Y}_p$	0
6,000–8,000	7,000	5,700	5,700	6,630	370
8,000–10,000	9,000	7,100	7,100	8,250	750

points, $(0,0)$ and $(\bar{Y}_p, \bar{C}_p)$, lie on the consumption function, the consumption function $0C_p$ can be drawn. The slope of $0C_p$ is $\bar{C}_m \div \bar{Y}_m = \bar{C}_p \div \bar{Y}_p = 0.86 =$ APC $=$ MPC. A function determined by the method of least squares using measured data must pass through the measured consumption function, where $\bar{C}_m = \bar{C}_p$ and $\bar{Y}_m = \bar{Y}_p$. At this point assumptions (6-25) and (6-26) become critical to the analysis, because as pointed out by equation (6-27), they allow us to state that the average transitory consumption of all households in any income bracket will be zero. If we know the measured consumption of a bracket, then we also know its permanent consumption, because these two values are the same.

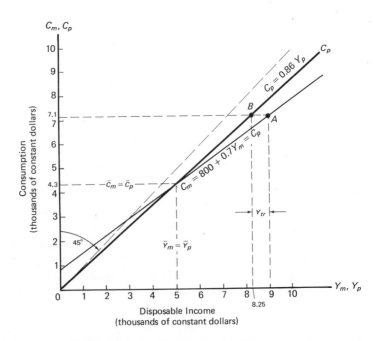

FIGURE 6-11   Estimation of Permanent and Measured Income Consumption Functions Based on Cross-sectional Data

If we now compute the regression of C_m on Y_m, we obtain a measured consumption function of the general form

$$C_m = a + bY_m = C_p \tag{6-28}$$

which also gives us the level of permanent consumption at any measured income level, assuming that $C_m = C_p$. For our "measured" data in Table 6-1, the measured consumption function is

$$C_m = C_p = 800 + 0.7Y_m \tag{6-29}$$

This measured consumption function is graphed in Figure 6-11. Because its APC > MPC, we can conclude that the permanent income hypothesis is not inconsistent with empirically observed cross-sectional budget studies of the type illustrated in Figure 6-3.

We can now solve for the level of permanent income that corresponds to each level of permanent consumption. Taking equation (6-20) and solving for Y_p, we obtain

$$Y_p = \frac{1}{k}C_p = \frac{1}{0.86}C_p \tag{6-30}$$

which can be used to compute the level of permanent income for the previously estimated values of permanent consumption. For example, for a measured income of $9,000 the level of permanent consumption is $7,100, as given in Table 6-1. This permanent consumption is not based on the measured income but on a permanent income of $7,100 ÷ 0.86 = $8,250, which is less than the observed income. In this case Y_{tr} = $750, which is positive. At levels of income less than Y_m, transitory income will be negative. Perhaps this can be more clearly seen by referring again to Figure 6-11. Starting with a measured income of Y_m = $9,000, we can determine the level of measured consumption by reading horizontally across this graph from point A on the measured consumption curve to obtain the corresponding measured consumption, $7,100. Because measured consumption is considered to be equal to permanent consumption, we can determine the level of permanent income corresponding to a permanent consumption of $7,100 by reading vertically downward from point B on the permanent income consumption curve to obtain Y_p = $8,250. The horizontal distance between points A and B measures the transitory income Y_{tr}, which is $ 9,000 − $8,250 = $750.

The permanent income hypothesis has been subjected to many empirical tests, the most common of which involve the use of cross-sectional studies. Friedman computed the APC of different communities that were fairly homogeneous in all respects except income. Because the transitory component of measured income can be expected to be canceled out for the entire community, $\bar{Y}_m = \bar{Y}_p$ and $\bar{C}_m = \bar{C}_p$ for each community. If the absolute income hypothesis were correct, a declining APC would be observed as we moved from the lower- to higher-income communities; in other words, there would be a negative correlation. If Friedman's permanent income hypothesis were correct, the APC would remain almost con-

TABLE 6-2   Income and Consumption Data for Non-self-employed
Homeowners, Bracketed According to Value of Home

Value of Home	Average Income $\overline{Y}_m = Y_p$	Average Consumption $\overline{C}_m = C_p$	$\dfrac{\overline{C}_m}{\overline{Y}_m} = \dfrac{C_p}{Y_p} = APC$
$1–4,999	$3,606	$3,530	0.98
5,000–7,499	4,274	4,190	0.98
7,500–9,999	4,649	4,600	0.99
10,000–12,499	5,191	5,140	0.99
12,500–14,999	5,729	5,610	0.98
15,000–17,499	5,948	5,949	1.00
17,500–19,999	7,547	7,170	0.95
20,000–24,999	9,607	9,500	0.99
25,000–above	11,267	11,100	0.99

SOURCE—F. Modigliani and A. Ando, "The 'Permanent Income' and the 'Life-cycle' Hypothesis of Saving Behavior: Comparisons and Tests," I. Friend and R. Jones, (eds.) Vol. II in *Consumption and Saving* (Philadelphia: University of Pennsylvania Press, 1960), p.154.

stant; there would be zero correlation. The results of Friedman's testing and of other studies indicate that the correlation is indeed zero, thus supporting the permanent income hypothesis.

One criticism of the foregoing test is that it assumes that all households in a given community have approximately the same permanent income or that households with high incomes are canceled out by households with low incomes. This may not actually be the case. To overcome this criticism, Franco Modigliani and Albert Ando proposed another method of identifying the permanent income of groups of households.[10] Arguing that expenditure on housing is based on what each household considers to be its permanent income, they conjectured that to obtain homogeneous groupings of households whose main differentiating characteristic is permanent income, these households should be divided into segments of renters and owners, each segment in turn being subdivided into categories of self-employed and non-self-employed.

Let us consider the non-self-employed homeowner subgroup. Each household in this subgroup is classified according to the valuation of its house. The average measured income $\overline{Y}_m$ and the average measured consumption $\overline{C}_m$ are then computed for each house-valuation bracket. Dividing $\overline{C}_m$ by $\overline{Y}_m$ gives us the APC of homogeneous households by house-expenditure bracket. If housing is a good proxy for permanent income, then $\overline{Y}_m = Y_p$ and $\overline{C}_m = C_p$ for each bracket. If the permanent income hypothesis is correct, then permanent consumption will be proportional to permanent income, so that APC is a constant for all households. The results of Modigliani and Ando's study of non-self-employed homeowners

[10] F. Modigliani and A. Ando, "The 'Permanent Income' and the 'Life-cycle' Hypothesis of Savings Behavior: Comparisons and Tests," in I. Friend and R. Jones (eds.), *Consumption and Saving*, Vol. II, (Philadelphia: University of Pennsylvania Press, 1960).

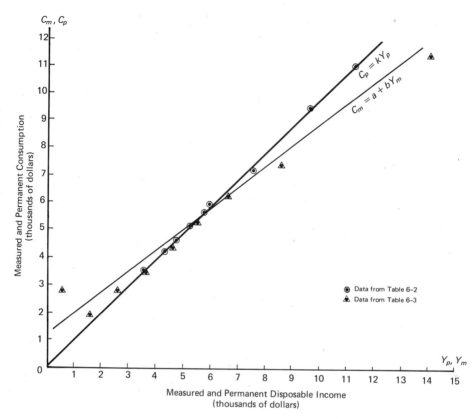

FIGURE 6-12   *Modigliani and Ando's Test of the Permanent Income Hypothesis*

appear in Table 6-2, where we can see that the APC is approximately the same for all brackets. The consumption data in Table 6-2 are plotted in Figure 6-12, and a consumption function C_p that is proportional to permanent income is drawn through these points. If the same households in Table 6-2 are grouped according to their measured income, as is the normal procedure in most budget studies, we obtain the results shown in Table 6-3. The consumption function C_m from this table is also plotted in Figure 6-12, where we can see that measured consumption is not proportional to measured income. The consumption curves resulting from this empirical study are strikingly similar to the hypothetical curves in Figure 6-11.

When Friedman investigated the long-run aggregate consumption function, he assumed that aggregate measured consumption is equal to aggregate permanent consumption and that aggregate permanent income is equal to a geometrically weighted average of present and past measured income. Specifically

$$Y_{p,t} = wY_{m,t} + w(1 - w)Y_{m,t-1} + w(1 - w)^2 Y_{m,t-2} + \cdots$$
$$+ w(1 - w)^n Y_{m,t-n} + \cdots$$

(6-31)

TABLE 6-3 Income and Consumption Data for Non-self-employed Homeowners, Bracketed According to Measured Income

Measured Income Bracket	Average Measured Income Y_m	Average Measured Consumption C_m	Measured APC $\dfrac{C_m}{Y_m}$
$ 0–999	$556	$2,760	4.79
1,000–1,999	1,622	1,930	1.19
2,000–2,999	2,664	2,740	1.03
3,000–3,999	3,587	3,515	0.98
4,000–4,999	4,535	4,350	0.96
5,000–5,999	5,538	5,320	0.96
6,000–7,499	6,585	6,250	0.95
7,500–9,999	8,582	7,460	0.87
10,000–above	14,033	11,500	0.82

SOURCE   F. Modigliani and A. Ando, "The 'Permanent Income' and the 'Life-cycle' Hypothesis of Saving Behavior: Comparisons and Tests," I. Friend and R. Jones (eds.) in *Consumption and Saving,* Vol. II (Philadelphia: University of Pennsylvania Press, 1960), p. 154

where w = the weight attached to this year's level of measured income.[11] Equation (6-31) is rather unwieldy, but fortunately, it can be transformed into a simpler version. First, we write the equation of permanent income for the time period $t - 1$

$$Y_{p,t-1} = wY_{m,t-1} + w(1 - w)Y_{m,t-2} + w(1 - w)^2 Y_{m,t-3} + \cdots$$
$$+ w(1 - w)^{n-1} Y_{m,t-n} + \cdots$$
(6-32)

Multiplying equation (6-32) by $(1 - w)$, we then obtain

$$(1 - w)Y_{p,t-1} = w(1 - w)Y_{m,t-1} + w(1 - w)^2 Y_{m,t-2} + w(1 - w)^3 Y_{m,t-3} + \cdots$$
$$+ w(1 - w)^n Y_{m,t-n} + \cdots$$
(6-33)

Subtracting (6-33) from (6-31) gives us

$$Y_{p,t} - (1 - w)Y_{p,t-1} = wY_{m,t}$$
(6-34)

Rearranging equation (6-34), we obtain the simplified definition of permanent income

$$Y_{p,t} = (1 - w)Y_{p,t-1} + wY_{m,t}$$
(6-35)

[11] The derivation of this equation is much too difficult for us to examine here. Friedman himself does not even derive it in *A Theory of the Consumption Function.* For the derivation, see Hal R. Varian, "Friedman's Permanent Income Estimate," in Thomas Mayer, *Permanent Income, Wealth, and Consumption* (Berkeley: University of California Press, 1972), pp. 362–64.

Friedman estimated that the weight attached to this year's level of measured income w is equal to 0.33. By limiting the series of past measured incomes to 16 years, Friedman could then estimate permanent income for the 1905–1951 period (excluding 1917–1918 and 1942–1945) by using equation (6-31). Next, by assuming that aggregate measured consumption is equal to aggregate permanent consumption, he estimated the long-run consumption function

$$C_p = 0.88 Y_p \qquad (6\text{-}36)$$

Friedman's estimate of $k = 0.88$ is remarkably close to the estimate of $k = 0.86$ obtained independently by Raymond Goldsmith for the 1897–1949 period (excluding 1917–1918 and 1942–1945).[12] Thus the permanent income hypothesis is consistent with the empirically observed long-run aggregate consumption function, that is, APC = MPC.

Friedman's formulation of the long-run aggregate consumption function can also be adapted to explain the short-run aggregate behavior of the economy during the business cycle. For example, consider the situation represented by the data in Table 6-4, where in year t measured income $Y_{m,t}$ is \$10,000 and is equal to $Y_{p,t-1}$, or permanent income in year $t - 1$. When $Y_{m,t} = Y_{p,t-1}$, equation (6-35) reduces to

$$
\begin{aligned}
Y_{p,t} &= (1 - w) Y_{p,t-1} + w Y_{p,t-1} \\
&= Y_{p,t-1} = Y_{m,t}
\end{aligned}
\qquad (6\text{-}37)
$$

Thus permanent income in time period t is equal to \$10,000. Now suppose that in time period $t + 1$, measured income decreases to \$9,000. Using equation (6-35) and letting $w = 0.33$, we can compute

$$
\begin{aligned}
Y_{p,t+1} &= (1 - 0.33) Y_{p,t} + 0.33 Y_{m,t+1} \\
&= \$9,670
\end{aligned}
\qquad (6\text{-}38)
$$

If $k = 0.88$, then we obtain

$$C_{p,t+1} = C_{m,t+1} = 0.88(\$9,670) = \$8,510 \qquad (6\text{-}39)$$

Assuming that measured income decreases further, to \$8,000 and \$7,000 in time periods $t + 2$ and $t + 3$, respectively, then measured consumption in these periods can also be calculated in the manner outlined in equations (6-38) and (6-39). The results of these calculations appear in Table 6-4.

The long-run consumption function given by equation (6-36) is graphed in Figure 6-13. The points given by the data in Table 6-4 that correspond to consumption and measured income when there is a short-run decline in income are also illustrated in Figure 6-13. If a statistical consumption function were fitted to the circled points

[12] Raymond W. Goldsmith, *A Study of Saving in the United States*, Vol. III (Princeton, N.J.: Princeton University Press for the National Bureau of Economic Research, 1956). In accordance with the permanent income hypothesis, Goldsmith used consumption figures that excluded expenditure on consumer durables but that included an estimate of the value of the services rendered by the stock of durable goods.

**TABLE 6-4   Aggregate Measured Consumption and Permanent Income
Given a Cyclical Decline in Measured Income**

Period	Measured Income Y_m	Permanent Income Y_p	Measured Consumption = Permanent Consumption $C_m = C_p = 0.88\,Y_p$
$t-1$	–	$10,000	$8,800
t	$10,000	10,000	8,800
$t+1$	9,000	9,670	8,510
$t+2$	8,000	9,120	8,030
$t+3$	7,000	8,420	7,410

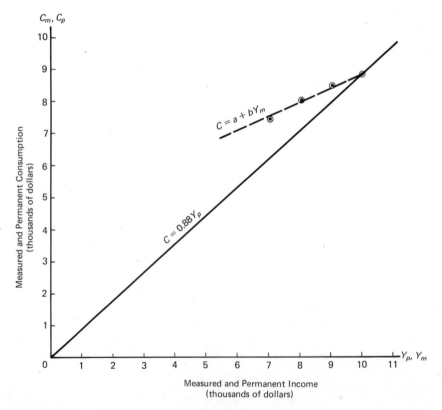

**FIGURE 6-13   The Effect of a Decline in Measured Income on Consumption
as a Function of Permanent Income**

in this graph, we would obtain both a nonproportional consumption function of the form

$$C = a + bY_m \qquad (6-40)$$

and the short-run consumption curve illustrated by the dashed line in Figure 6-13. This short-run consumption function is quite similar to the function graphed in Figure 6-2. Therefore, the permanent income hypothesis is compatible with the short-run aggregate consumption function where APC > MPC.

Friedman's permanent income hypothesis has not been accepted without criticism. Most of the controversy surrounds the assumption that $R_{Y_{tr},C_{tr}} = 0$. In other words, will a household that receives a windfall income spend any of it or save it all? Many tests purport to disconfirm Friedman's assumption that all transitory income is saved. But as Thomas Mayer points out, all these tests are invalid, because they do not distinguish between the consumption of transitory income and the consumption of the permanent income that transitory income produces.[13] The most serious challenge to the permanent income hypothesis also comes from Mayer, who employed 11 different tests to determine whether consumption is proportional to permanent income. Can we correctly assume that the "taste" for saving by low-income groups is the same as it is for high-income groups? Stated another way, "is a rich man ... simply a poor man with more money and ... given the same income, [will] the poor man ... behave exactly like the rich man?"[14] The results of Mayer's tests, which apply to the life-cycle hypothesis as well, disconfirmed the hypothesis that consumption is proportional to permanent income across income brackets. Fortunately, the fact that proportionality does not hold in the strict interpretation of the theory does not prevent the use of the permanent income hypothesis in most practical policy applications. This is due to the fact that in many cases we are interested only in what happens to APC as we move from one permanent income bracket to another; we are not concerned about whether these movements are due to differences in permanent income or differences in taste.

6-7   Concluding Remarks

It is not yet certain whether the relative income hypothesis, the life-cycle hypothesis, the permanent income hypothesis, or perhaps some other hypothesis best explains consumer behavior. However, the present consensus on this matter is perhaps expressed by Michael K. Evans:

> Without making final judgment on whether the strict terms of the permanent income hypothesis all hold, it can be fairly said that the weight of evidence supports this theory. Even if parts of the hypothesis are ultimately shown to be incorrect, Friedman's formulation has reshaped and redirected much of the research on the consumption function. It is unusual today to discuss the consumption function without referring to Friedman's terms of reference.[15]

[13] Mayer, Thomas, *Permanent Income, Wealth, and Consumption* (Berkeley: University of California Press, 1972), pp. 38–41.
[14] Pierre Martineau, quoted in Mayer, p. 10.
[15] Michael K. Evans, *Macroeconomic Activity* (New York: Harper and Row, 1969), p. 34.

In the remainder of this book we assume that the long-run consumption function is specified by

$$C = kY_p \qquad (6\text{-}41)$$

and that the short-run consumption function is specified by

$$C = a + bY_m . \qquad (6\text{-}42)$$

Because the major portion of the remainder of this book is concerned with the problems associated with the attainment and maintenance of full-employment equilibrium in the short run, we will primarily be using the short-run consumption function. When we examine the theory of economic growth, the long-run consumption function will be used.

7 Equilibrium in the Product Market

7-1 Introduction

In Chapters 3 and 4 we constructed a theory of aggregate demand that treated net investment as an exogenous variable. However, our analysis in Chapter 5 produced a theory that posits that investment is a function of the interest rate. In this chapter we incorporate this investment relationship into our general model of aggregate demand.

7-2 Derivation of the *IS* Curve (Excluding Government)

We have already learned that aggregate demand in an economy without a government (for which $T = 0$ and $G = 0$) can be expressed as

$$Y = C + I \tag{7-1}$$

where

$$C = a + bY_d$$
$$= a + bY \tag{7-2}$$

From our analysis in Chapter 5 we learned that investment is a negatively sloped, nonlinear function of the interest rate, as graphed in Figure 5-4(b). For our present

121

purposes the most important aspect of this relationship is the negative slope. To simplify the following analysis, we assume that net investment is a linear function of the interest rate and is specified by

$$I = j + ki \qquad (7\text{-}3)$$

where i = rate of interest
$k < 0$

Substituting (7-2) and (7-3) into (7-1) and solving for Y gives us

$$Y = \frac{1}{1 - b}(a + j + ki) \qquad (7\text{-}4)$$

which is not solvable because it contains two unknown variables Y and i. To understand this more clearly, assume that the consumption and investment functions are given by

$$I = 50 - 10i \qquad (7\text{-}5)$$

where the rate of interest is in percent and

$$C = 5 + 0.8Y \qquad (7\text{-}6)$$

Substituting (7-5) and (7-6) into (7-1) and solving for Y then gives us

$$Y = \frac{1}{1 - 0.8}[5 + 50 + (-10i)] \qquad (7\text{-}7)$$

which reduces to

$$Y = 5(55 - 10i) = 275 - 50i \qquad (7\text{-}8)$$

It is now clear that unless we know the interest rate, the equilibrium level of aggregate demand cannot be calculated. We can, however, select various interest rates and obtain corresponding values of Y. For example, if i = 1%, then Y = $225 billion; if i = 4%, then Y = $75 billion. Equation (7-8) is simply an expression of the functional relationship between the interest rate and the equilibrium level of aggregate demand. The graph of this relationship is shown in Figure 7-1(d). This curve is the product-market equilibrium curve and is generally referred to by most economists as the *IS curve.*[1]

The *IS* curve is derived graphically in Figure 7-1. Beginning in Figure 7-1(a), the investment function (7-5) is plotted. At this point we should recall equation (3-23)

$$I = S$$

which expresses a necessary condition for an equilibrium level of aggregate demand. This condition is represented in Figure 7-1(b) by the 45° line intersecting the origin. If the interest rate is, say, 4%, then the MEI curve in Figure 7-1(a) specifies that net investment will be $10 billion. The investment–savings equality condition in Figure 7-1(b) specifies that savings will also be $10 billion. Figure 7-1(c)

---

[1] Sir John Hicks first used this term in his famous article "Mr. Keynes and the 'Classics': A Suggested Interpretation," *Econometrica* **5** (1937), 147–59.

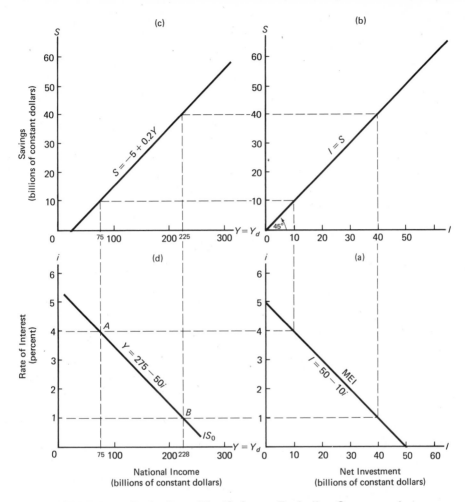

FIGURE 7-1   Derivation of the IS Curve, Excluding Government

graphs the savings function that is derived directly from the consumption function $C = 5 + 0.8Y$, which is given by equation (7-6). Using the equation

$$S = Y - C \qquad (7\text{-}9)$$

we can obtain the savings relationship simply by subtracting the consumption relation (7-6) from the income variable Y. In other words we substitute (7-6) into (7-9) to obtain

$$S = Y - (5 + 0.8Y) = -5 + 0.2Y \qquad (7\text{-}10)$$

The plot of this savings function in Figure 7-1(c) shows that savings is a monotonically increasing function of Y, so that for any given value of S there can be only one value of Y. This means that only one level of income can induce the community to produce a given level of savings. In the numerical example being considered, the level of national income must be $75 billion; otherwise, people would not save the $10 billion required for savings to equal investment. Thus at an interest rate of 4%, the corresponding equilibrium level of Y is shown graphically to be $75 billion. This interest rate and level of national income give us the coordinates of point A in Figure 7-1(d). If we select another interest rate, say, $i = 1\%$, for the purpose of illustration, then we can see that investment will be $40 billion and, for savings to be equal to this level, national income must be $225 billion. This result is represented by point B in Figure 7-1(d). Other interest rates generate a locus of points that together constitute the IS curve drawn in Figure 7-1(d). This curve is comprised of the plots of all combinations of interest rate and income at which $I = S$, or at which planned investment is equal to planned savings.

7-3   Derivation of the IS Curve (Including Government)

When government is included in our model, aggregate demand is defined as

$$Y = C + I + G \tag{7-11}$$

Government expenditure and taxation are initially assumed to be exogenous.
    Retaining the assumptions given in equations (7-2) and (7-3) and recalling that if $G > 0$, then $T > 0$ as well, we express aggregate demand as

$$Y = a + bY_d + j + ki + \overline{G} \tag{7-12}$$

However, using the relationship

$$Y_d = Y - \overline{T} \tag{7-13}$$

we can rewrite equation (7-12)

$$Y = a + b(Y - \overline{T}) + j + ki + \overline{G} \tag{7-14}$$

Rearranging terms and solving for Y then gives us

$$Y = \frac{1}{1 - b}(a - b\overline{T} + j + ki + \overline{G}) \tag{7-15}$$

Substituting the values of the parameters given by equations (7-5) and (7-6), we obtain

$$Y = \frac{1}{1 - 0.8}(5 - 0.8\overline{T} + 50 - 10i + \overline{G})$$
$$= 275 - 4\overline{T} + 5\overline{G} - 50i \tag{7-16}$$

For $G = \$10$ billion and $T = \$20$ billion, for example, equation (7-16) reduces to

$$Y = 245 - 50i \tag{7-17}$$

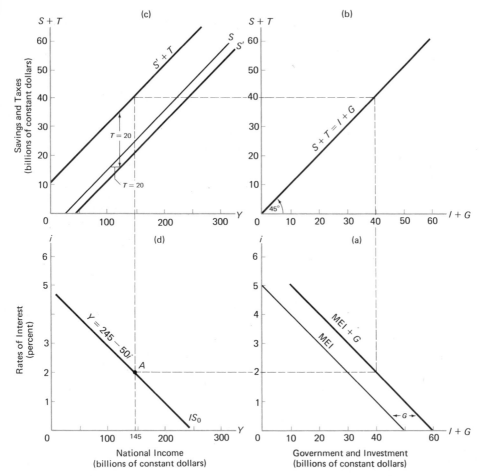

FIGURE 7-2   *Derivation of the* IS *Curve, Including Government and Exogenous Taxes*

which is the equation of a linear *IS* curve and is similar to the *IS* curve given by equation (7-8).

Figure 7-2 shows the derivation of the *IS* curve given by equation (7-17); this derivation is similar to the one in Figure 7-1. The MEI curve $i = 5 - 0.1I$ is plotted in Figure 7-2(a). Recalling equation (4-13), which specifies the necessary condition $S + T = I + G$ for an equilibrium level of aggregate demand, we can obtain an MEI + *G* curve graphically by adding the level of government expenditure horizontally to the MEI curve in Figure 7-2(a). The horizontal axis of this figure is labeled $I + G$ to indicate that for any interest rate *i* the corresponding level of net investment and exogenous government expenditure can be read from the horizontal axis.

Figure 7-2(b) graphically expresses the necessary condition for equilibrium specified by equation (4-13). The horizontal axis is the sum of net government spending and investment, and the vertical axis is the sum of savings and taxation. The 45° line drawn through the origin in Figure 7-2(b) is the graph of equation (4-13). The savings function given by equation (7-10) is graphed and labeled S in Figure 7-2(c). At this point, we must remember that equation (7-10) is derived on the assumption that $T = 0$, and therefore $Y_d = Y$. In this section we are assuming that $T > 0$, so that the savings function, which is theoretically specified in terms of disposable income, must be adjusted if it is to be plotted against national income. In Section 4-3 we saw that this can be done by shifting the savings function to the right by an amount that is equal to the tax. Curve S' in Figure 7-2(c) is the resulting adjusted savings function when $T = \$20$ billion. The relationship between savings *plus* taxes and national income is derived simply by vertically adding the amount of the tax to S'; this curve is designated $S' + T$ in Figure 7-2(c). (The apparent visual discrepancy between the horizontal and the vertical shifts occurs because different scales are used on the horizontal and vertical axes.) The *IS* curve in Figure 7-2(d) is derived by initially selecting a rate of interest, say $i = 2\%$. At this interest rate the sum of net investment and government expenditure will be \$40 billion per year, as specified by the MEI $+$ G curve in Figure 7-2(a). Figure 7-2(b) equates $S + T$ with $I + G$, so that the rate of savings *plus* taxes consistent with $i = 2\%$ must be \$40 billion. In Figure 7-2(c), $S' + T$ is equal to \$40 billion at an income level of \$145 billion. We can now locate point A ($Y = \$145$ billion, $i = 2\%$) on the *IS* curve in Figure 7-2(d). By selecting various interest rates and determining the requisite level of income that corresponds to each f these rates, we derive the *IS* curve shown in Figure 7-2(d).

If the government imposes an income tax of the form

$$T = h + tY = 10 + 0.1Y \tag{7-18}$$

then an equation for the equilibrium level of aggregate demand can be obtained by substituting (7-18) into (7-14) to obtain

$$Y = a + b[Y - (h + tY)] + j + ki + \bar{G} \tag{7-19}$$

Solving for Y gives us

$$Y = \frac{1}{1 - b + bt}(a - bh + j + ki + \bar{G}) \tag{7-20}$$

which reduces to

$$Y = \frac{1}{1 - 0.8 + (0.8)(0.1)}[5 - (0.8)(10) + 50 - 10i + 10] \tag{7-21}$$

$$= 204 - 35.7i$$

This is the equation for an *IS* curve.

The graphic derivation of the *IS* curve specified by equation (7-21) is essentially identical with the derivation of the exogenous tax case shown in Figure 7-2. The only difference occurs in the derivation of the savings *plus* taxes function. The method used in the graphic derivation of this curve is identical to the derivation method used in Figure 4-5.

7-4   Shifting the *IS* Curve

Excluding Government

The *IS* curve in Figure 7-1(d) is essentially determined by the MEI curve shown in Figure 7-1(a) and by the savings function given in Figure 7-1(c). Shifts in either of these curves will cause a displacement of the *IS* curve.

Beginning with all the assumptions embodied in Figure 7-1, we can now analyze the effects on the *IS* curve of shifting the MEI curve or the savings function curves. The curves shown in Figure 7-1 are reproduced as solid lines in Figure 7-3. However, here we graphically investigate only the effect of changes in the marginal efficiency of investment. Suppose that net investment increases by $10 billion at all rates of interest due to a new technological innovation. The MEI curve given in Figure 7-3(a) will then shift to the right by $10 billion. This new curve for the marginal efficiency of investment is drawn with a dashed line and labeled MEI′ in the figure. The investment–savings identity in Figure 7-3(b) must remain unchanged, and in this example we also hold the savings function constant, as illustrated in Figure 7-3(c). The new product-market equilibrium curve IS_1 is derived in the same manner as the original IS_0 curve.

An examination of Figure 7-3(c) reveals that an increase in net investment for a given interest rate, which shifts the MEI curve to the right, also shifts the *IS* curve to the right. Moreover, if $\Delta \bar{I} = \$10$ billion, then the resulting shift in the *IS* curve will be a constant ($\Delta Y = \$50$ billion). These magnitudes acquire a new significance when we recall our discussion in Chapter 3 of the investment multiplier.

$$\mu_I = \frac{\Delta Y}{\Delta \bar{I}} = \frac{1}{1 - b} \qquad (3\text{-}35)$$

In our example, MPC = 0.8, so that for constant interest rates equation (3-35) implies that

$$\Delta Y = \Delta \bar{I} \left(\frac{1}{1 - b} \right) = 10 \left(\frac{1}{1 - 0.8} \right) = \$50 \text{ billion} \qquad (7\text{-}22)$$

As we saw in Figure 7-3(d), this is actually what occurs. At any given interest rate, the *IS* curve shifts to the right by exactly $50 billion. Once again, if we know the interest rate, then we know the equilibrium level of aggregate demand.

A shift in the savings function will also cause a shift in the *IS* curve. If the savings function shifts downward, then the *IS* curve will shift outward to the right. This occurs because at any given interest rate the income level required to produce a level of savings equal to planned investment will be greater than the preceding income level. The graphic demonstration of this statement is left as an exercise for the student.

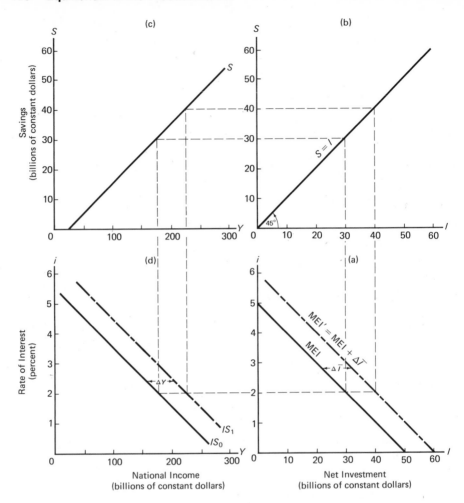

FIGURE 7-3   *The Effect of an Increase in Investment on the* **IS** *Curve*

Including Government

When government expenditure and taxation are added to our product-market model, the conclusions just derived are basically unaffected. Thus in this subsection we need to consider only the effects of changes in government expenditure and taxation.

The curves given in Figure 7-2 are reproduced in Figure 7-4 as solid lines. Suppose that government spending increases by $5 billion to pay for new mass-transit systems and that this expenditure increase is undertaken without modifying the level of taxation. This will cause the MEI + $\overline{G}$ curve in Figure 7-4(a) to shift to

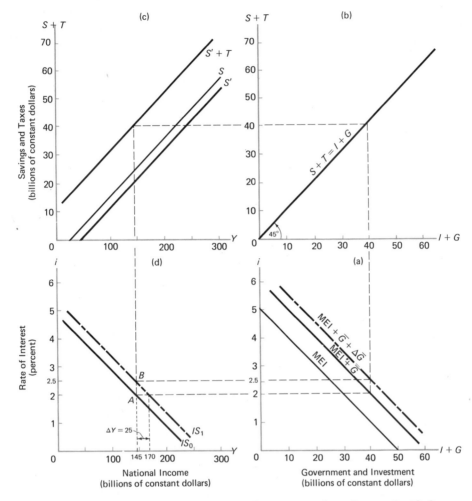

FIGURE 7-4   *The Effect of an Increase in Government Spending on the* IS *Curve*

the right by $5 billion and to become the dashed curve MEI $+ \bar{G} + \Delta \bar{G}$. Given that Figures 7-4(b) and 7-4(c) remain constant, a new product-market equilibrium curve IS_1 can be derived in Figure 7-4(d). This new *IS* curve has shifted to the right by $25 billion.

This $25 billion shift in the *IS* curve can be predicted from our study of the government expenditure multiplier in Chapter 4. When taxes are exogenous, the government expenditure multiplier derived in equation (4-18) is

$$\mu_G = \frac{\Delta Y}{\Delta G} = \frac{1}{1 - b} \tag{4-18}$$

In our example, the marginal propensity to consume *b* is equal to 0.8. Thus for any given interest rate, the change in aggregate demand will be

$$\Delta Y = \Delta \bar{G} \frac{1}{1-b} = 5\left(\frac{1}{1-0.8}\right) = \text{\$25 billion} \qquad (7\text{-}23)$$

At this point it is important to note that aggregate demand does not actually increase by this amount if the interest rate changes as government expenditure increases. For example, if the interest rate is initially 2%, then the level of aggregate demand prior to the increase in government spending will be $145 billion; this is designated by point A in Figure 7-4(d). When government expenditure increases by $5 billion, the product market equilibrium curve will then shift to IS_1. If the interest rate remains at 2%, then aggregate demand will increase by $25 billion to $170 billion. But suppose that as government spending increases, the interest rate simultaneously rises to 2.5%. In this case aggregate demand remains constant at $145 billion at point B on IS_1 in Figure 7-4(d).

An income tax will reduce the amount by which the IS curve shifts after an increase in government expenditure. Our analysis in Chapter 4 produced a government spending and investment multiplier

$$\mu'_G = \mu'_I = \frac{1}{1-b+bt}$$

for the case in which an income tax is levied. Using the values assigned to b and t in Figure 7-2, we obtain for these multipliers the numerical value

$$\mu'_G = \mu'_I = \frac{1}{1-0.8+(0.8)(0.1)} = 3.57 \qquad (7\text{-}24)$$

In Figure 7-4 an income tax with a marginal rate of taxation equal to 0.1 would produce only an $18.2 billion shift in the product-market equilibrium curve, rather than a $25 billion shift. One conclusion that we can draw from our discussion of the effect of an income tax is that this type of tax reduces the amount by which aggregate demand will change at a given interest rate when the level of government spending or investment changes.

The last example to be considered in this section is the effect of changes in taxation on the IS curve. Once again, the curves given in Figure 7-2 are reproduced as solid lines in Figure 7-5. Taxes are equal to a constant $20 billion, and government expenditure is equal to $10 billion. If taxes are reduced by 50% (that is, if $\Delta \bar{T} = -\$10$ billion), then the adjusted savings function S' in Figure 7-5(c) will shift to the left by $10 billion to a new adjusted savings function S''. Taxes are now equal to $\bar{T} + \Delta \bar{T}$. By adding this amount to S'', we obtain a new savings *plus* taxes curve $S'' + (\bar{T} + \Delta \bar{T})$, which represents the new relation between savings *plus* taxes and national income. The new product-market equilibrium curve, graphically derived in the usual manner, is labeled IS_1 in Figure 7-5(d). When taxes are reduced, the IS curve shifts to the right. For the example illustrated in Figure 7-5, the tax is exogenous and the IS curve shifts to the right by an amount determined by the tax multiplier given by

$$\mu_T = \frac{\Delta Y}{\Delta T} = \frac{-b}{1-b} \qquad (4\text{-}21)$$

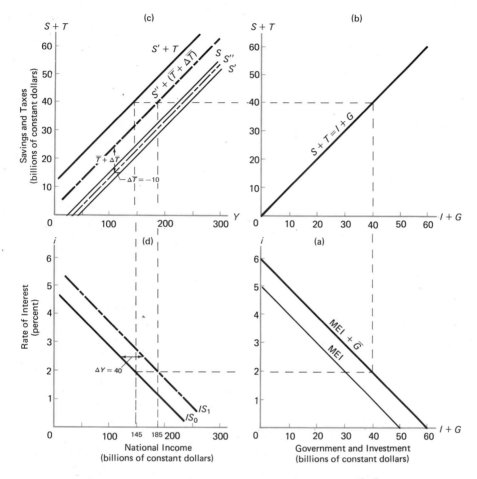

FIGURE 7-5   *The Effect of Reduced Taxation on the IS Curve*

Solving for the amount of the shift ΔY, we obtain

$$\Delta Y = \Delta \bar{T}\left(\frac{-b}{1-b}\right) = (-10)\left(\frac{-0.8}{0.2}\right) = \$40 \text{ billion} \tag{7-25}$$

which is in agreement with Figure 7-5(d).

When an income tax is issued by the government, reductions in taxes, either in the constant term h or in the marginal rate of taxation t, shift the IS curve to the right. For the simplest case where h is reduced, the IS curve shifts by a constant amount that is equal to

$$\Delta Y = \Delta h\left(\frac{-b}{1-b+bt}\right) \tag{7-26}$$

This result is a direct consequence of our definition of the income tax multiplier given by equation (4-40).

For the more complicated case in which the marginal rate of taxation is reduced by a small amount, the rightward shift in the *IS* curve will be

$$\Delta Y = \Delta t \left(\frac{-bY}{1 - b + bt} \right) \tag{7-27}$$

The presence of Y in the numerator means that the amount of shift in the *IS* curve depends on the level of national income, so that the amount of the shift cannot be a constant but must increase as Y increases. Equation (7-27) necessarily follows from the income tax multiplier defined by equation (4-41).

All other things remaining constant, an increase in taxes or a reduction in government expenditure will produce a leftward shift in the *IS* curve.

7-5   Concluding Remarks

In this chapter we have been concerned primarily with the implications of incorporating the theory of investment into a general model of aggregate demand. In the model that we have derived thus far, treating investment as an endogenous variable makes the level of aggregate demand indeterminate. This indeterminacy occurs because the model does not yet reflect the interest rate. However, we derived a functional relationship between the rate of interest and the equilibrium level of aggregate demand—the *IS* curve. The effects on the *IS* curve of varying levels of investment, savings, government expenditure, and taxation were also explored in detail.

In the next three chapters we will develop a theory of the money market that in conjunction with our theory of the *IS* curve will enable us to determine the interest rate and, subsequently, the level of aggregate demand. Given this general model, we will then be able to investigate such problems as unemployment, inflation, and macroeconomic policy.

8 The Supply of Money

8-1 Introduction

We are now ready to determine the level of aggregate demand when only the interest rate is known. In this and the next two chapters we will construct a theory of the money market. By combining our theories of the money market and the product market, we will then be able to determine the level of aggregate demand and the interest rate simultaneously. Given this sophisticated model of aggregate demand and our models of aggregate supply, we will then analyze the two major problems in macroeconomics: unemployment and inflation.

8-2 Money and Its Functions

Money can be defined as anything that actually functions as a generally accepted medium of exchange for goods, services, assets, and repayment of debts. In the United States today, coins, paper currency, and demand deposits (checking accounts) are the generally accepted media of exchange.[1] In addition to this necessary function, money can also serve as a store of wealth, a unit of account, and a standard for deferred payment.

Money as a Medium of Exchange

The most important characteristic of money is its function as a medium of exchange. Without a medium of exchange, the modern industrial state, which is

---

[1] Some economists also include traveler's checks. To simplify our analysis, we subsume traveler's checks, which are a small fraction of the total money supply, under checking accounts.

based on the specialization and division of labor, could not exist. In the absence of money, labor would be paid in terms of the real product it produced. For example, a worker on an automobile assembly line might be given two front fenders and three tires for a week's labor. To convert these real wages into required goods and services, this worker would have to find persons who wanted the fenders and tires and who also offered the required goods and services. Clearly, in a modern society, making all the necessary barter arrangements would be extremely time consuming at best, and probably impossible. The use of money eliminates these problems and enables a complicated economic society to exist.

The money used as a medium of exchange should possess characteristics that facilitate its exchange. First and foremost, the money must be readily acceptable by almost all members of society. Second, the money must have a high value in relation to its weight so that the cost of carrying it around is virtually zero. Third, the money must be readily divisible into smaller amounts, so that low-priced as well as high priced items can be purchased. Last, the money must be in a form that is not easy to counterfeit. The value of money is determined by its limited supply, and if this supply is greatly increased by counterfeiters, then the money will lose its value and cease to be a readily accepted medium of exchange.

Money as a Store of Wealth

Money represents generalized purchasing power over the goods and services produced by society. To the extent that an individual chooses to refrain from spending money, he or she holds a claim over present and future production. All such claims originate from the nation's stock of wealth, and because money is one form of claim, it must also be one form of wealth. Whether or not money represents *net wealth*—that is, assets of the community for which there is no offsetting liability—is a question that has concerned economists for many years and one that we will examine in greater detail in Chapter 11.

Wealth, the source of income, can be divided into two forms: *nonhuman,* or physical, and *human.* Nonhuman wealth is comprised of such tangible assets as land, machines, buildings, dams, and highways. Human wealth can be the knowledge and skill of a physician, the attractive face of a model, or the muscular coordination of a great golfer.

Individuals can store their wealth in any of its nonhuman forms and, less readily, in its human form. Money is a desirable medium for storing wealth, because it exhibits the property of perfect liquidity. *Liquidity* is the ease and certainty with which any asset can be converted into money. Normally, a fairly *illiquid* asset, such as a piece of land, can be quickly converted to money only if the owner is willing to sell the asset for less than its market value. An asset that is close to money in liquidity is a government bond, which can be converted directly into money. Furthermore, converting a bond into money requires a visit to a bank, so that there is some cost to the conversion process. Money assets, on the other hand, do not need to be converted to money; their value (in money terms) is known with certainty.[2] Money is therefore said to have *perfect liquidity*; it is the only asset that possesses this property. Assets that are relatively easy to convert into money with little or no loss have somewhat less than perfect liquidity and are known as *near monies*. Time deposits, savings and loan shares, and treasury bills are considered to be near monies.

If money is the only asset that has perfect liquidity, then why do people hold their wealth in other forms as well? The reason becomes obvious when we realize that assets that are less liquid than money yield higher rates of return than money. The real value of money declines when the price level rises, so that money yields a negative rate of return in this situation. As a hedge against inflation, it is wise for individuals to place a portion of their wealth in assets such as land that will increase in value if the price level rises. Conversely, in the event of deflation, it is prudent for individuals to shift the distribution of their portfolios from assets whose money value falls with the general price level to money, whose real value rises when prices fall. The degree to which people shift the distribution of their asset portfolios into or out of money naturally depends on the anticipated rate of price change and on the market rate of interest.

Money as a Unit of Account

Money is also the unit of account used to measure value in all but the most primitive societies. The values of two goods can be compared if their valuation in money terms is known. If good *A* sells for $2 and good *B* sells for $4, then we can say that the market value of *B* is twice that of *A*. By placing prices in terms of a unit of account on all goods and services produced by society, individuals and firms can more easily and efficiently make rational choices concerning the goods and services they purchase.

Money as a Standard for Deferred Payment

When an individual, a firm, or a government incurs a debt, the repayment of that debt is usually figured in terms of money. Money is used as a unit of account to measure the value of the future repayment of the debt. In this capacity money functions basically as a unit of account, given the added dimension of time.

8-3   Kinds of Money Used by the Public

In the United States today the public uses two basic kinds of money to conduct transactions: *currency* and *bank deposits subject to check.*

Currency

Currency is comprised both of paper money and of coins. Almost all paper currency is in the form of Federal Reserve notes, which are issued by the Federal

---

[2] If the price level should change, then the real value of money (its purchasing power) will move inversely with the change. Thus the *real* value of money is uncertain.

Reserve System. At one time a legal fiction was maintained that these notes were fractionally backed by the gold stock held in the U.S. Treasury. This fiction does not hold today; all Federal Reserve notes are simply *fiat money*, whose value depends on the public's confidence and willingness to accept them. A very small fraction of the paper currency in circulation today is in the form of Treasury currency. This currency is primarily the remnant of fiat money issued during the Civil War (greenbacks) or silver certificates once backed by government-owned silver and redeemable in silver. This portion of the money supply is slowly declining due to its retirement from circulation and will probably disappear in the near future.

Coins are metallic tokens minted by the Treasury to represent fractional amounts of a dollar. Originally, metallic coins had a commodity value, but today they are fiat money: their monetary values greatly exceed the commodity value of their metallic content. Today coins are desirable because they provide us with a form of money that is readily divisible into smaller amounts and because they simplify the design and operation of vending machines. Table 8-1 shows that the total sum of all currency in circulation in October 1975 amounted to $82,215 million.

It is important to note here that not all currency in circulation is held by the public. Some is held by the Treasury, the Federal Reserve System, and commercial banks. To determine the quantity of money held by the public, this portion of the currency in circulation is subtracted from the sum of government and commercial bank money, as shown in Table 8-1.

Commercial bank deposits with the Federal Reserve also appear in Table 8-1 in

**TABLE 8-1   U.S. Money Supply, October 1975
(in millions of dollars)**

Government or high-powered money	
Federal Reserve deposits of commercial banks	$ 27,254
Currency in circulation (Federal Reserve notes and Treasury currency)	82,215
Commercial bank money	
Demand deposits	221,500
	$330,969
Less: currency held by the Treasury, Federal Reserve banks, and commercial banks	−9,715
Less: Federal Reserve deposits of commercial banks	−27,254
Money supply held by nonbank public	$294,000

SOURCE   *Federal Reserve Bulletin* (January 1976), pp. A3 and A12.

the category of government money. These deposits, which are simply accounting entries, serve as reserves for member commercial banks and are considered equivalent to Federal Reserve notes, because notes and reserves can be interchanged at any time at virtually zero cost. These deposits are treated as accounting entries rather than as Federal Reserve notes purely for the sake of efficiency. Commercial bank deposits with the Federal Reserve rarely change ownership, and the use of accounting entries eliminates the cost of the paper, printing, and storage required to prepare actual notes. As Table 8-1 indicates, these deposits are not part of the money supply held by the public and therefore must be subtracted from government and commercial bank money. The reason for including them in Table 8-1 will become apparent later in the chapter.

Commercial Bank Deposits

A bank deposit is simply the accounting record of the money deposited in a bank by an individual. There are two types of bank deposits: *bank deposits subject to checking on demand* and *time (savings) deposits*. At present, economists disagree as to whether the definition of the money supply should include all bank deposits or only demand deposits. A broad definition of the money supply includes time deposits; a narrow definition excludes them. By investigating the characteristics of these two types of deposits, we can reach a tentative conclusion for our limited purposes here.

Deposits subject to checking on demand are exactly that: the bank that holds the deposit is obligated by law to return the depositor's money immediately on demand. More important, however, the depositor is not required to be present at the bank to make a payment; the depositor can write a check to transfer money to another person. Demand deposits are considered to be money because checks can be drawn on these deposits to conduct transactions. The ability to transfer deposits by check makes these deposits a medium of exchange, which satisfies our definition of money.

Time deposits are created in exactly the same manner as demand deposits: money is deposited in a bank account. Time deposits differ from demand deposits, however, in that the depositor, if requested by the bank, must give 30 days notice before withdrawing money, from a time deposit. In actual practice in the recent past, banks have not enforced this legal aspect of the time deposit, but the fact that they can do so reduces the liquidity of such deposits. (For some types of large savings deposits, usually reffered to as *certificates of deposit*, or CDs, withdrawals can be made without penalty only at specified times. These deposits are therefore highly illiquid and should not be considered part of the money supply.) A much more important difference is that the money in time deposits cannot be transferred by check. To make a transaction, you must transfer your time deposit either into cash or into your demand deposit.

Recently, however, competition between commercial banks and thrift institutions (mutual savings banks, savings and loan associations, and credit unions) for the deposits of customers has led to commercial banks automatically transferring funds from savings accounts to demand deposit accounts to cover overdraft checks. In actuality, these banks are paying interest on demand deposits. The competition between commercial banks and thrift institutions sharply increased in 1974, when thrift institutions in New England were allowed to offer customers a negotiated order of withdrawal (NOW) account. NOW accounts in effect pay interest on a form of checking account. To remain competitive, commercial banks were forced to offer similar services. Although NOW accounts are still offered only in the Northeast, they are having an increased impact on commercial banking in the rest of the United States.

Because the former distinction between demand deposits and other forms of deposits is much less clear today, economists have suggested several alternative definitions for money, which are defined by the shorthand notation M_1, M_2, M_3, M_4, and M_5. The differences between these definitions are given in detail in Table 8-2. When we refer to money in general in the remainder of this book, we will mean assets that serve as a medium of exchange, regardless of where they reside. When we refer to a particular type of money, we will specify which definition of money we are using. (For example, in Table 8-1 we employ the M_1 definition of money.)

8-4   The Central Bank and High-powered Money

The central bank controls the issue of its liabilities. These liabilities in turn become the monetary assets that commercial banks hold as reserves against their loans and investments. These assets are either currency or commercial-bank deposits in the central bank, which are equivalent to and interchangeable with currency. The public also holds central bank liabilities, but only in the form of currency. These assets of the central bank are an important determinant of the money supply, because they comprise the base on which commercial banks create demand deposits by the institution of fractional reserve banking. Changes in the quantity of central bank assets can produce much larger changes in the volume of demand deposits. For this reason, they are called *high-powered money.*

In the United States the central bank is the Federal Reserve System.[3] The Federal Reserve controls the quantity of high-powered money through the operation of buying or selling government securities. A government security (a treasury bill or bond) can be bought from either the Department of the Treasury or the public on the open market. When the security is purchased, a Federal Reserve deposit is created in the name of the seller, thus increasing the volume of high-powered money. When the Federal Reserve sells a government security from its asset portfolio, the opposite chain of events occurs and the quantity of high-powered money is reduced. These operations, referred to as *open-market operations,* are the most effective tool the Federal Reserve has for controlling the quantity of high-powered money and subsequently the quantity of money held by the public.

---

[3] The historical development of the Federal Reserve System and the details of its institutional operation will not be examined in this book. Any good introductory economics text will discuss these matters in sufficient detail.

TABLE 8-2   Definitions of the Quantity of Money

M_1	Currency *plus* demand deposits.
M_2	M_1 *plus* savings deposits *minus* negotiable Certificates of Deposit (CD's) of $100,000 or more.
M_3	M_2 *plus* mutual savings bank deposits, savings and loan shares, and credit union shares.
M_4	M_2 *plus* negotiable CD's of $100,000 or more.
M_5	M_3 *plus* negotiable CD's of $100,000 or more.

One institutional fact concerning the Federal Reserve's function as a central bank should be mentioned at this point: only about 45% of all commercial banks are members of the Federal Reserve System. This is not a critical point, however, because Federal Reserve banks handle about 85% of all bank deposits. In addition, most nonmember banks maintain balances in member banks and are therefore indirectly influenced by the Federal Reserve. For simplicity, we will assume that *all* commercial banks are members of the Federal Reserve System and are subject to its legal control.

8-5   Commercial Banks and Creation of Demand Deposits

Like other private corporations, commercial banks seek to maximize the profits of their stockholders. Banks earn some of their revenue by providing customer services, including checking accounts, trust management, and safe-deposit boxes. But more than 80% of a bank's profits are derived from the interest on loans and investments that the bank earns by using its depositors' money. Commercial banks can use their depositors' money in this way because during a normal banking day the difference between total withdrawals and total deposits is usually quite close to zero. To be prepared for those rare days when withdrawals exceed deposits, a bank maintains *reserves* (cash or immediate claims to cash) that are equal to a fraction of its deposit liabilities. This fraction is called the *reserve ratio*. If it were not maintained, then a failure to meet the withdrawal request of one depositor could precipitate a run on the bank and cause it to fail. In the United States, runs on commercial banks are a thing of the past due to the establishment of the Federal Deposit Insurance Corporation (FDIC), which insures each depositor's account in a commercial bank up to $40,000.

The reserve ratio under which commercial banks operate greatly exceeds the requirements of sound banking practice. This ratio is established by the Federal Reserve under the powers granted by the Banking Act of 1935.

We now examine how commercial banks create money in the form of demand deposits and how the Federal Reserve controls the money supply by determining the quantity of high-powered money and the commercial bank reserve ratio.

Creation of Money by a Monopoly Bank

The simple model of money creation we are going to develop here is based on the primary assumption that there is only one commercial bank (that is, a monopoly bank). We also assume that:

1. The public holds all the currency that it desires, so that any additional money that is created will *all* be placed on deposit.
2. The bank lends all deposits up to the legal reserve requirement established by the Federal Reserve; that is, the bank maintains no reserves in excess of the legal minimum.
3. The legal reserve ratio is 20%.
4. The bank's only assets are in reserves and loans; its only liabilities are in demand deposits.

Suppose that the name of our monopoly bank is the Commercial Bank and that its initial balance sheet is shown in Table 8-3. We can see that the bank is completely "loaned up"; its reserves are exactly equal to the minimum legally required by the central bank. Now suppose that the central bank, via an open-market operation, purchases a $100 government bond held by an individual. By assumption 1, the person who sold the bond to the central bank immediately places the money received from the sale of the bond in a checking account at the Commercial Bank. The bank's new balance sheet is shown in Table 8-4. The bank now has a reserve ratio R_r of 0.273, which is greater than the required reserve ratio RR_r of 0.20, and the bank is said to have *excess reserves XR*. The excess reserve ratio XR_r is equal to $R_r - RR_r$, or $0.273 - 0.20 = 0.073$. The bank is not maximizing its profits; it can legally increase its assets by extending additional loans. Clearly, the bank is not in an equilibrium position and will increase its loans, either by

TABLE 8-3 Commercial Bank: Initial Balance Sheet

Assets		Liabilities	
Reserves (including vault cash)	$ 200	Demand Deposits	$1,000
Loans	800		
	$1,000		$1,000

Reserve ratio $= R_r = \dfrac{\$200}{\$1,000} = 0.20 =$ Required reserve ratio $= RR_r$

TABLE 8-4 Commercial Bank: Balance Sheet After a Deposit of $100

Assets		Liabilities	
Reserves	$ 300	Demand deposits	$1,100
Loans	800		
	$1,100		$1,100

$R_r = \dfrac{\$300}{\$1,100} = 0.273 > RR_r$

reducing its interest rate or by being less selective in extending loans at the existing interest rate.

When the Commercial Bank extends a loan from its excess reserves, no matter who receives the loan or how it is spent, the full amount of the loan will soon be deposited in the bank. (This follows from our assumptions that the public has all the cash it desires and that there is only one commercial bank.) Thus for all practical purposes the bank deposit created by the loan never leaves the bank, and as a result the bank's reserves remain unchanged. Given this knowledge, the bank is faced with the task of determining the maximum amount by which it can increase its loans (create demand deposits) without permitting its reserve ratio to drop below the legally required minimum.

Given our previous assumptions, we can easily derive a simple formula to determine the amount by which the Commercial Bank should increase its loans. Initially, if the bank is in equilibrium (if it has no excess reserves), then the reserve ratio

$$\frac{\text{Reserves}}{\text{Deposits}} = \frac{R}{D} = R_r = RR_r = \text{Required reserve ratio}$$

(8-1)

$$= \frac{\$200}{\$1,000} = 0.20$$

Keeping in mind that RR_r is a constant established by the central bank and that the actual or working reserve ratio R_r must be equal to RR_r if the bank is to be in equilibrium, we can rewrite equation (8-1)

$$D = \frac{R}{RR_r}$$

(8-2)

Now if reserves increase by an amount equal to ΔR and if the bank is maximizing profits, then the increase in deposits ΔD must be

$$\Delta D = \frac{\Delta R}{RR_r}$$

(8-3)

In our example, $\Delta R = \$100$ and the equilibrium increase in deposits is

$$\Delta D = \frac{\$100}{0.20} = \$500$$

(8-4)

But ΔD in Table 8-4 is only $100. To achieve equilibrium, the Commercial Bank should therefore increase its loans (remember that all loans immediately become deposits) by $500 − $100 = $400. The balance sheet for the Commercial Bank after loans of this amount are made appears in Table 8-5.

When the individual sold the $100 bond, the money supply initially increased by this amount. This is apparent if we consider the difference in demand deposits between Tables 8-3 and 8-4. The central bank increases both the public's money supply and the quantity of high-powered money by $100. The Commercial Bank, as a byproduct of its profit-maximizing behavior, further increases the public's money supply by $1,500 − $1,100 = $400, as we can see by comparing Tables 8-4 and 8-5. Hence the total increase in the money supply resulting from an open-market purchase of $100 is $500.

TABLE 8-5   Commercial Bank: Balance Sheet After Loans of $400

Assets		Liabilities	
Reserves	$300	Demand deposits	$1,500
Loans	1,200		
	$1,500		$1,500

$$R_r = \frac{\$300}{\$1,500} = 0.20 = RR_r$$

It is not difficult to find the number of times the public's total money supply will increase (given our initial set of assumptions) as a result of a $1.00 increase in high-powered money. Simply rearrange equation (8-3) to obtain

$$\frac{\Delta D}{\Delta R} = \frac{1}{RR_r} \qquad (8-5)$$

This is sometimes referred to as the *monetary multiplier*. For our simple example

$$\frac{1}{RR_r} \Rightarrow \frac{1}{0.20} = 5 \qquad (8-6)$$

With a $100 increase in high-powered money, the money supply increases by (5)($100) = $500.

Now suppose that instead of purchasing a bond, the central bank initially sells a $100 bond. The immediate result of the purchase is shown in the Commercial Bank's balance sheet in Table 8-6. When the bond is bought by an individual, that person pays for the bond by writing a check on demand deposits payable to the central bank. Unlike individuals or firms, the central bank does *not* replace the receipt of the bond sale in the Commercial Bank, but instead deposits the money into itself. It does this by simply reducing the reserves of the Commercial Bank, which are on deposit in the central bank, by $100. The assets of the Commercial Bank, are still equal to its liabilities, of course, but its reserve ratio has fallen below the legally required minimum. To correct this situation, the Commercial Bank must either increase its reserves or reduce its loans.

One way the Commercial Bank can increase its reserves is to borrow $100 from

TABLE 8-6   Commercial Bank: Balance Sheet After a Withdrawal of $100

Assets		Liabilities	
Reserves	$100	Demand deposits	$900
Loans	800		
	$900		$900

$$R_r = \frac{\$100}{\$900} = 0.111 < RR_r$$

the central bank. This operation is not achieved without cost to the Commercial Bank, however, because the central bank charges interest on such loans. The interest rate charged by the central bank is called the *discount rate*. By varying this rate, the central bank can encourage or discourage borrowing by the Commercial Bank. As we shall learn in greater detail in Section 8-7, the ability to vary the discount rate provides the central bank with a third tool (in addition to open-market operations and the reserve ratio) with which to control the supply of money.

Borrowing from the central bank to meet reserve requirements is not a long-run solution if the discount rate exceeds the net rate of return on the loan or, as is usually the case in the United States, if the central bank will not allow the loan to be extended indefinitely. The central bank takes this position because it originally sold the government bond so that the Commercial Bank would be forced to contract its liabilities and therefore to reduce the money supply. The central bank lends reserves to the Commercial Bank so that the Commercial Bank will have time to adjust its portfolio and to reduce its deposits. Now suppose that the Commercial Bank has highly liquid assets and does not need additional time to bring its reserve ratio back up to the required level. The Commercial Bank will then reduce its demand deposits by not renewing its loans. We can calculate the required reduction in demand deposits by using equation (8-3) to obtain

$$\Delta D = \frac{\Delta R}{RR_r} = \frac{-\$100}{0.20} = -\$500 \tag{8-7}$$

This means that for demand deposits to decline $500, loans must be reduced $400. This follows because assets must equal liabilities, and the assets in the form of reserves remain constant at $100. The end result of this liquidation of assets appears in Table 8-7. There we can see that the Commercial Bank is once again maintaining its legal reserve ratio, but note that the money supply has been reduced $500.

We can use this simple model to examine one additional and very important monetary phenomenon: the effect on the money supply of a change in the required reserve ratio.

Suppose that once again the initial conditions are shown in Table 8-3 and that the central bank reduces the required reserve ratio to 15%. Immediately, the Commercial Bank has excess reserves amounting to 5%, or $50, and must expand its loans if it is to maximize profits. Using equation (8-3), we see that the amount by which loans and, concomitantly, the money supply will be expanded is given by

TABLE 8-7   Commercial Bank: Balance Sheet After a $400 Liquidation of Loans

Assets		Liabilities	
Reserves	$100	Demand deposits	$500
Loans	$400		
	$500		$500

$R_r = \frac{\$100}{\$500} = 0.20 = RR_r$

$$\Delta \text{ Loans} = \Delta D = \frac{\Delta R}{RR_r} = \frac{\$50}{0.15} = \$333 \tag{8-8}$$

The resulting situation after the money supply has increased $333 is shown in Table 8-8. If the central bank raises the required reserve ratio instead, then the opposite situation will occur and the money supply will contract.

From our simple analysis of commercial banking we have learned that:

1. Through a system of fractional reserve banking, a monopoly bank such as the Commercial Bank that seeks to maximize its profits will create money from excess reserves as it expands its loans.
2. By the operation of buying and selling bonds or other assets on the open market, a central bank can affect the level of the money supply. If the central bank buys (sells) bonds in its open market operations, then the money supply expands (contracts) by a multiple of this operation. The value of the monetary multiplier depends on the required reserve ratio.
3. The discount rate that a central bank charges on loans to a commercial bank affects the commercial bank's level of profits and its willingness to borrow from the central bank. When the discount rate is low relative to the loan rate, the commercial bank will be more willing to borrow from the central bank.
4. The central bank can vary the money supply by changing the required reserve ratio. Lowering (raising) the RR_r will expand (contract) the money supply.

Points 2, 3, and 4 describe the most powerful tools that a central bank can use to control the money supply. The manner in which open market operations and changes in the required reserve ratio affect the money supply should by now be clear. Exactly how changes in the discount rate affect the money supply is explained later, in Section 8-7.

Creation of Money by Competitive Banks

We now demonstrate that the conclusions we just reached in the context of our example of a monopoly commercial banking system also apply when perfect competition exists among commercial banks. When there are many commercial banks, the process of creating bank deposit money becomes more complicated, because when a bank extends a loan the ultimate receiver of the lending bank's cashier's check may deposit the check in one of several banks. For the purposes

TABLE 8-8 Commercial Bank: Balance Sheet After a Reduction in RR_r

Assets		Liabilities	
Reserves	$ 200	Demand deposits	$1,333
Loans	1,133		
	$1,333		$1,333

$R_r = \dfrac{\$200}{\$1,333} = 0.15 = RR_r$

of our analysis here, we assume that the deposit is *always* made in a different bank. All of our previous assumptions still hold, the required reserve ratio is 20%, and the banks are called Commercial Bank 1, Commercial Bank 2, and so forth.

Suppose that Commercial Bank 1 initially has a balance sheet identical to the one for the monopoly Commercial Bank given in Table 8-3. Once again, we assume that the central bank buys a $100 bond on the open market and that the seller of the bond deposits a $100 check from the central bank in Commercial Bank 1. The balance sheet for Commercial Bank 1 is still identical to the balance sheet for the monopoly Commercial Bank given in Table 8-4. At this point, however, the similarity between these balance sheets ceases.

Commercial Bank 1 cannot expand its loans by $400, because the deposits it would create in extending these loans would *all* have to be placed in different commercial banks. This would cause the reserve ratio of Commercial Bank 1 to fall below the required reserve ratio. In this situation Commercial Bank 1 can increase its loans only by an amount equal to the excess reserves created by the $100 deposit, or

$$\$100(1 - RR_r) = \$100(1 - 0.20) = \$80$$

as shown in Table 8-9. The deposit this $80 loan creates is placed in Commercial Bank 2, and the reserves of Commercial Bank 1 are reduced by $80. The R_r of Commercial Bank 1 is now equal to the RR_r, and this bank ceases to extend loans.

We assume that prior to this $80 deposit Commercial Bank 2 had no excess reserves, so that it now has excess reserves of $80. For simplicity, Table 8-10 shows only the net change in the assets and liabilities of Commercial Bank 2

TABLE 8-9   Commercial Bank 1: Balance Sheet After a Loan of $80

Assets		Liabilities	
Reserves	$ 220	Demand deposits	$1,100
Loans	880		
	$1,100		$1,100

$R_r = \dfrac{\$200}{\$1,100} = 0.20 = RR_r$

TABLE 8-10   Commercial Bank 2: Changes in Balance Sheet After a Deposit of $80

Δ Assets		Δ Liabilities	
Δ Reserves	+ $80	Δ Demand deposits	+ $80
Δ Loans	0		
	+ $80		+ $80

Excess reserves $XR = \$80 - (\$80)(0.20) = \$64$

TABLE 8-11   Commercial Bank 2: Changes in Balance Sheet After a Loan of $64

Δ Assets		Δ Liabilities	
Δ Reserves	+ $16	Δ Demand deposits	+ $80
Δ Loans	+ $64		
	+ $80		+ $80

Excess reserves = 0

TABLE 8-12   Summary of Net Loan and Deposit Creation by n Commercial Banks

Commercial Bank	Net Additional Money (Demand Deposits)	Net Additional Loans	Net Addition to Reserves
1	$100.00	$ 80.00	$ 20.00
2	80.00	64.00	16.00
3	64.00	51.20	12.80
4	51.20	40.96	10.24
5	40.96	32.77	8.19
6	32.77	26.22	6.55
7	26.22	20.98	5.24
8	20.98	16.78	4.20
.	.	.	.
.	.	.	.
.	.	.	.
n	00.00	00.00	00.00
Total Commercial banking system	$500.00	$400.00	$100.00

immediately after the deposit of the $80 check. Commercial Bank 2 must maintain reserves of ($80)(0.20) = $16 to support an $80 increase in deposits. This means that it has excess reserves of $80 − $16 = $64, which it can and does lend. The balance sheet for Commercial Bank 2 after lending $64 appears in Table 8-11.

The loan of Commercial Bank 2 becomes the deposit of Commercial Bank 3, which then has excess reserves of $64 − ($64)(0.20) = $51.20. Commercial Bank 3 can then lend these excess reserves, which become the net positive deposits of Commercial Bank 4, and so on. The sequence of this infinite but diminishing chain of deposit and loan creation is summarized in Table 8-12.

This example illustrates the important point that the final result of creating demand deposits when there are many commercial banks is exactly the same as it is when there is only one commercial bank.

This result can also be demonstrated algebraically. If $1.00 is deposited in a commercial bank, then the value of the second deposit ρ will be equal to the excess reserves generated by the first deposit, or

$$\rho = 1 - (1)RR_r = 1 - RR_r \qquad (8\text{-}9)$$

The value of the third deposit will be the value of the second deposit ρ *minus* the required reserves on the second deposit, or

$$\rho - \rho(RR_r) = \rho(1 - RR_r) = \rho^2$$

Similarly, the value of the fourth deposit will be the value of the third deposit ρ^2 *minus* the required reserves on the third deposit, or

$$\rho^2 - \rho^2(RR_r) = \rho^2(1 - RR_r) = \rho^3$$

and the fifth deposit will be

$$\rho^3 - \rho^3(RR_r) = \rho^3(1 - RR_r) = \rho^4$$

Generalizing, we can now write a series that represents the total change in the money supply ΔM after n deposits resulting from the deposit of a single dollar, or

$$\Delta M = 1 + \rho + \rho^2 + \rho^3 + \rho^4 + \cdots + \rho^{n-1} \qquad (8\text{-}10)$$

This is a geometric series. Since $RR_r < 1$, it follows from our definition of ρ that $\rho < 1$, so that this series has a limit. Using exactly the same method that we employed in Chapter 3 to find the sum of a similar series [see equation (3-39), page 44], we obtain

$$\Delta M = \frac{1}{1 - \rho} \qquad (8\text{-}11)$$

Now, since $\rho = 1 - RR_r$, equation (8-11) reduces to

$$\Delta M = \frac{1}{1 - 1 + RR_r} = \frac{1}{RR_r} \qquad (8\text{-}12)$$

which is identical to the monetary multiplier for a monopoly bank derived in equation (8-5). Thus we have shown that a banking system comprised of many individual commercial banks, each operating in its own self-interest, will create the same amount of demand-deposit money that a single monopoly bank will create, given our set of initial assumptions.

8-6   Determinants of Nominal Money Supply

In Section 8-5 we made two strong assumptions about the behavior of the public and commercial banks: (1) that the public's demand for currency is constant, and (2) that commercial banks always seek to maintain zero excess reserves. In reality, these two conditions do not hold; the actual behavior of the public and commercial banks is such that they *can* influence the money supply. In this section we derive a simple accounting model to show how the joint behavior of the central bank, commercial banks, and the public determines the money supply.[4]

From our discussion of the definition of money in Section 8-3, we can denote the supply of money held by the public

$$M_s = C + D \tag{8-13}$$

where M_s = the nominal money supply
C = nominal currency
D = nominal demand deposits.

From the discussion in Section 8-4 we can denote high-powered money

$$H = C + R \tag{8-14}$$

where H = the nominal supply of high-powered money
R = the nominal reserves of the commercial banks

The reserves of commercial banks in the United States comprise both Federal Reserve deposits and vault cash.

Dividing both sides of (8-14) by M_s gives us

$$\frac{H}{M_s} = \frac{C}{M_s} + \frac{R}{M_s} \tag{8-15}$$

The last term of equation (8-15) can be written

$$\frac{R}{M_s} = \frac{R}{D} - \frac{R}{D} + \frac{R}{M_s} \tag{8-16}$$

because we are simultaneously adding and subtracting identical terms. We can multiply the second term on the right-hand side of equation (8-16) by M_s/M_s and the third term by D/D without altering the equality, and we obtain

$$\begin{aligned}
\frac{R}{M_s} &= \frac{R}{D} - \frac{RM_s}{DM_s} + \frac{RD}{M_s D} \\
&= \frac{R}{D} - \frac{R(M_s - D)}{M_s D}
\end{aligned} \tag{8-17}$$

Now from equation (8-13) we know that $(M_s - D) = C$, so that we can write equation (8-17)

$$\frac{R}{M_s} = \frac{R}{D} - \frac{CR}{M_s D} \tag{8-18}$$

Substituting (8-18) into (8-15) then gives us

$$\frac{H}{M_s} = \frac{C}{M_s} + \frac{R}{D} - \frac{CR}{M_s D} \tag{8-19}$$

[4] This analysis of the money stock and its determinants is based on that used by Philip Cagan in his *Determinants and Effects of Changes in the Stock of Money 1875–1960* (New York: Columbia University Press, 1965), p. 12.

Finally, dividing both sides of equation (8-19) by H and taking its reciprocal, we obtain

$$M_s = \frac{H}{\frac{C}{M_s} + \frac{R}{D} - \frac{CR}{M_s D}} \tag{8-20}$$

which is an expression for the nominal money supply held by the public in terms of the behavior of the central bank, commercial banks, and the public.

The central bank determines the supply of nominal high-powered money. Given the behavior of the public and commercial banks, the nominal supply of money will vary directly with the nominal supply of high-powered money.

The behavior of the public is specified by the ratio of currency to the money supply C/M_s, which is called the *currency ratio*. By necessity, the currency ratio is less than 1.0.

The behavior of a commercial bank is specified by the ratio of its reserves to its deposits R/D. We already know that this is called the *reserve ratio* and that it can be alternatively expressed by the symbol R_r. We also know that the Federal Reserve has the authority to establish the minimum legal value of this ratio, called the *required reserve ratio* RR_r. In actual banking practice, R_r has always been less than 1; for the commercial banking system as a whole, R_r is usually greater than RR_r, as will be explained in Section 8-7.

Letting the *currency ratio* C_r be equal to C/M_s, we can write equation (8-20) in the slightly more convenient notation

$$M_s = \frac{H}{C_r + R_r - C_r R_r} \tag{8-21}$$

where R_r is our previously defined reserve ratio.

Because C_r and R_r are both less than unity, their product must be less than either of their individual values. This means that if either C_r or R_r increases and H remains constant, then the nominal money stock will decrease. Thus we can conclude that the nominal money supply varies directly with the quantity of high-powered money and inversely with the currency and reserve ratios. These three variables do not completely explain variations in the nominal money supply, but they do serve as useful devices in analyzing such variations. For this reason these variables are called the *proximate determinants* of the nominal money supply.

Economists Milton Friedman, Anna Jacobson Schwartz, and Phillip Cagan, among others, who have studied monetary history, find the preceding classification of the channels through which changes in the money supply occur to be quite useful, because the three determinants are not rigidly linked by either accounting or institutional arrangements. Some interdependency no doubt exists between these three variables, but this approach implies that such interdependency is the result of certain behavior on the part of the central bank, commercial banks, and the public. By examining data that measure the actions of these three sectors, it is possible to determine the nature of the interdependency among the determinants. We shall consider this interdependency in greater detail in Chapter 13, where we examine the explanations of recession and inflation offered by Friedman, Schwartz, and Cagan.

8-7   Behavior of Commercial Banks

In the preceding section we mentioned the historically observed fact that the aggregate reserve ratio of commercial banks is usually greater than the required reserve ratio established by the Federal Reserve. On first inspection this fact may seem to be at odds with our earlier assumption that commercial banks are profit-maximizing businesses. It seems that a commercial bank cannot possibly maximize its profits as long as

$$XR = R - RR > 0 \qquad (8\text{-}22)$$

where XR is the excess of reserves over required reserves. This conclusion is incorrect, however, because the simple model we derived in Section 8-5 ignores the facts that commercial banks do not have perfect knowledge of the future and that all assets and loans acquired by a commercial bank do not have the same degree of liquidity, yield, and risk. A bank faced with the decision of acquiring assets will not place all its excess reserves into assets that yield the highest rate of return, because those assets will also be the least liquid and the riskiest. Instead, a bank will diversify its investment portfolio, basing its choices on considerations of yield, liquidity, and risk. Its portfolio will range from high-yield, risky, illiquid assets to the perfectly liquid asset, money. A bank must maintain some liquid assets, because it lacks perfect knowledge of the future. If a bank with zero excess reserves loses reserves due to some random or unforeseeable event, then it must borrow to meet the legal reserve requirement. A bank can borrow on short notice from other commercial banks or from the Federal Reserve, but because borrowing requires interest payments, the bank's costs rise and its profits fall. To maximize its profits, the bank must maintain excess reserves in conjunction with some of its assets in the form of highly liquid, low-risk, relatively low-yield U.S. Treasury bills. As the cost of acquiring reserves decreases in relation to the return on the bank's asset portfolio, the bank will shift the asset distribution of its portfolio toward less liquid, higher-yield assets. This means that the reserve ratio will be reduced and that the nominal money supply will expand, given that the nominal stock of high-powered money and the currency ratio remain constant.

This can easily be shown in a more rigorous manner. Rearranging equation (8-22) and dividing both sides by D, we obtain

$$\frac{R}{D} = \frac{XR}{D} + \frac{RR}{D} \qquad (8\text{-}23)$$

or

$$R_r = XR_r + RR_r \qquad (8\text{-}24)$$

where XR_r is the *excess reserve ratio*. Substituting equation (8-24) into equation (8-21) yields

$$M_s = \frac{H}{C_r + XR_r + RR_r - C_r XR_r - C_r RR_r} \qquad (8\text{-}25)$$

Because C_r and XR_r are both less than unity, their product must be less than either of their individual values, so that the nominal money stock is inversely related to either of them.[5]

It follows from the explanation of commercial bank behavior just described that the excess reserve ratio will decline when the cost of acquiring reserves decreases relative to the return on bank loans and investments. If all other determinants remain constant, this means that the nominal money stock will increase. But what factors determine the relative cost of acquiring reserves? Two important determinants are the market rate of interest and the Federal Reserve discount rate. If the market rate of interest *rises* and the discount rate remains constant, then the relative cost of obtaining reserves from the Federal Reserve *decreases*. If the discount rate *falls* and the market rate of interest remains constant, then the relative cost of obtaining reserves from the Federal Reserve *decreases*. Thus the excess reserve ratio varies inversely with the market rate of interest and directly with the discount rate.

Another way to interpret this theory is to regard the market rate of interest as the opportunity cost of holding excess reserves and the discount rate as the penalty that must be paid to the Federal Reserve when a commercial bank extends too many loans and its reserves fall below the minimum legal requirement. When the difference between the market rate of interest and the discount rate increases, banks are motivated to lend their excess reserves and to assume a more risky position with respect to their required reserves.

The effect of changes in the market rate of interest i and in the discount rate i_d on the excess reserve ratio can be represented symbolically by

$$XR_r = XR_r(i, i_d) \tag{8-26}$$

where

$$\frac{\Delta XR_r}{\Delta i} < 0 \quad \text{and} \quad \frac{\Delta XR_r}{\Delta i_d} > 0$$

Equation (8-26) merely states that the excess reserve ratio is a function of the market rate of interest and the Federal Reserve discount rate. As the market interest rate rises (falls), the excess reserve ratio falls (rises); as the discount rate rises (falls), the excess reserve ratio also rises (falls).

From equation (8-25) we know that the nominal money supply varies inversely with the excess reserve ratio. Therefore, as the relative cost of extending loans decreases, the excess reserve ratio falls and the quantity of the nominal money supply increases. Because the desired amount of excess reserves is determined by the market rate of interest and by the Federal Reserve discount rate, the nominal money supply is a function of these variables as well as of high-powered money, the currency ratio, and the required reserve ratio. We can now graphically derive the nominal money supply curve based on these assumptions.

The relationship between the rate of interest and the nominal money supply curve is graphed in Figure 8-1, based on the assumption that the currency ratio is held

[5] The same argument holds for the relationship between C_r and RR_r.

constant. Figure 8-1(a) illustrates the hypothesized behavior of commercial banks with respect to the excess reserve ratio when the rate of interest rises and the discount rate remains constant. As the interest rate increases, the XR_r becomes smaller and finally reaches zero at i_3. As the market rate of interest falls, the XR_r increases and reaches a maximum of $1 - RR_r$ when $i = 0$.

The graph in Figure 8-1(b) is simply the curve of the relationship between the XR_r and the value of the money multiplier $1/(C_r + XR_r + RR_r - C_rXR_r - C_rRR_r)$, which is the reciprocal of the denominator of equation (8-25), holding C_r and RR_r constant. As we have previously demonstrated, the money multiplier is inversely related to the excess reserve ratio. The money multiplier reaches a maximum when $XR_r = 0$ and a minimum when $XR_r = 1 - RR_r$. Substituting the maximum value of XR_r into equation (8-25), we obtain

$$M_s = \frac{H}{C_r + 1 - RR_r + RR_r - C_r + C_rRR_r - C_rRR_r} = \frac{H}{1.0} \qquad (8\text{-}27)$$

Thus the money multiplier is equal to unity when the rate of interest is zero. Figure 8-1(c) graphs the relationship between the money multiplier and the quantity of

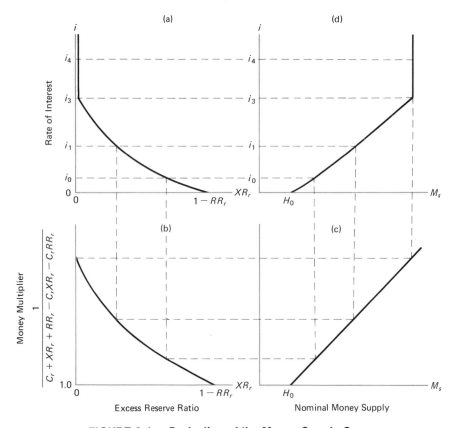

FIGURE 8-1   *Derivation of the Money Supply Curve*

money supplied for a given quantity of high-powered money. Because the money multiplier is equal to unity when $i = 0$, the curve in Figure 8-1(c) intersects the horizontal axis at a value of the money supply that is equal to the quantity of high-powered money. By selecting interest rates of i_0, i_1, i_3, and i_4 in Figure 8-1(a), we can, with the assistance of Figures 8-1(b) and 8-1(c), derive the money supply curve in Figure 8-1(d). The nominal money supply curve M_s becomes perfectly interest inelastic at i_3, because XR_r becomes zero at that rate of interest.

Using the money supply model illustrated in Figure 8-1, it is easy to demonstrate how other factors can affect the nominal money supply curve. The effect of lowering the discount rate is illustrated in Figure 8-2, where the derivation of the initial money supply curve M_s with an initial discount rate of i_{d_1} is represented by the solid curves. Now suppose that the discount rate falls to i_{d_0}. This means that the relative cost of holding excess reserves at a given interest rate will decline, that commercial banks will reduce their excess reserves, and that the excess reserve ratio will decrease. This behavior is indicated by the dashed excess reserve ratio function in Figure 8-2(a). The effect of the downward shift in the excess reserve ratio function on the money supply curve is shown by the dashed money supply

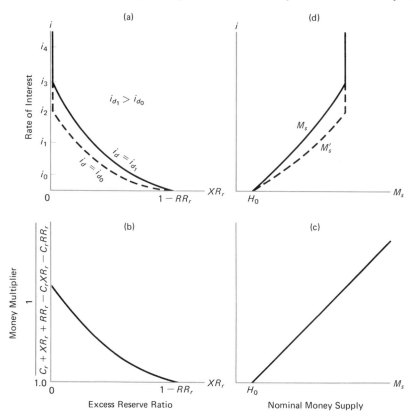

FIGURE 8-2   *The Effect of a Reduction in the Discount Rate on the Money Supply*

curve M'_s in Figure 8-2(d). Below an interest rate of i_3, the money supply curve shifts to the right at the lower discount rate. For interest rates equal to or greater than i_3, the money supply curve M'_s becomes equal to M_s, because the excess reserve ratio is equal to zero at both discount rates.

Thus far we have assumed that the currency ratio is not affected by the rate of interest. We now disregard this assumption and argue that as interest rates rise, individuals and firms try to economize on their cash balances, which causes the currency ratio C_r to fall and the money supply to increase. Symbolically, we can state this hypothesis as

$$\frac{\Delta C_r}{\Delta i} < 0 \tag{8-28}$$

The effect of this relationship between i and C_r on the nominal money supply curve is illustrated in Figure 8-3. As the interest rate rises in Figure 8-3(a), the currency ratio must fall according to (8-28). This is shown graphically in Figure 8-3(b), where a money multiplier curve corresponding to the appropriate C_r for each interest rate is drawn. For increasing interest rates, the currency ratio must fall, shifting the

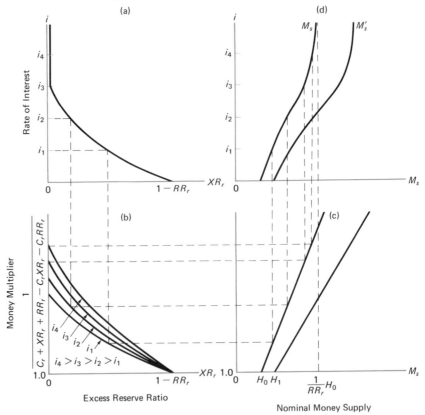

FIGURE 8-3   *The Money Supply When the Currency Ratio Is a Function of the Interest Rate*

money multiplier curves outward to the right, with each successive curve corresponding to a higher interest rate. The lower limit on C_r is obviously zero, and thus in the limit as $i \to \infty$ and $C_r \to 0$, the money multiplier approaches $1/RR_r$. Hence the nominal money supply curve M_s in Figure 8-1(d) does not become perfectly interest inelastic, as it did in the two previous examples, but instead asymptotically approaches $(1/RR_r)H_0$ as $i \to \infty$. We can therefore conclude that if C_r is a function of the interest rate, then the nominal money supply curve will have increased interest elasticity.

Finally, the effect of a central bank open-market purchase is also shown in Figure 8-3. An increase in the quantity of high-powered money from H_0 to H_1 is illustrated by the rightward shift of the curve in Figure 8-3(c). This in turn increases the nominal money supply, as indicated by the new dashed money supply curve M'_s in Figure 8-3(d). A reduction in the quantity of high-powered money would clearly have the opposite effect.

We have not shown that a reduction of the required reserve ratio also increases the money supply by shifting the money supply curve to the right. This is left as an exercise for the student.

An important characteristic of the nominal money supply function that we have just derived is that the money supply is not simply an exogenous variable controlled by the Federal Reserve. It is partially an endogenous variable whose value is jointly determined by the Federal Reserve, commercial banks, and the public. This characteristic of the money supply is of more than passing interest; the extent of its endogeneity is an extremely important factor in determining the influence that money can exert on economic activity. The full implication of this endogeneity will become apparent in our critical discussion of the importance of money in Chapter 14.

8-8   Concluding Remarks

In this chapter we have been concerned with the definition, function, creation, and wealth aspect of money. We defined money as currency *plus* demand deposits and listed money s functions as a medium of exchange, a store of wealth, a unit of account, and a standard of deferred payment. The role of the central bank as the supplier of high-powered money and the controller of the nominal money supply was examined. We learned that the Federal Reserve System, which is the central bank of the United States, controls the nominal money supply by employing three policy instruments: (1) open-market operations, (2) the required reserve ratio, and (3) the discount rate. We also saw how commercial banks, through the institution of fractional reserve banking, create demand deposits that comprise the bulk of the money supply. A simple accounting model was derived that showed that the nominal money supply is affected by three proximate determinants: (1) the nominal supply of high-powered money, (2) the reserve ratio, and (3) the currency ratio. Finally, in this chapter it was demonstrated that the money supply is not perfectly exogenous but partially endogenous, being jointly determined by the central bank, commercial banks, and the public.

9 The Demand for Money

9-1　Introduction

In Chapter 8 we learned how the money supply is determined by the central bank, in conjunction with the commercial banking system and the public. We also derived the supply curve, which is an upward sloping function of the interest rate. If we could demonstrate that conversely, the demand for money is a simple downward sloping function of the interest rate, then we could easily determine both the equilibrium rate of interest and (using the *IS* curve derived in Chapter 7) the equilibrium level of aggregate demand. Unfortunately, the demand for money cannot be graphed as a simple function of the rate of interest, because it is a function of several variables, some of which interact directly with the interest rate. This complexity has caused considerable controversy among economists concerning the exact nature of the demand for money and has generated many approaches to the analysis of this issue. In this chapter we take an essentially historical approach to the evolution of the modern theory of the demand for money.

9-2　The Theory of Money Demand Before Keynes

Prior to the publication of Keynes's *The General Theory*,[1] theories of the demand for money were variations on the quantity theory of money that David Hume

---

[1] J. M. Keynes, *The General Theory of Employment, Interest, and Money* (New York: Harcourt Brace Jovanovich, Inc., 1936). Hereafter referred to as *The General Theory*.

advanced as early as 1752 to explain the balance-of-payments adjustment mechanism. Irving Fisher, writing in 1911, presented one of the first modern statements of the quantity theory.[2]

Irving Fisher's Transactions-demand Theory

In his theory of the demand for money, Fisher placed primary emphasis on the use of money as a *medium of exchange.* He based his theory on a simple accounting identity, namely, that whenever a transaction occurs between a buyer and a seller, there is an exchange of money for a good, service, or security. It then follows as a truism that the value of the money must equal the value of the good, service, or security exchanged for the money. In any given time period, the value of all goods, services, or securities sold must equal the number of transactions in the time period T multiplied by the *average price* of the transactions P. Corresponding and identically equal to the value of PT is the value of the money flow, which is equal to the *nominal quantity of money* in circulation M multiplied by the average number of times the quantity of money in circulation turns over per period. Fisher called the average number of times the quantity of money is exchanged the *transactions velocity* of money V. Symbolically, this accounting identity is expressed as

$$MV \equiv PT \tag{9-1}$$

Because (9-1) is an identity, it is always true, and at first glance it may appear to be of little theoretical value. However, an examination of each of its four component variables will reveal that this identity can be transformed into a theoretical relationship that describes the demand for money.

Following Fisher's approach, we assume that the nominal quantity of money in circulation is determined by the central bank and can be treated as an exogenous variable. The number of transactions is considered to be a function of the level of income and if, with Fisher, we assume that income is always at the full-employment level, then the value of T is fixed in the short run. Thus far, Fisher's approach is not inconsistent with identity (9-1) if we assume that P and V can take on any values required to maintain the identity. It is at this juncture that Fisher's theory departs from an accounting identity and becomes an equation, because the value of V, according to Fisher, is a constant and is independent of M, P, and T. Fisher reached this conclusion because he believed that the velocity of transactions is determined by the *institutional* and *technological* factors of the transaction process, which can be assumed to be fixed in the short run.

The impact of institutional and technological factors can be explained readily with the aid of the following examples. Assume that we have an economy that is comprised of only one firm and only one individual. The individual works for the firm to earn income, which is then spent on the firm's products. First, we explore the institutional aspect of Fisher's assumption of constant velocity.

[2] Irving Fisher, *The Purchasing Power of Money* (New York: Macmillan, 1911).

Suppose that the individual is paid only twice a year, once on January 1 and once on July 1. The individual receives $100 in cash each time and spends all this money in a steady stream during each six-month period. To pay the individual on each payday, the firm needs $100 from the money it has acquired prior to each payday by selling its goods to the individual. Figure 9-1 shows the flow of expenditures and receipts over time for the firm and for the individual. The firm pays the individual $100 on January 1; its cash balance therefore decreases to zero, and the individual's cash balance rises to $100. As the individual spends income in a steady stream during the six-month period, the cash balance of the firm rises as the individual exchanges cash for the firm's products. By midnight on June 30, the individual's cash balance is zero and the firm's cash balance is $100, at which time the process repeats itself. During the six-month period, the average cash balance for both the individual and the firm is $50. The sum of these averages is, as it must be, the total cash in the economy, or $100. Now suppose that the individual is paid

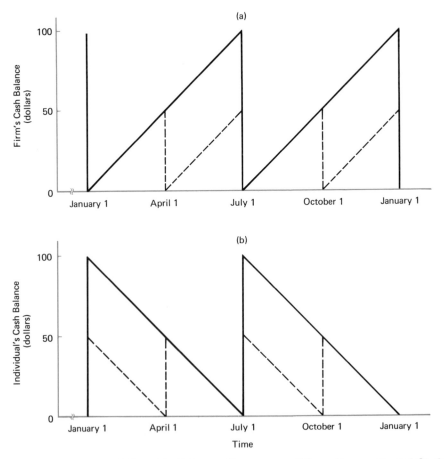

FIGURE 9-1   *The Relationship Between Frequency of Wage Payments and Cash Balances*

four times instead of twice a year (an institutional change). The individual's real income remains constant at $200, so that each income payment is now $200 ÷ 4 = $50, rather than $200 ÷ 2 = $100. The firm now needs a cash balance of only $50, shown by the dashed lines in Figure 9-1(a), to meet its payroll. The individual does not have to alter the rate at which income is spent (represented in Figure 9-1(b) by the slope of the expenditure line) and is quite content to be paid twice as often. Prior to the institutional change, the money stock was exchanged twice during the year, so that the transactions velocity of money was two turnovers per year. After the institutional change the money stock is smaller but the total stock is exchanged more often, resulting in a velocity of four turnovers per year. This example demonstrates that institutional changes, such as frequency of income payment, can alter the velocity of circulation of the money stock. Fisher held that such institutional changes occur slowly, so that V can be assumed to be constant in a short-run analysis.

As an example of a technological change, let us now consider a situation in which all the initial assumptions of the preceding example are retained, but let us make the additional assumptions that the individual spends each income payment in various places throughout the country and that it takes an average of 18 days for $1 to be returned to the firm after being spent. This produces a lag in the receipts of the firm, as shown in Figure 9-2(a). Thus on July 1 the firm finds that only $90 of the $100 it paid on January 1 has been returned. Because it must pay the individual $100 on this date, the required cash balance is $110 and the transactions velocity of circulation is $200 ÷ $110 = 1.82. Now suppose that due to a technological change, money can be returned to the firm in only 9 days, as indicated by the dashed lines in Figure 9-2(a). The required cash balance now decreases to $105, and the transactions velocity of circulation increases to $200 ÷ $105 = 1.90. (Examples of such a technological change are air mail, telegraphic transfers, computerized check clearing, and credit cards.) Here, as in the case of the institutional change in the preceding example, Fisher assumed that in the short run the technology of the transaction process is constant and therefore that the velocity of transactions can be considered fixed.

Given our earlier assumptions regarding M, V, and T, we can transform identity (9-1) into a theory of the determination of the price level, where

$$P = \frac{MV}{T} \tag{9-2}$$

Equation (9-2) states that the general price level is determined exclusively by the nominal quantity of money and in fact is proportional to it. In other words, if the nominal quantity of money doubles, then the price level will double but V and T will remain constant.

We know that the nominal quantity of money supplied must be equal to the nominal quantity demanded to maintain money-market equilibrium, a requirement symbolized by

$$M_s = M_d = M \tag{9-3}$$

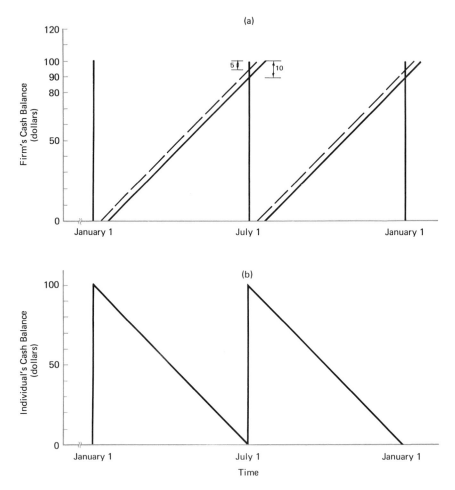

FIGURE 9-2   *The Effect of Check Clearing in Transactions Demand for Cash Balances*

Hence equation (9-2) can be solved for the real quantity of money demanded, or

$$m_d = \frac{M_d}{P} = \frac{1}{V} T \qquad (9\text{-}4)$$

Equation (9-4) states that the real quantity of money demanded is *inversely* proportional to the *velocity* of transactions and *directly* proportional to the *number* of transactions. Because V and T are assumed to be fixed in the short run, m_d is a constant. If a disequilibrium occurs in the money market due to an increase in the nominal money supply, then initially $m_s > m_d$ and the price level will rise while the real quantity of money decreases until $m_s = m_d$. Conversely, if $m_s < m_d$, then the real quantity of money will increase and the price level will fall until equilibrium is restored in the money market. The important factor to note here is that as long as V and T remain constant, the real quantity of money demanded will also be constant and the price level will fluctuate to maintain equilibrium when nominal increases or decreases in the money supply occur.

As the economy grows, the volume of transactions T will increase and the quantity of real money demanded will grow in direct proportion to the increase in transactions. This growth in the quantity of real money can occur with a fixed nominal quantity of money and a falling price level, or with an increasing nominal quantity of money and a constant price level, or with some combination of the two. Given a technological innovation such as the introduction of credit cards, the velocity of transactions will increase and the quantity of real money demanded will decrease. As with changes in T, equilibrium will be restored through changes in the nominal quantity of money, or in the price level, or in some combination of the two.

Although conceptually elegant, Fisher's transactions-demand theory presented two serious problems when used in empirical research. The first problem was that Fisher's transactions included those arising from current production as well as those that occur when capital assets are transferred. The known volatility of the capital market makes it rather difficult to assume that T will remain constant even at a full-employment level. The second problem centers around the difficulty of defining a general price level that encompasses goods and services as well as assets. These two problems were never completely overcome by Fisher or his followers.

The advent of national income accounting changed the direction of economic thought about the quantity theory and circumvented the need to solve these problems. Instead of concentrating on gross transactions, economists began to stress income transactions. Real national income Y replaced T, and the average price of transactions became the implicit national income price index P. Fisher's equation for the quantity of money was redefined as

$$MV = PY \qquad (9\text{-}5)$$

The nominal quantity of money is defined as before, but V is now the number of times per year that the money stock is used to purchase the annual production of goods and services. In other words, V is now the *income velocity of circulation* (computed using only income transactions), rather than the velocity of gross transactions, and the difference between the volume of these transactions and total gross transactions is ignored. Because the quantity of nominal money supplied must be equal to the quantity demanded to maintain money-market equilibrium, the nominal demand for money can be written

$$M_d = \frac{1}{V}PY \qquad (9\text{-}6)$$

Dividing both sides of equation (9-6) by P, we obtain

$$m_d = \frac{1}{V}Y \qquad (9\text{-}7)$$

which is the Fisherian equation for the income demand for real money.

While this income formulation greatly reduces the empirical problems just discussed, it does raise certain theoretical problems. Recalling that Fisher based his theory of the demand for money on the technology of the execution of transactions, we see that the income formulation of the quantity theory presents a new problem: it does not include all transactions. For example, the exchange of an asset such as land or stock is excluded from Y because, as we explained in Chapter 1, the exchange of assets does not produce income. Moreover, if vertical integration occurs in industry, then the volume of transactions will decline but the level of real national income may remain unchanged. (*Vertical integration* is the merging of a firm with one of its suppliers. This occurs, for example, when an automobile manufacturer merges with a steel firm.) Equation (9-2) emphasizes the role of money in the transaction process, whereas equation (9-5) emphasizes the role of money in the production of national income. Thus the income formulation of the quantity of money is theoretically incompatible with the transactions approach to the demand for money. This difference was to be further emphasized in the Cambridge cash-balances approach.

The Cambridge Cash-balances Demand Theory

The Cambridge cash-balances approach differs from Fisher's transactions approach in that the former places primary emphasis on money as a *store of wealth* rather than as a medium of exchange.[3] You should recall from Chapter 8 that the exchange function of money eliminates the need to barter and the accompanying inefficient requirement of double coincidence of wants. In its function as a store of wealth, money serves as a *temporary abode of generalized purchasing power* for individuals over the time interval between the sale of a good or service and the subsequent purchase of a good or service. The Cambridge cash-balances approach places primary emphasis on this function of money.

The Cambridge approach concentrates its analysis on the factors that determine the individual's demand to hold cash balances. Cambridge economists Alfred Marshall and A. C. Pigou, who developed this theory, acknowledged that such factors as interest rate, wealth owned by the individual, convenience of purchase, and expectations of future interest rates and prices all influence the individual's decision to hold money. But they argued that over short time periods, the movements of such factors are fixed or proportional to changes in the individual's income. Thus the Cambridge economists hypothesized that an individual's demand for nominal money balances is proportional to that individual's nominal income and that the aggregate demand for nominal money balances is specified by

$$M_d = ky \qquad (9\text{-}8)$$

where y = the nominal national income
k = the proportionality factor

[3] A.C. Pigou, "The Value of Money," *The Quarterly Journal of Economics* **XXXII** (November 1917), 38–65.

Because real aggregate income is defined as

$$Y = \frac{y}{p} \tag{9-9}$$

we can rewrite equation (9-8)

$$M_d = kPY \tag{9-10}$$

Dividing both sides of equation (9-10) by P then gives us

$$\frac{M_d}{P} = m_d = kY \tag{9-11}$$

which is the Cambridge equation for the demand for real cash balances. Equation (9-11) is mathematically equivalent to the Fisherian income demand for money given by equation (9-7), since

$$k = \frac{1}{V} \tag{9-12}$$

However, the two equations are *not theoretically equivalent:* the economic line of reasoning behind (9-7) is based on Fisher's transactions approach, whereas (9-11) evolves from the Cambridge cash-balances approach. Figure 9-3 graphically depicts the Cambridge equation, showing that as real national income increases, the real quantity of money demanded increases proportionally.

It should be noted that the Cambridge approach does not exclude the institutional and technological factors of the transactions process emphasized in Fisher's quantity theory. Changes in these factors can be accounted for by changes in the proportionality factor, which is implicitly assumed to be a function of other variables which in turn are assumed to be constant in the short run. For example, if the time period between wage payments to workers decreases, then the demand for money will be reduced, as we have seen, and k will become smaller. The transactions

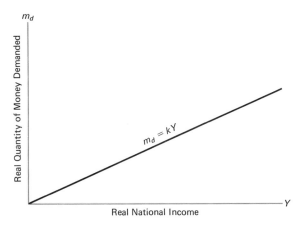

FIGURE 9-3   *The Relation Between Real Income and Real Cash Balances as Specified by the Cambridge Equation*

approach is useful here, because it is easier to consider the impact of institutional or technological changes in terms of velocity and then to ascertain whether the demand for money will increase or decrease, realizing that changes in V affect k inversely.

To the casual observer, the fine distinction drawn between equations (9-7) and (9-11) may seem unimportant, but this distinction allows us to bypass the theoretical reservations concerning the exclusion of many non-income-producing transactions that the Fisherian income approach entailed and to base the demand for money on logically consistent theoretical grounds.

Another reason for stressing the differences between the theoretical developments of equation (9-7) and equation (9-11) is that the Cambridge approach emphasized the economic variables that determine the *asset value of money* (that is, the interest rate and expectations of future prices and interest rates). These variables, in contrast to the institutional and technological variables stressed by Fisher, can fluctuate greatly in a short period of time, thereby changing the demand for money in the short run. This is a conclusion that cannot be derived from Fisher's transactions approach. However, although the Cambridge approach is conceptually richer than the transactions approach, the former is incomplete because it does not formally incorporate the influence of the economic variables just mentioned on the demand for cash balances. As we shall see in Section 9-3, John Maynard Keynes first attempted to eliminate this shortcoming.

9-3   Keynes's Theory of the Demand for Money

John Maynard Keynes studied under Alfred Marshall at Cambridge, so it is not surprising that Keynes's theory of the demand for money is based on the Cambridge cash-balances approach and emphasizes the asset role of money. Prior to the publication of *The General Theory*, Keynes's approach to the demand for money was entirely within the Cambridge tradition. In *The General Theory*, however, he extended the Cambridge approach to include variables that had previously been mentioned only in passing. Keynes formulated his theory of the demand for money in terms of three motives that individuals and firms have for holding cash balances: the *transactions demand*, the *precautionary demand*, and the *speculative demand*.

The Transactions Demand for Money

Keynes's transactions demand for money by individuals and firms is basically the same as the motive for holding money that the Cambridge approach emphasized. It results from the existence of an asset—money—that is unique in being the only generally accepted medium of exchange. Individuals and firms hold money because it is convenient and expedites the planned purchase of goods and services. Keynes argued that the demand to hold money for making transactions is determined by the level of income and by institutional factors. In this respect, Keynes is completely within the Cambridge tradition, and his transactions motive is indistinguishable from the Cambridge cash-balances equation (9-11).[4]

The Precautionary Demand for Money

In his theory of transactions demand, Keynes placed primary emphasis on the planned purchases of goods and services. The precautionary demand, he argued, was the result of providing for *contingencies* and *unforeseen opportunities* to make advantageous purchases, or in other words, *unplanned expenditures.* To understand the concept of a precautionary demand to meet a contingency, consider the amount of money that an individual would require to take a vacation by automobile. Clearly, the amount of cash balances would have to be sufficient to meet all planned or anticipated expenditures, such as food, lodging, gasoline, oil, and so on. A wise traveler would also prepare for the possibility of unanticipated expenditures, such as the replacement of a fan belt or physician's fees in the event of illness. Meeting these unforeseen contingencies would demand additional cash balances.

The remainder of our traveler's precautionary demand would be for the purpose of taking advantage of unforeseen bargains that may be encountered on the trip. A collector of antique clocks, for example, would no doubt prepare for the unlikely but possible event of stumbling across a Willard banjo clock at a bargain price and would carry additional cash balances for this unplanned purchase. According to Keynes, preparations for planned and unplanned expenditures determine the traveler's precautionary demand for money.

Using the same basic argument for the precautionary demand that he used for the transactions demand, Keynes hypothesized that the precautionary demand is determined by an individual's income and institutional factors that could be considered fixed in the shortrun. To understand how an institutional change could affect both the transactions demand and the precautionary demand of our imaginary traveler, consider the introduction of credit cards. By carrying one or more credit cards, our traveler could greatly diminish the cash balances required for both planned and unplanned expenditures; thus the value of k would decrease, or equivalently, the income velocity of transactions would increase.

Assuming that all individuals and firms behave in a similar manner, Keynes argued that the aggregate transactions demand, including precautionary demand, is given by

$$m_t = kY \qquad (9\text{-}13)$$

where m_t = the combined transactions and precautionary demand for real cash balances and k and Y are defined as before. A graph of equation (9-13) would be identical to Figure 9-3, except that the quantity of money demanded for transactions and precautionary balances instead of the total quantity of money demanded would appear on the vertical axis.

---

[4] Keynes mentioned in *The General Theory* (p. 126) that the interest rate probably influenced the transactions demand, but he paid little attention to this possibility thereafter. It was largely ignored until 1953, as we will learn in Section 9-4.

The Speculative Demand for Money

In our discussion of the differences between the Cambridge cash-balances approach and Fisher's transactions approach, we pointed out that the Cambridge economists were aware of the possibility that expectations of future prices and interest rates could affect the demand for money. However, they did not pursue this point, and it remained for Keynes to make a major contribution to monetary theory by extending their analysis of the demand for money using this line of reasoning.

In his analysis, Keynes limited his attention to one variable, the interest rate, and to the effect that expectations concerning the future value of this variable would have on the demand for money. For simplicity, Keynes assumed that individuals could hold their wealth in only two ways: in cash balances in excess of those needed to meet transactions demand or in bonds. He further assumed that all bonds are *consols* and therefore that their present value P_v, originally derived in Chapter 5 and given by equation (5-18), is

$$P_v = \frac{R}{i} \tag{9-14}$$

where R = the annual fixed revenue from the consol
$\quad\ i$ = the interest rate
$\quad P_v$ = the purchase price of consols

We also learned in Chapter 5 that the amount an individual is willing to pay for a bond, its *present value*, is inversely related to the interest rate because the annual revenue R is fixed for the life of the bond. In the case of a consol, whose life is infinite, R is paid in perpetuity, so that its selling price P_v can be easily calculated using equation (9-14). For example, if a consol pays $10 per year and the market rate of interest is 5%, then a person will pay up to, but no more than, $200 for the consol. If the interest rate rises to 10%, then the selling price of the consol will decrease to $100. Conversely, if the interest rate falls to 2.5%, then the selling price will increase to $400. Thus changes in the interest rate affect the value of consols, and their owners experience capital gains or losses. If an individual buys the consol just described when the interest rate is 5% and then sells it when the interest rate has fallen to 2.5%, then the owner will earn a capital gain of $400 − $200 = $200. On the other hand, if the same consol is sold when the interest rate has risen to 10%, then the owner will incur a capital loss of $100. A rational investor attempts to avoid capital losses and holds cash as a precaution against such losses, but this action precludes earning interest income and the possibility of acquiring capital gains. Keynes based his speculative demand for money on this difference between the effects of interest rate changes on bonds and on money.

We have just reviewed how changes in the interest rate produce capital gains and losses and why holders of wealth seek to avoid capital losses. We now return to the individual who is faced with the choice of storing wealth in money or in consols. Assuming that the interest rate never changes, consols are preferable to money, because they yield a positive rate of return; thus in this case all wealth will be held in consols. If we relax our assumption of a fixed interest rate, consols are still preferable to money if the value of the future interest rate is expected to fall, because they will enable our wealth holder to reap a capital gain in addition to interest income. Conversely, if the interest rate is expected to rise, our wealth holder will incur a capital loss, but consols will still be preferable to money *as long as the capital loss does not exceed the income from the consol.* When the capital loss is exactly equal to the income from the consol, the individual wealth holder will be indifferent to holding bonds or cash. When the capital loss is expected to exceed the annual return, the wealth holder will sell all bonds and store wealth only in the form of money.

Until this point Keynes's theory of the speculative demand for money seems reasonable enough, but how does the individual wealth holder determine the future rate of interest? Keynes solved this problem by positing that every individual at each moment in time has some definite opinion of the *normal* or long-run interest rate and that the individual compares the current rate to this normal rate to determine whether interest rates will rise or fall in the future. If the normal interest rate is lower than the current rate, then the future interest rate is expected to be lower than the current rate. Conversely, if the normal interest rate exceeds the current rate, then the future interest rate is expected to be higher than the present rate. Thus the current interest rate and an estimate of the normal rate enable the individual to make judgments about the potential capital gain or loss that can be incurred by holding consols. These expectations of capital gain or loss in turn determine the individual wealth holder's decision to store assets in *either* money or bonds.

This verbal argument can be easily stated mathematically. Suppose that we have a consol whose current present value P_{v_0} is exactly \$1. By equation (9-14), the annual return on this consol is

$$R = i_0 P_{v_0} = i_0(1) = i_0 \tag{9-15}$$

where i_0 = the current interest rate. The capital gain or loss Γ is the difference between the current present value of the consol and the present value of the consol one year later; or

$$\Gamma = P_{v_1} - P_{v_0}$$

$$= \left(\frac{i_0(P_{v_0})}{i_n} - P_{v_0} \right) \tag{9-16}$$

since

$$P_{v_1} = \frac{R}{i_n} = \frac{i_0 P_{v_0}}{i_n} \tag{9-17}$$

where i_n = the normal interest rate. Now by dividing both sides of equation (9-16) by P_{v_0}, we obtain the capital gain or loss expressed on an annual percentage basis as

$$\gamma = \frac{\Gamma}{P_{v_0}} = \left(\frac{i_0}{i_n} - 1 \right) \tag{9-18}$$

Our decision to hold wealth either all in cash or all in consols depends on the sum of i_0 and γ. Adding i_0 to both sides of equation (9-18) gives us

$$i_0 + \gamma = i_0 + \left(\frac{i_0}{i_n} - 1 \right) \tag{9-19}$$

If the result of equation (9-19) is greater than zero, we will hold all wealth in consols; if it is less than zero, we will hold all wealth in cash. The value of i_0 when the result of equation (9-19) is exactly equal to zero is the *critical rate of interest* i_c; at this point we are indifferent to holding either all cash or all bonds. Setting the left-hand side of equation (9-19) equal to zero and letting $i_0 = i_c$, we obtain

$$i_c + \frac{i_c}{i_n} - 1 = 0$$

which can be transformed into

$$i_c \left(\frac{i_n + 1}{i_n} \right) = 1$$

and in turn reduces to

$$i_c = \frac{i_n}{i_n + 1} \tag{9-20}$$

As long as the current rate of interest lies above the critical rate i_c, a wealth holder's portfolio will consist of only consols. Should i fall below i_c, the wealth holder's portfolio will be composed entirely of cash. When i is equal to i_c, the wealth holder is indifferent to holding either cash or consols.

The discontinuous portfolio decision that we have just described mathematically is illustrated graphically in Figure 9-4. When the interest rate is above the critical rate, all wealth is held in the form of bonds. If the interest rate falls below i_c, then the individual sells all consols and holds all wealth W in speculative cash balances.

When we change our focus from individual to aggregate speculative demand for money, the discontinuous nature of the individual's demand disappears and we obtain what can be considered for all practical purposes a continuous downward sloping function that describes the relationship between the current rate of interest and the speculative demand for money. This transformation occurs because every individual in the economy estimates the normal interest rate slightly differently, and any given individual's stock of wealth is insignificant relative to the economy's total stock of wealth.

In functional notation, Keynes's aggregate speculative demand for real cash balances m_{sp} can be expressed as

$$m_{sp} = h(i) \tag{9-21}$$

The aggregate speculative demand for money curve is graphed in Figure 9-5.

Extending this line of reasoning even further, Keynes made another extremely

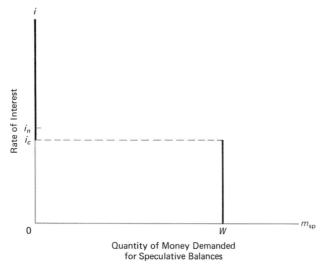

FIGURE 9-4   *The Speculative Demand for Money by an Individual Wealth Holder*

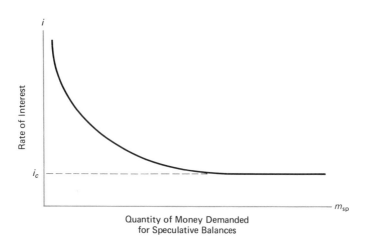

FIGURE 9-5   *The Aggregate Speculative Demand for Money*

important contribution to the theory of the demand for money. He argued that as the interest rate falls toward zero, more and more individuals will estimate that the current rate of interest is below the critical rate, so that the speculative demand for money will become greater at an increasing rate. Keynes believed that eventually the interest rate could become so low that every individual wealth holder would believe it was below the critical rate and would want to hold wealth in the form of cash. In other words, Keynes felt that the interest elasticity of the demand for money defined by

$$\eta_i = \frac{\% \text{ change in } m_{sp}}{\% \text{ change in } i} = \frac{\Delta m_{sp}/m_{sp}}{\Delta i/i} \tag{9-22}$$

becomes infinite at some low rate of interest. This is shown in Figure 9-5, where at an aggregate critical rate of interest i_c, the slope of the speculative demand curve becomes zero.[5] This condition has come to be known in macroeconomics literature as the *liquidity trap*, because if the central bank were to expand the money supply, then all additional real cash balances would be held as speculative hoards while individual wealth holders waited for the interest rate to return to its normal level. This means that all new money is trapped in *idle* hoards instead of finding its way into *active* transaction balances. In Chapter 11 we will learn that the liquidity trap can critically affect the full-employment stability of a perfectly competitive economy.

According to Keynes, then, the total aggregate demand for real money m_d is the sum of transactions demand and speculative demand, or

$$m_d = m_t + m_{sp} = kY + h(i) \tag{9-23}$$

A graphic derivation of equation (9-23) appears in Figure 9-6. The transactions demand for money is shown in Figure 9-6(a) for four levels of real national income, where $Y_1 < Y_2 < Y_3 < Y_4$. This transactions demand is graphed as a function of the interest rate, and the fact that each curve is a vertical line means that the interest rate does not affect transactions demand. Figure 9-6(b) is a graph of the speculative demand for money, where a liquidity trap is shown to exist at the critical rate of interest i_c. By summing horizontally for each income level, total aggregate demand for money curves (one for each level of real national income) are derived in Figure 9-6(c). When the interest rate reaches the liquidity-trap level, these separate curves all merge into one single curve; as we will learn in Chapter 11, this represents the

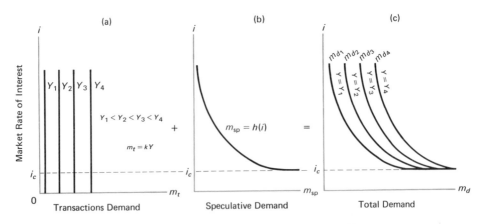

FIGURE 9-6   *Derivation of the Demand for Money*

[5] If you do not understand why $\eta_i = \infty$ when the slope of the speculative demand curve is zero, consult Appendix B.

floor below which the rate of interest cannot fall.

Defining the income velocity of money as

$$V = \frac{Y}{m_d} \tag{9-24}$$

Keynes then rejected the idea that V can be treated as a constant in the short run. The existence of speculative balances that are sensitive to interest rate changes means that m_d is not fixed in the short run, so that V can fluctuate for a given Y.

9-4   The Demand for Money After Keynes

Keynes's theory of the speculative demand for money was a radical departure from the orthodox theory of the day and was not without its challengers. Two significant criticisms were raised. The first argued that the speculative demand for money derived by Keynes depended on the difference between the current interest rate i_0 and the normal interest rate i_n, and that the difference $(i_0 - i_n)$ would disappear if i_0 were to remain constant long enough. In other words, Keynes's critics believed that any rate of interest, no matter how small, will become the normal interest rate if it prevails long enough, resulting in the disappearance of expectations of capital loss and therefore of the speculative demand for money. The second criticism argued that empirical evidence has revealed that individuals do not keep all their financial assets in either bonds or money but in some combination of the two. In a brilliant article, James Tobin demonstrated that these two criticisms can be overcome by a more sophisticated analysis than the one Keynes used.[6]

Tobin's Theory of Liquidity Preference[7]

In Keynes's analysis of the speculative demand for money, the individual makes discrete decisions concerning the management of the financial asset portfolio; that is, the wealth holder is motivated to hold either bonds or money. In his analysis, Tobin demonstrated that rational behavior dictates a portfolio comprised of both bonds and money.

Assume that at the beginning of some time period an individual has a portfolio of a given size W_0. If we also make the intuitively appealing assumption that this individual prefers more wealth to less, then the wealth holder is faced with the problem of deciding what fraction of the portfolio to place in consols (the only type of bond we assume is available) and what fraction to hold in money. In Keynes's analysis the individual holds either all money or all consols based on the estimated value of the future interest rate—what Keynes called the *normal rate*. But following Tobin, suppose that we make the more realistic assumptions that a wealth holder is uncertain about the future interest rate and that the average individual will be just

[6] James Tobin, "Liquidity Preference as Behavior Toward Risk," *Review of Economic Studies* 25 (February 1958), 65–86.

[7] The exposition used here is a simplified variation of Tobin's original analysis developed by D.E.W. Laidler in *The Demand for Money: Theories and Evidence* (Scranton, Pa.: International Textbook Co., 1969), pp. 67–76.

as likely to underestimate as to overestimate this rate, so that after many years the average capital gain is zero. Although the expected capital gain or loss is zero, either a capital loss or a capital gain will occur in any given period. The extent to which a loss or a gain does occur is determined by the amount of uncertainty associated with the future interest rate. Tobin showed that for a given uncertainty concerning the future interest rate, the wealth holder assumes a greater risk as a greater proportion of the portfolio is placed in consols.

A wealth holder operating under the conditions just outlined who places the entire portfolio in consols will maximize the expected growth of wealth and simultaneously assume the maximum risk of a possible capital loss or gain.

On the other hand, if all of the wealth is held in money, then the individual's portfolio will exhibit zero risk but also zero growth. Now if we assume that the wealth holder is a risk averter—preferring less risk to more risk at a given rate of return—then the decision as to what fraction of the portfolio to place in consols hinges on the individual's attitude toward the tradeoff between certainty with no growth and risk with growth.

The individual wealth holder's attitude toward risk and portfolio growth is illustrated in Figure 9-7 using indifference curves, where I_2 is preferred to I_1 and I_1 is preferred to I_0. The vertical axis in Figure 9-7 measures the expected value of the portfolio at the end of the time period in question; the horizontal axis measures the amount of portfolio risk. As we just pointed out, increasing portfolio risk means that an increasing fraction of the portfolio is being held in consols and a decreasing fraction is being held in money. The slope of the indifference curves is positive due to our assumptions that increased risk is not desirable for a given level of wealth at the end of the period and that greater growth of wealth is preferred for a given level of portfolio risk. The curves are concave from above due to the plausible

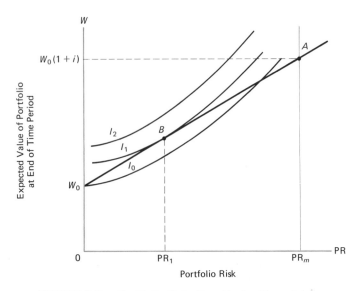

FIGURE 9-7   Portfolio Selection Under Uncertainty

assumption that as wealth increases, the marginal utility of wealth declines, and the individual is less willing to bear greater risk to increase the stock of wealth.

If an individual took a position of zero risk and held all of the initial stock of wealth W_0 in money, then at the end of a given time period the stock of wealth would remain at point W_0 in Figure 9-7. The individual's welfare also remains constant on indifference curve I_0. If all the wealth is placed in consols, then the expected wealth at the end of the time period will be $W_0(1 + i)$, where i is the rate of return on consols. Note, however, that the expected wealth is not what the individual has acquired at the end of this time period, but rather what the average wealth is at the end of many similar time periods. At the end of any given time period, the stock of wealth is just as likely to be above $W_0(1 + i)$ as it is to be below this value. The attitude of our wealth holder, who is a risk averter, toward capital gain or loss is not symmetrical. This individual considers the marginal utility of a dollar's worth of capital gain to be worth less than the absolute value of the marginal disutility of a dollar's worth of capital loss.

For a given amount of uncertainty about the future interest rate, the maximum amount of portfolio risk occurs when all of W_0 is in the form of consols. This maximum amount of risk is designated PR_m in Figure 9-7. The expected value of the portfolio at the end of the time period and the portfolio risk are necessarily simultaneously maximized, as indicated by point A in Figure 9-7. For a given interest rate, the expected gain in wealth from all possible portfolio combinations between holding only money (point W_0) and holding only consols (point A) is represented by the straight line drawn between points W_0 and A in Figure 9-7. This graph is linear because the expected gain in wealth is proportional to the number of consols held; due to our assumption that portfolio risk is proportional to the number of consols held, the expected gain in wealth will be proportional to portfolio risk. Borrowing from the theory of consumer choice, we call this line the *budget constraint line*.

We have now reduced the determination of portfolio composition to the familiar microeconomic problem of constrained welfare maximization. The wealth holder wants to obtain the highest level of indifference subject to the constraint of remaining on the budget line $W_0 A$. This is achieved at point B in Figure 9-7, where indifference curve I_1 is just tangent to the line $W_0 A$, indicating that the portfolio of the wealth holder is diversified between money and consols.

Tobin's liquidity preference function (Keynes's speculative demand function) for an individual wealth holder can now be derived by analyzing the effect on the portfolio of varying the interest rate. In Figure 9-8, we assume the same original endowment of wealth W_0, and the same uncertainty about the future interest rate as before. This gives us the same maximum portfolio risk PR_m. Inspection of the budget constraint line in Figure 9-7 reveals that the vertical intercept of any such constraint line is W_0 and that its slope is given by

$$\frac{W_0(1 + i) - W_0}{PR_m} = \frac{iW_0}{PR_m} \tag{9-25}$$

Since W_0 and PR_m are constants, the slope of any budget constraint will increase as the rate of interest expected to be paid on consols increases.

Three budget constraint lines are drawn in Figure 9-8 for three rates of interest

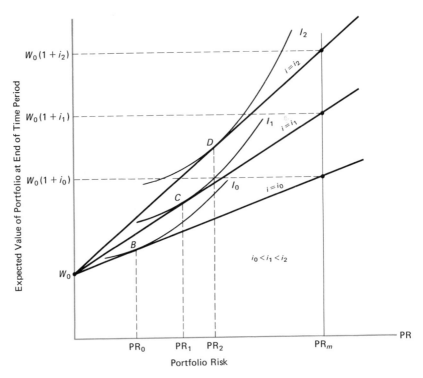

FIGURE 9-8   *The Effect of Changes in the Interest Rate on Portfolio Selection*

i_0, i_1, and i_2, where $i_0 < i_1 < i_2$. Recall that increasing portfolio risk implies that a greater fraction of W_0 is being held in the form of consols. Thus as we increase the interest rate from i_0 to i_1 to i_2, the individual wealth holder maximizing utility under these various alternatives moves from tangency point B to C to D as welfare increases. In this case, the increase in welfare evidenced by movements to higher indifference curves is accompanied by an increase in portfolio risk. Thus as the interest rate rises, our wealth holder's demand for money decreases. The liquidity preference curve for this individual is the continuous downward sloping curve shown in Figure 9-9. The horizontal axis measures the demand for money as an asset, and the symbol that we used for the speculative demand for money m_{sp} is retained here to indicate the relationship between the approaches of Keynes and of Tobin.

Unfortunately, all of this is not as cleanly and neatly executed as Figure 9-8 and 9-9 seem to indicate. Figure 9-10 is essentially the same as Figure 9-8, except that the points of tangency indicate decreasing rather than increasing portfolio risk as the interest rate rises. This implies that the portfolio's percentage of cash increases as the interest rate rises, or in other words that the liquidity preference curve is sloping upward, as shown in Figure 9-11. Only empirical research can determine which of these conditions is better, because both are consistent with the theory.

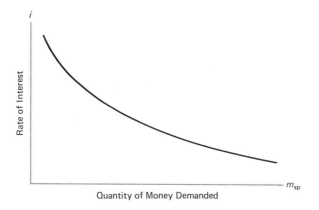

FIGURE 9-9   *The Individual Wealth Holder's Liquidity Preference Curve Derived from Figure 9-8*

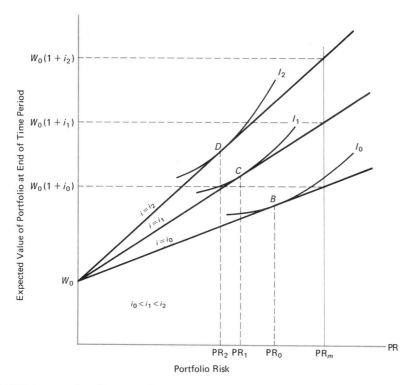

FIGURE 9-10   *The Effect of Changes in the Interest Rate on Portfolio Selection*

Many studies have been conducted to measure the interest elasticity of the demand for money, and all of them have concluded that the aggregate liquidity preference curve is negatively sloped. Thus we can presume that most individuals in the

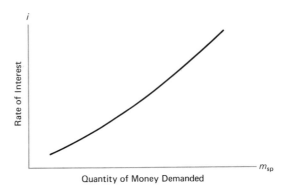

Quantity of Money Demanded

FIGURE 9-11   *The Individual Wealth Holder's Liquidity Preference Curve Derived from Figure 9-10*

economy exhibit liquidity preference curves similar to the one shown in Figure 9-9.[8]

Thus Tobin's approach yields conclusions that answer the criticisms of Keynes's theory mentioned earlier. Individual wealth holders behave rationally, exhibiting a continuous liquidity preference function. Moreover, their simultaneous holding of bonds and cash is not based on the belief that the interest rate will move in only one direction, but rather on the simple assumption that individuals do not know with certainty which way the interest rate will move.

Tobin's theory that liquidity preference is determined by behavior toward risk need not be limited to the simple case we discuss here; it can be extended to the problem of asset choice when there are more than two alternatives.

Baumol's Inventory Approach to Transactions Demand

William J. Baumol approached the theory of transactions demand for money from the view point of *business inventory control*.[9] An inventory of money is demanded because it facilitates exchange, but by holding this inventory the firm or the individual incurs costs in the form of interest income forgone. The problem here is inventory management; its solution entails determining the optimal inventory of money that should be held to minimize cost.

It is assumed that the individual or the firm knows exactly what transactions are to be made in the future. Thus we exclude the demand for speculative and precautionary balances and concentrate on the transactions demand. In addition, it is assumed that payments are made in a steady stream and that in the period of time under consideration (one year) y nominal dollars' worth of income transactions will be made. To simplify the argument without altering its final conclusions, it is also assumed that the individual (or firm) obtains money to meet the transactions

---

[8] Some of these studies are summarized later in the book, in Table 15-1.

[9] W.J. Baumol, "The Transactions Demand for Cash: An Inventory Theoretic Approach," *Quarterly Journal of Economics* **66** (November 1952), 545–56. Working independently, James Tobin also constructed a theory of the transactions demand for money that yielded conclusions similar to those of Baumol; see Tobin, "The Interest Elasticity of Transactions Demand for Cash," *Review of Economics and Statistics* **38** (August 1956), 241–47.

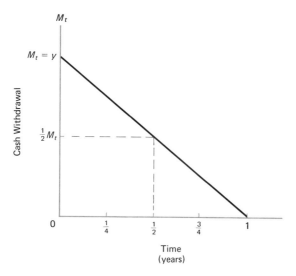

FIGURE 9-12   *Stream of Transactions Payments When One Cash Withdrawal Is Made per Year*

by selling bonds. When a dollar's worth of bonds is converted into cash, an opportunity cost of i dollars per dollar per year is incurred. If at the beginning of the year the individual converts bonds to an amount of cash M_t that will cover all the transactions made during the year, then the interest opportunity cost O_c will be

$$O_c = yi/2 = M_t i/2 \qquad (9\text{-}26)$$

where i = annual interest rate.

The opportunity cost is $M_t i/2$ rather than $M_t i$ because it is assumed that transactions are made in a steady stream, as shown in Figure 9-12. At the beginning of the year the individual has $M_t = y$ dollars; at the end of the year, zero dollars. Therefore, the wealth holder possesses an average of $M_t/2$ dollars at any given time.

If withdrawals are made twice a year, the amount of cash withdrawn will be

$$M_t = \frac{y}{2} \qquad (9\text{-}27)$$

and the average quantity of dollars held will be $M_t/2 = (y/2)/2$. The opportunity cost over six months will be $(y/2)(i/2)/2$, and hence the annual opportunity cost will be

$$O_c = \frac{1}{2}\left(\frac{y}{2}\right)\left(\frac{i}{2}\right) + \frac{1}{2}\left(\frac{y}{2}\right)\left(\frac{i}{2}\right) = \left(\frac{y}{2}\right)\left(\frac{i}{2}\right) \qquad (9\text{-}28)$$

where $i/2$ = the semiannual interest rate. In this case $y = 2M_t$, so that equation (9-28) can be rewritten

$$O_c = \frac{M_t i}{2} \qquad (9\text{-}29)$$

which is the same result given in equation (9-26). By induction we can see that for any number of withdrawals per year y/M_t, the interest opportunity cost can be calculated using equation (9-29).

Interest opportunity cost is not the only cost incurred by the individual. There is also a fixed cost of b dollars per withdrawal. This cost includes all noninterest costs and can include anything from the broker's fee for converting bonds to cash to the required walk around the corner to the bank to make a withdrawal. As long as disutility is attached to the process of conversion to cash, there will be an associated cost. Because y/M_t withdrawals are made each year, the annual noninterest cost is by/M_t.

The sum of interest opportunity cost and noninterest cost is

$$\sigma = \frac{by}{M_t} + \frac{iM_t}{2} \tag{9-30}$$

The problem is to determine the amount M_t such that σ is minimized. Baumol showed that this occurs when[10]

$$M_t = \sqrt{\frac{2by}{i}} \tag{9-31}$$

Dividing both sides of equation (9-31) by the price level, we obtain the transactions demand for real money

$$m_t = \sqrt{\frac{2(b/P)(y/P)}{i}} = \sqrt{\frac{2BY}{i}} \tag{9-32}$$

where B = the real noninterest cost
$\quad\quad\; Y$ = real income

Equation (9-32) states that the loss-minimizing individual or firm demands real money balances for transaction purposes that are directly proportional to the square root of real income and inversely proportional to the square root of the interest rate. This is often referred to as the *square root rule*. Aggregating equation (9-32) over all individuals and firms gives us the aggregate transactions demand for money. Because this will be identical to equation (9-32), we simply refer to equation (9-32) as the aggregate demand as well. In functional notation equation (9-32) can be expressed as

$$m_t = g(i, Y) \tag{9-33}$$

Baumol's contribution yields two important theoretical conclusions. First, the demand for transactions balances is shown to be interest elastic. As the interest rate rises for a given level of income, the demand for real transactions balances

---

[10] This can easily be proved by differentiating σ with respect to M_t, which gives us

$$\frac{d\sigma}{dM_t} = -\frac{by}{M_t^2} + \frac{i}{2}$$

Setting this result equal to zero and solving for M_t, we obtain equation (9-31).

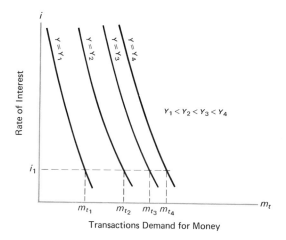

FIGURE 9-13   *The Transactions Demand for Money Specified by the Square Root Rule*

declines. This is shown in Figure 9-13, where transactions-demand curves for four different income levels are illustrated. Second, equation (9-32) states that the demand for transactions money rises less than proportionally to the volume of income. This implies that there are economies of scale in the use of money, a conclusion that contradicts both Fisher's transactions-demand approach and the Cambridge cash-balances approach. The contradiction becomes evident when we inspect Figure 9-14, which shows the demand for transactions balances vs. real income for a given interest rate. This demand curve for transactions balances is obtained by mapping points from Figure 9-13 onto Figure 9-14 when the interest rate in Figure 9-13 is held constant at $i = i_1$. The transactions-demand curve in Figure 9-14 is concave from below, whereas the transactions-demand curve in Figure 9-3 (page 163) is linear. The concavity in the curve in Figure 9-14 is the result of the economies of scale.

Friedman's Modern Quantity Theory[11]

Friedman's approach to the demand for money is in the mainstream of the Cambridge tradition: the demand for money is not analyzed from the viewpoints of all the possible motives for holding money. Instead, Friedman considers the demand for money simply as an application of a more general theory of the demand for capital assets, and by specifying the variables that determine this demand, he derives a demand for money function.

Friedman divides demanders of money into two groups. The first group is comprised of the ultimate owners of all wealth—individuals who consider money

---

[11] Milton Friedman, "The Quantity Theory of Money: A Restatement," in M. Friedman (ed.), *Studies in the Quantity Theory of Money* (Chicago: University of Chicago Press, 1957), pp. 3–21. This exposition is based on Friedman's simplified formulation in "A Theoretical Framework for Monetary Analysis," *Journal of Political Economy* **78** (March/April 1970), 193–238.

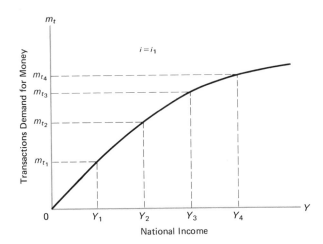

FIGURE 9-14   *The Transactions Demand for Money at a Constant Interest Rate*

one of the forms in which to hold their wealth. We refer to these individuals simply as *wealth holders.* The second group is comprised of business enterprises to whom money is a factor of production. We refer to these enterprises as *firms.* The demand for money by wealth holders will be treated first; then the demand for money by firms will be shown to be almost equivalent, so that a single aggregate function is possible.

Friedman argues that the demand for money by wealth holders is a function of the following variables:

1. *Total real wealth.*   As we saw in Figure 9-7, the nonhuman wealth held by an individual represents the maximum amount of money that he or she can demand. It is the basis of the individual's budget constraint at any moment in time. The definition of wealth used by Friedman is the same definition we encountered in reviewing his permanent income hypothesis in Chapter 6. The wealth Friedman refers to is total wealth W; that is, human wealth *plus* nonhuman wealth. As wealth rises, permanent income will rise. Thus the demand for money will increase if, as seems likely, money is a normal good.

2. *Percentage of total wealth in nonhuman form.*   In our review of Tobin's contribution in Section 9-4, we assumed that all the wealth held by an investor could be converted to money. With Friedman's definition of wealth, encompassing its human as well as nonhuman forms, the substitution of human wealth for money is quite limited in the absence of slavery. Limited substitution is possible by selling nonhuman wealth to finance education or by neglecting education to earn money for the purchase of nonhuman assets. Clearly, such a possible substitution is small in relation to the total amount of wealth. Since human wealth exhibits much less liquidity than nonhuman wealth, Friedman argued that as the percentage ratio of nonhuman wealth to total wealth Ω decreases, there may be an increased demand for money to compensate for the illiquidity of human wealth.

3. *The opportunity cost of holding money.* The opportunity cost of holding money depends on the rate of interest and the rate of change in the price level. In deciding to hold cash balances, an individual forgoes income that could be earned on an interest-bearing asset, such as a bond. As the market rate of interest rises, the the amount of forgone interest income increases, and therefore the opportunity cost of holding cash balances increases. If the demand for money is similar to the demand for other assets, we expect less of it to be demanded as its cost increases. Thus the demand for money is inversely related to the interest rate.

When the price level rises, the real value of nominal cash balances falls; as the rate of price rise $\Delta P/P$ increases, the opportunity cost of holding money also increases. In this situation, it is helpful to consider money to be similar to a bond that pays a negative interest rate. As the rate of inflation increases, the negative rate of return becomes absolutely larger. On the other hand, if prices are falling, the opportunity cost of holding money decreases as the rate of deflation increases. In this case money is analogous to a bond that pays a positive rate of return; an increasing rate of deflation is equivalent to an increasing rate of return on a bond. Thus the opportunity cost of holding cash balances is directly related to the rate of change in the price level, and we expect the demand for money to diminish as the rate of change in price level increases.

4. *Other variables that determine the utility of money.* The overall economic outlook can influence the demand for money. If a war or recession is anticipated, then the demand for cash balances will increase. Instability in capital markets that results in an increased turnover of bonds and equity shares will also increase the demand for money. Other factors can influence the utility of money and subsequently affect its demand. To account for these additional factors, Friedman includes the *portmanteau variable u.*

In functional notation, Friedman's demand for money by individual wealth holders can be symbolized

$$m_d = f\left(W, \Omega, i, \frac{\Delta P}{P}, u\right) \tag{9-34}$$

where m_d = the demand for real cash balances. A major problem encountered while using this formulation is that no reliable data exist for W. Friedman suggests that since $W = Y_p \div i$, permanent income Y_p can be used as a surrogate variable for total wealth. Incorporating this modification, equation (9-34) can be rewritten

$$m_d = f\left(Y_p, \Omega, i, \frac{\Delta P}{P}, u\right) \tag{9-35}$$

The aggregate demand function of wealth holders is the summation of individual demand functions. Equation (9-35) can also be used to represent the aggregate demand function, because it is identical to that function.

We have already stated that firms view money as a factor of production, whereas wealth holders treat it as an asset in their portfolios. There is another difference between Friedman's two types of demanders. In contrast to wealth holders, firms can·convert the total amount of their wealth into money, because the only wealth they own is nonhuman in form. Thus, the variable Ω, the ratio of nonhuman wealth to total wealth, is unity and can be dropped from the firm's demand function. In addition, firms can borrow money to maximize profits, so that the constraint of total wealth does not have the same implication for the firm that it has for the individual. Nonetheless, Friedman believes that some variable should be included in a firm's demand function to reflect the scale of its business activity and its resulting demand for money. Variables such as total transactions, net value added, net income, total capital in nonmoney form, and net worth have been suggested. Until further empirical research has been conducted, the best indicator remains unknown. To simplify his argument and in the absence of a better variable, Friedman used business income Y as a measure of this demand.

Like individuals, firms are sensitive to changes in the interest rate and in the price level. Because firms borrow money, the interest rate on business loans will affect a firm's demand for money. Rising prices during a period of inflation will increase the firm's cost of holding cash balances; therefore, the firm will seek to reduce the quantity of money it holds. This in turn will reduce the demand for money by firms. During periods of deflation, the opposite effects will occur.

Friedman concluded that the aggregate money demand function of firms will differ from equation (9-35) only to the extent that the variable Ω is excluded. The total aggregate demand for money can therefore approximated by this equation.

Now if we assume, as we have in our previous money demand models, that prices are constant and that Ω and u are institutional variables assumed to be fixed in the short run, then equation (9-35) can be simplified to

$$m_d = f(Y_p, i) \qquad (9\text{-}36)$$

We can simplify this function even further if we recall from Chapter 6 that permanent income is the weighted average of past measured incomes and that if measured income Y remains constant long enough, then

$$Y_p = Y \qquad (9\text{-}37)$$

Thus we can rewrite equation (9-36)

$$m_d = f(Y, i) \qquad (9\text{-}38)$$

The similarity between Friedman's formulation expressed in equation (9-38) and the Keynes–Tobin–Baumol synthesis becomes apparent if we combine equations (9-21) and (9-33) to obtain

$$m_d = m_t + m_{sp}$$
$$= g(i, Y) + h(i) \qquad (9\text{-}39)$$

Equation (9-39) is a synthesis of the approaches to the demand for money via the motives for holding money of Keynes, Tobin, and Baumol. Because this equation is separated into two parts, it is often referred to as a *dichotomized money demand function.* There is no mathematical reason for maintaining this dichotomy, and equation (9-39) can be more simply expressed as

$$m_d = f(i, Y) \tag{9-40}$$

Although equations (9-38) and (9-40) appear to be exactly the same, it would be a serious mistake to infer that they are theoretically identical. Remember that Friedman's demand function given by equation (9-38) has been drastically simplified. It employs measured income as a surrogate variable for total wealth, and its use is applicable only after a sustained period of constant income. Using equation (9-38) to predict money demand in a recession when $Y_p > Y$ will underestimate the demand for money compared to the use of equation (9-36). During periods of inflation, on the other hand, the exclusion of the rate of change in price level in equation (9-38) and the fact that $Y_p < Y$ will result in an overestimation of the demand for money compared to the result obtained from equation (9-36).

9-5   An Expository Money Demand Model

The money demand model we will use in Chapters 10–16 is based on the dichotomized Keynes–Tobin–Baumol motive approach expressed in equation (9-39). We choose this approach instead of Friedman's because the dichotomized approach is formulated in terms of the interest rate and measured income. Using a money demand function based on these variables produces a general equilibrium model of the economy that is flexible, illuminating, and not too complicated.[12] Moreover, such a model will not necessarily produce qualitative conclusions that diverge from those drawn from a more complicated model based on Friedman's modern quantity theory.

The dichotomized formulation of the Keynes–Tobin–Baumol money demand function is preferable to the nondichotomized version of equation (9-40), because the former serves as a better expository device to illuminate certain historical controversies in macroeconomic theory. The explanation of such controversies is automatically simplified in a model that explicitly includes the transactions and speculative motives for holding money.

In subsequent chapters, we will use the money demand curves derived in Figure 9-15. Figure 9-15(a) graphs the transactions demand for money curves that result from the Keynes–Baumol approach. Figure 9-15(b) is the speculative demand for money curve that results from the Keynes–Tobin approach to the demand for nontransactions balances. If we horizontally sum the speculative demand curve with each transactions demand curve, one at a time, then we obtain the total money demand curves in Figure 9-15(c). Each curve represents total money demand at a given income level. These total demand curves merge at an interest rate of i_c,

---

[12] For a quite complicated macroeconomic model that includes Friedman's theories of the demand for money and the consumption function, see Fred R. Glahe, "A Permanent Restatement of the *IS–LM* Model," *The American Economist* **XVII** (Spring 1973), 158–67.

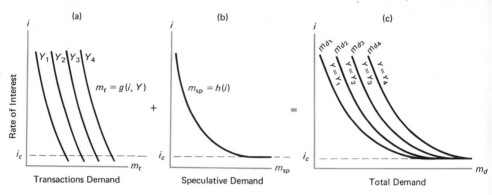

FIGURE 9-15   *Derivation of the Total Demand for Money*

showing that in this particular money demand function the liquidity trap hypothesized by Keynes exists at i_c.

For a given speculative demand curve, the curves in Figure 9-15(c) differ from those in Figure 9-6(c) in that for any given interest rate the slope of the total demand curves, when measured in absolute value, will be smaller in Figure 9-15(c) than in Figure 9-6(c). A visual comparison of these two curves should make this apparent. The effect results from the fact that the transactions demand curves in Figure 9-15(a) are interest elastic.

9-6   Concluding Remarks

In this chapter we have traced the historical development of the modern theory of the demand for money. Irving Fisher's transactions equation led to the Cambridge cash-balances equation. At this point, the development of the theory becomes divided: Keynes, Tobin, and Baumol constructed increasingly complex theories based on the motives for holding money; Milton Friedman approached the demand for money in the same general manner in which economic theory treats the demand for any durable asset. Using a simpler technique, Friedman derived a money demand function that is practically equivalent to the Keynes–Tobin–Baumol theory in certain situations but is significantly different in other situations. Both approaches, however, when incorporated into a general equilibrium model yield essentially the same qualitative equilibrium results. Because the motives approach to the theory of the demand for money produces a model that has greater expository power, this theory will be used in Chapters 10-16.

Combining the theory of the demand for money developed in this chapter with the theory of the supply of money developed in Chapter 8, we can derive a theory of money-market equilibrium in Chapter 10. This theory of the money market combined with the theory of the product market already developed in Chapter 7 will determine the equilibrium level of aggregate demand in our sophisticated economic model.

10
General Equilibrium of National Income and The Price Level

10-1   Introduction

In Chapters 8 and 9 we examined in detail the factors that determine the supply of and the demand for money to prepare for a study of the conditions under which equilibrium prevails in the money market. In this chapter we unite the theories of the supply of and the demand for money to determine their implications in terms of money-market equilibrium. Combining the concept of money-market equilibrium with that of product-market equilibrium examined in Chapter 7 enables us to derive a price-elastic aggregate demand curve. This aggregate demand curve, in conjunction with the aggregate supply curves studied in Chapter 2, gives us an equilibrium level of income and a determinate price level.

10-2   Money-market Equilibrium

Equilibrium in the money market exists when the demand for real money m_d is equal to the supply of real money m_s. This concept is exactly equivalent to equilibrium in a product market, where the quantity supplied is equal to the quantity demanded. In our analysis of the money market, we consider the simple case first, and then slowly increase the complexity of our assumptions to develop a fairly sophisticated model for use in our study of macroeconomic problems.

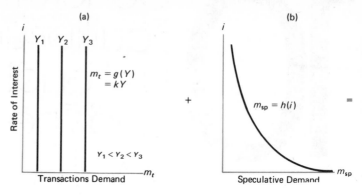

FIGURE 10-1   *Derivation of the LM Curve: First Model*

In our first model of the money market, we assume that

$$m_d = m_t + m_{sp}$$

$$= g(Y) + h(i) \qquad (10\text{-}1)$$

$$= kY + h(i)$$

where m_t = transactions demand for real cash balances
m_{sp} = speculative demand for real cash balances
k = the Cambridge k

Also by definition

$$m_s = \frac{M_s}{P} \qquad (10\text{-}2)$$

where M_s = nominal supply of money
P = general price level

Note that the implicit assumption in equation (10-1) is that the transactions demand is *not* a function of the interest rate. In addition, we assume initially that

$${}^{9}M_s \neq f(i) \qquad (10\text{-}3)$$

and that

$$P = P_0 \quad \text{(a constant)} \qquad (10\text{-}4)$$

Assumption (10-3) simply states that the nominal money supply is not a function of the interest rate, or in other words, that the nominal money supply curve plotted against the interest rate is a vertical line. Hence, the supply curve for real money m_s is also a vertical line.

Figure 10-1 graphs the workings of the money market under these assumptions. Figures 10-1(a) and 10-1(b) show the transactions-demand curves and the speculative demand curve, respectively. Summing these two graphs horizontally gives us

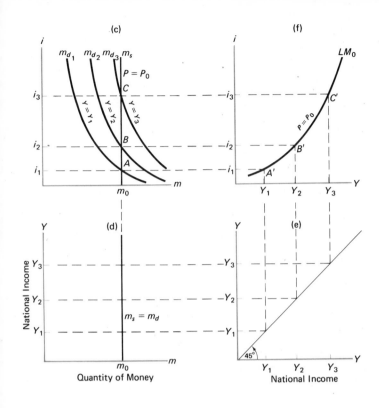

the total money demand curves (one for each level of real income) in Figure 10-1(c). By assumption (10-3), the real money supply m_s at price level P_0 is a constant at m_0. Equilibrium in the money market dictates, as we just mentioned, that

$$m_s = m_d = m_0 \tag{10-5}$$

This occurs in Figure 10-1(c) at points A, B, and C, where each equilibrium point corresponds to a different rate of interest and level of income.

Because we know that the money market is in equilibrium at (Y_1, i_1), (Y_2, i_2), and (Y_3, i_3), we can construct a curve that shows all possible combinations of Y and i consistent with equilibrium in the money market. This curve, generally referred to as the *LM curve*, is derived in Figure 10-1 in the following manner.[1] Directly below Figure 10-1(c) in Figure 10-1(d) is a curve showing the levels of income that must accompany the equilibrium quantities of money. In this example there is only one equilibrium quantity of money m_0, because the money supply is assumed to be interest inelastic; therefore, the curve in Figure 10-1(d) is also vertical. Figure 10-1(e) is simply a geometric device that permits us to rotate the axes. In Figure 10-1(f) the points (Y_1, i_1), (Y_2, i_2), and (Y_3, i_3) are located by transferring the income levels that correspond to the equilibrium quantity of money via Figure 10-1(e) to the

[1] Like the *IS* curve, the *LM* curve was first derived by J.R. Hicks in his famous article "Mr. Keynes and the 'Classics': A Suggested Interpretation," *Econometrica* **5** (1937), 147–59.

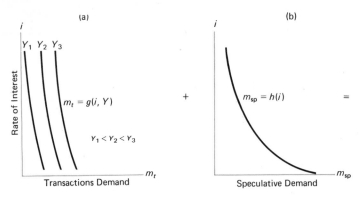

FIGURE 10-2 *Derivation of the* **LM** *Curve: Second Model*

horizontal axis in 10-1(f) and then plotting these income levels against the corresponding interest rates. In this example the three points are labeled A', B', and C'. The LM curve LM_0 is constructed by drawing a smooth curve through these points. The slope of the LM curve, as we can observe in Figure 10-1(f), is positive, because the quantity of money demanded is directly related to the income level and inversely related to the interest rate. Because the quantity of money supplied at price level P_0 is constant, as income increases the rate of interest must rise to maintain money-market equilibrium.

In our second model of the money market, the money demand function is assumed to be

$$m_d = g(i, Y) + h(i) \qquad (10\text{-}6)$$

and assumptions (10-3) and (10-4) continue to prevail. The only difference in this model is that we include the interest rate in the transactions demand for money. Thus our transactions-demand curves are now interest elastic, and our money demand function is the same as that specified by equation (9-39).

The LM curve is derived under these assumptions in Figure 10-2. The transactions-demand curves in Figure 10-2(a) are shown to be interest elastic according to equation (10-6). As before, equilibrium in the money market can occur at only one quantity of money m_0, as shown in Figure 10-2(c), but the equilibrium rates of interest corresponding to income levels Y_1, Y_2, and Y_3 are *not* the same interest rates as in Figure 10-1, as the difference in subscripts indicates. The three points in Figure 10-2(f) corresponding to the three money-market equilibrium points are labeled A', B', and C', and the LM curve LM_0', representing all possible combinations of income level and interest rate that are consistent with money-market equilibrium when at price level P_0, is constructed by drawing a smooth curve through these three points.

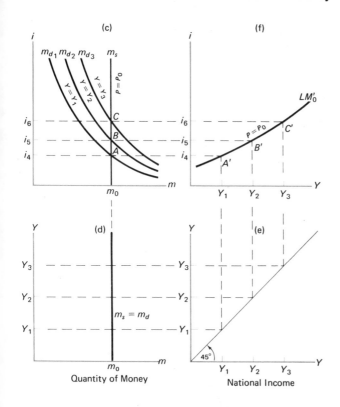

Our last model, which is the one we apply most consistently throughout the remainder of the book, combines the money demand function of equation (10-6) and the money supply function derived earlier in equation (8-25), or

$$M_s = \frac{H}{C_r + XR_r + RR_r - C_r XR_r - C_r RR_r} \tag{10-7}$$

where H = quantity of high-powered money
   C_r = currency ratio
   XR_r = excess reserve ratio
   RR_r = required reserve ratio

as before. In this money supply model, if H, RR_r, and the discount rate i_d are assumed to be constant, then an increase in i will cause C_r and XR_r to decrease, and the quantity of money supplied will therefore increase. Hence the money supply curve is interest elastic. If H increases or if RR_r or i_d decreases, then the money supply will increase; that is, the money supply curve will shift to the right.

The *LM* curve derivation under these assumptions is graphed in Figure 10-3. Because the money demand function in this model is exactly identical with the one in the preceding model, the graphs in Figures 10-2(a) and 10-2(b) are eliminated

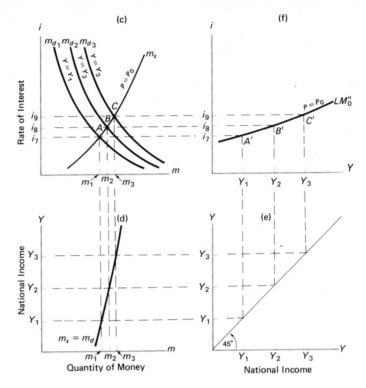

FIGURE 10-3   *Derivation of the* **LM** *Curve: Third Model*

from Figure 10-3. However, for clarity we retain the same corresponding alphabetical designations on the four remaining graphs. The *LM* curve for this model of the money market LM_0'' is derived in Figure 10-3(f) in exactly the same manner that we derived the previous two *LM* curves.

The important difference between Figure 10-3(c) and Figure 10-2(c) is that in 10-2(c) there is only one equilibrium quantity of money m_0, whereas in 10-3(c) there are an infinite number of equilibrium quantities of money (only three of which, m_1, m_2, and m_3, are shown at their respective interest rates i_7, i_8, and i_9). The corresponding income levels Y_1, Y_2, and Y_3 are the same as those in the previous two models. An infinite number of equilibrium quantities of money exist, because the money supply in this model is assumed to be interest elastic; in both of the previous models it is assumed to be interest inelastic.

Our derivation of the *LM* curve using three increasingly complex models of the money market is useful because it permits us to examine the concept of the *LM* curve at a leisurely pace. A second purpose of this derivation is revealed in Figure 10-4, where the *LM* curves that we derived in our three models, LM_0, LM_0', and LM_0'', are drawn. A comparison of these curves reveals that when the transactions demand is assumed to be interest elastic in the second model, the resulting *LM* curve LM_0' has a smaller slope than LM_0 at any given interest rate. Moreover, when the money supply is assumed to be interest elastic in the third money-market model, the slope of this model's *LM* curve LM_0'' has an even smaller slope than LM_0' at any given interest rate. This reduction of the slope of the *LM* curve at a given interest rate is of more than passing theoretical interest; as we shall learn in Chapters 14, 15, and 16, the actual slope of the *LM* curve is a critical factor in the prescription of appropriate macroeconomic policy.

10-3   The *LM* Curve and the Liquidity Trap

In Chapter 9 we pointed out during the explanation of Keynes's theory of the speculative demand for money that Keynes made an extremely important contribution to monetary theory when he hypothesized the possibility of a liquidity trap. Recall that this trap occurs when the demand to hold cash balances becomes perfectly interest elastic at the critical rate of interest. At this critical rate, individuals are indifferent to the choice between holding bonds or cash and will simply hoard money if the central bank increases the money supply.

The effect of the liquidity trap on the *LM* curve is illustrated in Figure 10-5. The same transactions-demand curves appear in Figure 10-5(a) that are graphed in Figure 10-2(a). However, the speculative demand for money curve is drawn in Figure 10-5(b) so that a liquidity trap is present at the critical rate of interest i_c. The resulting money demand curves in Figure 10-5(c) all merge to become horizontal at the liquidity-trap interest rate i_c. As before, equilibrium in the money market occurs at those income levels and interest rates where $m_s = m_d$.

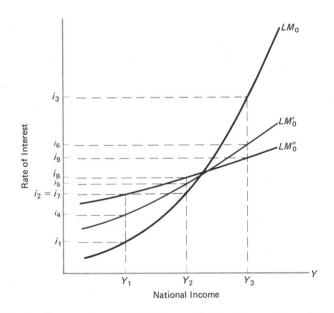

FIGURE 10-4   *Comparison of* **LM** *Curves Derived from Three Different Models*

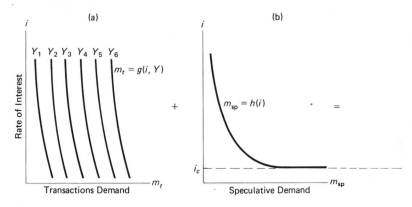

FIGURE 10-5   *The Effect of the Liquidity Trap on the LM Curve*

The *LM* curve derived in Figure 10-5(f) has a slope of zero at income levels below Y_2, because the money supply curve in Figure 10-5(c) intersects the money demand curves corresponding to all income levels below Y_2 at an interest rate that is equal to i_c. The full significance of the horizontal position of the *LM* curve that results from the presence of a liquidity trap in the speculative demand for money will not be apparent until Chapter 11, where we discuss the possibility of having an economy without a stable equilibrium at full employment.

10-4   Shifting the *LM* Curve

The position of the *LM* curve can be changed in a variety of ways. Because the intersection of the *LM* and *IS* curves determines the level of aggregate demand, as we learn in greater detail later in this chapter, it should be apparent that by shifting the *LM* curve we can change the level of aggregate demand. For this reason we now examine the various factors that can cause the *LM* curve to be displaced.

Change in the Transactions Demand

Changes in the technological and institutional aspects of the transaction process can decrease or increase the transactions demand for cash balances, as we saw in Chapter 9. Such a change in the dichotomized money demand function we are presently using can be interpreted as a change in the average number of times per year that transactions cash balances turn over, or in other words, the *transactions income velocity*. To simplify our explanation by backtracking slightly, we assume that the demand function for money is

$$m_d = m_t + m_{sp}$$
$$= g(Y) + h(i)$$

(10-8)

and specifically that

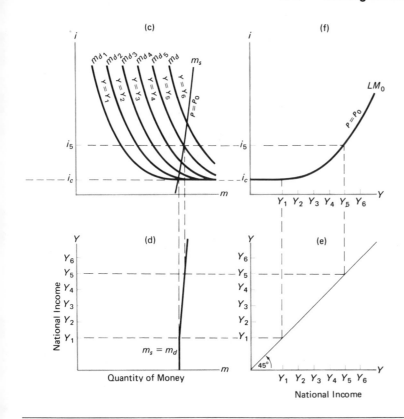

$$g(Y) = kY$$
$$= \frac{1}{V_t} Y$$

(10-9)

where equation (10-9) is basically the Cambridge cash-balances equation and V_t is the transactions income velocity. As V_t rises, the demand for cash balances for transactions purposes falls.

The effect of an increase in V_t is illustrated in Figure 10-6, where the solid curves represent the situation prior to the increase in V_t and the dashed curves represent the situation after the increase. The demand curve for transactions balances is given in Figure 10-6(g). To find the transactions-demand curves in Figure 10-6(a) prior to the increase in V_t, we simply select an income level on the national income axis in Figure 10-6(g)—say, Y_2—and then use the transactions-demand curve $m_t = kY$ to determine the corresponding level of m_t demanded. This gives us the transactions-demand curve in Figure 10-6(a), which is a vertical line by assumption (10-8). Summing the resulting set of transactions-demand curves in Figure 10-6(a) and the speculative demand curve in Figure 10-6(b) gives us the total demand for money curves in Figure 10-6(c). Given a money supply curve m_s at price level P_0, money-market equilibrium produces the *LM* curve LM_0 in Figure 10-6(f).

Now suppose that a technological innovation speeds up the check-clearing process in commercial banks, thereby reducing the demand for transactions cash balances. This would result in an increase in transactions income velocity from V_t

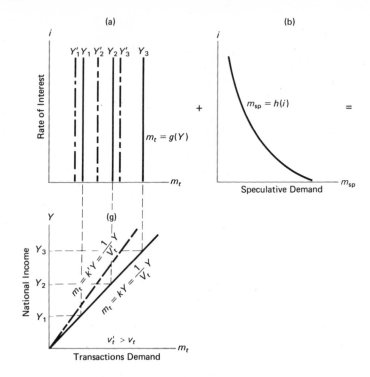

FIGURE 10-6   *The Effect of an Increase in Transactions Income Velocity on*

to V'_t, which is represented by the new dashed transaction-demand curve in Figure 10-6(g). The effect of an increase in V_t is to rotate the transactions-demand curve counterclockwise about the origin. This rotation in turn shifts the transactions-demand curves to the left in Figure 10-6(a), as shown by the new dashed curves. As we would expect, all the new total money demand curves in Figure 10-6(c) also shift to the left. However, the increase in transactions velocity causes the *LM* curve to shift it downward to the right to LM'_0 in Figure 10-6(f). If we assumed that V_t has fallen instead of risen, then we would reach the opposite conclusion, that the *LM* curve would shift upward to the left. If we include Baumol's more sophisticated formulation of the transactions motive in our analysis of the effects of changing technological and institutional characteristics of the transactions process, then our general conclusions would not change, but our graphic explanation would be much more complex.

Change in the Speculative Demand

As we learned in discussing Friedman's restatement of the quantity theory of money, it is possible for random and unforeseen events such as war or collapsing financial markets to alter the demand for money. We can demonstrate how such factors can affect this demand by using Tobin's theory of portfolio selection, which we developed in Chapter 9.

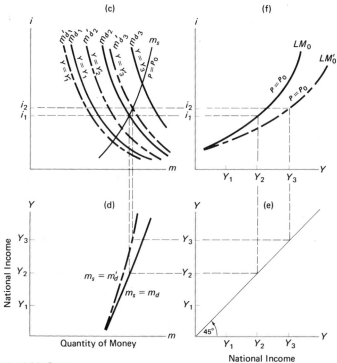

the **LM** *Curve*

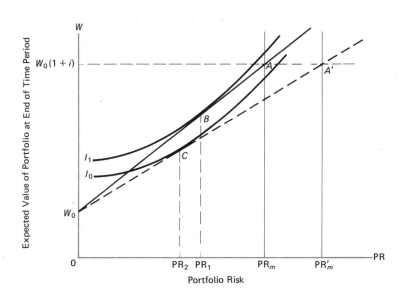

**FIGURE 10-7   *The Effect on Portfolio Selection of Increasing the Risk
Involved in Holding Bonds***

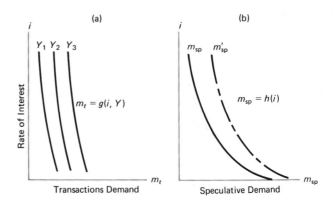

FIGURE 10-8   *The Effect on the* **LM** *Curve of Increasing the Risk Involved in Holding Bonds*

Either of these events would increase the risk involved in bond holding. The effect of this increased risk on the demand for cash balances is illustrated in Figure 10-7. Prior to the expected occurrence of an event such as a war, if the interest rate is i, an individual with wealth W_0 at the end of a given time period can be assured of W_0 or a maximum expected growth of wealth equal to $W_0(1 + i)$. The wealth holder's budget constraint line $W_0 A$ will then have a slope of

$$\frac{W_0(1 + i) - W_0}{PR_m} \qquad (10\text{-}10)$$

where PR_m = maximum portfolio risk, that is, the risk the individual would incur by placing total wealth in bonds. Being a risk averter, our wealth holder maximizes personal welfare by selecting the combination of money and bonds that provides a portfolio with a risk of PR_1. This combination is determined by the point of tangency between indifference curve I_1 and the budget constraint line $W_0 A$ (point B in Figure 10-7).

During a war (or even when there are rumors of war), for a given interest rate i, the expected wealth at the end of the time period will still be $W_0(1 + i)$ if all wealth is held in bonds, but the risk associated with holding such a portfolio will increase. In Figure 10-7 this maximum portfolio risk increases from PR_m to PR'_m. Because the numerator of the slope of the new budget constraint line $W_0 A'$ is identical to the numerator in equation (10-10) and the denominator is larger than the denominator in this equation, it follows that the slope of $W_0 A'$ is smaller than the slope of $W_0 A$, as Figure 10-7 shows. The individual, once again maximizing welfare and averting risk, selects the portfolio corresponding to point C in Figure 10-7 when maximum portfolio risk increases to PR'_m. That portfolio has a risk of PR_2 and is comprised of a smaller percentage of bonds than PR_1 before the increase in maximum portfolio risk, because $PR_2/PR'_m < PR_1/PR_m$. Thus for a given interest rate, an increase in the risk involved in holding bonds increases the demand for money. If the risk involved in holding bonds declines, then the demand for money at any given interest rate will be reduced.

We can now relate such changes to both the speculative demand for money

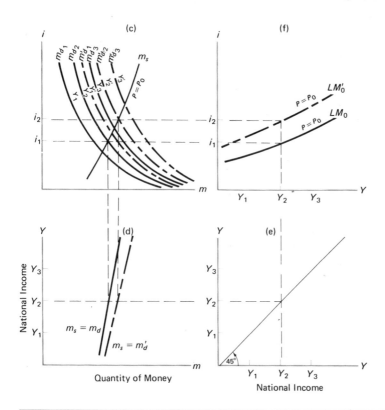

curve and the *LM* curve. Two speculative demand for money curves are graphed in Figure 10-8(b). The first curve m_{sp} represents the initial condition. The second curve m'_{sp} represents the speculative demand for money after an increase in the risk involved in holding bonds. The total demand for money curves before (solid) and after (dashed) the crisis are graphed in Figure 10-8(c) with the real money supply curve m_s consistent with a price level of P_0. The *LM* curve existing before the shift in speculative demand LM_0 and the *LM* curve existing after the shift LM'_0 are derived graphically via Figures 10-8(d) and 10-8(e), and we see that LM'_0 lies above and to the left of LM_0. We can now conclude that an increase in speculative demand shifts the *LM* curve upward and to the left, whereas a decrease in speculative demand produces the opposite effect.

Change in the Money Supply

An increase in the money supply will shift the money supply curve to the right; a decrease will shift it to the left. Because we are dealing with the real quantity of money supplied, it is obvious that changes in this real quantity can be created by changes either in the nominal money supply M_s or in the price level P. As we learned in Chapter 8, the nominal money supply can be increased if the central bank (1) increases the quantity of high-powered money by buying government securities, (2) reduces the required reserve ratio, or (3) lowers the discount rate. In

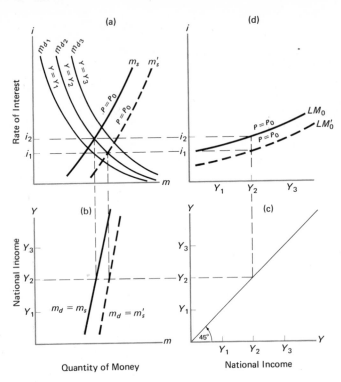

FIGURE 10-9   *The Effect of an Increase in the Nominal Money Supply on the LM Curve with the Price Level Constant*

addition, the nominal money supply can be increased if the public decides to hold less currency at a given interest rate and the currency ratio drops.

Because the price level and the real quantity of money are inversely related, a decline in the price level will increase the real money supply. Clearly, if any of these factors move in the opposite direction, then the real money supply will be reduced.

Let us suppose that the real supply of money increases due to an open-market purchase that increases the nominal money supply from M_s to M'_s. If we maintain assumption (10-4), so that the price level is fixed at P_0, then the real money supply curve shifts from m_s to m'_s, as shown in Figure 10-9(a). The LM curve corresponding to the initial money supply curve LM_0 is derived graphically in Figure 10-9(d) via Figures 10-9(b) and 10-9(c). The new LM curve corresponding to the increased money supply LM'_0 is derived in the same manner in Figure 10-9(d), where it lies below and to the right of LM_0. From this analysis we can therefore conclude that an increase in the real money supply shifts the LM curve downward and to the right and that a decrease in the real money supply shifts the LM curve upward and to the left.

We can now draw analogies between the movement of the money supply curve and changes in the transactions income velocity and the speculative demand for money. In Figure 10-6 we saw that an increase in V_t shifts the LM curve downward and to the right. This same movement results from an increase in the money supply, so that we can regard an increase in V_t as analogous to an increase in the money supply. This statement is intuitively appealing, because such an increase in V_t is due to increased efficiency in the use of money for transactions purposes and is therefore a quality change in money that is not reflected in a change in the price level. In Figure 10-8, an increase in the speculative demand for money produces an upward and leftward shift in the *LM* curve that is similar to a decrease in the real money supply. Thus we can say that an increase in the speculative demand for money is analogous to a decrease in the money supply. Once again, this result is intuitively appealing, because an increase in the speculative demand for money results in an increase in the amount of money that is hoarded by the public, thereby reducing the amount of money available for the purchase of goods and services that can be produced.

The Liquidity Trap and Shifting of the LM Curve

In Section 10-3 we learned that when the speculative demand for money exhibits the liquidity trap hypothesized by Keynes, the *LM* curve is horizontal if the interest rate is equal to the critical rate of interest i_c. We now analyze how changes in the money supply affect the *LM* curve under this condition. Remember that changes in the money supply are analogous to changes in V_t and shifts in the speculative demand for money, so that any conclusions we reach concerning changes in the money supply are applicable to these changes as well.

As before, we assume that the increase in the real money supply is the result of an open-market purchase. The money demand curves in Figure 10-10(a) all become horizontal at the critical rate of interest i_c, indicating that this is also the critical rate of interest for the speculative demand for money (not shown in the figure). Given an initial real money supply curve m_s at price level P_0, the *LM* curve LM_0 is graphically derived in Figure 10-10(d) via Figures 10-10(b) and 10-10(c). This *LM* curve is horizontal at interest rate i_c for all levels of national income below Y_2. When the nominal money supply increases from M_s to M_s', the real money supply will increase from m_s to m_s' if the price level remains constant. The *LM* curve LM_0' corresponding to this increased real money supply moves downward and to the right for interest rates above i_c, as we would expect based on our previous analysis. However, at the liquidity-trap interest rate, LM_0' also becomes horizontal; it therefore shifts only to the right, leaving the interest rate for all points on LM_0' less than Y_4 equal to the critical rate of interest i_c. If the money supply contracts, then the opposite effect results.

One implication of the liquidity trap should now be apparent. Its existence means that the floor of the interest rate is greater than zero. Therefore, monetary policy, which determines the nominal money supply, is completely incapable of generating an *LM* curve below the critical rate of interest. As we shall learn in Section 10-5, the intersection of the *LM* and *IS* curves determines the market rate of interest; because the *LM* curve is horizontal at i_c, the *IS* curve cannot intersect the *LM* curve at *any* interest rate below i_c. This means that the minimum market rate of interest is

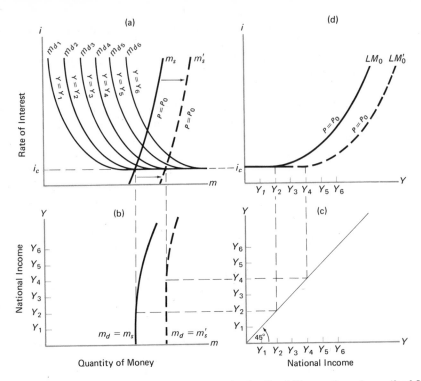

FIGURE 10-10 *The Effect of an Increase in the Real Money Supply on the LM Curve When the Liquidity Trap Exists*

the critical interest rate. The theoretical and policy implications of this fact are discussed later, in Chapter 11.

10-5   The Aggregate Demand Curve

In Chapter 3, where we first combined the aggregate supply and demand curves, we discovered that in our simple model of aggregate demand an equilibrium level of national income and a determinate price level can coexist only at less than the full-employment level and only in the presence of downwardly rigid wages. Moreover, we learned that when aggregate demand is equal to aggregate supply at the full-employment level, no single price level is consistent with this income level for either labor supply case. Indeed, an infinite number of price levels become possible and the price level is indeterminate.

To eliminate these major shortcomings in our theory and to prepare for the investigation of several macroeconomic problems, we then embarked on a lengthy and detailed construction of a more sophisticated theory of aggregate demand. At this point in our analysis, we can combine all the diverse elements of this theory to produce a new aggregate demand curve that is price elastic and that will, when combined with our aggregate supply models, yield a general equilibrium of national income and a determinate price level.

The *IS* curve is the locus of the points corresponding to rates of interest and levels of income that produce equilibrium in the product market. The *LM* curve is the locus of the points corresponding to rates of interest and levels of income that produce equilibrium in the money market. The *IS* curve tells us the equilibrium level of aggregate demand if the interest rate is known, whereas the *LM* curve tells us the interest rate if the level of aggregate demand is known. Clearly, this presents us with the problem of solving two equations in two unknowns. The graphic solution to this problem lies at the intersection of the *IS* and *LM* curves. Typical *IS* and *LM* curves are illustrated in Figure 10-11, where the intersection of the *IS* and *LM* curves determines the equilibrium level of aggregate demand Y_e.

When we first used our simple model in Chapters 3 and 4 to determine the level of aggregate demand, the resulting aggregate demand curve was perfectly price inelastic and we were unable to determine the price level at full employment. We can now demonstrate that our sophisticated model produces an aggregate demand curve that is price elastic and that yields a determinate price level at full employment.

Thus far, certain assumptions about the manner in which the different sectors of the economy react to changes in the price level have been implicit in our theory. Before we can make these assumptions more explicit, we must explain the implications of a change in the price level.

When the price level changes, we assume that all prices change in the same proportion; in other words, we assume that relative prices for all goods and services remain constant. We also assume that a change in the price level does not produce a change in the income distribution of the economy. This means that wages,

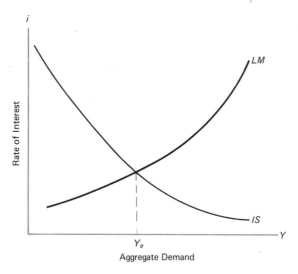

FIGURE 10-11   *Determination of Aggregate Demand*

contracts, pensions, mortgages, and all other such flows are negotiated in real terms, so that they are adjusted proportionally in money terms to changes in the price level. Finally, for simplicity we assume that firms and individuals consider each price change permanent. In other words, we assume that the expected future price level is always the same as the current price level. In the real world it is unlikely that the economy will behave in this manner, especially when there is a high inflation rate. However, this simplifying assumption is acceptable for our purposes here, because its adoption does not significantly alter the validity of the conclusions we reach in Chapter 11. When we examine certain aspects of inflation later, in Chapter 12, we will assume that individuals and firms are able to form, with varying degrees of perfection, positive expectations about future price increases.

At this point, we can proceed to an explicit examination of the assumptions we have made concerning the underlying functions of the IS and LM curves.

Both the short-run function specified in equation (6-32) and the long-run consumption function stated in equation (6-41) are expressed in terms of real variables, an approach justified by the reasonable assumption that households do not suffer from money illusion and react only to real changes in income. Therefore, for changes in the price level that are consistent with our assumptions in the preceding paragraph, we now assume explicitly that consumption in real terms is unaltered and that the consumption curve does not shift.[2] Similarly, there is no reason to suppose that government expenditures or revenue policies suffer from money illusion, and we also assume that they are invariant in real terms with respect to the price level.

We based our analysis of the investment behavior of firms on the assumption that firms seek to maximize profits. It is reasonable to assume that firms measure these profits in real terms and that the expected profits and risk associated with any investment are not affected by changes in the price level, given our previous assumption that whenever the price level changes the new price level is expected to continue indefinitely. Then we can assume that the nominal rate of interest is analogous to the expected real rate of interest, and the investment function is represented by

$$I = I(i) \tag{10-11}$$

where both net investment I and the interest rate i are measured in real terms and are unaffected by changes in the price level. Thus the MEI curve does not shift with changes in the price level.

The demand for money is assumed to reflect the command that the ownership of cash balances gives individuals and firms over goods and services. Given our assumption that every price change is expected to be permanent, the demand for cash balances in nominal terms will rise and fall in proportion to changes in the price level. The demand for money in real terms will be invariant with respect to the price level. In functional notation this can be specified by

---

[2] As we will show in Chapter 11, this assumption is incorrect, because changes in the price level can affect the net wealth of individuals and thereby alter consumption. The role prices play in net wealth is not required in our analysis in the rest of this chapter.

$$m_d = f(i, Y) \tag{10-12}$$

The only relationship that now remains is the money supply. In Chapter 8 we showed that for a given nominal quantity of high-powered money, a given required reserve ratio, and a given discount rate, the real money supply is a function of the interest rate, assuming the currency ratio and the excess reserve ratio decline as the interest rate rises. Given these assumptions, the nominal money supply curve can be expressed in functional notation as

$$M_s = j(i) \tag{10-13}$$

Since

$$m_s = \frac{M_s}{P}$$

the real money supply curve for a given price level can then be expressed as

$$m_s = j(i) \tag{10-14}$$

What happens to the real supply of cash balances when the price level changes depends on how the central bank reacts to these changes. Here, we assume that the central bank does not alter the nominal quantity of high-powered money when the price level changes, so that for a given interest rate the nominal supply of cash balances is unaltered. Of course, this implies that the *real money supply curve shifts to the right when the price level falls and to the left when the price level rises*.

The implications that these assumptions have for the level of aggregate demand are illustrated in Figure 10-12. For a given nominal money supply M_s when the price level is P_3, the real money supply curve is m_{s_3}, as shown in Figure 10-12(a). The intersection of m_{s_3} with the set of money demand curves in Figure 10-12(a) produces the *LM* curve LM_3 in Figure 10-12(b). Because this *LM* curve results when the price level is P_3, it follows that this curve holds only for this price level; thus the subscript signifies the relevant price level. The intersection of LM_3 with the *IS* curve in Figure 10-12(b) determines the equilibrium level of aggregate demand Y_1 when the price level is P_3. If the price level declines from P_3 to P_2, then the real quantity of money supplied will increase from m_{s_3} to m_{s_2}. By our previous assumptions all other underlying functions remain unaffected in real terms, so that the *LM* curve shifts to the right to LM_2, the *IS* curve remains fixed, and aggregate demand increases to Y_2. A further decline in the price level to P_1 will once again increase the real quantity of money, shifting the money supply curve from m_{s_2} to m_{s_1}. This will shift the *LM* curve further to the right to LM_1, and the level of aggregate demand will increase to Y_3.

The level of aggregate demand that corresponds to each price level is plotted in Figure 10-12(c). The curve drawn through these points is our new aggregate demand curve AgD. This curve is price elastic, because a decline in the price level increases the real supply of money, and at the initial interest rate and income level the new quantity of cash balances supplied exceeds the demand. As individuals and firms seek to reduce the real quantity of the cash balances they hold by buying financial assets such as bonds, the price of these assets rises, the interest rate falls,

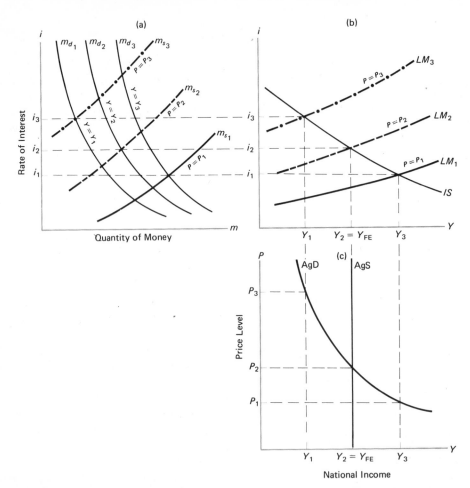

FIGURE 10-12   Determination of Aggregate Demand and General Equilibrium

net investment increases via a downward movement along the MEI curve, and the quantity of national income demanded increases via the multiplier process.

Whenever a change in the real quantity of cash balances produces a change in the demand for commodities, the effect is called, after Patinkin, a *real-balance effect*.[3] The particular real-balance effect described here occurs via a decline in the price level that increases the real quantity of money supplied and shifts the *LM* curve to the right. This particular type of real-balance effect is generally referred to in economic literature as the *Keynes effect*, because Keynes mentions its occurrence in *The General Theory*.

The Keynes effect is only one of several possible economic effects that can be grouped under our definition of the real-balance effect. Another type of real-

[3] Don Patinkin, *Money, Interest, and Prices*, Second Edition (New York: Harper & Row, 1965), p. 19.

balance effect occurs when the central bank increases the nominal money supply by means of an open-market purchase.

10-6   General Equilibrium

General equilibrium occurs at full employment, and the price level is determined by the intersection of the aggregate demand curve and the aggregate supply curve. To understand how our sophisticated theory of aggregate demand enables us to determine the general equilibrium of national income and price level, we can again consider Figure 3-6 (page 39). Given a price-inelastic aggregate demand curve, there is no equilibrium level of income or price when the aggregate demand curve is either AgD or AgD'. When the aggregate demand curve is AgD", the equilibrium level of income is equal to the full-employment level, but there is no determinate price level.

Now consider Figure 10-12(c), where the aggregate supply curve is the one we derived using our model of perfect competition in Chapter 2. Aggregate supply in this model is a function only of real variables and is therefore perfectly price inelastic at the full-employment level of output. Suppose that initially the level of aggregate demand is Y_1 at price level P_3, as determined in Figure 10-12(b) by the intersection of the *IS* and LM_3 curves. Figure 10-12(c) shows that at price level P_3 aggregate demand is Y_1 and aggregate supply is Y_{FE}, so that an excess aggregate supply prevails. Given an excess aggregate supply, the price level will fall and the real quantity of money will increase, shifting the *LM* curve downward to the right. As long as aggregate demand is less than aggregate supply, the price level will fall, real cash balances will increase, and the level of aggregate demand will rise. The price level will continue to fall until the aggregate demand curve intersects the aggregate supply curve. This situation is shown in Figure 10-12(c) at price level P_2, where AgD is equal to AgS. In Figure 10-12(b) the level of aggregate demand at price level P_2 is determined by the intersection of LM_2 (the *LM* curve corresponding to the supply of real money at price level P_2) with the *IS* curve. This level of aggregate demand is equal to the full-employment level. The interest rate that prevails at full employment is called the *natural rate of interest;* in the example illustrated in Figure 10-12 the natural rate of interest is equal to i_2. The condition illustrated in Figure 10-12 when AgD is equal to AgS at full employment is called a condition of *general equilibrium*. When general equilibrium prevails, supply is equal to demand in all markets; this condition can last indefinitely provided the underlying functions remain unaltered.

If the aggregate demand is initially Y_3 at price level P_1, then excess demand will be present and the price level will rise. As the price level rises, the real money supply will decline, the *LM* curve will shift to the left from LM_1, and the level of aggregate demand will diminish via the real-balance effect. Movement upward along the aggregate demand curve will continue as long as any excess demand persists. At full employment, the level of excess demand is zero and the general equilibrium levels of national income, price, and interest rate prevail.

In our analysis of general equilibrium in this chapter we have used the perfectly competitive, flexible-wage aggregate supply model. In Chapter 11, we will examine the implications of using an imperfectly competitive, rigid-wage aggregate supply model, and we will modify the conclusions drawn in this section.

10-7   Concluding Remarks

In this chapter, we have shown that equilibrium in the money market exists when the quantity of money supplied is equal to the quantity of money demanded. Because the quantity of money demanded is a function of the level of national income as well as of the interest rate, as long as the money supply is a function of the interest rate there will be not just one equilibrium quantity of money, but one for each interest rate and level of national income. The curve described by the locus of these points is called the *LM curve*. We have seen that the position of the *LM* curve depends on the transactions demand, the speculative demand, and the real money supply. Except for the special case of the liquidity trap, the *LM* curve can be shifted downward as close to the horizontal axis as desired. However, when the *liquidity trap* exists, there is a minimum interest rate above the zero rate below which the *LM* curve cannot shift.

We have also shown that the intersection of the *IS* and *LM* curves determines the level of aggregate demand. Variations in the price level shift the *LM* curve and create a different level of aggregate demand for each price level. The curve derived from the points whose coordinates are the price level and the level of aggregate demand is the *aggregate demand curve;* it is price elastic due to the presence of the *real-balance effect.* The intersection of the aggregate demand curve with the aggregate supply curve at full employment yields the *general equilibrium* levels of income and price; the interest rate that prevails in general equilibrium is called the *natural rate of interest.*

At this point, we have essentially completed our task of developing a sophisticated model of aggregate demand and supply. In Chapters 11–17 we will employ this model in examining some of the major problems that macroeconomics seeks to answer.

11

Unemployment and Disequilibrium

11-1 Introduction

We have already noted that John Maynard Keynes published his most famous work, *The General Theory of Employment, Interest, and Money,* in 1936. In writing *The General Theory,* Keynes's goal was to explain and find a cure for the chronically high levels of unemployment existing in Great Britain and the United States at the time and to refute the theories and policy prescriptions of the prevailing orthodoxy. This ambitious attempt by one of the foremost economists of the era touched off a revolution in macroeconomic thought, the effects of which are still being felt.

Unfortunately or fortunately, depending on viewpoint, *The General Theory* was not without flaws. Its two most serious problems were that its theoretical model suffered in places from errors in logic and that, in marked contrast to Keynes's previous published works, it was poorly organized and written. A minor work containing similar flaws would soon be forgotten, but because of the importance of the ideas it set forth, *The General Theory* spawned a large number of critics and apologists. In addition, it was inevitable that later economists would assume the role of redactors and attempt to correct the flaws. As might be expected in any humanly inspired revision, the suggested corrections and additions to *The General Theory* often reflected the redactor's view of the world rather than Keynes's view. These economists have come to be generally known as *Keynesians*; among the most famous are John R. Hicks, Alvin H. Hansen, and Lawrence R. Klein.[1]

It is hardly surprising that the views of the Keynesians are not homogeneous. However, their sometimes divergent theories are united by a common denominator: the general adoption and extension of the *IS–LM* framework and the reliance on fiscal policy as the most powerful instrument with which to control macroeconomic problems.

In recent years a growing body of economic thought has developed to challenge the Keynesian interpretation of *The General Theory*.[2] This debate in exegetical scholarship will not be examined in this book, because for our purposes the correctness of the Keynesian interpretation of Keynes is not of primary importance. What is important here is the theoretical framework and the resulting policy prescriptions that have dominated macroeconomics since the 1940s. This is the product of the Keynesians and their critics.

In this chapter we first review the Keynesian interpretation of Keynes's contention that under certain special conditions a perfectly competitive economy may not have a stable full-employment equilibrium. Using this analysis as a base, we then consider the Keynesian argument that fiscal policy should be the primary instrument of macroeconomic countercyclical policy. Finally, we examine the theoretical and empirical counterarguments of the anti-Keynesians and present the grounds on which it has been argued that the theoretical bases of the Keynesian emphasis on fiscal policy prescriptions are incorrect.

11-2 Macroeconomic Models Without Stable Full-employment Equilibrium

Before the appearance of *The General Theory* it was a universally accepted tenet of economic theory that a perfectly competitive economy has only one equilibrium level of employment—the full-employment level—and that this equilibrium is stable.[3] The Keynesians suggested two special conditions to demonstrate that a perfectly competitive economy may not have a stable full-employment equilibrium. The first condition deals with the nature of the MEI (marginal efficiency of investment) curve; the second condition is concerned with the demand for money. To determine how these conditions can prevent a stable full-employment equilibrium, we will examine the consequences of each in turn within the context of our macroeconomic model.

[1] J.R. Hicks, "Mr. Keynes and the 'Classics:' A Suggested Interpretation," *Econometrica* (April 1937), 147–59; A.H. Hansen, *A Guide to Keynes* (New York: McGraw-Hill, 1953); L.R. Klein, *The Keynesian Revolution* (New York: Macmillan, 1947).

[2] Axel Leijonhufvud, *On Keynesian Economics and the Economics of Keynes* (New York: Oxford University Press, 1968). For rebuttals to Leijonhufvud's contentions, see Herschel I. Grossman, "Was Keynes a 'Keynesian'?, A Review Article," *Journal of Economic Literature* **X** (March 1972), 26–30; Leland B. Yeager, "The Keynesian Diversion," *Western Economic Journal* (June 1973), 150–63; and Richard Jackman, "Keynes and Leijonhufvud," *Oxford Economic Papers* **26** (July 1974), 259–72.

[3] By *equilibrium* we mean that excess demand and excess supply in a market are both equal to zero. By *stable equilibrium* we mean that if there is a small deviation from equilibrium, market forces will automatically restore that equilibrium.

Investment Insufficiency

The point where the *IS* curve intersects the income axis represents the maximum attainable aggregate demand. This fact was not important in any of our previous analyses, because we assumed that income at the point of intersection was greater than the full-employment income level. If the *IS* curve intersects the income axis at less than full employment, then no amount of shifting of the *LM* curve will ever produce a level of aggregate demand that is equal to full-employment aggregate supply.

The first special condition suggested by the Keynesians occurs when the *IS* curve intersects the income axis at less than full employment, as may happen when the MEI curve becomes perfectly or almost perfectly interest inelastic at a level of net investment that is insufficient to equal the desired full-employment level of savings. This means that business cannot be induced to borrow and increase investment by reduction in the interest rate, even if the rate declines to zero. The interest inelasticity of the MEI curve in turn can be produced by severely pessimistic business expectations, by idle capital already in existence, or by general economic stagnation.

In Figure 11-1(a) the MEI curve becomes perfectly interest inelastic at investment level I_0 and at interest rates of less than i_0. This produces the *IS* curve in Figure

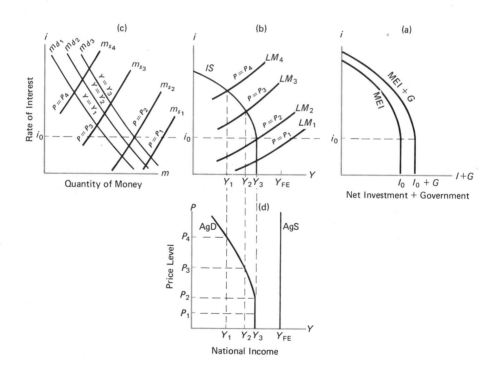

FIGURE 11-1   *A Competitive Economy Without a Full-employment Equilibrium, Resulting from Investment Insufficiency*

11-1(b), which is perfectly inelastic at income level Y_3 and interest rates below i_0. If the initial LM curve is LM_4 at price level P_4, then total aggregate demand will be Y_1, which as we can see in Figure 11-1(d) is less than the aggregate supply produced by labor hired in a purely competitive labor market. Given an excess aggregate supply, the price level will decline, increasing the real supply of money, as shown in Figure 11-1(c); this in turn will cause the LM curve in Figure 11-1(b) to shift to the right. At the lower price level P_3, aggregate demand Y_2 will be greater than Y_1 but less than Y_{FE}. An excess supply will still exist, producing a further decline in the price level. When the price level falls to P_2, aggregate demand will again increase from Y_2 to Y_3, but this is the limit to which aggregate demand will expand via the Keynes effect. Further reductions in the interest rate as the LM curve continues to shift to the right will not result in net investment increases, because the MEI curve is perfectly inelastic at rates of interest below i_0.

The significance of the MEI curve graphed in Figure 11-1(a) is revealed in Figure 11-1(d), where the aggregate demand curve becomes perfectly price inelastic at price levels below P_2. The maximum quantity of national income demanded is Y_3, which is less than the full-employment output. This model of a perfectly competitive economy does not have a stable full-employment equilibrium.

The Liquidity Trap

The second special condition that the Keynesians suggest can prevent a stable full-employment equilibrium in a perfectly competitive economy is the occurrence of a liquidity trap. You should recall from our discussion of the demand for money in Chapter 9 that Keynes argued that if the interest rate fell to a sufficiently low value, called the critical interest rate, then the demand to hold money would become perfectly interest elastic. In this situation, if the real quantity of money increases as a result of a decline in the price level, holders of these additional real cash balances will not use them to purchase bonds, because individuals are indifferent to the choice between holding their wealth in bonds or in cash balances when the interest rate is equal to the critical rate. No investor wishes to purchase bonds at a price in excess of the prevailing market price, so that the interest rate cannot fall below the existing rate, which is the critical interest rate. The money demand curves become horizontal at the critical rate of interest, and the LM curve derived from this money-market condition also becomes horizontal at the critical rate. A further decline in the price level under this liquidity-trap condition shifts the LM curve to the right as the real money supply increases, but this shift merely extends the horizontal portion of the curve. Because the interest rate cannot decrease any further, it is possible for the level of desired investment *plus* government spending at this rate to be less than the level of desired saving *plus* taxes at full employment. Thus a stable full-employment equilibrium is not possible.

To clarify this situation, consider Figure 11-2. The money demand curves in Figure 11-2(a) all become perfectly interest elastic at the critical rate of interest i_c. Given a price level of P_5, the real quantity of money supplied is m_{s_5} and the resulting LM curve is LM_5. The intersection of LM_5 with the IS curve in Figure 11-2(b) results

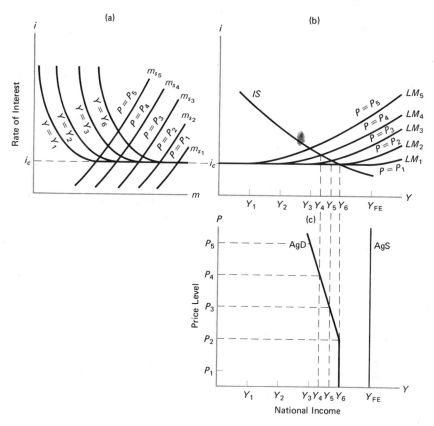

FIGURE 11-2   *A Competitive Economy Without a Full-employment Equilibrium, Resulting from a Liquidity Trap*

in a level of aggregate demand of Y_3. At these levels of aggregate demand and price there is an excess aggregate supply of $Y_{FE} - Y_3$, as shown in Figure 11-2(c). In this situation the price level in a perfectly competitive economy must fall. When the price level reaches P_4, the real quantity of money increases to m_{s_4}, the *LM* curve shifts to LM_4, and the level of aggregate demand increases to Y_4. At these levels of aggregate demand and price there is still an excess supply, and the price level continues to decline, accompanied by increases in the real money supply and aggregate demand, until the level of aggregate demand reaches Y_6 at price level P_2. At this combination of price and aggregate demand, an excess supply still persists, as shown in Figure 11-2(c). Therefore, prices will continue to fall, but aggregate demand will stop increasing and will become perfectly price inelastic at Y_6. The reason for this price inelasticity is illustrated in Figure 11-2(b). As the price level falls from P_5 to P_2, the *LM* curve shifts to the right, intersecting the *IS* curve at successively lower rates of interest. As the interest rate falls, the amount of net investment increases and aggregate demand increases. When the price level falls to P_1, however, the resulting shift in the *LM* curve from LM_2 to LM_1 does not produce a reduction in the interest rate, because the interest rate has reached the liquidity-trap rate. Therefore, the *IS* curve intersects LM_1 at exactly the same rate of interest and level of income at which it intersects LM_2. Without a reduction in the interest rate, net investment will not increase; there is no Keynes effect. Further reductions in the price level will not alter the interest rate, so that the aggregate demand curve shown in Figure 11-2(c) becomes perfectly price inelastic at price levels below P_2. Because the maximum aggregate demand induced by the Keynes effect is Y_6, an excess aggregate supply will always be present. Thus this model of a perfectly competitive economy will not have a stable full-employment equilibrium.

In summary, in this section we have examined two models of a perfectly competitive economy that do not exhibit stable full-employment equilibria. However, we have *not* demonstrated that there is a competitive equilibrium at less than full employment, and neither did the Keynesians, contrary to what many economics textbooks say. We merely showed that, given our assumptions, it is possible for a competitive economy to have no stable price equilibrium either at full employment or at less than full employment. As Gottfried Haberler pointed out many years ago, the price level in the models just described will fall to zero and the system will presumably collapse.[4] To eliminate the necessity for this collapse and thus rescue the model, Keynesians introduced the assumption of downwardly rigid money wages. This assumption results in a model that is no longer perfectly competitive in all markets. Even before publication of *The General Theory,* an economy characterized by such a model was long recognized as not having a stable full-employment equilibrium; however, it was generally held that if price and wage flexibility could be attained, then full employment would automatically occur. The importance of the preceding examples is that they challenge this pre-Keynesian notion by demonstrating that policies designed to increase price and wage flexibility may actually worsen rather than improve economic conditions.

11-3   Keynesian Policy for an Unstable Economy

From the foregoing analysis of a perfectly competitive economy, the Keynesians reached the following conclusions regarding government policies to be pursued in a depression:

1. Policies designed to increase wage and price flexibility are ineffective and possibly incapable of returning the economy to full employment. Moreover, they may only aggravate the situation.
2. Monetary policy is likely to be an inefficient if not ineffective policy tool.
3. Fiscal policy is the only effective tool that can restore full employment with certainty.

We now examine the reasoning behind each of these conclusions.

---

[4] Gottfried Haberler, *Prosperity and Depression* (Geneva: League of Nations, 1941), p. 500. Franco Modigliani was also aware of this result, as shown in his famous article "Liquidity Preference and the Theory of Money," *Econometrica* **12** (January 1944), 74.

Wage and Price Flexibility

The Keynesians believed that even in the perfectly competitive economy of the textbook world, a stable full-employment equilibrium may be impossible once a depression occurs. Even if wage and price flexibility can be increased, in the imperfectly competitive economy of the real world there is no guarantee that a stable full-employment equilibrium will result. In fact, the Keynesians felt that policies designed to increase wage and price flexibility could even worsen economic conditions and therefore discouraged such policies. From a practical point of view, an increase in the short-run flexibility of wages and prices would require a restructuring of the economy—a difficult and time-consuming process. The economic conditions of the times dictated the pursuit of only those policies that would quickly and surely bring about an increase in national income.

Monetary Policy

If we assume that wages and prices are inflexible downward, then there is no reason why the real quantity of money cannot be increased by an expansionary monetary policy that increases the nominal money supply. In this situation, monetary policy can shift the money supply curve to the right to produce a real-balance effect that in turn shifts the *LM* curve to the right, increasing aggregate demand. However, if either of the two special conditions discussed in Section 11-2 hold, then monetary policy will not achieve full-employment equilibrium. Instead, there will be what we can call a *less than full-employment stable disequilibrium condition*.[5]

This less than full-employment stable disequilibrium is possible because money wages are assumed to be rigid downward, producing an aggregate supply curve like the one we derived in Figure 2-8(c), page 27. But before we can explain why monetary policy may have only a limited influence on aggregate demand, we must determine what happens to the aggregate demand curve when the nominal money supply is increased.

In Figure 11-3(a) money demand curves are graphed for the special Keynesian condition where a liquidity trap is present at the critical rate of interest i_c. If the initial nominal money supply is M_s, we can vary the price level to obtain various real money supply curves, as shown in Figure 11-3(a). Each of these real money supply

---

[5] We call this a disequilibrium condition because in a market where money wages are rigid downward, if the real wage exceeds the equilibrium real wage, then the quantity of labor supplied exceeds the quantity of labor demanded. If less than full employment exists, the market is not cleared. An excess supply of workers exists at the going money-wage rate, but there is no tendency for the money wage to decrease, so that this market remains uncleared. The definition of equilibrium given in footnote 3 is not satisfied, and hence we are in disequilibrium. In terms of our aggregate demand and supply curves, however, this condition of disequilibrium is stable, because any small deviation from the point of their intersection automatically produces forces that return the economy to the original disequilibrium. Many economists call this *underemployment equilibrium,* because their definition of equilibrium is a condition in which "there will be no tendency for income, employment, and output to change" (Modigliani, "Liquidity Preference and the Theory of Interest and Money," p. 66).

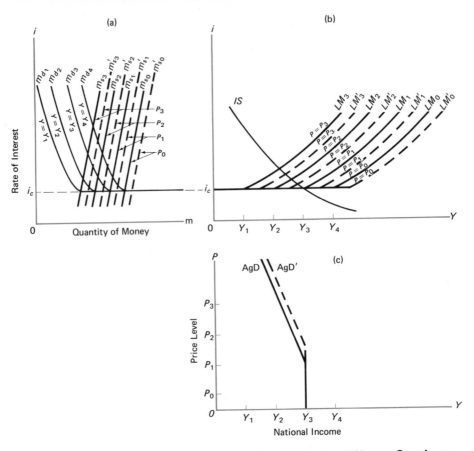

FIGURE 11-3 *The Effect of an Increase in the Nominal Money Supply on Aggregate Demand*

curves m_{s_0}, m_{s_1}, m_{s_2}, and m_{s_3} corresponds to one of four price levels P_0, P_1, P_2, and P_3. We can now construct the respective LM curves LM_0, LM_1, LM_2, and LM_3 in Figure 11-3(b) just as we did in Figure 10-12. The intersections of these LM curves with the IS curve in Figure 11-3(b) determine the levels of aggregate demand that correspond to the assumed price levels. When these levels of aggregate demand are plotted against their respective price levels, we obtain the solid aggregate demand curve AgD graphed in Figure 11-3(c). This curve becomes price inelastic at price levels below P_1, because at and below this price level the IS curve intersects the LM curves in their horizontal or liquidity-trap portions.

Now suppose that the central bank increases nominal high-powered money by means of an open-market operation that increases the nominal money supply from M_s to M_s'. This will shift *all* the real money supply curves in Figure 11-3(a) to the right, as indicated by the dashed curves m_{s_0}', m_{s_1}', m_{s_2}', and m_{s_3}'. These new real money supply curves, one for each of our four assumed price levels, produce the new LM curves LM_0', LM_1', LM_2', and LM_3', which are graphed as dashed lines in Figure 11-3(b). The intersections of these new LM curves with the IS curve will produce an increase in aggregate demand as long as the LM curves intersect the IS curve at a rate of interest above i_c, which is the liquidity-trap rate. Once the IS curve intersects these new LM curves in the liquidity-trap region, any further increase in aggregate demand is impossible. The new aggregate demand curve resulting from this increase in high-powered money is graphed as the dashed line AgD′ in Figure 11-3(c). We can now see that increasing the nominal money supply causes the aggregate demand curve to shift upward to the right, being limited in its rightward movement in this instance by the liquidity trap. Thus AgD′ becomes perfectly price inelastic at a price level somewhere between P_2 and P_1 and at national income level Y_3. Additional increases in the nominal quantity of money will produce aggregate demand curves that will be higher than AgD′ and that will also become price inelastic at income level Y_3 but at higher price levels. Under conditions of investment insufficiency rather than of the liquidity trap, the effect of expansionary monetary policy on the aggregate demand curve will produce essentially the same results. Demonstration of this is left as an exercise for the student.

We can now investigate the effectiveness of monetary policy when any of the special Keynesian conditions hold. A downwardly rigid money-wage aggregate supply curve AgS is graphed in Figure 11-4. Now suppose that a rather severe depression has occurred. The marginal efficiency of investment curve has dropped inward toward the origin, and the resulting aggregate demand curve is AgD_1. The level of national income is Y_1 at price level P_1.

Because the intersection of AgD_1 and AgS occurs in the price-elastic portion of the aggregate demand curve, expansionary monetary policy can increase the level of income by shifting the aggregate demand curve upward, as shown in Figure 11-3. Suppose that the nominal money supply is increased, shifting the aggregate demand curve from AgD_1 to AgD_2. As we can see in Figure 11-4, this monetary policy increases the stable disequilibrium level of national income to Y_2 via the real-balance effect and raises the price level to P_2. If money wages are held constant, a rise in the price level produces a decline in the real wage of workers. This means that additional workers are employed, increasing the quantity of output supplied from Y_1 to Y_2. An additional increase in the nominal money supply will shift the aggregate demand curve upward to AgD_3, and a stable disequilibrium will prevail at the higher price level P_3 and at a national income level of Y_3. At this higher price level more workers will be employed as the real wage continues to decrease, but an excess labor supply will still exist.

Further increases in the nominal money supply cannot continue to expand output and employment as a result of either investment insufficiency or the liquidity trap. If the nominal money supply is increased so that the aggregate demand shifts upward to AgD_4 in Figure 11-4, then the point at which this curve intersects AgS will be the same point at which the aggregate demand curve AgD_3 intersects AgS. The expansion of the stable disequilibrium level of national income reaches its maximum at Y_3 when the aggregate supply curve intersects the aggregate demand

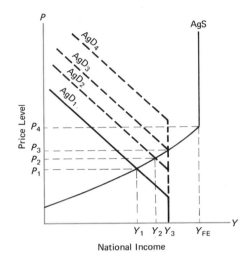

FIGURE 11-4 *The Effect of Monetary Policy on the Level of Less Than Full-employment Stable Disequilibrium Income When Keynesian Conditions Prevail*

curve in its perfectly inelastic portion. The price level reaches a maximum at P_3, and increases in employment cease as the real wage stops falling.

In this subsection we have shown that under either of the two special Keynesian conditions, monetary policy *may* be incapable of restoring the economy to full-employment equilibrium. Obviously, if the vertical portion of the aggregate demand curve were positioned to the right of full-employment national income, then nothing could prevent monetary policy from eliminating unemployment caused by rigid money wages, but the Keynesians did not feel that this condition would occur in a severe depression. While not completely discounting the help that monetary policy might provide in returning the economy to the full-employment level, the Keynesians, following the foregoing reasoning, advocated fiscal policy as the only *certain* method of returning to full-employment equilibrium.

Fiscal Policy

After eliminating increased price and wage flexibility and monetary expansion as effective monetary tools, the Keynesians were left with fiscal policy. At this point they proceeded to demonstrate that fiscal policy exhibits great leverage in effecting changes in aggregate demand, that is, that a very small change in fiscal policy can produce a large change in aggregate demand. Moreover, the Keynesians argued that fiscal policy would always be successful in restoring full employment.

Now suppose that a condition of less than full-employment stable disequilibrium prevails and that the interest rate is equal to the critical rate of interest i_c. In other

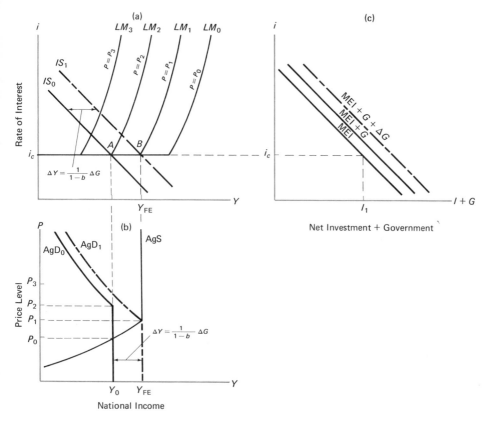

FIGURE 11-5   *The Effect of Fiscal Policy on Aggregate Demand: the Level of Investment Remaining Constant*

words, suppose that we are in the liquidity trap. This situation is illustrated in Figure 11-5(a), where the initial *IS* curve IS_0 intersects the given set of *LM* curves in the liquidity trap at all price levels less than or equal to P_2. The resulting aggregate demand curve AgD_0 in Figure 11-5(b) is, as we have previously demonstrated, perfectly price inelastic at all price levels less than or equal to P_2. The aggregate supply curve AgS intersects AgD_0 in its perfectly price-inelastic portion at price level P_0 and at the less than full-employment level of income Y_0.

To return the economy to full employment it is necessary to increase income by

$$\Delta Y = Y_{FE} - Y_0 \tag{11-1}$$

Now suppose that this increase in income is to be produced by fiscal policy in the form of increased government expenditure. By how much should G be increased? We can use the government spending multiplier derived in Chapter 4 to calculate the required increase. Assuming that we have exogenous taxes, the relevant government spending multiplier, given by equation (4-18), is

$$\mu_G = \frac{\Delta Y}{\Delta G} = \frac{1}{1-b} \tag{4-18}$$

If this multiplier is correct, then the required increase in government expenditure will be

$$\Delta G = (1-b)\Delta Y = (1-b)(Y_{FE} - Y_0) \tag{11-2}$$

From our discussion of the properties of the *IS* curve in Chapter 7, we know that if government expenditure is increased by ΔG, then the *IS* curve will shift horizontally to the right by an amount equal to $\Delta Y = [1/(1-b)]\Delta G$. This shift is shown in Figure 11-5(a) by the dashed post-government-expenditure *IS* curve IS_1. Because IS_1 intersects the *LM* curve LM_1 at the critical rate of interest i_c, IS_1 simultaneously intersects all other *LM* curves that represent price levels less than P_1. The aggregate demand curve AgD_1 produced by the intersections of IS_1 with the set of *LM* curves is shown in Figure 11-5(b). The price-inelastic portion of AgD_0 shifts to the right by $\Delta Y = [1/(1-b)]\Delta G$ and becomes price elastic at exactly the same price level at which the aggregate supply curve becomes perfectly price inelastic. Thus we have achieved full-employment equilibrium at price level P_1 and at interest rate i_c.

We can now see why the Keynesians considered fiscal policy such a powerful instrument. If the marginal propensity to consume b is 0.8, for example, then a $1 increase in government spending will produce a $5 increase in income, since

$$\Delta Y = \frac{1}{1-0.8}(\$1) = \$5 \tag{11-3}$$

If the government chooses to increase national income by means of a tax cut rather than by increased expenditure, the required reduction will be

$$-\Delta T = \frac{1-b}{b}\Delta Y \tag{11-4}$$

if taxes are exogenous. If we assume once again that $b = 0.8$, then a $1 reduction in taxes will produce a $4 increase in income.

Suppose, however, that neither of the investment insufficiency and liquidity-trap conditions discussed in Section 11-2 exists and that the situation illustrated in Figure 11-6 prevails instead. The *LM* curves LM_0, LM_1, LM_2, and LM_3 in Figure 11-6(a) are asymptotic to the horizontal axis, indicating that no liquidity trap occurs at any positive rate of interest. Similarly, the initial *IS* curve IS_0 is asymptotic to the horizontal axis, indicating that investment insufficiency cannot occur. The resulting initial aggregate demand curve AgD_0 is shown in Figure 11-6(b), where it intersects the aggregate supply curve AgS at price level P_0 and at a less than full-employment stable disequilibrium level of income Y_0.

Now suppose that the fiscal policy prescription in the preceding example is followed here. Because the desired increase in the level of income, which is

$Y_{FE} - Y_0$, is the same as before, it seems logical to assume that the same increase in government expenditure ΔG will restore full employment. Suppose that this increase in government expenditure does take place, shifting the IS curve to the right by an amount equal to $[1/(1 - b)]\Delta G$ to give IS_1 in Figure 11-6(a), just as in Figure 11-5(a). The newly produced aggregate demand curve AgD_1 lies to the right of AgD_0 in Figure 11-6(b), but the horizontal shift ΔAgD is less than $[1/(1 - b)]\Delta G$, unlike the perfectly price-inelastic portion of the aggregate demand curve in Figure 11-5(b), which shifts to the right by exactly $[1/(1 - b)]\Delta G$. Furthermore, the actual increase in income $Y_1 - Y_0$ is even less than the amount by which the aggregate demand curve shifts horizontally.

Thus we have not achieved full employment as our multiplier theory postulated. This theory seems to work satisfactorily when a liquidity trap exists; so why has it failed here? The answer can be found by comparing the intersection points A and B of the IS and LM curves in Figure 11-5(a) with intersection points A' and B' in Figure 11-6(a). In Figure 11-5(a), point A, which determines the original less than

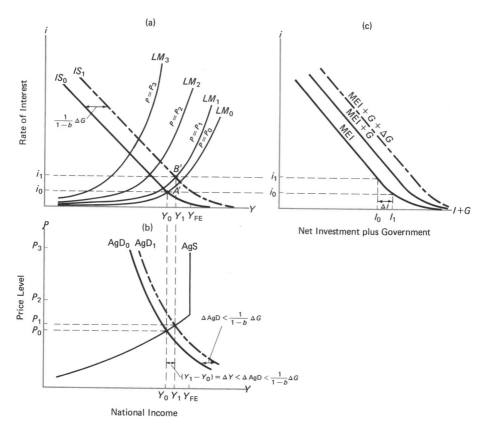

FIGURE 11-6   *The Effect of Fiscal Policy on Aggregate Demand: the Level of Investment Declining*

full-employment level of income, and point B, which determines the new level of income after fiscal policy is employed, both occur in the liquidity trap and therefore at the same rate of interest i_c. On the other hand, points A' and B' in Figure 11-6(a), which correspond to points A and B in terms of fiscal policy, do *not* occur at the same interest rate. The implication of this observation is that the government spending multiplier μ_G in Figure 11-5 is an accurate predictor of changes in income level, because interest rates and therefore net investment remain constant, as shown in Figure 11-5(c). In Figure 11-6, however, when government spending increases, the interest rate rises from i_0 to i_1. This rise in the interest rate occurs because the *LM* curves are positively sloped and also because the accompanying rise in the price level causes the real money supply to decrease. The increase in the interest rate causes a movement upward along the MEI curve in Figure 11-6, and net investment declines by ΔI. Thus government expenditure rises by ΔG, but investment falls by ΔI, and the net expansionary effect of ΔG on income is reduced. Given this line of reasoning, the results in Figure 11-6 are not at all surprising and serve to emphasize the fact that the multipliers we derived in Chapters 3 and 4 are in fact *naive* in that they yield correct results only when the level of net investment remains constant.

If we had chosen to examine the investment insufficiency case rather than the liquidity-trap case, we could have used the naive multipliers to predict the required increase in government expenditure or the reduction in taxation, provided the accompanying rise in the interest rate remained within the range of rates where the MEI curve is vertical. The demonstration of this statement is left as an exercise for the student.

Although Keynes himself was aware that fiscal policy could have an adverse effect on investment and that it would not produce the results indicated by the naive multipliers, the Keynesians tended to overlook this fact. They often made exaggerated claims regarding the leverage that fiscal policy can exert, at the same time denigrating the effectiveness of monetary policy. Only in recent years have these claims begun to disappear from the literature.

11-4   Price Flexibility and Full Employment Revisited

After the Keynesians had demonstrated that a perfectly competitive economy may not have a stable equilibrium at full employment, other economists, particularly Gottfried Haberler and A.C. Pigou, came forward to challenge this conclusion.[6] They suggested that the Keynesians had neglected the real-balance effect on the behavior of individuals. Basically, Haberler and Pigou argued that if we assume that both disposable income and wealth influence the level of consumption, then we can write the consumption function

---

[6] Gottfried Haberler, *Prosperity and Depression* (Geneva: League of Nations, 1941), pp. 242, 389, 403, and 491–503; and A.C. Pigou, "The Classical Stationary State," *Economic Journal* **LIII** (1943), 343–51.

$$C = C(Y_d, W) \qquad (11\text{-}5)$$

Real cash balances are part of an individual's stock of wealth, but unlike physical wealth (the nominal value of which rises or falls with the general price level), the nominal value of money remains constant and its real value moves inversely with the price level.[7] For example, if prices double, the purchasing power of $100 is cut in half, and vice versa. If these real cash balances are net financial assets of the entire economy (that is, financial claims against which there are no offsetting liabilities), then changes in the price level will affect net wealth. If the price level were to fall, as it would during a depression in a perfectly competitive economy, then the magnitude of real cash balances would increase, net wealth would rise, and the desire to consume out of a given income would rise.

As consumption increases, the *IS* curve shifts to the right and aggregate demand increases. In other words, a real-balance effect occurs in the household sector, increasing aggregate demand as the price level falls. If the price level rises, then the opposite effect will occur and aggregate demand will fall. This particular form of the real-balance effect has become known as the *Pigou effect*.

The Pigou effect has great theoretical importance, because once our model has been modified to incorporate this real-balance effect, the Keynesians' demonstration that a perfectly competitive economy may not have a stable full-employment equilibrium is undermined. To understand why this is true, consider the special Keynesian case of the liquidity trap, which in the absence of the Pigou effect prevents a stable full-employment equilibrium, as we saw in Figure 11-2.

Figure 11-7 demonstrates the result of adding the Pigou effect to the consumption–savings relationship. As the price level falls from P_3 to P_0, real cash balances and net wealth rise, the short-run consumption function shifts upward, and concomitantly the short-run savings function shifts downward. As the savings function shifts in Figure 11-7(a) with each change in price level, a new *IS* curve corresponding to each new price level is produced in Figure 11-7(b). Each new change in the price level also produces the money-market equilibrium curves LM_0, LM_1, LM_2, and LM_3 graphed in Figure 11-7(b). The intersection of an *IS* curve for a given price level with the corresponding *LM* curve gives us the level of aggregate demand at that price level. These points of intersection are labeled A, B, C, and D in Figure 11-7(b). The respective points on the aggregate demand curve, which is generated by variations in the price level, are labeled A', B', C', and D' in Figure 11-7(c).

An inspection of Figure 11-7(c) reveals that the presence of the Pigou effect in the commodity market gives us a price-elastic aggregate demand curve and produces a perfectly competitive model that is stable at the full-employment level, despite the presence of a liquidity trap. If instead of using the liquidity-trap case, we

---

[7] There is some debate at present as to what portion of the total money supply should be considered net wealth. The majority opinion is that currency, coin, and some as yet undetermined fraction of demand deposits can be considered representative of net wealth. For a more detailed discussion of this issue see: Harry G. Johnson, "Inside Money, Outside Money, Income, Wealth, and Welfare in Monetary Theory," *Journal of Money Credit and Banking*, 1: 1 (February 1969), 30–45.

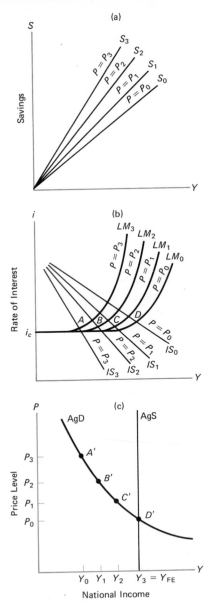

FIGURE 11-7   The Pigou Effect and Full-employment Equilibrium

had chosen to examine the consequences of the presence of the Pigou effect in the investment insufficiency case, our conclusions would have been the same.

In summary, we can say that the Pigou effect is of extreme theoretical importance, because it produces a stable full-employment equilibrium in a perfectly

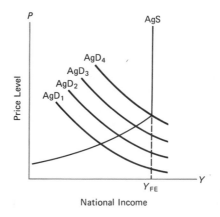

FIGURE 11-8   *Monetary Policy Implications of the Pigou Effect*

competitive economy. In an economy characterized by money wages that are rigid downward, the addition of the Pigou effect does not ensure full-employment equilibrium, and it is possible for such an economy to be in a state of stable disequilibrium at less than full employment. However, the importance of the Pigou effect is not diminished even when wages are rigid downward; its presence ensures that monetary policy will always be effective, because this policy can directly increase the net wealth of households. This conclusion is evident when we consider the aggregate demand curve in Figure 11-7(c). The addition of the Pigou effect to the model results in an aggregate demand curve that is price elastic everywhere, even if either the liquidity trap or investment insufficiency exists. Thus, expansionary monetary policy, which shifts the aggregate demand curve to the right, will never produce the results illustrated in Figure 11-4, but will produce the results given in Figure 11-8. Therefore, the Pigou effect destroys the Keynesian argument against monetary policy.

11-5   Likelihood of Investment Insufficiency and the Liquidity Trap

In Section 11-2, we examined two special conditions suggested by the Keynesians that might, in the absence of the Pigou effect, prevent a stable full-employment equilibrium. The first condition hypothesizes a situation in which the level of desired investment at full employment, even at a zero rate of interest, is less than the level of desired savings at full employment. The second condition is an aggregate demand curve for money that becomes infinitely elastic at some interest rate greater than zero. In this section we analyze the likelihood that either of these special conditions will hold in reality.

Investment Insufficiency

In our analysis of the theory of investment in Chapter 5 we demonstrated that any capital project, such as land reclamation, that is long-lived and has an annual positive net rate of return will become profitable at some positive rate of interest. For the investment project we considered (creating farming land along the continental shelf in the Gulf of Mexico), the cost of the project is equivalent to about 50 years' worth of full-employment investment. In addition to this project there are several others of equal magnitude available. As Martin Bailey has observed: All these investments together assure a huge backlog of investment opportunities at low rates of yield on equity investment. Even if expectations were so bad that gross investment of the current types fell to zero, and even if business were not expected to improve for 10 or 20 years, there would be some positive rate of interest low enough to make these investments worthwhile given their durability.[8] It is therefore unlikely that an MEI curve of the type illustrated in Figure 11-1 could occur in the foreseeable future.

Liquidity Trap

The liquidity-trap concept has been labeled by many Keynesians as one of Keynes's most important contributions. Keynes himself, however, did not believe that the occurrence of absolute liquidity preference was particularly likely. Writing in 1935, when the interest rate in the United States was 0.137% per annum on 90-day treasury bills, Keynes could still remark that "whilst this limiting case [the trap] might become practically important in the future, I know of no example of it hitherto."[9]

For decades theoretical economists have discussed whether a liquidity trap is even possible. Theoretical models have been constructed that purport to prove that the trap is impossible; alternative models purport to prove that the trap can exist. However, this issue cannot be settled by a priori reasoning; it can be resolved only by empirical research.

Early empirical research by James Tobin on liquidity preference functions seemed to indicate that a liquidity trap was present in the United States during the great depression at an interest rate of about 2%.[10] Later work by Bronfenbrenner and Mayer reversed this finding.[11] They tested the hypothesis that the interest elasticity of the demand for money increased as interest rates decreased. The results of their research, which included data from the great depression when interest rates were quite low, indicated no tendency for the interest elasticity of the demand for money to increase, much less become infinite, as the interest rate became smaller. Subsequent empirical research on the nature of the demand for money has supported the basic findings of Bronfenbrenner and Mayer.

[8] M.J. Bailey, *National Income and the Price Level*, Second Edition (New York: McGraw-Hill, 1971), pp. 143–44.

[9] J.M. Keynes, *The General Theory*, p. 207.

[10] James Tobin, "Liquidity Preference and Monetary Policy," *Review of Economics and Statistics* **29** (May 1947), 124–31.

[11] Martin Bronfenbrenner and Thomas Mayer, "Liquidity Functions in the American Economy," *Econometrica* **28** (October 1960), 810–34.

In summary, it does not appear likely that either of the two special conditions hypothesized by the Keynesians have occurred in the past or that can they be expected to occur in the foreseeable future. Thus even in the absence of the Pigou effect, a perfectly competitive economy will be stable at the full-employment level of income. But this does not settle the issue as a practical matter. Even if it is true that the free market forces will eventually restore full employment if left to themselves, it should be emphasized that reliance on price and wage flexibility to accomplish this from the depths of a *severe recession* in an imperfectly competitive real world may require a time interval that is far too long to be acceptable. In this situation, monetary and fiscal policy should be employed.

11-6   Concluding Remarks

In this chapter we have examined the modern macroeconomic analysis of employment, which is rooted in *The General Theory* of John Maynard Keynes. However, in this chapter we have based our analysis mainly on the interpretations, revisions, and extensions of the *Keynesians*.

According to the Keynesians, two special conditions—*investment insufficiency* and the *liquidity trap*—could prevent a perfectly competitive economy from having a stable full-employment equilibrium and produce an economy with no equilibrium at all. Introducing the premise of downwardly rigid wages ensured the Keynesians of a model with a stable price and income level, but this model was in permanent disequilibrium because the labor market was never cleared. As a result of this analysis the Keynesians reached the conclusion that fiscal policy was the only feasible method for controlling what they believed to be a basically unstable economy. Critics of the Keynesians countered with the Pigou effect, which undermined the theoretical Keynesian arguments related to long-run equilibrium in a perfectly competitive economy. However, when wages and prices are rigid downward, both the Keynesians and their critics agreed that the Pigou effect contributes virtually nothing to an automatic return to full-employment equilibrium. Even if prices and wages are somewhat flexible, the magnitude of the Pigou effect is probably too small to be of practical significance. However, the Pigou effect does mean that monetary policy can restore full employment even if the special Keynesian conditions prevail. Moreover, recent research indicates that neither of these conditions has actually held in this century, and it seems unlikely that they will be encountered in the foreseeable future. Thus there appears to be little basis for the views of those who reject monetary policy completely and who advocate a virtually exclusive reliance on fiscal instruments of stabilization policy.

12 Inflation

12-1 Introduction

In the preceding chapters we have concentrated primarily on the problem of unemployment for three reasons. First, the development of the branch of economic theory now known as macroeconomics began with the publication in 1936 of Keynes's *The General Theory.* At that time unemployment was the primary economic problem in the industrial nations and therefore the topic to which Keynes addressed himself. Keynes was well aware that the policy prescriptions he offered to alleviate unemployment could not be successfully employed during inflationary periods, but his followers, the so-called Keynesians, erroneously believed that fiscal policy could cure inflation as well. Second, many economists and politicians since the 1930s have considered the problem of unemployment to be of greater social importance than the problem of inflation. This judgment was not shared by Keynes, who observed that "There is no subtler, no surer means of overturning the existing basis of society than to debauch the currency. The process engages all the hidden forces of economic law on the side of destruction ...." Third, the simultaneous occurrence of unemployment *and* inflation was an event most economists felt was unlikely to occur—until it happened.

In this chapter we explore the theory of inflation, examine some of the possible causes of inflation, and consider the relationship between unemployment and inflation.

226

12-2   Demand-pull Inflation

When there is a high level of employment, an increase in aggregate demand usually produces inflationary pressures in the economy. Inflation caused by a shift in the aggregate demand curve is called *demand-pull inflation.* An increase in demand can originate in the real sector or in the monetary sector, or in some combination of these two. First, we examine an increase in demand that originates in the real sector. Throughout this and the next section we retain our earlier assumption that the expected future price level is always the existing price level. In addition, to simplify our analysis without altering any of its basic conclusions, we assume that the Pigou effect portion of the real-balance effect is not present.

Inflation Originating in the Real Sector

When an economy is at or near full employment, an increase in aggregate demand usually results in an excess aggregate demand that in turn causes the price level to rise until equilibrium is restored. Although it is possible for this increase in aggregate demand to originate in the household sector or the business sector (rather than in the government sector), this does not usually happen, because the private sectors lack the authority to tax and to print money. Households and business firms can increase their aggregate demand only by drawing on accumulated savings or by borrowing. Both of these methods are self-limiting and will probably produce only a minor increase in demand. Because government has the power to tax and to print money as well as the ability to borrow from the public, it can often be a source of inflationary pressure. For this reason, in this subsection we concentrate on inflation that originates in the government sector.

Suppose that we are initially in the state of full-employment equilibrium illustrated in Figure 12-1. The level of investment *plus* government expenditure is given by the MEI + G curve in Figure 12-1(a). The savings function, plotted against national income when there are no taxes, is given by curve S in Figure 12-1(c). Given that taxes T are equal to G, the relevant savings function becomes S'. This is simply curve S shifted to the right by an amount T, so that savings, which is a function of disposable income, can be plotted against national income. The curve giving the level of savings *plus* taxes for any level of income is $S' + T$, which is obtained by adding the amount of the tax T vertically to S'. The MEI + G and the $S' + T$ curves yield the initial IS curve IS_1 graphed in Figure 12-1(d). Also shown in Figure 12-1(d) are the three LM curves LM_1, LM_2, and LM_3, whose subscripts designate the respective price levels P_1, P_2, and P_3 to which each curve applies. The intersection of these LM curves with the initial IS curve IS_1 produces the initial aggregate demand curve AgD_1 in Figure 12-1(e). The intersection of AgD_1 with the full-employment aggregate supply curve AgS in Figure 12-1(e) gives us our initial full-employment equilibrium conditions. Specifically, the level of income is Y_{FE} at price level P_2. The interest rate is the natural rate of interest i_N that prevails in Figure 12-1(d).

Now suppose that there is an increase in autonomous government expenditure by an amount ΔG, as shown in Figure 12-1(a), and that this increase is financed by

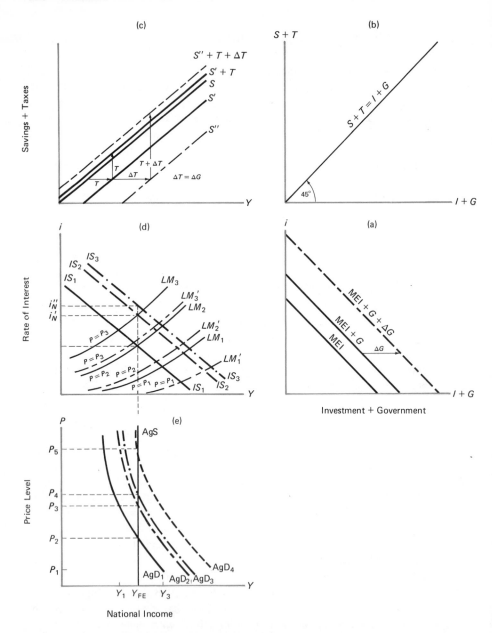

FIGURE 12-1   The Effect of Increased Government Expenditure on the Price Level When Alternative Methods of Financing Are Employed

an increase in taxes of $\Delta T = \Delta G$. Because total taxes are now $T + \Delta T$, the relevant savings function in Figure 12-1(c) becomes S'' and the curve that represents savings *plus* taxes is therefore $S'' + T + \Delta T$. This curve in conjunction with the

MEI + G + ΔG curve gives us the new IS curve IS_2. The intersection of IS_2 with the original set of LM curves yields a new aggregate demand curve AgD_2, which intersects the AgS curve in Figure 12-1(e) at the higher equilibrium price level P_3. The natural rate of interest now becomes i'_N, which is given by the point at which IS_2 intersects the LM curve LM_3 that exists at this price level at the full-employment level of aggregate demand.

Instead of financing its increased expenditure by raising taxes, the government could raise the necessary revenue by the sale of bonds to the public sector. This means that the relevant savings *plus* taxes curve reverts to $S' + T$ in Figure 12-1(c), and using the MEI + G + ΔG curve, we now obtain the IS curve IS_3. The intersection of IS_3 with the original set of LM curves increases aggregate demand, shifting the curve to AgD_3. The equilibrium price level now rises to P_4, and the natural rate of interest increases to i''_N.

The government can also raise the money needed for the increased expenditure by a method equivalent to printing it. In the United States, the Department of the Treasury can sell government bonds to the Federal Reserve, which in return creates bank deposits in the Treasury's account, or equivalently, prints Federal Reserve notes and exchanges them for the bonds. Whereas theoretically the government must pay interest on these bonds, in practice it does not. The Federal Reserve pays its stockholders (the member commercial banks) a fixed percentage on their investment and, after deducting operations costs, returns *all* excess revenue to the Treasury. Thus, in effect, the sale of bonds by the Treasury to the Federal Reserve is a costless operation identical to merely printing money, provided the Federal Reserve is willing to absorb these additional bonds and does not sell them to the public. All such money is high-powered money, which becomes part of the monetary base from which commercial banks can expand the money supply.

Let us assume that the government deficit is financed by simply printing the money, so that the resulting inflation originates in the real sector but is produced by a combination of monetary and fiscal operations. High-powered money will increase by an amount equal to ΔG, so that the nominal money supply increases by some multiple of ΔG, as we saw in Chapter 8. As we demonstrated in Chapter 11, an increase in the nominal money supply will shift the set of LM curves in Figure 12-1(d) to the right, producing the new set of curves LM'_1, LM'_2, and LM'_3. The intersection of these new LM curves with IS_3 gives us the new aggregate demand curve AgD_4, which determines the new and higher equulibrium price level P_5. Because the IS curve does not shift but remains at S_3, the interest rate at the full-employment level of income remains at i''_N.

From the preceding analysis we can conclude that the least inflationary means of financing an increase in government expenditure is to increase taxes by an equal amount, but even such an increase is inflationary. The only way to avoid inflation is to increase taxes by some amount greater than the increase in expenditure. The next least inflationary method is to obtain the required money by selling bonds to the public and thereby maintain a constant nominal money supply. By far the most inflationary method is to print an amount of money equal to the increase in government expenditure. In fact, this method of financing the deficit is even more inflationary than the one just described, because we have shown only what Friedman calls the "first-round effect."[1] As long as the deficit persists, the government will increase the quantity of high-powered money in each successive expenditure period and the price level will continue to rise. This will not be the case if either of the other two methods of expenditure financing is employed, and the first-round inflationary effect illustrated in Figure 12-1 will be the final effect.

It is important to keep in mind that these conclusions are based on a model of an economy whose output is constant in the short run. As long as we have net investment, the capital stock will grow and, with it, income. Thus it is entirely possible that within a dynamic framework, increases in government expenditure may be less than or more than those required to maintain a stable price level.

In this subsection we have limited our analysis of inflation originating in the real sector to government expenditure. Of course, a shift of the *IS* curve to the right could also be produced by a rightward shift to the MEI curve or a downward shift of the savings function. However, neither firms nor individuals have the legal power to tax or to print money, so that their increased expenditures would have to be taken either from past and present savings or from borrowed funds. The net effect on the aggregate demand curve would be analogous to the case when increased government expenditure is financed by the sale of bonds. Because private savings are fixed and rising interest rates limit the borrowing capacity of the private sector, it is unlikely that the private sector will be a source of major and sustained inflation. However, one condition can invalidate this generalization. Suppose that the central bank pursues a policy of maintaining the interest rate below a specified value. If there is an increase in aggregate demand originating in the private sector and the market rate of interest rises above the central bank's maximum allowable rate, then the bank will increase the nominal money supply in an attempt to lower the interest rate. The increase in the money supply allows aggregate demand to increase, so that once again the price level and the interest rate rise, and once again the central bank increases the nominal money supply. As long as the central bank pursues this policy, inflation will persist.

Inflation Originating in the Monetary Sector

We have analyzed how an increase in aggregate demand originating in the government, household, or business sectors can cause inflation when the economy is at or near full employment. We have also learned how this inflation will be worsened if the actions of government, business, or households are aided and abetted by an increase in the money supply. We now demonstrate how the monetary authorities can initiate an increase in aggregate demand that subsequently causes inflation.

Suppose that we are originally in a state of full-employment equilibrium, as depicted in Figure 12-2. The equilibrium rate of interest is the natural interest rate

[1] Milton Friedman, "Comments on the Critics," in "Symposium on Friedman's Theoretical Framework," *Journal of Political Economy* **80** (September/October 1972), 916–17.

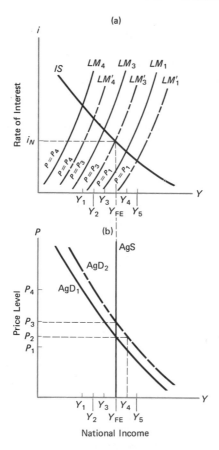

FIGURE 12-2   *The Effect of an Increase in the Nominal Money Supply on the Equilibrium Price Level and the Interest Rate*

i_N shown in Figure 12-2(a); the equilibrium price level P_2 is shown in Figure 12-2(b). Now assume that for some reason the nominal money supply is increased by the central bank, so that the original LM curves LM_1, LM_3, and LM_4 all shift to the right[2] to become LM'_1, LM'_3, and LM'_4.

As an immediate consequence of the increase in the nominal money supply, the aggregate demand curve shifts to AgD_2, where at price level P_2 the excess aggregate demand is $Y_4 - Y_{FE}$ and individuals hold excess real cash balances. As individual wealth holders attempt to dispose of their excess real cash balances, the price level rises. The market rate of interest is below the natural interest rate immediately after the increase in the nominal money supply, producing a rise in desired investment that further increases the pressure on the price level. As the

[2] The LM curve corresponding to price level P_2 (that is, LM_2) is omitted from Figure 12-2(a) for clarity. If it were drawn, it would coincide with LM'_3.

price level rises, the real money supply shrinks and the market rate of interest begins to return to the natural interest rate. This process continues as long as there is any excess demand. When the economy achieves equilibrium again, the price level is determined by the intersection of the aggregate demand curve and the aggregate supply curve, or P_3 in this example. The price level must rise in proportion to the increase in the nominal money supply; otherwise, an excess of real cash balances would continue to exist. As long as there are excess real cash balances, the price level will continue to rise. However, the interest rate returns to the equilibrium or natural interest rate determined by the *IS* curve when income is at the full-employment level. Thus the natural interest rate in this model is determined exclusively by the real sector and cannot be influenced by the monetary sector. If the central bank refuses to accept this result and attempts to peg the interest rate below the natural rate, then continuous inflation will result as the monetary authorities repeatedly increase the nominal money supply in their attempt to prevent the interest rate from rising.

12-3   Cost-push Inflation

Thus far all the inflations we have analyzed have resulted from a shift in the aggregate demand curve. For this reason we call them *demand-pull inflations.* In this section we consider inflation that results from a shift of the aggregate supply curve, which is usually referred to as *cost-push inflation.* Cost-push inflation arguments are usually associated with nonmonetary forces and imperfectly competitive aggregate supply models. Here we examine two cost-push arguments that are based on market imperfections in either the demand for labor or the supply of labor.

Imperfect Competition and the Demand for Labor

Many people view the American economy as a far cry from the textbook economy of perfect competition. It is argued that economic power is concentrated in the hands of a few sellers, enabling monopolistic firms to raise prices whenever they please; mass advertising based on motivational psychology is then employed to persuade the consumer to buy products at these prices.[3]

Initially, we assume that perfect competition prevails in both the demand for and the supply of labor. These assumptions are illustrated in Figures 12-3(a) and

---

[3] An exposition of this view can be found in John Kenneth Galbraith, *The New Industrial State* (Boston: Houghton Mifflin, 1967). For a critical microeconomic examination of this view, see P.L. Burgess and F.R. Glahe, "Pricing in the American Automobile Industry and the Galbraith Hypothesis," *Rivista Internazionale di Scienze Economiche e Commerciali* **XVII** (December 1970), 1176–86.

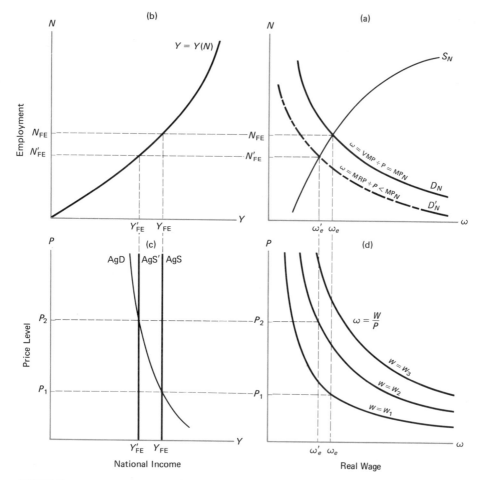

FIGURE 12-3   *Cost-push Inflation Produced by Business Monopoly Power*

12-3(d). The demand for labor curve D_N in Figure 12-3(a) specifies that the real wage paid to labor ω is equal to the value of the marginal product of labor VMP *divided by* the price level, and this in turn is equal to the marginal product of labor MP_N. In Chapter 2 we showed that in perfect competition the real wage of labor would be equal to its marginal product. This means that the D_N curve in Figure 12-3(a) is a perfectly competitive demand for labor curve. The intersection of the labor supply curve S_N with D_N in Figure 12-3(a) determines the labor market equilibrium real wage ω_e. Figure 12-3(d) tells us that money wages are flexible upward or downward and therefore that perfect competition exists in the supply of labor.

Because we have perfect competition in the demand for and the supply of labor, the level of employment will be the full-employment level N_{FE}. With employment at N_{FE}, the production function in Figure 12-3(b) specifies that the level of output is equal to the full-employment level of national income Y_{FE}. Thus, the perfectly competitive aggregate supply curve AgS in Figure 12-3(c) is produced. Given an aggregate demand of AgD, the equilibrium price level under perfect competition is P_1 and the nominal wage is W_1, as shown in Figure 12-3(d).

We now modify our assumption that the business sector is perfectly competitive and assume that imperfect competition prevails in this sector. In Chapter 2 we showed that a perfectly competitive firm will hire workers up to the point when the money wage paid to workers is exactly equal to the value of their marginal product VMP. In the context of our aggregate economic model

$$W = VMP = P \cdot MP_N \tag{12-1}$$

For a profit-maximizing, imperfectly competitive firm, however, the money (or nominal) wage paid to workers is equal to the *marginal revenue product* of labor[4] MRP. The MRP is defined as the net addition to the firm's total revenue TR due to the additional employment of one unit of labor, or

$$W = MRP = \frac{\Delta TR}{\Delta N} \tag{12-2}$$

Equivalently,

$$MRP = MR \cdot MP_N \tag{12-3}$$

where MR, the marginal revenue of the firm, is defined as the net addition to the firm's total revenue that results from a one-unit increase in the sale of the firm's total product TP, or

$$MR = \frac{\Delta TR}{\Delta TP} \tag{12-4}$$

We have previously defined the marginal product of labor by

$$MP_N = \frac{\Delta TP}{\Delta N} \tag{12-5}$$

We now can rewrite equation (12-4)

$$\Delta TR = \Delta TP \cdot MR \tag{12-6}$$

and equation (12-5)

$$\Delta N = \frac{\Delta TP}{MP_N} \tag{12-7}$$

Substituting equations (12-6) and (12-7) into (12-2), we obtain

$$W = MRP = \frac{\Delta TP \cdot MR}{\Delta TP/MP_N} = MR \cdot MP_N \tag{12-8}$$

---

[4] For a proof of this profit-maximizing condition, see C.E. Ferguson and J.P. Gould, *Microeconomic Theory*, Fourth Edition (Homewood, Ill.: Richard D. Irwin, 1975), p. 403.

This proves that equation (12-3) is equivalent to equation (12-2).

One of the most important characteristics that differentiates the imperfectly competitive firm from the perfectly competitive firm is that the former has a negatively sloped product demand curve but the latter has a horizontal one. This means that the MR of the imperfectly competitive firm is always *less than* product price and the MR of the perfectly competitive firm is always *equal to* product price.[5]

Now if we divide equation (12-8) by the price level, we obtain

$$\frac{W}{P} = \omega = \frac{MR}{P} \cdot MP_N \qquad (12\text{-}9)$$

the real wage that an imperfectly competitive firm pays to labor. Because MR is less than price in imperfect competition, it follows that the real wage paid to labor will be less than its marginal product, or

$$\omega < MP_N \qquad (12\text{-}10)$$

The extent to which ω is less than MP_N is directly related to the degree of monopolistic imperfection existing in the economy. As monopolistic imperfection increases and the economy moves further away from perfect competition, the real wage paid to workers declines relative to their marginal productivity.

We can now examine the inflationary effect of going from perfect competition to imperfect competition. We assume that there is no change in the supply side of the labor market; that is, perfect competition in the supply of labor still prevails. The demand for labor is altered, however, because firms are now imperfectly competitive. This causes the demand for labor curve in Figure 12-3(a) to shift downward to D'_N, because the real wage paid to labor will be less than its marginal product. The imperfectly competitive demand for labor curve now intersects S_N at a lower equilibrium real wage ω'_e, and the level of full employment falls to N'_{FE}. This decline in the level of full employment produces an accompanying decline in aggregate supply, and the aggregate supply curve shifts to the left, to AgS'. The equilibrium price level now rises to P_2, as shown in Figure 12-3(c), and the money wage rises to W_2, as shown in Figure 12-3(d).

---

[5] PROOF: Total revenue is price × quantity sold, or

$$TR = P \cdot Q$$

Marginal revenue is the derivative of total revenue with respect to output, or

$$MR = \frac{dTR}{dQ} = P + Q\frac{dP}{dQ}$$

Since dP/dQ is the slope of the demand curve, in perfect competition $dP/dQ = 0$ and therefore

$$MR = P$$

In imperfect competition, the slope of the demand curve is negative; that is, $dP/dQ < 0$, so that

$$MR < P$$

If we had chosen to assume in this analysis that imperfections did exist in the supply of labor (that is, that money wages are rigid downward), then it would not have altered our conclusions here in any way. This is so because the aggregate demand curve would continue to intersect the aggregate supply curve in its vertical portion after it shifts to the left.

We have just demonstrated that introducing market imperfection into our model causes a reduction in output and an increase in the price level, but it is quite another thing to attribute an observed secular rise in the price level to this phenomenon. For any given degree of market imperfection there will be a unique equilibrium price level, and profit-maximizing firms will not be motivated to increase prices. A secularly rising price level can be attributed to monopoly power only if the extent of this power continually increases over time.

There appears to be little or no empirical evidence that the extent of monopoly power in the United States has significantly increased since 1900. One way of measuring an increase or a decrease in market imperfection in an industry over time is the so-called *concentration ratio*. The concentration ratio is simply the percentage of an industry's assets (or sales, or value added, or employment) that can be assigned to the industry's four largest firms. Because an increase in monopoly power over time in an industry is generally recorded as an increase in the concentration ratio, this ratio can serve as an index of market imperfection in that industry. This is admittedly a crude measure, but it is, unfortunately, one of the best available.

Data required to calculate concentration ratios accurately did not become available until 1947; however, in a pioneering study G. Warren Nutter estimated the trend in market concentration from 1899 to 1939.[6] Nutter considered industries in which the four largest firms were responsible for at least one-half the output and then estimated the fraction of national income produced by these four firms in each industry. He concluded that from 1899 to 1939 market concentration increased only in finance, declined in transportation, manufacturing, communications, and mining, and remained constant in retail trade, services, agriculture, public utilities, and construction. In a similar study, George Stigler examined the trend of market concentration from 1900 to 1939 and reached essentially the same conclusions Nutter did.[7] In a review of the work of Nutter and Stigler, Solomon Fabricant pointed out numerous contradictions and analytical problems but nevertheless concluded that:

> . . . the essential validity of their conclusion must stand. All the doubts that can be raised do not destroy, rather they support, the conclusion that there is no basis for believing that the economy of the United States is largely monopolistic and has been growing more monopolistic.[8]

---

[6] G. Warren Nutter, *The Extent of Enterprise Monopoly in the United States, 1899–1939: A Quantitative Study of Some Aspects of Monopoly* (Chicago: University of Chicago Press, 1951).

[7] George J. Stigler, "Competition in the U.S.," *Five Lectures on Economic Problems* (London: Longmans, Green and Co., 1949).

[8] Solomon Fabricant, "Is Monopoly Increasing?" *Journal of Economic History* (Winter 1953), 93.

TABLE 12-1   Average Concentration Ratios by Type of Industry, 1947–1966

	213 Total Industries	132 Capital Goods Industries	81 Consumer Goods Industries
1966	41.9	43.4	39.6
1963	41.4	43.3	38.2
1958	40.2	43.1	35.5
1954	40.6	43.8	35.4
1947	41.2	45.1	34.8
Change, 1947–1966	0.7	-1.7	4.8

SOURCE   *Studies by the Staff of the Cabinet Committee on Price Stability* (Washington, D.C. : U.S. Government Printing Office, January 1969) , p. 58.

Since 1947 the availability and quality of data classified by industry has improved significantly, primarily due to the Census of Manufacturers conducted by the Bureau of the Census. In Table 12-1, data on the change in market concentration between 1947 and 1966 in 213 manufacturing industries are summarized. These data indicate that the average level of concentration for all industries shows no marked tendency to increase or to decrease over the period. In 1947 the average market concentration ratio was 41.2%; in 1966 it was 41.9%. If we categorize these industries by capital-goods production and consumer-goods production, then the results indicate that market concentration declined in the former and was offset by a rise in the latter.

Another way to measure the degree of competitiveness in the economy is to compute the fraction of value added in manufacturing by industries in which the four largest firms produce at least 50% of the output. The results of this computation appear in Table 12-2 for selected years from 1901 to 1970. This approach indicates that the trend in monopoly concentration in this century has been

TABLE 12-2   The Trend in Concentration in Manufacturing

	1901	1947	1954	1958	1963	1966	1970
Percentage of value added in industries with a four-firm concentration greater than 50%	32.9	24.4	29.9	30.2	33.1	28.6	26.3

SOURCE   Paul W. McCracken and Thomas Gale Moore, *Competition and Market Concentration in the American Economy*, Reprint No. 25 (Washington, D.C.: American Enterprise Institute, June 1974), p.4.

downward and, most important to the discussion in this section, that monopoly power increased from 1954 to 1963, when price stability existed in the American economy, and decreased from 1963 to 1970, when inflation prevailed. This evidence directly contradicts the theory that monopolistic firms have been the source of the recent inflation.

A different approach to the question of market concentration and inflation is to compare pricing behavior in concentrated industries with that in nonconcentrated industries. Steven Lustgarten did just this for the period from 1954 to 1973 and concluded that an inverse correlation exists between industry concentration and price increase.[9] In other words, according to Lustgarten, prices in concentrated industries rise more slowly than they do in nonconcentrated industries. Once again we see that evidence directly contradicts the theory.

In summary, we can conclude that no overall increase in market concentration appears to have occurred in the American economy since the turn of the century. With respect to recent U.S. inflation, the evidence from market concentration and pricing behavior directly contradicts the theory. It therefore does not seem reasonable to attribute periods of inflation in the twentieth century to monopolistic business power.

Imperfect Competition in the Labor Sector

Another popular explanation for inflation can be summarized as follows. Labor unions are powerful enough to monopolize the supply of labor. Union leaders who are anxious to remain in office must negotiate labor contracts that grant union members ever-increasing money wages. Employers faced with the monopolistic power of unions must give in, and when wage increases exceed productivity gains, as it is believed they often do, production costs also rise. Increased production costs are passed on to the consumer in the form of higher prices, causing inflation. Of course, certain difficulties arise when this explanation is applied to the American experience, but before exploring them we examine this form of cost-push argument to see if it contains any kernels of truth.

Let us assume that there is a perfect monopoly in the labor sector; that is, there is only one labor union, every worker is a member of that labor union, and all workers are paid the union money wage, which is perfectly inflexible downward. The aggregate supply curve that results under these conditions is identical to the one we derived in Figure 2-8 (page 27).

Suppose that initially we are in the condition of full employment depicted in Figure 12-4(c). Given an initial imperfectly competitive aggregate supply curve AgS and an initial aggregate demand curve AgD, the full-employment price level is P_0 and the nominal wage is W_1, as shown in Figure 12-4(d). Now suppose that the monopolistic labor union demands and is given an increase in the nominal wage to W_2. Because W_2 is the lowest money wage that workers can now accept, the aggregate supply curve in Figure 12-4(c) shifts upward to AgS'. At the initial price

[9] Steven Lustgarten, *Industrial Concentration and Inflation* (Washington, D.C.: American Enterprise Institute, 1975).

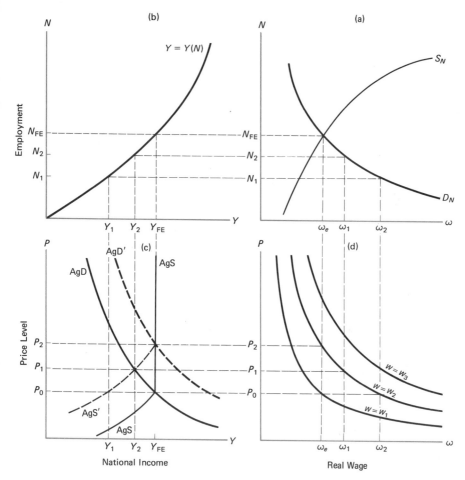

FIGURE 12-4   *Cost-push Inflation Produced by Monopolistic Labor Power*

level P_0, the real wage is ω_2, N_1 workers are employed, and the level of national income supplied is Y_1. An excess aggregate demand exists that is equal to $Y_{FE} - Y_1$, and the price level consequently rises to P_1, where aggregate demand is equal to aggregate supply at the less than full-employment stable disequilibrium level of income Y_2. The rise in the price level is less than proportional to the increase in money wages, and the real wage paid to employed workers ω_1 is therefore greater than the equilibrium real wage ω_e, as shown in Figure 12-4(d). Since $\omega_1 > \omega_e$, the quantity of workers employed is $N_2 < N_{FE}$, as shown in Figure 12-4(a); the level of national income supplied is therefore $Y_2 < Y_{FE}$, as shown in Figure 12-4(c).

The labor union can create full employment by demanding a reduction in money wages. However, this is unlikely to occur, because it would worsen conditions for most workers and a union leader who advocated such a policy would soon be voted out of office. The most probable course of action would be to demand government action via monetary or fiscal policy. If a government pledges to maintain full employment, as the U.S. government did in the 1946 Employment Act, then the pressure to take action will shift to the government. One possible policy would be to apply antitrust action against the monopolistic union, thereby moving toward perfect competition in the labor market. But in an elected government, antitrust action might not be popular with the electorate, most of whom are union members. The only alternative for the government would then be expansionary monetary or fiscal policy.

Expansionary fiscal or monetary policy shifts the aggregate demand curve in Figure 12-4(c) to AgD′ and restores full employment at the higher price level P_2. As a result of this increase in the price level, real wages return to the equilibrium real wage ω_e as shown in Figure 12-4(d), the level of employment rises to N_{FE}, and national income once again achieves the full-employment level.

The mechanism that produced the inflation in this analysis is not necessarily self-limiting, as it is in the business-sector monopoly example in Figure 12-3. In fact, we could expect workers who suffered due to the price rise from P_1 to P_2, which reduced their real wage from ω_1 to ω_e, to demand a return to their former real wage. This would pressure union leaders to demand increased money wages from business, and the whole cycle would repeat itself.

The degree to which the model of cost-push inflation is applicable to the American economy is debated by economists. Those who feel that this model is unrealistic point out that only 25% of all workers in the United States are members of labor unions and that there are many different independent unions. Thus, they argue, the actual performance of the labor market is much closer to perfect competition than to perfect monopoly. Other economists view the situation quite differently. They argue that if a single union represents workers in a major industry (for example, the United Auto Workers) and if many major industries are organized in this way, then unions will have the power to drive up wages beyond the equilibrium rate in those industries. This will increase the prices of the commodities produced by these industries, and because many of them are basic industries such as steel and chemicals, the cost and price of other products will rise as well. Thus the monopolistic power of less than one-fourth of the labor force can create aggregate cost-push inflation. This form of inflation also produces unemployment, as we demonstrated in the preceding analysis. If the government pledges to maintain full employment, then aggregate demand is increased, and this sets the stage for another inflationary period. For this reason, the resulting continuous inflation is sometimes referred to as a *wage-price spiral*. Not surprisingly, economists who hold this view of union power recommend that some form of wage controls be imposed on labor.

Empirical evidence tends to refute the conclusion that labor unions are the source of inflation in the United States. Because the power of American unions is greatest in highly concentrated industries, we would expect prices in these industries to increase faster in the beginning stages of inflation. However, Lustgarten's study, cited in the preceding subsection, indicates exactly the opposite result: concentrated industries with greater union power exhibited relatively smaller price increases than did the less concentrated and less unionized industries.

12-4   Employment and Inflation

Thus far we have considered full employment to be a condition in which everyone who wishes to work at the prevailing wage has a job. A labor market that exhibits this characteristic is frictionless or, as we have called it, perfect. In the real world, however, this perfection is impossible to obtain due to imperfections in the product and labor markets, the training and skills required for most jobs, the cost of obtaining and providing information regarding job vacancies, and the time and cost involved in transferring from one job to another. Due to these imperfections, the labor market can remain uncleared and exhibit no change in the wage rate. This condition holds when the number of workers seeking employment is equal to the number of job vacancies. The resulting unemployment is defined as *frictional unemployment*.[10] When the *unemployment rate* (the number of workers seeking employment *divided by* the number of workers employed *plus* those seeking employment) is equal to the frictional unemployment rate (the number of frictionally unemployed workers *divided by* the number of workers wishing to work at the market wage rate), full employment is said to exist.

Figure 12-5 illustrates this concept. In a frictionless market, N_2 workers are

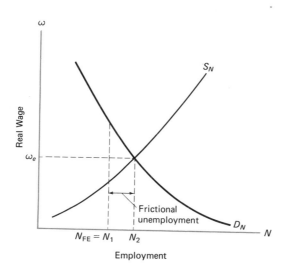

FIGURE 12-5   *Full Employment When Frictional Imperfections Exist in the Labor Market*

---

[10] This is not a necessary condition; for example, individuals may be unemployable for various reasons. We ignore this possibility here to simplify exposition.

employed when the real wage is ω_e, but due to imperfection in the market the maximum amount of employment consistent with an equilibrium wage of ω_e is N_1. At employment level N_1, the number of job vacancies is exactly equal to the number of job seekers. Thus excess supply is equal to excess demand, and there is no tendency for the wage rate to change. The frictional unemployment rate is therefore $(N_2 - N_1) \div N_2$. If the prevailing level of employment is N_1, then the unemployment rate $(N_2 - N_1) \div N_2$ is identical with the frictional rate and full employment exists. For a smaller degree of market imperfection, there is a decline in both the frictional rate of unemployment and the rate of unemployment consistent with the definition of full employment.

In the early 1960s the full-employment rate of unemployment was estimated at about 4%. This percentage is now considered to have been a low approximation; a more realistic figure for the period would be closer to 5%. Since the 1960s the composition of the labor force has shifted to include a greater fraction of demographic groups such as teen-agers and women that tend to have relatively high unemployment rates. Members of these groups change jobs more often and remain unemployed longer while searching for new jobs, so that the full-employment rate of unemployment has increased in the last decade.[11] Franco Modigliani and Lucas Papademos estimate that the full employment rate is currently about 5.6%.[12]

As we have just seen, the rate of frictional unemployment is not immutable. To the extent that imperfections in the market influence this rate, they should be reduced. To achieve this end, policy should be directed toward reducing the monopolistic power of unions and corporations, providing already existing educational and job-training subsidies to all individuals equally, eliminating minimum-wage laws, and ensuring that information concerning job vacancies and people seeking jobs is available at the lowest possible cost.

In recent years an economic debate has evolved over the policy measures required to achieve full employment in our imperfect real world. This debate was sparked by empirical research into the relationship between unemployment and wages by British economist A.W. Phillips,[13] who concentrated on the relationship between the rate of change in money wages and the rate of unemployment. Phillips discovered that periods of low unemployment were highly correlated with periods of rapidly rising money wages in the United Kingdom. This relationship was also found to hold for U.S. data. In Figure 12-6, annual unemployment and money-wage data are plotted for the American economy from 1961 to 1969. The rounded L-

[11] For a fuller discussion of this phenomenom, see Robert E. Hall, "Why Is the Unemployment Rate So High at Full Employment?" *Brookings Papers on Economic Activity* **3** (1970), 369–402.

[12] Franco Modigliani and Lucas Papademos, "Monetary Policy for the Coming Quarters: The Conflicting Views," *New England Economic Review* (March/April 1976), 12.

[13] A.W. Phillips, "The Relationship Between Unemployment and the Rate of Change of Money Wage Rates in the United Kingdom, 1861–1957," *Economica* **XXV** (November 1958), 283–99. Actually, the pioneer in this area was Irving Fisher, not Phillips. See Fisher's "A Statistical Relation Between Unemployment and Price Changes," *International Labor Review* (June 1926), 785–92. Reprinted in the *Journal of Political Economy* (March/April 1973), 496–502.

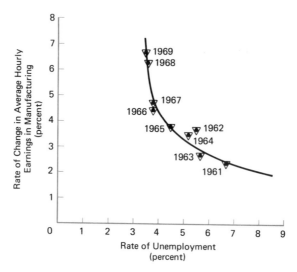

FIGURE 12-6   *The Relationship Between the Rate of Change in Money Wages and the Rate of Unemployment: 1961–1969*

shaped curve that is fitted to these data points is called a *Phillips curve*, and we can visually ascertain that it fits the data quite well.

Phillips's original contribution was subsequently extended to an examination of the relationship between the rate of unemployment and the rate of change in the price level. Annual data for the rate of unemployment and the rate of change in the GNP implicit price deflator are plotted in Figure 12-7. The L-shaped curve that is fitted to these data points is also called a Phillips curve. Here again it is visually apparent that this curve fits the data quite well.

It is not surprising that this similarity between Figures 12-6 and 12-7 should hold. In a period of rising prices, money wages must increase at a faster rate than the secular growth rate in real wages, or real wages will experience a relative decline. In the long run, the growth in real wages closely parallels the growth in labor productivity. The rate of change in labor productivity in U.S. manufacturing has averaged about 3% per year since 1947. Therefore, in a period of approximately stable prices, the rate of change in money wages should be about 3%, which was indeed the case in 1961, as indicated in Figure 12-6. When the price level starts to rise, workers, after some lag, demand and receive increases in money wages in excess of 3% per year. Thus there tends to be a strong relationship between a rising price level and rising money wages.

The extremely good fit of the data to the Phillips curves drawn in Figures 12-6 and 12-7 led many economists (who have not read Fisher's forgotten work) to conclude that the relationships depicted are stable. As a result of this analysis these economists also felt that full employment, which they defined as approximately 4% unemployment, cannot be reached unless it is accompanied by a rate of

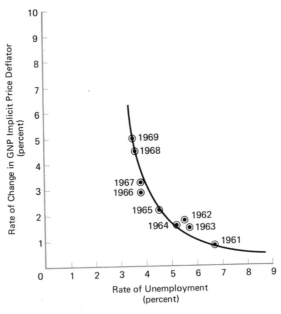

FIGURE 12-7 *The Relationship Between the Rate of Change in Prices and the Rate of Unemployment: 1961–1969*

inflation close to 2–3%. They considered this rate of inflation a small price to pay for the benefits of low unemployment. To reach the goal of full employment, they argued, the goal of price stability must be abandoned. In other words, they believed that the traditional macroeconomic policy goals of full employment *and* price stability are incompatible *if* the tradeoff between the rate of change in the price level and the rate of unemployment is stable.

These revolutionary conclusions were short-lived, however. As the inflation of the mid-1960s and 1970s unfolded, data generated in the United States and elsewhere destroyed all faith in the alleged stability of the Phillips curve. In Figures 12-8 and 12-9 annual American data for the period 1970–1975 are superimposed on the data originally given in Figures 12-6 and 12-7. The 1970–1975 data reveal that there is no predictable tradeoff between unemployment and inflation. In fact, these data suggest that rather than reducing unemployment, inflation may actually increase it. Given hindsight, we can now see that the original formulation and policy conclusions of the Phillips curve were faulty.

Fortunately, some economists did not need hindsight to recognize the shortcomings of the original Phillips-curve analysis. One such economist was Milton Friedman.[14] We can better understand his new view of the Phillips curve if we begin with a review of the original explanation of the unemployment–wage tradeoff

[14] Milton Friedman, "The Role of Monetary Policy," *The American Economic Review* **58** (March 1968), 1–17; see also Edmund S. Phelps, "Money Wage Dynamics and Labor Market Equilibrium," in E.S. Phelps (ed.), *Microeconomic Foundations of Employment and Inflation Theory* (New York: Norton Press, 1970).

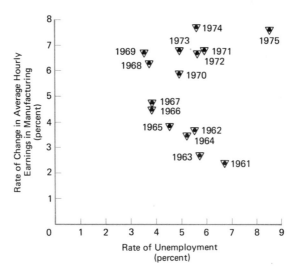

FIGURE 12-8   *The Relationship Between the Rate of Change in Money Wages and the Rate of Unemployment: 1961–1975*

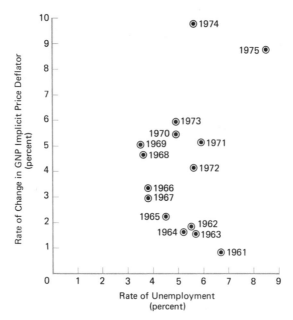

FIGURE 12-9   *The Relationship Between the Rate of Change in Prices and the Rate of Unemployment: 1961–1975*

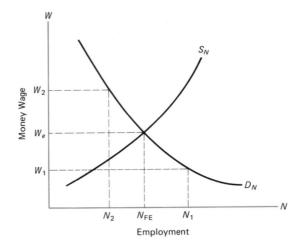

FIGURE 12-10   *The Labor Market of A.W. Phillips*

offered by Phillips.[15] The supply of and the demand for labor curves are graphed as functions of the nominal wage in Figure 12-10. When these two curves intersect, the nominal wage is the equilibrium wage W_e and the level of employment is the full-employment level N_{FE}. (Frictional unemployment exists in this analysis, but it is not explicitly illustrated as it is in Figure 12-5.) Now suppose that the money wage is W_1, which is less than the equilibrium wage. At this wage there is an excess demand for labor, wages increase, and the level of employment rises (that is, unemployment declines). On the other hand, if the money wage is W_2, then the quantity demanded is N_2, there is an excess supply of labor, and wages decrease as unemployment increases (as employment decreases). Phillips theorized that the rate at which the money wage changes over time is a function of the level of excess demand: the greater the excess demand, the more rapidly money wages will increase; conversely, the greater the excess supply, the more rapidly money wages will decrease.

It follows from the line of reasoning embodied in Figure 12-10 that when unemployment is equal to the full-employment rate, the rate of change in nominal wages $\Delta W/W$ is zero. At less than the full-employment rate of unemployment, money wages increase at a rate that becomes greater as unemployment decreases. Conversely, if unemployment exceeds the full-employment rate, then money wages decrease at a rate (the rate of negative increase) that becomes greater as unemployment increases. These results are illustrated in Figure 12-11. At an

---

[15] The theoretical explanation that follows draws heavily on Milton Friedman's *Unemployment versus Inflation?—An Evaluation of the Phillips curve*, Occasional Paper 44 (London: The Institute of Economic Affairs, 1975).

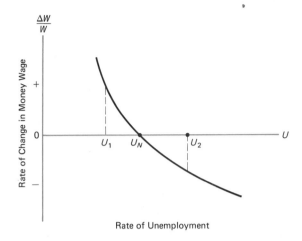

$$\frac{\Delta W}{W}$$

(y-axis label: Rate of Change in Money Wage, with + above 0 and − below)

0

U_1 U_N U_2 U

Rate of Unemployment

FIGURE 12-11   *Phillips's Relation Between the Rate of Change in Money Wages and the Rate of Unemployment*

unemployment rate of U_N corresponding to an employment level of N_{FE}, the rate of change in money wages is zero. When unemployment reaches U_1, the demand for labor exceeds the full-employment rate and the rate of wage increase is positive. The greater the demand (the less the unemployment), the greater the rate of change in money wages. The opposite results are obtained when unemployment exceeds U_N.

Although our analysis of the Phillips theory seems to be reasonable and correct thus far, it contains a fatal flaw: Phillips assumed that the demand for and the supply of labor are functions of the *nominal wage*. Throughout this book, we have argued that the quantities of labor that are demanded and supplied are functions of the *real wage*. This case is presented in Figure 12-5, where the equilibrium real wage ω_e is consistent with both money wages and the price-level constant, rising, or falling at the same rate. For Example, if prices were rising at 5% and the money wage was also rising at 5%, the real wage would nevertheless remain constant. The same result would occur if prices and wages were both falling at a constant rate.

The fact that we have rejected Phillips's theoretical explanation of the obvious tradeoffs illustrated in Figures 12-6 and 12-7 is only the first step toward understanding these tradeoffs and their subsequent breakdown in Figures 12-8 and 12-9. The clue required to solve our problem can be found in the earlier work of Irving Fisher, who wrote:

> When the dollar is losing value, or in other words when the price level is rising, a business man finds his receipts rising as fast, on average, as the general rise in prices, but not his expenses, because his expenses consist, to a large extent, of things that are contractually fixed. . . . Employment is then stimulated—for a time at least.[16]

---

[16] Fisher, "Unemployment and Price Changes," p. 786.

In other words, the price of goods and services responds more quickly to increased demand that is generated by a monetary expansion, for example, than does the wage for the labor employed to produce these goods and services. This lag is the result of either formal contractual agreements such as union contracts or informal arrangements such as customary money wages. Of course, this means that the prices workers pay for the products they buy are increasing faster than their money wages and their real wages are decreasing, so that we observe an increase in employment and output in the *short run*.

This decrease in real wages occurs because workers do not correctly anticipate the future behavior of prices when they enter into their wage bargains. For example, if prices have been stable for a long time, workers will expect the rate of change in the price level to be zero. When business activity increases due to monetary stimulation, firms attract additional workers by offering higher money wages. Because workers expect the price level *not* to rise, they interpret these higher money wages as higher real wages. The traditional Phillips curve can therefore be interpreted as a relationship between the rate of change in money wages and the rate of unemployment for a given expectation about future inflation. This result is illustrated in Figure 12-12, where the Phillips curve is now drawn for a given expected rate of change in the price level $\Delta P^*/P$, where ΔP^* is the expected change in the price level and P is the current price level. In Figure 12-12 $\Delta P^*/P = 0$, so that if money wages are constant, unemployment remains at the equilibrium level U_N, or what Milton Friedman calls (after Wicksell) the *natural rate of unemployment*. When the rate of change in money wages is greater than zero, workers expect real wages to increase and the unemployment rate then falls below the natural rate. Conversely, when money wages decline, wookers expect real wages to decrease and unemployment increases as workers seek jobs that pay the expected real wage they require to remain in the labor force.

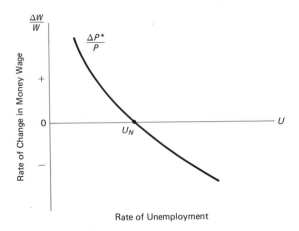

FIGURE 12-12   *The Short-run Phillips Curve*

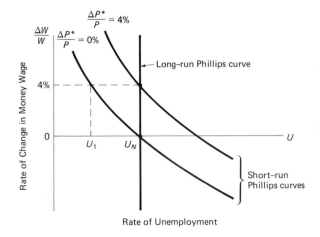

FIGURE 12-13   *The Long-run Adjustment of the Phillips Curve*

Obviously, it is unreasonable to argue that the tradeoff described in Figure 12-12 is permanent. Workers eventually recognize that the expected real wage will never materialize, and the rate of unemployment returns to the natural rate. For this reason, the Phillips curve in Figure 12-12 has become known as the *short-run Phillips curve.*

The end result of the adjustment process, as worker expectation about the rate of change in the price level $\Delta P^*/P$ becomes equal to the actual change in the price level $\Delta P/P$, is shown in Figure 12-13. The short-run Phillips curve for an expected price increase of 0% in Figure 12-12 is redrawn in Figure 12-13. Initially, the rate of inflation is zero. Suppose that a monetary expansion then occurs that is consistent with an annual rise in the price level of 4%. At first, unemployment declines from U_N to U_1 as we move to the left along the Phillips curve of expected zero price rise. This rate of unemployment is not stable, and as inflationary expectations adjust upward, the rate of unemployment increases until the expected rate of inflation is equal to the actual inflation rate of 4%. This result is represented in Figure 12-13 by the short-run Phillips curve, whose expected rate of price-level increase is 4%. Because worker expectation is now in accord with reality, the money wage is rising at the same rate as the expected rate of inflation, and the rate of unemployment returns to the natural rate U_N.

We can draw several conclusions from the foregoing analysis. First, when expectations adjust fully to the actual rate of price-level change, the rate of unemployment for any rate of inflation is the natural rate. The *long-run Phillips curve* is then a vertical line that passes through U_N, as shown in Figure 12-13, and there is no tradeoff between unemployment and inflation. Second, because the long-run Phillips curve is vertical, a monetary policy that is designed to produce a constant rate of inflation cannot permanently reduce the rate of unemployment. Expectations will adjust, and unemployment will return the natural rate. Unemployment can be held below the natural rate only by an ever-accelerating rate of inflation, because this produces an actual rate of inflation that is always in excess of the anticipated rate.[17] Of course, the end result of this process would be hyperinflation and the political collapse of any government that attempts to pursue such a policy. Third, if the central bank realizes the drawbacks of its policy of reducing unemployment below the natural rate, then a move on its part to reduce the growth rate of the money supply to a noninflationary rate would produce unemployment in *excess* of the natural rate. And as a corollary to this conclusion, the higher the rate of inflation, the greater the resulting unemployment becomes as the inflation is brought under control.

The conclusions we have drawn here are contingent on the correctness of the Fisher–Friedman–Phelps approach. The key issue in this approach is the extent to which long-run expectations adjust to the actual rate of inflation. If there is no realignment of expectations with reality, then what we have termed the short-run Phillips curve actually becomes the long-run Phillips curve. If expectations adjust completely to reality, then, the long-run curve is vertical. If the adjustment of expectations to reality is less than complete, then the long-run Phillips curve is steeper than the short-run curve, but not vertical. It is extremely complicated to determine empirically whether anticipations of the rate of price increase completely adjust to the actual increase, and a detailed discussion of the subject is beyond the scope of this book. However, we can sketch the evidence that has been developed to date. Early empirical studies primarily produced results indicating that the adjustment of expectations to reality was less than complete.[18] But these results are suspect for several reasons, the primary one being that early studies were not based on an independently determined measure of expected inflation. The results are therefore biased and indicate a less than complete adjustment in expectations. In a more recent study, Parkin, Sumner, and Ward used independently derived expected rates of inflation for retail prices, domestic wholesale prices, and export prices.[19] For each of these measures of expected inflation, their results indicated that the expected rate fully adjusted to the actual rate. All the evidence is not yet in (and in fact may never be, due to complex estimating problems), but the results strongly suggest that the long-run Phillips curve is quite steeply sloped if not actually vertical.

---

[17] Due to this conclusion, the new view of the Phillips curve has also become known as the *accelerationist hypothesis.*

[18] For a listing of these studies and a discussion in greater detail of the issues involved, see David Laidler and Michael Parkin, "Inflation: A Survey," *The Economic Journal* **85** (December 1975), 741–809.

[19] J.M. Parkin, M.T. Sumner, and R. Ward, "The Effects of Excess Demand, Generalized Expectations, and Wage–Price Controls on Wage Inflation in the U.K.," in Karl Brunner and Allan H. Meltzer (eds.), *The Economics of Price and Wage Controls*, Carnegie-Rochester Conference Series on Public Policy, Vol. 2 (New York: North-Holland Publishing Co., 1976).

12-5   Unemployment and Inflation

Until recently, many economists believed that a simultaneous combination of high unemployment and high inflation was impossible. However, this phenomenon, termed *stagflation*, has occurred in the last few years. Here we examine two possible theoretical reasons for stagflation. Together they probably explain much of what has been observed about this phenomenon.

The first explanation follows directly from our analysis of the Phillips curve. Suppose that a 10% rate of inflation has existed long enough for inflationary expectations to adjust fully to the actual rate. The relevant short-run Phillips curve is illustrated in Figure 12-14, where the rate of unemployment is the natural rate U_N. The rate of increase in money wages at which the short-run Phillips curve intersects the long-run curve (at point A in the figure) is 10%. Now suppose that the monetary authorities reduce the rate of growth of the money supply in an effort to reduce the rate of inflation to 6%. The initial effect of this action is to decrease the aggregate demand for goods and services, so that inventories begin to accumulate. The rate of price increase decelerates as firms attempt to reduce their inventories, and workers are laid off to eliminate new inventory accumulation. In the short run, workers who are laid off expect prices to continue to rise at the 10% rate and are therefore reluctant to accept jobs that promise money-wage increases at less than a rate of 10%. The excess supply of workers does exert some downward pressure on the rate of increase in money wages, but because expectations of future price increases remain at 10%, the rate of unemployment is dictated by a movement to the right from point A to point B on the short-run Phillips curve in Figure 12-14. Unemployment then exceeds the natural, or full-employment, rate by the amount $U_2 - U_N$, and we now have high unemployment *and* inflation.

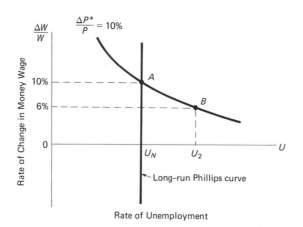

FIGURE 12-14   *The Creation of Stagflation*

The second explanation of stagflation was originally offered in 1931 by Friedrich A. von Hayek, the 1974 cowinner of the Nobel prize in economics.[20] According to Hayek, the monetary expansion that produces inflation temporarily lowers the interest rate below the natural rate in the initial stages, as we saw earlier in this chapter. This temporary decline in the interest rate makes previously unprofitable marginal investment projects appear profitable. These projects are undertaken because this temporary decline in the interest rate is assumed to be sufficiently permanent for these projects to become profitable. Resources are therefore invested in these projects, and when the interest rate returns to its natural rate, many projects that are not yet complete appear unprofitable and are abandoned. Workers employed in either the construction or the operation of such projects find themselves suddenly unemployed. In addition to the erroneous allocation of resources in these new investment projects due to false interest-rate signals, the whole spectrum of rational decision making on the part of households and firms becomes increasingly difficult, if not impossible. In the case of hyperinflation, the result can be a general breakdown of the market economy.

12-6   Concluding Remarks

In this chapter we learned that inflation can originate in either the real sector or the monetary sector of the economy. We saw that sustained long-run inflation is possible if excessive growth in the nominal money supply is maintained by the monetary authorities and that cost-push inflation results when imperfections exist in the demand for or the supply of labor. Monopolistic power in the hands of business can cause the price level to rise but cannot be a source of sustained inflation unless the concentration of power continues to increase. Monopolistic labor unions can cause the price level to rise by demanding a real wage in excess of the equilibrium real wage, but this cannot cause sustained inflation unless the government increases the nominal money supply in the pursuit of full employment. We also discussed the Phillips curve, which indicates the relationship between the rate of unemployment and the rate of inflation, in terms of its short- and long-run properties. In the short run the Phillips curve shows that there is a significant tradeoff between unemployment and inflation and that full employment must be accompanied by continuous inflation. The new view of the Phillips curve is that no such tradeoff occurs in the long run, so that the joint policy goals of full employment and price stability are compatible. The phenomenon of high unemployment accompanied by high rates of inflation was then explained in terms of the Phillips curve analysis and the earlier theory of F.A. von Hayek.

[20] Friedrich A. von Hayek, *Prices and Production* (London: Routledge and Kegan Paul, 1931).

13 The Monetarist Interpretation of History

13-1 Introduction

In Chapters 11 and 12 we examined certain aspects of unemployment and inflation. In our discussion of unemployment in Chapter 11 we purposely bypassed the problem of how an economy that is initially at full employment can be transformed into an economy at high unemployment, and in our analysis of inflation in Chapter 12 we argued that inflation could result from expansionary fiscal or monetary policy. We now consider the growing debate that centers around the monetarist explanation of both of these phenomena and the criticism opposing it.

In recent years a growing number of economists, following the pioneering lead of Milton Friedman, have become advocates of the view that periods of high unemployment and sustained inflation result exclusively from disturbances originating in the monetary sector. Due to their emphasis on the causal role of money in depression and inflation, these economists have been labeled *monetarists*.

The monetarist interpretation of history has been flatly rejected by some economists and only partially accepted by others. The group of economists who flatly reject monetarist claims, who can probably be most accurately labeled *extreme Keynesians,* are relatively few in number. The extreme Keynesians, typified by Nicholas Kaldor of Cambridge University, generally advocate the theoretical and policy views that dominated macroeconomics in the early 1950s. In direct contrast to the monetarists, extreme Keynesians believe that the quantity of money does not play a critical role in the economy. The second group of antimonetarists is comprised of the majority of economists today, and its members are usually called neo-Keynesians. Led by Yale University's James Tobin, the neo-Keynesians accept the proposition that money plays an important role in economic activity, but they object to the primary role the monetarists have assigned it.

In this chapter we examine a small portion of the empirical evidence that the monetarists have amassed to support their position. We then consider the objections that the Keynesians and the neo-Keynesians have raised regarding the validity of this evidence. Our discussion of the debate between monetarists and antimonetarists is continued in Chapter 14, where the underlying theoretical arguments of both sides are examined in greater detail. The implications of this debate with respect to policy are then evaluated in Chapter 16.

13-2   The Monetarist Interpretation of Recessions

Economic *recessions* are short-run downward departures from the long-run economic growth path; economic *expansions* are exactly the opposite. The point at which a turnaround occurs—when recession ceases and expansion begins—is called the *trough*; its counterpart—the point at which expansion ceases and recession begins—is called the *peak*. This terminology is illustrated in Figure 13-1.

Because of its concentration on the business cycle, the National Bureau of Economic Research has become the final arbiter in the exact dating of peaks and troughs in the American business cycle. Table 13-1 contains peak and trough dates for the U.S. business cycle for 1854–1975. Although such data give us a superficial idea of the periodicity of the historical business cycle, they shed no light on the

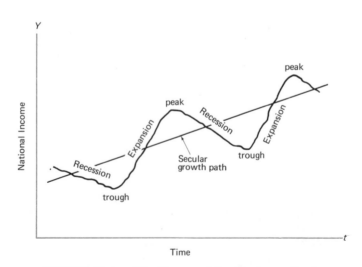

FIGURE 13-1   *The Phases of the Business Cycle*

severity of the observed recession or expansion. In addition, they do not tell us whether the peak of the expansion phase is less than, equal to, or greater than the previous peak. To obtain a rough idea of the severity of the business cycle, the index of industrial production for 1870–1975 is plotted in Figure 13-2. The time spans covering the major recessions designated by the National Bureau of Economic Research are illustrated by the shaded bars in Figure 13-2. The remaining deviations in trend are due to minor business cycles and to nonbusiness events such as demobilization after World Wars I and II.

Table 13-1   Troughs and Peaks of the Business Cycle Estimated by the National Bureau of Economic Research: 1854–1975

Trough		Peak	
Dec.	1854	Jun.	1857
Dec.	1858	Oct.	1860
Jun.	1861	Apr.	1865
Dec.	1867	Jun.	1869
Dec.	1870	Oct.	1873
Mar.	1879	Mar.	1882
May	1885	Mar.	1887
Apr.	1888	Jul.	1890
May	1891	Jan.	1893
Jun.	1894	Dec.	1895
Jun.	1897	Jun.	1899
Dec.	1900	Sep.	1902
Aug.	1904	May	1907
Jun.	1908	Jan.	1910
Jan.	1912	Jan.	1913
Dec.	1914	Aug.	1918
Mar.	1919	Jan.	1920
Jul.	1921	May	1923
Jul.	1924	Oct.	1926
Nov.	1927	Aug.	1929
Mar.	1933	May	1937
Jun.	1938	Feb.	1945
Oct.	1945	Nov.	1948
Oct.	1949	Jul.	1953
Aug.	1954	Jul.	1957
Apr.	1958	May	1960
Feb.	1961	Nov.	1969
Nov.	1970	Nov.	1973
Mar.	1975		

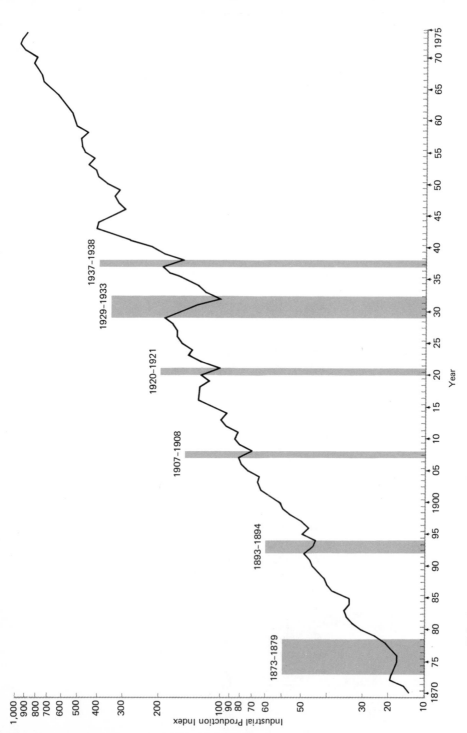

FIGURE 13-2   The Index of Industrial Production and Major Business Cycles (1913 = 100)

Note: Shaded areas represent major recessions as dated by the NBER.

SOURCE: U.S. Department of Commerce, *Long-term Economic Growth, 1860–1965*,

TABLE 13-2   Time Periods Prior to 1948 Over Which the U.S. Money Supply Exhibited Decline and the Rate of Decline

Time Period	Rate of Decline*
1873–1879	4.9
1892–1894	5.8
1907–1908	3.7
1920–1921	5.1
1929–1933	35.2
1937–1938	2.4

* All figures are based on the M_2 definition of money.

SOURCE   M. Friedman and A.J. Schwartz, "Money and Business Cycles," *Review of Economics and Statistics* **45**, No. 1, Part 2, Supplement (February 1963), 34.

The Major Recessions

In their monumental study of the monetary history of the United States, Milton Friedman and Anna Schwartz found that the monetary supply of the United States generally exhibited a tendency to rise in both the expansionary and contractionary phases of the business cycle from 1867 to 1948, *except* in the years listed in Table 13-2.[1] The percentage of absolute decline in the money supply in those exceptional years is also given in Table 13-2.

A comparison between Figure 13-2 and Table 13-2 reveals the striking observation that major business-cycle periods correspond to exceptional periods in which the money supply experienced an absolute decline. Of course, the critical question related to this coincidence is, Does the decline in the money supply cause the business cycle, or does the business cycle cause the decline in the money supply, or does some third factor cause a joint decline in business activity and the money supply?

By examining the historical circumstances that brought about the decline in the supply of money shown in Table 13-2, Friedman and Schwartz hoped to demonstrate conclusively that for the most part the causation flowed from money to business. Their analysis of the factors that caused a decline in the money supply during each of the periods mentioned in Table 13-2 is as follows.

1873–1879: To finance the costs of the Civil War, the U.S. government printed fiat money, which became generally known as *greenbacks.* Inflation occurred to such an extent due to the rapid growth in the number of greenbacks that prices rose about 250% during the Civil War. At this rate of inflation it was impossible for the federal government to continue to convert paper money into gold at the prewar fixed rate, because a large import surplus due to the lower European prices would have occurred. This in turn

[1] M. Friedman and A.J. Schwartz, *A Monetary History of the United States 1867–1960* (Princeton, N.J.: Princeton University Press, 1963).

would have been offset in the balance of payments by the export of gold. After the Civil War political pressure was exerted to resume specie conversion into paper currency at the prewar rate, but because the price-level differential continued to exist between New York and London, this resumption would soon have led to an outflow of gold and, quite clearly, to the cessation of specie conversion once again. For conversion to occur successfully at the prewar rate, it was first necessary to deflate the postwar price level to the prewar price level.[2] This was accomplished by decreasing high-powered money H, which in turn precipitated the banking crisis of 1873. This crisis produced many bank failures, which in turn caused a rise in the currency ratio C_r and in the reserve ratio R_r as both the public and the banks scrambled for liquidity. Recall equation (8-21), which expresses the nominal money supply M_s as

$$M_s = \frac{H}{C_r + R_r - C_r R_r} \qquad (8\text{-}21)$$

With a decline in H and increases in both C_r and R_r, it necessarily follows that the money supply must decrease. The decline of these proximate determinants and their effect on the money supply are illustrated in Figure 13-3.

Friedman and Schwartz argue that this basically political move to resume gold specie conversion at the prewar rate produced a net decline of 4.9% in the money supply, and the result of this decline was the major recession of 1873–1879.

1893–1894: After returning to the gold standard, the United States—a relatively minor country on the gold standard—was required to subordinate movements of the domestic price level to movements of foreign price levels. A generally declining world price level from 1891 to 1897 meant that the U.S. money supply had to grow at a slower rate than output, and this produced the effect of *tight money*. The effect was felt particularly in the rapidly expanding West, and this led to political pressure urging the abandonment of the gold standard and the adoption of the bimetallic standard of gold and silver. Had this happened, foreigners who held dollar balances in New York or American securities would have suffered capital losses as they reconverted their dollars back into their domestic currency, because the dollar would then have been worth less in gold. Owners of dollar deposits and securities would therefore be motivated to convert their dollars into gold if the likelihood of such an event were to increase. Such an increase did occur when the Sherman Silver Act of 1890 was passed. This act allowed the Treasury to double its monthly purchase of silver and increased the doubts of foreigners about the American government's commitment to the gold standard. In fact, gold started to flow out of the country at a rapid rate in 1891, but this trend was temporarily reversed by the European crop failure of the same year, as U.S. food exports increased 250%. This gold inflow was short-lived, however; in 1892 gold

---

[2] Of course, it would have been possible and economically more desirable to resume conversion at a new and higher exchange rate consistent with the post-Civil War price level differential existing between the United States and Europe.

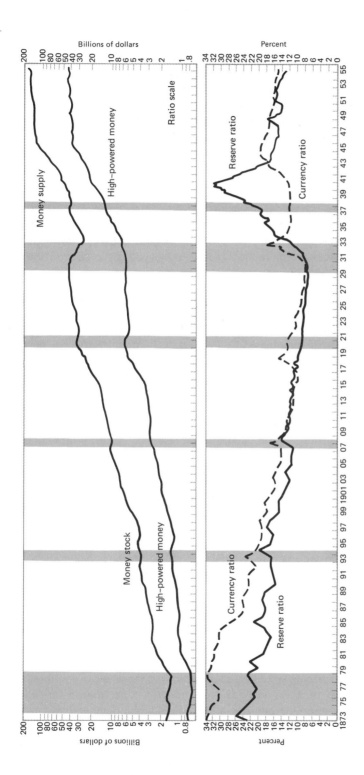

FIGURE 13-3 *The Money Supply and Its Three Proximate Determinants: 1873–1955*

Note: Shaded areas represent major recessions, and all figures are based on the M_2 definition of money.

SOURCE P. Cagan, Determinants and Effect of Changes in the Stock of Money, 1875–1960, Chart 1, and M. Friedman and A.J. Schwartz, A Monetary History of the United States, 1867–1960, Tables A-1 and B-3.

outflow resumed as it appeared that the political forces seeking the monetization of silver might succeed. The Treasury and commercial banks pursued policies to prevent the loss of gold reserves as the public, both domestic and foreign, sought simultaneously to increase theirs. The resulting runs on commercial banks produced many bank failures and the suspension of deposit withdrawal privileges. As might be expected under these conditions, the public wished to hold a larger fraction of its money in the form of currency and commercial banks wished to increase their reserve ratios. As can be seen in Figure 13-3, the result was an absolute decline in the money stock of almost 6%.

Friedman and Schwartz contend that this contraction in the money supply was produced by domestic political pressure that sought to achieve an easy money policy through the monetization of silver but that actually achieved the opposite result when high-powered money in the form of gold began to flow out of the country. The subsequent contraction of the money supply produced the major recession of 1893–1894, during which the index of industrial production fell from 38.8 to 33.7.

1907–1908: Having survived the onslaught of the silver forces, the United States remained on the gold standard with all its requisite price discipline. In the spring of 1907 gold began to flow out of the country, thereby producing a slight decline in the money supply. Little else would have occurred if the third largest trust company in New York, the Knickerbocker Trust, had not failed. This failure precipitated a classic run on the commercial banking system: the public wished to hold more currency; the banks, more reserves. As bank after bank failed, the scramble for currency and reserves intensified. The effect of rising currency and deposit ratios produced a rapid decline in the money supply, as reflected in Figure 13-3. It was not until banks suspended the conversion of deposits into currency that the monetary decline was halted. The decline in real output was rapid and severe: the industrial production index fell from 80.6 to 68.0. Fortunately, the recovery was equally dramatic: the industrial production index jumped to 80.2 in 1909, as shown in Figure 13-2.

As a result of such recurring bank panics, political pressure mounted to reform the banking system. This in turn led to passage by the U.S. Congress of the Federal Reserve Act, which created the Federal Reserve System. It was hoped (wrongly, as we shall soon see) that the Federal Reserve would prevent future financial panics.

1920–1921: After the downturn of economic activity following demobilization at the end of 1918, the inflation that had occurred during World War I promptly resumed. As its gold reserves declined, the Treasury feared that gold specie payments would be suspended and therefore urged the Federal Reserve Board to act quickly to stem inflation. The Board responded by increasing the discount rate from 4.75% to 6% at the beginning of 1920. This 1.25% rise is the sharpest single increase in the discount rate in the history of the Federal Reserve System. Dissatisfied with the rate of progress achieved in rolling back prices, the New York Federal Reserve Bank raised the discount rate to 7% in June 1920. This increase, combined with the lagged effects of the previous rate hikes, produced a decline in the money supply of 5.1%, and the index of industrial production dropped from 124.0 in 1920 to only 100.0 in 1921.

According to Friedman and Schwartz, this episode clearly demonstrated that the line of causality could be drawn directly from money to economic activity.

1929–1933 (The Great Contraction): Before the stock market crash of October 1929, the money supply declined slightly as the Federal Reserve reduced its portfolio of assets in an attempt to curb what was believed to be excessive speculation on the stock exchanges. This decline was accompanied by a minor decline in industrial production, which signaled the recession phase of the typical business cycle. The stock market crash greatly contributed to the uncertainty of the future and thus slightly increased the demand for currency by corporations and individuals. In October 1930, bank failures rapidly increased as depositors attempted to convert deposits into currency. In November, 256 banks failed; in December, 352. Although many of these were small country banks, some were not—in particular, the prestigious Bank of United States with deposits of over $200 million failed. Had there not been a Federal Reserve System, Friedman and Schwartz argue, the commercial banks would have suspended conversion of deposits into currency to prevent additional bank failures, as they did in the 1893 and 1907 banking crises. But due to the existence of the Federal Reserve, commercial banks deferred their traditional leadership and responsibility to the System. As the demands for currency were met, the banking crisis subsided, only to be reactivated in March 1931. This increased the decline in the money supply as the currency ratio shot upward (again, see Figure 13-3). The commercial banks that remained open took only minor action to increase their reserve ratios, believing that the Federal Reserve was taking sufficient action to increase the quantity of high-powered money. In fact, the Federal Reserve did virtually nothing to offset the decline in the money supply caused by a sudden increase in the public's desire for currency. However, the Federal Reserve did not remain passive when gold began to flow out of the country after Britain abandoned the gold standard in September 1931. Prompted by fears that the United States would soon follow Britain's lead, the Federal Reserve raised the discount rate sharply in October to stop the outflow of gold; this produced a contraction in the money supply that the Federal Reserve made no attempt to offset. The consequent third banking crisis resulted in the suspension of operations of 1,860 banks between August 1931 and January 1932. Deposits in these suspended banks amounted to $1,449 million, and the crisis drastically reduced the deposits of the banks that remained in operation as the currency ratio jumped even higher. Now commercial banks began to liquidate their assets, causing R_r to shoot upward and thereby reducing the money supply even further. During this period the money supply declined absolutely by 12% and fell at an annual rate of 31%!

Friedman and Schwartz contend that inept monetary policy on the part of the Federal Reserve caused the Great Contraction. As illustrated in Figure 13-2, the industrial production index declined from 188.3 in 1929 to only 100.5 in 1932. Throughout this period the money supply (defined to include time deposits) decreased 35.2%. Although some of this decrease was undoubtedly attributable to a decline in business activity, the bulk of this decrease was the direct result of the Federal Reserve's initial inaction and its subsequent inappropriate action. Thus the Federal Reserve System, which had been established to prevent bank crises, actually aggravated them.

> *1937–1938:* As a result of the widespread banking collapse during the Great Depression, which was wrongly attributed to improvident commercial bank management, Congress authorized the Federal Reserve System to vary the reserve requirements of member banks. The System exercised this power in 1937 to reduce the excess reserves held by commercial banks. It was argued that large amounts of excess reserves reduced the effectiveness of open-market operations and discount-rate adjustments. Reduction of these excess reserves, it seemed, could be quickly and painlessly achieved by raising the reserve requirements. Reserve requirements were raised in August 1936, March 1937, and May 1937. Unfortunately, commercial banks continued to maintain large quantities of excess reserves—a precautionary action resulting from the painful lessons learned in 1931 and 1932. Thus when the Federal Reserve raised the required reserve ratio in an attempt to reduce excess reserves, commercial banks, seeking to maintain a given level of excess reserves, simply raised their reserve ratios as well. At the same time the Treasury sought to offset the large inflow of gold from Europe, and the growth of high-powered money ceased. The combination of these two policies caused a decline in the money supply of 2.4%, as shown in Figure 13-3.

Friedman and Schwartz consider that this contraction of the money supply clearly resulted from forces that were unrelated to business activity. This gives additional support to their belief that the monetary contraction caused the economic contraction, rather than vice versa.

The Minor Recessions

If we subtract the six major recessions from the total number of recessions listed in Table 13-1, we are left with 23 minor recessions. Given their analysis of major recessions, Friedman and Schwartz believe it is not unreasonable to suppose that monetary change had some bearing on these cycles as well, rather than that they were completely influenced by business activity. As they put it, "If money plays an independent role in major movements, is it likely to be almost passive in minor movements?"[3]

The primary evidence that Friedman and Schwartz employ to support their view of the causal role of money in minor business cycles is based on the rate of change

---

[3] M. Friedman and A.J. Schwartz, "Money and Business Cycles," *The Review of Economics and Statistics* **XLV**, No. 1, Part 2, *Supplement* (February 1963), 55.

in the money supply. Because the money supply has declined absolutely only in major recessions, it necessarily follows that the money supply has maintained a positive growth rate during minor recessions. However, Friedman and Schwartz discovered that prior to almost all minor cycles the rate of growth in the money supply decreased. They argue that it is conceivable that many minor recessions were simply mild forms of major recessions. But Friedman and Schwartz stop short of claiming that this is an established fact. They acknowledge that before a complete explanation of the minor recessions is possible, a rigorous and explicitly stated theory of how changes in the monetary sector are transmitted to the real sector must be developed and tested.

In summary, Friedman and Schwartz argue that the severity of all major American recessions results from financial and/or political events that produce an absolute contraction in the money supply; this contraction in turn causes a decline in economic activity. Friedman and Schwartz recognize that economic activity can and probably did influence the money supply, but they believe that this reverse causation explains only a small fraction of the actual money supply contraction. Following this analysis, Friedman and Schwartz feel that the frequently observed contraction in the rate of growth of the money supply before minor recessions suggests a causal relationship between money and business activity in minor as well as in major recessions.

13-3   The Monetarist Interpretation of Inflation

In our theoretical analysis of inflation in Chapter 12, we demonstrated that continued inflation could be the result of either a pure fiscal policy or a pure monetary policy. Monetarists believe that sustained and severe inflation can be produced *only* by excessive increases in the money supply. In his academic writing, Milton Friedman expresses this premise as follows: "Long-period changes in the quantity of money relative to output determine the secular behavior of prices. Substantial expansions in the quantity of money over short periods have been a major *proximate* source for the accompanying inflation in prices."[4] In his more popular writings, Friedman is even more dogmatic, stating, "Inflation is always and everywhere a monetary phenomenon."[5]

To support their claim, the monetarists have produced an impressive body of research in monetary economics.[6] We could easily fill an entire book with examples of this research, but in this section we consider only three representative examples. Two are cases of moderate inflation; the third is a classic example of hyperinflation.

---

[4] M. Friedman, "Monetary Studies of the National Bureau," in *The Optimum Quantity of Money and Other Essays* (Chicago: Aldine Publishing, 1969), p. 277.

[5] M. Friedman, "Inflation and Wages," *Newsweek* (September 28, 1970), 77.

[6] For studies conducted under Milton Friedman's guidance, see particularly M. Friedman (ed.), *Studies in the Quantity Theory of Money* (Chicago: University of Chicago Press, 1956), and D. Meiselman (ed.), *Varieties of Monetary Experience* (Chicago: University of Chicago Press, 1970).

The World Gold Inflation of 1897–1914

When the United States returned to the gold standard in 1879, the Treasury was required by law to purchase all newly mined gold bullion at a fixed price with either gold coin or gold certificates, which were claims on the gold stock held by the Treasury. Because gold coin and gold certificates were freely used as currency, they were also high-powered money. Therefore, the purchase of newly mined gold would increase high-powered money and cause a multiple expansion of the money supply.

Two events of the early 1890s greatly increased world production of gold. The first was the discovery of major gold deposits in South Africa, Alaska, and Colorado. The second was the perfection of the cyanide process for extracting gold from low-grade ore. These two developments reduced the cost of mining gold relative to the fixed Treasury purchase price, and the world's gold stock more than doubled from 1890 to 1914.

Since most industrialized nations were on the gold standard, the money supply in these countries increased rapidly, resulting in worldwide inflation. In the United States, the gold stock rose from $502 million in 1896 to $1,891 million in 1914. The money supply (see Figure 13-4) grew from $3,434 million in 1896 to $14,316 million in 1914.[7] This represented an average annual growth rate of 8.25%. The increase in the money supply was accompanied by an average annual growth in the wholesale price index of 2.3% from 1897 to 1914. This represents the longest sustained period of peacetime inflation in the history of the United States.

The German Hyperinflation of 1922–1923

After World War I, the victorious Allies at Versailles ordered Germany to pay reparations. First, the Allies demanded that Germany pay the full cost of the war, but by 1921 they had reduced their demands to $33 billion, which the Germans agreed to pay in Allied currencies (for example, British pounds and French francs). Unfortunately for Germany—and the rest of the world—this proved impossible. In a vain attempt to purchase the necessary foreign currency, the German government, with the cooperation of the German central bank, started the printing presses rolling.

By August 1922 the price level was increasing at a rate of 50% per month, and according to Phillip Cagan's definition, hyperinflation was underway.[8] When this hyperinflation ended in November 1923, the price level had risen by a factor of 1.02×10^{10} and the money supply had increased about 7.32×10^9 times.[9] The hyperinflation was halted by the Commissioner for National Currency, Hjalmar Horace Greeley Schact, who promptly stopped printing of the mark and issued a new currency (the Rentenmark) that was equal to one trillion old marks.

---

[7] The money stock as defined here includes time deposits, because no data prior to June 1914 exist to differentiate time deposits from demand deposits.

[8] Phillip Cagan, "The Monetary Dynamics of Hyperinflation," in M. Friedman (ed.), *Studies in the Quantity Theory of Money* (Chicago: University of Chicago Press, 1956), p. 25.

[9] *Ibid.*, p. 26.

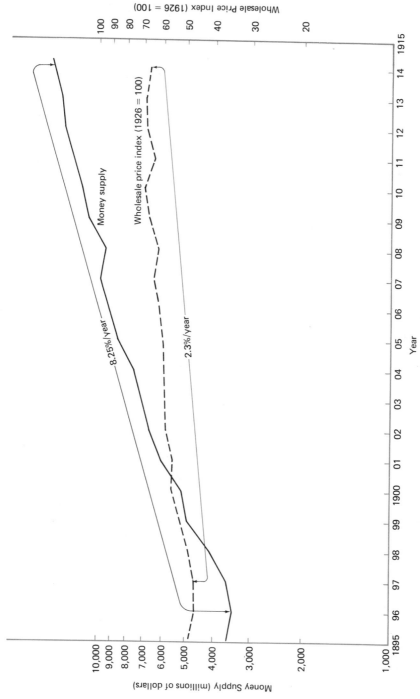

FIGURE 13-4   U.S. Money Supply and Wholesale Price Index: 1895–1914

DATA SOURCES   Money Supply: M. Friedman and A.J. Schwartz, A Monetary History of the United States, 1867–1960 (Princeton, N.J.: Princeton University Press, 1963), pp. 705–708; Wholesale Price Index: Historical Statistics of the United States, Colonial Times to 1957 (Washington, D.C.: U.S. Government Printing Office, 1960), pp. 116–17.

Recent American Inflation

Inflation occurs most often during periods of war, as deficit spending financed by the central bank produces a rapid growth in the money supply. In the United States, inflation accompanied the Revolutionary War, the Civil War, World Wars I and II, and the Korean War. The most recent American inflation resulted from two wars: the war in Vietnam and the war on poverty. As in previous wars, federal government spending was in excess of tax revenue. From fiscal year 1951 through 1960 the Federal deficit averaged only $1.46 billion per year, but from 1961 through 1976 the annual average deficit was $15.2 billion—a more than tenfold increase. Now as we learned in Chapter 12, such deficits can be financed either by selling government securities to the public or by creating money. When deficits are small—as they were, on the average, during the 1951–1960 period—the sale of bonds to the public does not place excessive upward pressure on interest rates, so that the Federal Reserve does not have to monetize the debt to maintain high bond prices (and low interest rates). As a result, the money supply during the 1951–1960 period grew at an average annual rate of only 1.9%. However, this situation changed dramatically in 1961 (for reasons that we will discuss in greater detail in Chapter 16), and due to the magnitude of the debt, approximately 40% of it was monetized by the Federal Reserve. For every dollar of debt monetized, the money supply held by the public increased approximately $2.50. Thus the money supply grew at an annual rate of 5.3% from 1962 to 1975. The behavior of the money supply from 1950 to 1975 is graphed in Figure 13-5.

The behavior of prices as measured by the wholesale price index is also graphed in Figure 13-5. The wholesale price index remained almost constant from 1951 through 1964. This is in agreement with the fact that the money supply from 1951 to 1962 grew at an annual rate that was slightly lower than the rate of growth in GNP. The rapid rate of growth in the money supply beginning in 1962 began to affect prices in 1964, after a two-year lag, as illustrated in Figure 13-5. In this instance the money supply increased at an annual rate of 5.3% during the period. This rate of growth in M_1 was almost twice the rate of growth in real GNP (2.8%), providing a classic example of too much money chasing too few goods, and the wholesale price index increased at an annual rate of 5.7%.

A common argument opposing the monetarist explanation is that at the time, the money supply was only responding to the increase in aggregate demand, or in other words, that the money supply is endogenous. Monetarists counter this argument by citing the published minutes of the Federal Reserve open-market committee, which reveal that in 1967 and 1968 the committee erroneously believed that the economy was slowing down and deliberately increased the growth of the money supply.[10] Another popular explanation is that the 1973 oil embargo produced the rapid increase in the price level. But as Figure 13-5 clearly shows, prices were already rising rapidly when the embargo occurred. This does not mean that a

---

[10] Phillip Cagan, *Recent Monetary Policy and the Inflation: From 1965 to August 1971* (Washington, D.C.: American Enterprise Institute for Public Research, 1971), pp. 12–15.

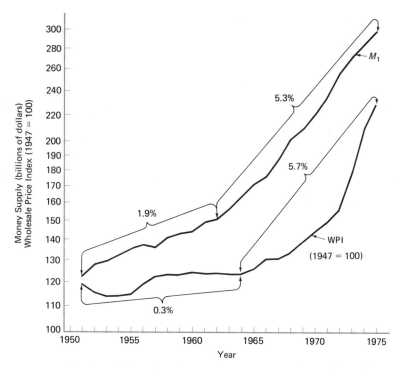

FIGURE 13-5   *Growth of the Money Supply and Prices: 1951–1975*

DATA SOURCE   Economic Report of the President, 1976 (Washington, D.C.: U.S. Government Printing Office, 1976), pp. 225 and 231.

doubling in the price of petroleum did not affect the price level; it simply indicates that this effect was minor in relation to the inflation produced by the rapid growth in M_1.

In summary, monetarists regard inflations as sustained periods of price increase that have historically resulted from the excessive expansion of the money supply. In its most extreme form, monetarism proclaims that expansionary fiscal policy financed by borrowing from the public has no net effect on aggregate demand. The increased government expenditure is simply offset by a reduction in private spending: If the government gets the funds by borrowing from the public, then those people who lend the funds to the government have less to spend or to lend to others. The effect of the higher government expenditures may simply be higher spending by government and those who receive government funds and lower spending by those who lend to government or by those to whom lenders would have loaned the money instead.[11]

---

[11] Milton Friedman, *The Counter-Revolution in Monetary Theory* (London: The Institute of Economic Affairs, 1970), p. 19.

In Chapter 14 we will present a detailed critical examination of the theoretical analysis underlying the monetarist position.

13-4   The Keynesian Critique

As we stated in the introduction to this chapter, only a few extreme Keynesians still exist, and for the most part their stronghold is in Britain. Foremost among the extreme Keynesians is Nicholas Kaldor of Cambridge University. In this section we briefly examine Kaldor's interpretation of monetary history.[12]

Basically, Kaldor argues that the money supply is for all practical purposes purely endogenous, or in other words that the money supply simply expands or contracts to meet the needs of trade. Thus it directly follows that there is a historically high correlation between money and money income.

Consider, for example, the seasonal increase in currency held by the public during the Christmas season. Kaldor reasons that in this situation the central bank expands its note circulation to meet the needs of trade. He then asks what the effect would be on the economy if the central bank did not supply all the currency that was demanded. Kaldor's answer: money substitutes such as credit cards, promissory notes, and scrip currency issued by corporations would replace central bank currency. The corporations issuing scrip currency would soon find it convenient to establish clearing houses to process the scrip and to provide credit facilities to handle net debit and credit balances after each clearing. Thus, "a complete surrogate money system and payments system would be established, which would exist side by side with 'official money.'"[13] We use this concept of an endogenous money supply to examine Kaldor's explanation of the high correlation between money and economic activity.

We now describe Kaldor's extreme Keynesian interpretation of the high correlation observed by Friedman and Schwartz between a reduction in the money supply and a reduction in income after a lag. Suppose that a recession is caused by a decision on the part of some firms to reduce their inventories and that as a direct consequence of this action these firms reduce their net borrowings as well. Suppliers to the firms with reduced inventories will then find their own inventories rising due to declining sales. To stop this unintended investment, the suppliers will institute production cutbacks to reduce their inventory and will also reduce their net borrowing. As the demand for credit decreases, the growth in the money supply will decline. However, the decline in the money supply does not create the subsequent decline in income; rather the investment multiplier works as inventories are reduced, and the measurable impact on income is not felt until the investment multiplier works itself out after 6 to 12 months. It follows from this line of reasoning that a decline in the money supply should of necessity precede the decrease in income. During a period of increasing aggregate demand the opposite effect should occur, and an increase in the money supply should precede increases in the price level.

[12] N. Kaldor, "The New Monetarism," *Lloyds Bank Review* (July 1970), 1–17.
[13] Ibid., p. 7.

For statistical evidence to support his view that the money supply is endogenous, Kaldor cites the same U.S. monetary statistics for the 1929–1933 period that are employed by Friedman and Schwartz. Kaldor acknowledges that the central bank can control the volume of high-powered money. However, he argues that this control is unimportant in determining the money stock, because the public and the commercial banks can and will offset any attempt to change the quantity of money against their wishes.

According to the monetary statistics compiled by Friedman and Schwartz, the quantity of high-powered money increased by 10% from October 1929 to June 1933. However, during this same period the money supply (defined to include time deposits) decreased by more than 35%. This occurred, Kaldor argues, for two reasons. First, the currency ratio C_r rose from 8% in October 1929 to 16% in June 1933. Second, the reserve ratio R_r rose from 7.5% to 12% in the same period. Rather than ascribe these two events to the banking crises, as Friedman and Schwartz do, Kaldor believes that these rises were caused by other factors. One reason Kaldor feels the currency ratio rose was that the stock market crash altered the volume of financial transactions, usually paid for by check, relative to income transactions, usually paid for with currency. Another reason was that due to the recession, the relative share of national income paid to workers increased and the relative share paid to owners of capital decreased. Because workers were paid in currency and owners of capital were paid by check, the relative demand for currency increased. These changes, according to Kaldor, produced changes in the pattern of expenditures between commodities usually paid for by check and those usually paid for in currency, thereby increasing the relative demand for currency and the currency ratio. The reserve ratio rose simply because no one wished to borrow under the adverse and uncertain business conditions that prevailed during the period. Kaldor's interpretation of the Great Contraction is perfectly in accord with his view that the money supply is purely endogenous.

Unfortunately, there is a major flaw in Kaldor's interpretation of the Great Contraction. Neither the currency ratio nor the reserve ratio began to rise until November 1930, which was concurrent with the first rash of banking failures. In fact, these ratios did not begin to increase rapidly until the second banking crisis occurred in March 1931. An inspection of Figure 13-3 reveals quite dramatically the rise in C_r and R_r after March 1931. Kaldor's hypothesis cannot account for this lag, but Friedman and Schwartz's confidence hypothesis can.

13-5   The Neo-Keynesian Critique

Among antimonetarist forces, the neo-Keynesians—those economists who have extended macroeconomics along the lines pioneered by Keynes and the Keynesians—are decidedly in the majority. Probably the most distinguished neo-Keynesian is James Tobin of Yale University. In this section we introduce and briefly discuss some of Tobin's more crucial arguments against monetarism; then in Chapter 14 we will present a more detailed examination of these concepts within the confines of a complete theoretical framework.

In his review of Friedman and Schwartz's *A Monetary History of the United States*[14] and in other publications, Tobin assumes a position between monetarism and extreme Keynesianism. First we consider some of the more important points on which Tobin and Friedman disagree and then the points on which they agree.

Tobin and the Monetarists: Points of Disagreement

You should recall that Friedman and Schwartz attach great significance to the observed fact that a declining (increasing) rate of growth in the money supply almost always precedes a recession (expansion). They consider this an indicator of the strength of the linkage between money and economic activity. In other words, they believe that the chain of causality from money to economic activity is so direct that the effect of business on money can be ignored. In the case of minor expansions or recessions, Tobin disagrees.

Tobin believes that in most minor recessions the observed decline in the rate of growth in the money supply prior to the peak is the result of the effects of business activity on money. According to Tobin, if the demand for currency in the short run is a function of the volume of the wage and retail transactions in which it is used, then as economic activity increases during the expansion phase of the business cycle, with H and R_r held constant, C_r will rise and the supply of money will decrease. Historically, however, the supply of money has not been observed to decline at the beginning of the expansion, because H is rising and R_r is falling. Thus their combined effect on the money supply offsets the movement in the currency ratio, and M_s increases. The quantity of high-powered money increases because in the recession phase of the cycle, the central bank, as part of its countercyclical policy, started to increase the quantity of high-powered money, and this policy usually continues well into the expansion phase. The reserve ratio decreases during the expansion because interest rates typically rise in this phase of the cycle, and this rise prompts commercial banks to reduce their excess reserve ratio XR_r. Now, according to equation (8-25)

$$M_s = \frac{H}{C_r + XR_r + RR_r - C_r XR_r - C_r RR_r} \qquad (8\text{-}25)$$

increasing H and reducing XR_r will increase the money supply M_s. Thus we have one force in the expansion phase that tends to reduce M_s and two other forces that tend to increase it. The net effect of these forces is to increase the money supply. After the economy is well into the expansion, the central bank reduces the rate of growth of high-powered money, commercial banks are unable to reduce XR_r much more because it is already close to zero, the still-rising C_r now becomes significant, and the rate of growth of M_s begins to decline. An opposite chain of events occurs during the recession phase of the cycle. From this analysis, Tobin concludes that a change in the rate of growth in the money supply is the *result* of change in economic activity, not its cause.[15]

---

[14] James Tobin, "The Monetary Interpretation of History," *The American Economic Review* **55** (June 1965), 646–85.

[15] For a more recent statement supporting the endogeneity argument, see J. Tobin, "Money and Income: Post Hoc Ergo Propter Hoc," and M. Friedman's "Comment on Tobin," both appearing in the *Quarterly Journal of Economics* (May 1970), 299–329.

Another important source of disagreement between the monetarists and the neo-Keynesians is the role that the interest rate plays in commercial bank behavior. Tobin believes that commercial banks have a liquidity preference function for excess reserves that is highly sensitive to the interest rate, and he feels that Friedman and Schwartz's belief that it is highly insensitive leads them to overemphasize the effectiveness of monetary policy.

The nature of this disagreement can be fruitfully explained in the context of U.S. monetary history. At the end of the Great Contraction the commercial banking system held extremely high excess reserves. In December 1929 the excess reserves of Federal Reserve member banks amounted to only $48 million and accounted for less than 0.5% of total reserves. By December 1935 these excess reserves had reached $3.0 billion and were equal to 52% of member bank reserves. According to Friedman and Schwartz's interpretation of this event, the large volume of excess reserves was primarily the result of a shift of bank liquidity preference functions, rather than of movement along the function. The shift of the function was in turn the result of the commercial banking system's attempt to raise the reserve ratio after the painful lessons learned during the financial crises of the Great Contraction.

We can easily illustrate this argument. The liquidity preference function of the member banks prior to the Great Contraction is depicted in Figure 13-6 by curve XR_0. The steepness of this curve indicates the minor importance that Friedman and Schwartz attach to the effect of the interest rate on the function. In other words, they believe that it is relatively interest inelastic. In December 1929 the interest rate of 4- to 6-month commercial paper was about 5.9% and the level of excess reserves was $0.048 billion; curve XR_0 is therefore drawn through the point with these coordinates in Figure 13-6. As a result of the bank crises of 1930 and 1931, by December 1935 the liquidity preference function had shifted to the right to XR_1, where $3 billion in excess reserves are demanded at an interest rate of 0.75%. Because of the assumed interest inelasticity of the liquidity preference function, Friedman and Schwartz ascribe the observed increase in excess reserves primarily to the shift of the function.

From the same set of data, Tobin reaches a different conclusion. He believes that the liquidity preference function of commercial banks is relatively interest elastic. Thus the increase in excess reserves can be shown to result primarily from a movement along the function. This line of reasoning is illustrated in Figure 13-7. The liquidity preference function for the excess reserves that are assumed to exist in December 1929 is XR_0', which is drawn so that it is highly interest elastic relative to curve XR_0 in Figure 13-6. At an interest rate of 5.9%, the demand for excess reserves is $0.048 billion. As a result of the ensuing financial crises, Tobin's liquidity preference function also shifts rightward to XR_1', where member commercial banks demand $3.0 billion in excess reserves at a 0.75% interest rate. A comparison of Figure 13-7 and 13-6 reveals that the shift of the liquidity preference curve in Tobin's hypothesis offers only a minor explanation for the large increase in excess reserves. This increase is primarily explained by the movement along the curve.

This difference in explanations of the observed liquidity of commercial bank

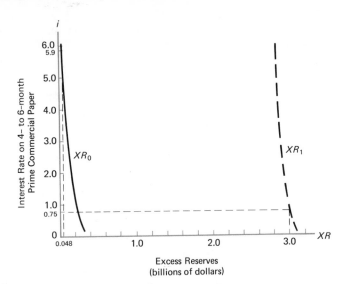

FIGURE 13-6   *The Liquidity Preference Function of Commercial Banks as Hypothesized by Friedman and Schwartz*

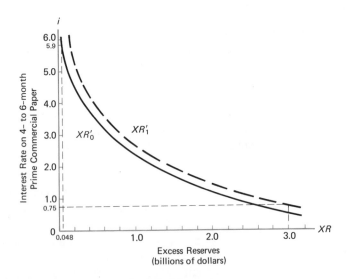

FIGURE 13-7   *The Liquidity Preference Function of Commercial Banks as Hypothesized by Tobin*

behavior may seem trivial, but in reality it is quite an important factor in understanding the monetarist–neo-Keynesian debate over the monetary interpretation of history and the effectiveness of monetary policy vis-à-vis fiscal policy.

If Tobin's analysis in terms of the monetary interpretation of history is correct, then expansionary monetary policy after the Great Contraction would have had a much smaller impact on the American economy than Friedman and Schwartz contend. The reason for this should be clear. If the Federal Reserve had increased the quantity of high-powered money through open-market purchases, this would have tended to depress the interest rate and virtually all high-powered money would have simply become part of the commercial banking system's portfolio holdings of excess reserves. Thus Friedman and Schwartz's severe criticism of Federal Reserve policy after the Great Contraction is far too strong if Tobin is correct. Tobin acknowledges that the economic policies of the 1930s were wrong, but this fact is unimportant because their negative effect on the economy was insignificant.

Regarding the debate over the effectiveness of monetary policy relative to fiscal policy, the extent of the interest elasticity of the commercial banking system's liquidity preference for excess reserves is an extremely important factor. Recall our discussion of the money supply curve illustrated in Figure 8-1 (page 152). If the liquidity preference function of commercial banks is highly interest elastic, as Tobin suggests, then the excess reserve ratio XR_r will also be highly interest elastic. In other words, when the rate of interest falls, XR_r will become quite large, and vice versa. This means that the money supply specified by equation (8-25) will also be highly interest elastic. This is significant because in our derivation of the LM curve in Chapter 10 we learned that increasing the interest elasticity of the money supply curve increases the interest elasticity of the LM curve. And as we shall learn in Chapter 14, the degree of interest elasticity of the LM curve is critical to the monetarist–neo-Keynesian debate.

Another source of disagreement between neo-Keynesians and monetarists revolves around the exact nature of the demand for money. Neo-Keynesians believe that the demand for money is highly interest elastic and that variations in the interest rate therefore have a strong inverse effect on the demand for money. Monetarists tend to believe that the effect of the interest rate on the demand for money is insignificant when the economy is near the full-employment level. If neo-Keynesians are correct in their appraisal of the interest elasticity of the demand for money, then their LM curve is much more interest elastic than that of the monetarists.

Tobin and the Monetarists: Points of Agreement

In contrast to Kaldor's extreme Keynesian view, Tobin does readily agree with some major points of the monetarist thesis. He is in accord with the view of Friedman and Schwartz that the absolute decline in the money supply during major American recessions has contributed significantly to the severity of these recessions and that appropriate monetary policy could prevent such a decline. Tobin also concurs with the monetarist view that excessive expansion of the money supply produces inflation, but he does not believe that this the only cause of inflation.

13-6   Nonmonetary Forces and the Great Depression

Peter Temin has also challenged Friedman and Schwartz's interpretation of the events that produced the Great Depression.[16] Temin believes that when the Federal Reserve raised the discount rate to offset gold outflows from October 1929 through September 1931, the general economic downturn resulted from reduced invest- ment and consumption expenditure rather than from the collapse of the banking system. As income decreased, less money was demanded, and "The money market was equilibrated by the fall in the stock of money following the bank panics, but these panics did not in any way cause the decline in income."[17] In other words, according to Temin, even if there had not been a banking collapse, the supply of money would have been reduced endogenously anyway, because the supply of money accommodates the demand for money.

In Chapter 8 we learned how the supply of money can theoretically be influenced by demand-related factors. In terms of Temin's analysis, as income decreased in the beginning stages of the Great Depression, interest rates also declined because the supply of money exceeded the demand for money. Decreasing interest rates produced increases in the currency and reserve ratios, which in turn reduced the supply of money and equilibrated the money market. Thus for Temin's interpreta- tion to be acceptable, it must be demonstrated empirically that these variables are quite sensitive to the factors that influence the demand for money. Gandolfi and Lothian have thoroughly examined the demand for money during this period and have concluded that "If demand and supply were interdependent, then in view of the substantial differences in conditions of supply over our sample period [1929–1968] we would expect to see a good deal of temporal instability in our estimated income and interest-rate coefficients. But since that was not the case, we suspect that the degree of interdependence has been small."[18] A study by Donald L. Kohn indicates that the demand for currency relative to the interest rate is highly inelastic.[19] Kohn's results for the 1952–1975 period show that a 1% change in the rate of interest will produce only a 0.002% change in the demand for currency. If we accept Gandolfi and Lothian's conclusion that the total demand for money remained stable over the 1929–1968 period, then it follows that the demand for currency was highly interest inelastic during the 1929–1931 period. In addition, the work of Phillip Cagan has shown that large movements in the currency and reserve ratios in all major recessions were caused by bank panics that were not in themselves the result of downturns in income. If this was not also true during the great depression, then behavior during this period is characterized by a one-time shift in the actions of the public and banking sectors of the economy. Because this

---

[16] Peter Temin, "*Did Monetary Forces Cause the Great Depression?*' (New York: W.W. Norton, 1976).

[17] Peter Temin, "Lessons for the Present from the Great Depression," *American Economic Review* **66** (May 1976), 41.

[18] Arthur E. Gandolf and James R. Lothian, "The Demand for Money from the Great Depression to the Present," *American Economic Review* **66** (May 1976), 51.

[19] Donald L. Kohn, "Currency Movements in the United States," *Monthly Review of the Federal Reserve Bank of Kansas City* (April 1976), 3–8.

seems unlikely and because there *was* a banking collapse, we tend to conclude that the reduction in the money supply produced the decrease in income, rather than the reverse.

13-7 Concluding Remarks

In this chapter we have reviewed the monetarist interpretation of history. Monetarists conclude that a strong and direct link exists between the money supply and economic activity in the short run. Absolute declines in the money supply have preceded every major American recession, and monetarists believe that these declines were the primary reason for the severity of the recessions, which could have been alleviated by appropriate changes in monetary policy. Based on their examination of major recessions, the monetarists conclude that money probably plays a causal role in most minor recessions as well. According to the monetarist viewpoint, sustained inflation always results from excessive expansion of the money supply by the central bank. Expansionary fiscal policies have little if any effect on inflation. The major criticism of this theory to be voiced by the extreme Keynesians is that the money supply is purely endogenous and that the entire monetarist explanation of history is therefore false. Correlation, these Keynesians argue, does *not* necessarily mean causation. The neo-Keynesians take a position somewhere between monetarism and extreme Keynesianism. They argue that the monetarist claims of a strong and direct link between money and business activity are incorrect. In reality, they claim, the link is much weaker, because economic activity can affect the money supply significantly and because the demand for money is more interest elastic than the monetarists realize. Neo-Keynesians, however, agree with the monetarist claims that the severity of major recessions results from the absolute decline in the money supply and that periods of major and sustained inflation result from overexpansion of the money supply.

14 How Much Does Money Matter?

14-1   Introduction

The single most important issue in macroeconomics today is the relative effectiveness of fiscal vs. monetary policy. This debate revolves around the nature of the demand for and the supply of money. If either the demand for money or the supply of money exhibits certain characteristics, then fiscal policy becomes the only effective means of altering aggregate demand. However, if the demand for and the supply of money combined exhibit other specific characteristics, then fiscal policy can have no effect on aggregate demand. In the first case monetary policy is ineffective; in the second case it becomes all powerful. Between these two extremes, monetary policy varies from very weak to very strong. Therefore, judging the exact nature of the demand for and the supply of money plays a critical role in the formulation of monetary policy.

The spectrum of opinion among economists concerning the nature of the supply of and the demand for money ranges from the *"money doesn't matter"* view of the *extreme Keynesians* to the *"only money matters"* view of the *extreme monetarists*. In this chapter we consider the central theoretical issues that surround the debate over the importance of money and examine how these issues influence the various economic models constructed by opposing factions to illustrate the basis of their policy conclusions. We then examine the current empirical evidence and extend it to reach some conclusions about the probable outcome of this monetary debate.

14-2   "Only Money Matters"

The *extreme monetarist* position, summarized in the phrase *"only money matters,"* is based on the joint validity of particular assumptions about the demand for and the supply of money. Specifically, the money demand and money supply functions are assumed to be perfectly interest inelastic. We now examine how these assumptions affect our basic *IS-LM* model and the conclusions that can be drawn from it. Figure 14-1(a) is a graph of four money demand curves that satisfy the assumption of perfect interest inelasticity. At any given level of real income, the demand for money is independent of the interest rate. The four curves are labeled m_{d_1}, m_{d_2}, $m_{d_{FE}}$, and m_{d_4}, where the subscripts refer to the corresponding levels of real income. Beginning with an initial perfectly interest-inelastic nominal money supply M_s, we show two perfectly interest-inelastic real-money supply curves m_{s_1} and m_{s_2} (out of the whole family of such curves) in Figure 14-1(a). These representative money supply curves apply at price levels P_1 and P_2 (as indicated by their subscripts) and are drawn so that m_{s_2} coincides with m_{d_1} and m_{s_1} coincides with m_{d_2}. Because only one quantity of real money can correspond to one level of real income under these assumptions, the loci of money-market equilibrium in Figure 14-1(b) are points instead of curves. For money supply curves m_{s_2} and m_{s_1} these points are labeled A and B, respectively. The LM curves LM_1 and LM_2 that are derived from the money supply curves m_{s_2} and m_{s_1} appear in Figure 14(d). We can now see the effect that the extreme monetarist money demand and money supply functions have on the LM curve: the curves are now perfectly interest inelastic.

Assuming an initial IS curve of IS_0, we derive the corresponding aggregate demand curve AgD in Figure 14-1(e). If we also assume an aggregate supply model in which wages are downwardly rigid, then a less than full-employment stable disequilibrium exists at price level P_1 and income level Y_2, as shown by point D in Figure 14-1(e).

We can now examine the impact of pure fiscal and pure monetary policies on national income and the price level. Suppose the government institutes an expansionary fiscal policy in which the nominal money supply M_s remains unchanged. Such a policy will shift the IS curve outward from IS_0 to IS_1. However, because the LM curves are vertical, the price levels and the income levels at which IS_1 intersects the LM curves LM_1 and LM_2 are identical with the levels prevailing when the relevant IS curve was IS_0. Therefore, in this model expansionary fiscal policy has no effect on the aggregate demand curve, which remains fixed at AgD. The only effects that an expansionary fiscal policy produces in this model are to raise the interest rate from i_0 to i_1 as shown in Figure 14-1(d), and to increase the share of national income consumed by government. In terms of national income and the price level, we can conclude from this model that the government spending multiplier is zero and therefore that *fiscal policy does not matter.*

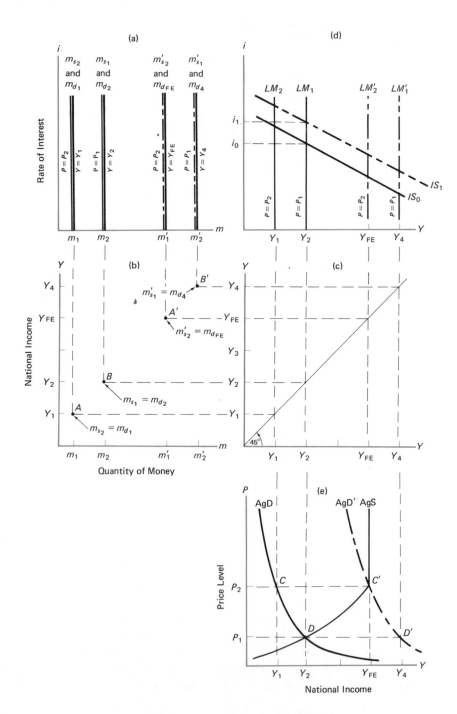

FIGURE 14-1   "Only Money Matters"

Now suppose that the relevant IS curve is once again IS_0 and that the central bank increases the nominal money supply from M_s to M_s'. At price levels P_1 and P_2, the new real-money supply curves become m_{s_1}' and m_{s_2}', respectively. As shown in Figure 14-1(a) these money supply curves coincide with money demand curves m_{d_4} and $m_{d_{FE}}$, respectively, giving us money-market equilibrium points B' and A' in Figure 14-1(b). The resulting LM curves LM_1' and LM_2', which are derived in Figure 14-1(d), lie to the right of the previous LM curves. The effect of an increase in the nominal money supply on the aggregate demand curve is shown in Figure 14-1(e), where the new aggregate demand curve AgD' lies to the right of AgD and now intersects the aggregate supply curve at the full-employment level of income.

It follows from the analysis of the preceding model, which embodies the extreme monetarist assumptions, that fiscal policy cannot affect national income or the price level, whereas the money supply can. Thus extreme monetarists conclude that *only money matters*.

14-3 "Money Doesn't Matter"

The *extreme Keynesians* are in direct opposition to the extreme monetarists. Whereas the extreme monetarist model requires both the money supply and money demand functions to possess certain characteristics simultaneously, the extreme Keynesian model can be based on any one of three assumptions. Specifically, the extreme Keynesian position is based on (1) a perfectly endogenous money supply, (2) a perfectly interest-elastic demand for money, or (3) a perfectly interest-inelastic MEI curve. Our purpose now is to learn how these assumptions affect our basic IS-LM model and the conclusions that can be drawn from it.

A Perfectly Endogenous Money Supply

Nicholas Kaldor's attack on the monetarist interpretation of economic history— and, to a lesser extent, Peter Temin's—are based on the argument that the quantity of money is determined by public demand and that the central bank is powerless to change the quantity of money. The graphic depiction of this argument is a real-money supply curve that is perfectly interest elastic at the normal rate of interest i_0, as shown in Figure 14-2(a). The horizontal position of the money supply curve at the normal rate of interest means that the central bank cannot alter the curve's position. Furthermore, this single curve is the real-money supply curve at all possible price levels.

Money demand curves m_{d_1}, $m_{d_{FE}}$, and m_{d_3} are also graphed in Figure 14-2(a). These curves are drawn perfectly interest inelastic, indicating that this particular extreme monetarist assumption is not in itself sufficient to yield the extreme monetarist conclusions. Given these particular assumptions about the demand for and the supply of money, we can derive the LM curve LM_0 shown in Figure 14-2(d). We can see there that LM_0 is perfectly interest elastic at i_0, signifying money-

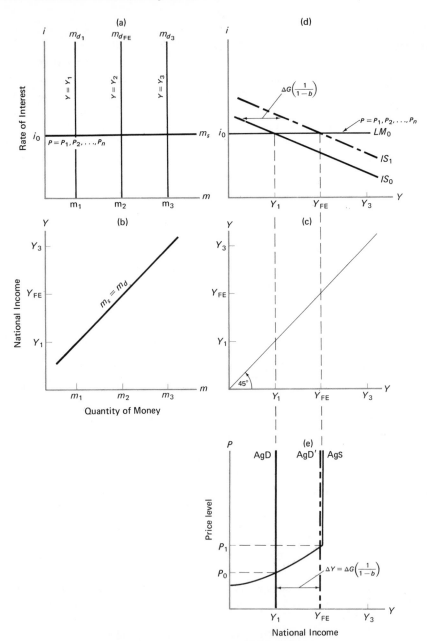

FIGURE 14-2   "Money Doesn't Matter"

market equilibrium at all price levels. This occurs because the money supply is perfectly endogenous.

If our initial *IS* curve is IS_0, then the level of aggregate demand will be Y_1 at all price levels. Hence the aggregate demand curve AgD is perfectly price inelastic at

Y_1 in Figure 14-2(e). The intersection of AgD with the downwardly rigid money-wage aggregate supply curve AgS determines the price level P_0.

Now suppose that the central bank attempts to increase aggregate demand by an open-market purchase. According to the extreme Keynesian assumption of endogeneity, this is impossible because the public will not accept more real cash balances than the "needs of trade" and portfolios require. Hence the real-money supply curve remains fixed at m_s, and the LM curve cannot be shifted from LM_0. Monetary policy is completely ineffective, and *money doesn't matter*.

On the other hand, fiscal policy will be extremely effective, because the actual multiplier resulting from an increase in government expenditure will be equal to the naive multipliers we developed earlier in Chapter 4. To restore full employment, the government need only increase government expenditure by

$$\Delta G = (1 - b)(Y_{FE} - Y_1) \tag{14-1}$$

if we assume taxes are exogenous. This will shift the IS curve by $\Delta G[1/(1 - b)]$, from IS_0 to IS_1, as shown in Figure 14-2(d). Since IS_1 now intersects LM_0 at Y_{FE}, the new aggregate demand curve AgD' intersects AgS at the full-employment level of income. Hence, the extreme Keynesian assumption that the money supply is perfectly endogenous leads to the conclusion that *only fiscal policy matters*.

Before examining the second extreme Keynesian model, we should point out that the model used in this analysis, like our models in Chapters 3 and 4, does not yield a determinate price level at full employment. This indeterminacy is evident in Figure 14-2(e), where AgD' coincides with AgS for all price levels greater than P_1. This is not a crucial criticism of the model, however, because if the Pigou effect is added, then the aggregate demand curve will become price elastic and a determinate price level will be reached.

A Perfectly Interest-elastic Demand for Money

Our discussion of the likelihood of a stable full-employment equilibrium in Chapter 11 included two conditions that the Keynesians suggested might preclude equilibrium. One of these conditions, the so-called *liquidity trap*, caused the interest elasticity of the demand for money to become infinite at some positive rate of interest. While virtually all present-day economists agree that a liquidity trap has never been observed and is unlikely to occur in the foreseeable future, a few extreme Keynesians still base their policy prescriptions on an implicitly assumed liquidity trap.

A detailed graphic analysis of this extreme Keynesian case was constructed in Figures 11-2, 11-4, and 11-5. You should recall from this discussion that the presence of the liquidity trap produced an aggregate demand curve that became perfectly price inelastic at the level of income consistent with product-market equilibrium at the critical rate of interest. Since (in the absence of the Pigou effect) an increase in the nominal money supply does not change the level of income specified by the IS curve at the critical rate of interest, the aggregate demand curve remains perfectly price inelastic at the same level of income. If the income level at which the aggregate demand curve becomes perfectly price inelastic is less than the full-employment level, then monetary policy cannot restore full employment.

A Perfectly Interest-inelastic Investment Function

The third condition that the Keynesians suggested could prevent full employment was investment insufficiency due to a vertical MEI curve. In this situation monetary expansion will produce no change in the level of income, whereas expansionary fiscal policy increases income by an amount equal to that predicted by the naive multipliers. Proof of this statement is left as an excercise for the student.

The important thing to observe in these examples is that expansionary monetary policy produces no changes in the relevant economic variables (the price level and the income level). These variables all remain at their pre-monetary-expansion values. On the other hand, fiscal policy is extremely powerful under the keynesian conditions, and the full force of the naive multipliers prevails. Hence the extreme Keynesian conclusion, *money doesn't matter,* and its corollary, *only fiscal policy matters,* are upheld.

14-4 "Money Matters"

As we stressed earlier, most economists hold neither the extreme monetarist nor the extreme Keynesian view. Most contemporary economists agree that money matters, but even within this broad spectrum of consensus there are varying degrees of dissent over the extent to which money matters. At one end of the spectrum, the Keynesians believe that money matters very little relative to real factors in the short run. At the other end of the spectrum, the monetarists believe that money matters very much relative to real factors in the short run, but not in the long run. In the middle of this spectrum, the neo-Keynesians assign comparable weight to both monetary and real factors. We now examine the theoretical arguments behind the Keynesian, monetarist, and neo-Keynesian views.

The Keynesian View

The Keynesians' view that *money matters very little* is based on their assumptions about the real and the monetary sectors of the economy. These assumptions determine the *IS* and *LM* loci and hence the effectiveness of monetary policy relative to fiscal policy.

Keynesians generally believe that the forms of real expenditure that are influenced by the interest rate are the tangible investments of business firms, whose behavior is summarized in the marginal efficiency of investment (MEI) curve. However, Keynesians also conclude that the interest rate plays only a minor role in investment decisions and therefore that the MEI curve is highly interest inelastic. A highly interest-inelastic MEI curve in turn produces a highly interest-inelastic *IS* curve. Such an *IS* curve, IS_0, is graphed in Figure 14-3(a).

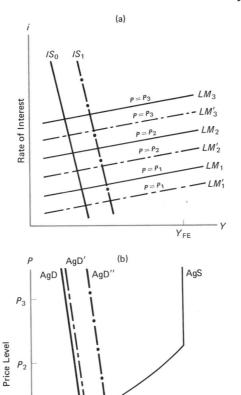

FIGURE 14-3   *The Keynesian View: Money Matters Very Little*

Keynesians assume that the demand for money is highly interest elastic. This means that an open-market purchase of bonds by the central bank will raise bond prices and lower interest rates by only a small amount. These interest-rate changes, Keynesians argue, are sufficient to maintain money-market equilibrium, so that the holders of these new cash balances have no strong desire to spend more for commodities whose purchase is not influenced by interest-rate changes. Keynesians also assume that the money supply is largely endogenous and that the real-money supply curves are therefore highly interest elastic. The net effect of interest-elastic money demand and money supply curves is to produce *LM* curves that are even more highly interest elastic. Such a family of *LM* curves, LM_1, LM_2, and LM_3, is graphed in Figure 14-3(a).

The *IS* and *LM* curves in Figure 14-3(a) produce the aggregate demand curve AgD in Figure 14-3(b). It follows from the Keynesian assumptions that the aggregate demand curve is relatively price inelastic. Now suppose that the nominal money supply is increased by the central bank, shifting the *LM* curves in Figure 14-3(a) to the right, to LM_1', LM_2', and LM_3'. This shift of the *LM* curves in turn causes the aggregate demand curve to shift to the right, to AgD'. As a result of the high interest elasticities of the *LM* curves and the low interest elasticity of the *IS* curve, aggregate demand shifts only slightly to the right and the consequent increase in national income is also slight.

Now suppose that we return to our initial nominal money supply, so that the relevant *LM* curves are once again LM_1, LM_2, and LM_3, and that the government initiates a tax cut. The tax cut shifts the *IS* curve from IS_0 to IS_1, as shown in Figure 14-3(a). The intersection of this new *IS* curve and the original set of *LM* curves then shifts the aggregate demand curve from AgD to AgD''. In this case fiscal policy has greatly affected national income due to the high interest elasticity of the *LM* curves and the low interest elasticity of the *IS* curve.

We can now comprehend the policy implications of the Keynesian view. Keynesians place major emphasis on fiscal policy and tend to ignore monetary policy, because fiscal policy is strong and monetary policy is weak. They advocate monetary policy primarily as a means for the monetary authorities to lower market rates of interest and thereby to reduce the fraction of tax dollars spent to service the national debt.

The Monetarist View

Like the Keynesians, the monetarists base their view on certain assumptions about the real and the monetary sectors of the economy. Monetarists accept Friedman's permanent income hypothesis and therefore include consumer durables in the spectrum of tangible assets whose purchase is a function of the interest rate. This means that the MEI curve includes consumer durables as well as business investment. The monetarists then argue that these expenditures are highly sensitive to variations in the interest rate and hence that the MEI curve is highly interest elastic. Moreover, the inclusion of consumer durables in the MEI curve greatly increases the absolute level of investment at any given interest rate. It then follows that the monetarists' *IS* curve will be highly interest elastic. Such a curve, IS_0, is shown in Figure 14-4(a).

As we might expect, monetarists assume a position that is closely related to the extreme monetarist view regarding the supply of and the demand for money. Although monetarists do not go as far as postulating that money demand and money supply curves are perfectly interest inelastic, they generally assume that these curves are highly inelastic and that the resulting family of *LM* curves will therefore be relatively interest inelastic as well. Typical *LM* curves exhibiting this characteristic, LM_1, LM_2, and LM_3, are graphed in Figure 14-4(a). The intersection of these *LM* curves with the IS_0 curve produces the aggregate demand curve AgD

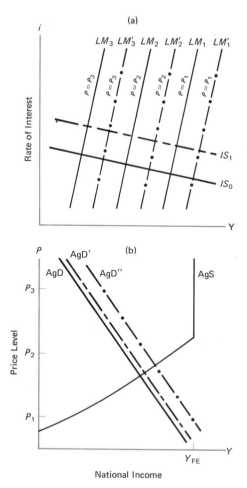

FIGURE 14-4   *The Monetarist View: Money Matters Very Much*

in Figure 14-4(b). A comparison between the aggregate demand curves in Figures 14-3 and 14-4 reveals that the monetarist curve is much more price elastic at a given price than the Keynesian curve.

As before, we examine the effectiveness of monetary policy relative to fiscal policy. Suppose that the government initiates an expansionary fiscal policy to restore full employment. This means that the *IS* curve shifts from IS_0 to IS_1, as shown in Figure 14-4(a). This shift in turn causes the aggregate demand curve to shift from AgD to AgD′. In this monetarist model, the resulting increase in national income is small due to the relative interest elasticities of the *IS* and *LM* curves.

Now suppose that instead of an expansionary fiscal policy, the government institutes an expansionary monetary policy. The central bank increases the nominal money supply via open-market purchases, and the set of *LM* curves shifts to LM_1', LM_2', and LM_3' in Figure 14-4(a). The intersection of these *LM* curves with the initial *IS* curve IS_0 produces the aggregate demand curve AgD". As we can clearly see from this example, monetary policy is much more effective than fiscal policy. Hence, in contradistinction to the Keynesian view, the monetarists believe that *money matters very much* and that it should be a primary concern of macroeconomic policy.

The Neo-Keynesian View

The neo-Keynesian view is sometimes called the *eclectic* view, because it embodies selected Keynesian and monetarist theories. From the Keynesians, the neo-Keynesians select the theories that argue that the demand for and the supply of money are highly interest elastic, so that the neo-Keynesian *LM* curve is also highly interest elastic. Neo-Keynesians believe that the transactions-demand motive is not the major reason the public holds money. They believe that an equally important reason the public holds money is as a *store of value*, or an asset. Because many financial assets approach the perfect liquidity of money, neo-Keynesians argue that these assets should be considered close substitutes for money. Moreover, unlike currency and demand deposits, these assets earn interest, making the desirability of holding money in portfolios highly sensitive to variations in the interest rate. Hence the demand for money should be highly interest elastic. For the same reason, the demand for currency is inversely related to the interest rate; when interest rates rise, the currency ratio C_r declines and the quantity of money supplied increases. In addition, the excess reserve ratio XR_r also varies inversely with the interest rate, as commercial banks seek to maximize profits. Hence, the neo-Keynesian money supply curve is partially endogenous and interest elastic. The total effect of these two theories produces a relatively interest-elastic family of *LM* curves, such as LM_1, LM_2, and LM_3 shown in Figure 14-5(a).

Like the Keynesians, the neo-Keynesians believe that the major impact of monetary changes is indirectly transmitted to the real sector. For example, suppose that the central bank increases the money supply by conducting open-market purchases of government securities. When these securities are purchased, their prices increase and their interest rates decline. The decline in interest rates produces an increase in investment, as businesses move downward along their MEI curves; increased investment in turn increases consumption and income via the investment multiplier. Because the neo-Keynesian definition of consumption includes the purchase of all consumer durables (with the exception of owner-occupied housing), the increased expenditure on consumer durables is an *indirect* result of monetary expansion. In contrast to the Keynesians, the neo-Keynesians believe, with the monetarists, that business investment is sensitive to interest-rate changes. Hence, the neo-Keynesian view of the MEI curve is midway between that of the Keynesians and that of the monetarists. Therefore, the interest elasticity of the neo-Keynesian *IS* curve lies somewhere between the interest elasticity of the monetarist and the Keynesian *IS* curves. Such an *IS* curve is illustrated by the IS_0 curve in Figure 14-5(a).

The aggregate demand curve produced by the intersection of IS_0 with LM_1, LM_2, and LM_3 is AgD, which is shown in Figure 14-5(b). A comparison of this aggregate demand curve with the AgD curves in Figures 14-3 and 14-4 reveals, as we might expect, that the relative price elasticity of the neo-Keynesian aggregate demand curve is approximately midway between that of the Keynesian and that of the monetarist AgD curves.

As in the two previous cases, we now examine the relative effectiveness of monetary and fiscal policy. Suppose that an expansionary fiscal policy is initiated by the government and that the *IS* curve shifts from IS_0 to IS_1 in Figure 14-5(a). This in turn causes the aggregate demand curve to shift to the right from AgD to AgD', as shown in Figure 14-5(b).

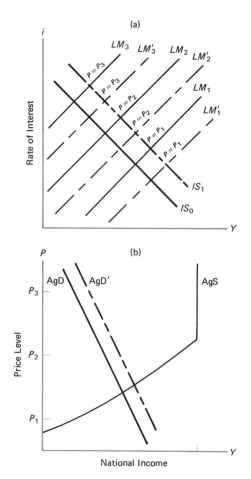

FIGURE 14-5 *The Neo-Keynesian View: Money Matters*

Now suppose that instead of an expansionary fiscal policy, the government adopts an expansionary monetary policy. The LM curves then shift to the right, to LM_1', LM_2', and LM_3' in Figure 14-5(a). The aggregate demand curve produced by the intersection of these curves with IS_0 is AgD′, which is the same aggregate demand curve produced by the fiscal policy. Clearly, the coincidence of these aggregate demand curves is the result of the geometric construction of Figure 14-5 and is not a necessary conclusion of the neo-Keynesian argument. We overlap these demand curves simply to emphasize the fact that monetary and fiscal policy achieve the same order of effectiveness in neo-Keynesian analysis. Hence the neo-Keynesian view places equal stress on the implementation of monetary and fiscal policy.

Summary of Views Discussed

In summary, we have examined the major theoretical differences that separate the Keynesians, monetarists, and eclectic neo-Keynesians. These theoretical differences produce the divergent policies emphasized by these three groups of economic theorists. Keynesians argue that money matters very little and that fiscal policy should be emphasized almost exclusively. Monetarists reach exactly the opposite conclusion, advocating that primary importance be placed on monetary policy. Neo-Keynesians adopt a midway position between these two extremes, concluding that both Keynesian and monetarist policy tools can be used with almost equal effectiveness.

Shortly, we will examine the current empirical evidence pertaining to these theoretical controversies to try to ascertain which, if any, of these views is most applicable to the American economy. But before we can do this, we must explore the monetary transmission mechanism in greater detail to obtain a fuller understanding of the implications of the empirical evidence.

14-5   The Transmission Mechanism

The *monetary transmission mechanism* is the mechanism by which changes in the money supply produce effects that interact with the real sector to create changes in income and in the price level. Two primary mechanisms are believed to be involved in this process: the *portfolio* or *relative price mechanism,* and the *wealth mechanism*. We examine both of these mechanisms in this section; in the next section we review the empirical evidence concerning their relative importance.

The Portfolio Mechanism

There are two major schools of thought regarding the manner in which monetary policy affects the asset portfolios of households and firms. One emphasizes the so-called *credit effects*, or the impact of monetary policy on certain well-defined market rates of interest, and is closely associated with the neo-Keynesian approach to the transmission mechanism. The second concentrates on the *monetary effects*, or the effect of monetary policy on the quantity of money, and is associated with the monetarist theory of the transmission mechanism.

The neo-Keynesian approach treats changes in the market rate of interest that result from changes in the money supply as the significant aspect of monetary policy. To the extent that investment expenditures on plant and equipment are sensitive to changes in the interest rate, the initial impact of monetary policy is felt in the capital goods industry. These variations in investment in turn produce changes in consumption and income via the investment multiplier.

The monetarist approach, on the other hand, views the direct change in the money supply as the most relevant aspect of monetary policy. This emphasis on changes in the money supply is based on the premise that households wish to maintain some desired stock of money relative to their income and that monetary policy, by causing the actual stock to differ from the desired stock, causes households to respond by attempting to return to the desired stock of money balances. In this attempt, households directly change the level of aggregate demand, income, and prices. Using this approach, monetary policy operates directly on the total spectrum of expenditures, rather than simply via investment expenditures, as in the neo-Keynesian approach.

At first glance these two approaches probably appear to be two clearly distinct views of the transmission mechanism, but a closer examination indicates that this is not the case. The two approaches are really quite similar, differing only in the range of interest rates considered. The neo-Keynesian transmission mechanism focuses on the narrow and well-defined range of interest rates associated with easily marketable assets, such as government securities, corporate stocks and bonds, commercial paper, savings and loan shares, and real estate mortgages. Neo-Keynesians argue that these assets are close substitutes for money, because they serve as a store of value in a manner equivalent to money. Hence a change in the money supply will have its initial impact on the interest rates associated with these assets, as individual wealth holders readjust their asset portfolios. For example, suppose that the Federal Reserve conducts an open-market purchase and increases the money supply. As a result of this operation, wealth holders exchange government securities for Federal Reserve notes and increase the quantity of cash balances in their individual portfolios, which in turn creates a temporary imbalance of excess cash in the portfolio. Because neo-Keynesians view liquid financial assets as close substitutes for money, portfolio equilibrium is restored as the excess money in individual portfolios is used to purchase dividend- or interest-bearing financial assets. As wealth holders attempt to adjust their portfolios by purchasing noncash financial assets, they drive up the price of these assets, thereby reducing the market rate of interest. This increase in the price of assets eventually encourages the issue of new financial assets. The money received from the sale of these assets is then used for the purchase of the real investment, which then expands income via the investment multiplier.

It should be noted here that the neo-Keynesian transmission mechanism makes a sharp distinction between households and firms. With the single exception of owner-occupied housing, households are assumed to hold their wealth in the form of money or financial assets, such as bonds or stocks, and to use income to increase their wealth or to purchase goods and services. All of the community's physical wealth, with the exception of owner-occupied housing, is assumed to be held by firms and is considered to be the real counterpart of the financial assets held by households. It follows from these assumptions that consumption expenditures include the purchase of all durable goods as well as current services and that saving can only take the form of cash balances, financial assets, or owner-occupied housing. Hence, a clear distinction is made between firms and households (with the exception of housing) regarding their respective roles in the transmission mechanism. If we ignore housing, then interest-rate changes resulting from monetary policy cause households to alter their portfolios of financial assets (there is no real effect), and this in turn, via interest-rate changes, causes firms to alter their level of investment (the initial real effect). In response to this change in investment, aggregate demand is further altered via the investment multiplier.

This narrow definition of physical assets embodied in the neo-Keynesian approach is clearly in opposition to that employed by the monetarist leader Milton Friedman. You should recall that Friedman, in his theories of the consumption function and of the demand for money, defined the physical assets of households to include, in addition to owner-occupied housing, every possible consumer durable good that produces a flow of services. As a result of this approach, households, which are consumers of these service flows, simultaneously behave as firms, because they purchase durable goods, which are really investment goods, and "sell" the services of these goods to themselves. From this point of view, it is impossible to differentiate clearly between firms and households. Keeping this distinction in the definition of physical assets in mind, we can now discover why there is little theoretical difference between the monetarist and the neo-Keynesian approaches.

According to the monetarist theory, every durable good owned by a household should be considered a physical asset that produces a flow of services, the present value of which is determined by some appropriate rate of interest, as we learned in Chapter 5. Like the business firm's portfolio, the household's portfolio of assets is in equilibrium when each asset's present value, as computed by the relevant interest rate, is equal to its purchase cost. Hence monetary policy, by altering the various interest rates, changes this equilibrium condition to a disequilibrium condition. Thus as households and business firms adjust their stock of assets in an attempt to return to an equilibrium stock, they jointly and directly affect the level of aggregate demand.

If the monetarist theory of the transmission mechanism can be reduced to a description of the effect of interest-rate variation on aggregate demand, then why is the money supply given primary emphasis? The answer to this question can be learned by asking another question: What relevant interest rates correspond to the portfolio of assets held by households, according to the opposing theories? According to the neo-Keynesian approach, the relevant assets, including owner-occupied housing, are all very narrowly and well defined and are associated with an equally well-defined set of market interest rates—the rates of return on government securities, corporate stocks and bonds, and housing mortgages, which are the assets households purchase—and all of these interest rates are readily observable. If the neo-Keynesian viewpoint is correct, then the market rates of interest corresponding to these assets are the appropriate indicators of monetary policy, and the central bank can determine whether to loosen or to tighten monetary policy by observing these rates.

The monetarist definition of the asset portfolio of households, which includes all consumer durable goods, is much broader than the neo-Keynesian definition. This creates a problem in the implementation of monetary policy that the neo-Keynesian approach cannot handle. The problem occurs because most of a household's durable assets are not bought and sold in organized financial markets, so that it is impossible to observe their corresponding rates of return, which take the form of a flow of subjective future benefits to the consumer. Hence, it is impossible to determine how monetary changes affect these rates. Furthermore, because of imperfections in the markets for these durable goods, the implicit rate of return that equates the present value of the flow of services with the initial purchase price of a durable good will probably differ markedly from the implicit rate of return that equates the flow of services of the durable good with the resale price of the second-hand good. For example, consider the difference between the purchase price of a new overcoat and the resale price of the overcoat after it has been worn only once. Clearly, the flow of services the overcoat will yield has not been appreciably affected by the fact that it has been worn once, but its much lower price when sold as a second-hand coat indicates that a higher implicit rate of return is necessary to equate its present value to its present cost. For these reasons, it is difficult or impossible to associate an observable set of interest rates with the portfolio adjustment of households. Because these subjective rates are a crucial factor in determining aggregate demand but are also unobservable, Friedman argues that the "second best" measure of monetary policy is the rate of change in the money supply, rather than the few narrowly defined market interest rates considered by the neo-Keynesians. The neo-Keynesian rejoinder to the monetarist emphasis on the quantity of money is that gauging the direction of monetary policy by observing changes in the money stock can be equally misleading, because the money supply is partially endogenous.

In summary, both monetarists and neo-Keynesians base their theories of the transmission mechanism on the portfolio approach, but the portfolio of assets held by households in the neo-Keynesian analysis is limited to money, financial assets, and owner-occupied housing, whereas the monetarist portfolio is based on the concept of total wealth outlined in Friedman's permanent income hypothesis and his restatement of the quantity theory of money. Therefore, the impact of monetary policy in the neo-Keynesian framework will affect aggregate demand via changes in the interest rate that determines the investment expenditures of firms, and these expenditures in turn will produce investment multiplier effects on the levels of consumption and income. Hence, these interest rates are the best indicators of monetary policy. According to the monetarist theory, however, monetary policy directly affects not only business investment expenditures but also household investment expenditures (durable goods purchased) by altering the implicit market rates of interest that households use to determine their optimal stock of assets. Because these implicit rates of return are the most relevant gauge of monetary policy but are unknown to monetary authorities, changes in the money supply are the "second best" indicator of monetary policy.

The Wealth Mechanism

The wealth mechanism is based on the manner in which changes in the quantity of money affect nonhuman net wealth and how this in turn affects aggregate demand. One definition of nonhuman nominal net wealth W_{NH} is

$$W_{NH} = H + P_v K \tag{14-2}$$

where H = quantity of nominal high-powered money
$\quad\quad P_v K$ = market or nominal present value of capital stock

In our discussion of a real-balance effect, called the *Pigou effect,* in Chapter 11 we argued that as the price level declined, the real value of high-powered money increased. This increase in the real value of H produces an increase in the net wealth of households, and because consumption is a function of wealth, consumption increases. The same increase in consumption results if the central bank increases the quantity of money held by the nonbanking public and the price level remains constant. In terms of equation (14-2), increases in H increase W_{NH}, and consumption out of current measured income increases. Hence, the real-balance effect we have just examined is one mechanism whereby monetary policy can affect aggregate demand by changing nonhuman wealth.

Another way monetary forces can affect nonhuman wealth—and therefore consumption—is via the market value of the capital stock $P_v K$. Suppose that the Federal Reserve conducts an open-market operation that increases the demand for Treasury securities, thereby raising their prices and lowering their interest rates. This in turn initially increases the desirability of equities (common stocks) relative to government bonds, and the prices of equities rise, causing an increase in $P_v K$. If the price level does not rise or if there is a significant lag in the price level increase, equity owners will consider themselves wealthier and consumption expenditures will rise.

14-6   The Empirical Evidence

The empirical evidence related to the issues discussed in this chapter can be divided into three areas: (1) the interest elasticity of expenditures, (2) the interest elasticity of the demand for money, and (3) the interest elasticity of the supply of money. We now examine some of the empirical findings pertaining to each of these areas and conclude with a tentative resolution of the debate regarding the importance of money.

Interest Elasticity of Expenditures

In our discussion of investment theory in Chapter 5 we were chiefly concerned with a theory of the behavior of business firms. We concluded from the theoretical and empirical results that firms attempt to invest up to the point where the internal rate of return on the marginal unit of capital is equal to the external rate of return. These same results also hold for households, if we make the monetarist assumption that consumer durables are a form of capital purchased by households. In other words, we can conclude that households seek to acquire a stock of durable goods such that the rate of return equating the money value of the flow of services of the marginal durable good with its purchase price is equal to the external rate of return. Hence, by altering the external rate of return, monetary policy can directly affect the purchase of consumer durable goods.

In Chapter 5 we also cited the results of empirical studies demonstrating that expenditures on capital goods and owner-occupied housing are sensitive to interest-rate changes. However, this is not a strong effect and in itself is insufficient to support the monetarist view that the *IS* curve is highly interest elastic. To substantiate the monetarist view, it is necessary to show that expenditures on consumer durables either are interest elastic or are directly affected by monetary policy via some other channel.

Michael J. Hamburger has examined the relationship between interest rates and the demand for consumer durable goods.[1] Hamburger found that in addition to the traditional variables of income and relative prices, the consumption of durable goods also exhibited a significant inverse relationship to the interest rate. Using a somewhat different approach, Colin Wright has estimated a consumption function in which one of the independent variables is the interest rate.[2] In his analysis, Wright found that an inverse relationship between consumption and the interest rate was consistent with historical data. His estimate of savings elasticity related to the interest rate was approximately 0.2, a much higher result than previously assumed values.

In a thorough and complex study of monetary effects, Frank deLeeuw and Edward M. Gramlich used a large econometric model to examine the channels through which monetary policy operates.[3] DeLeeuw and Gramlich postulated three possible channels: (1) movement along the MEI curve by business firms, state and local government, and households; (2) change in household wealth resulting from changes in bond and stock prices; and (3) credit rationing, or the availability of credit.

To study these channels, deLeeuw and Gramlich simulated the effect of a billion-dollar increase in high-powered money on the Federal Reserve Board–Massachusetts Institute of Technology econometric model. For tangible business investment

---

[1] Michael J. Hamburger, "Interest Rates and the Demand for Consumer Durable Goods," *American Economic Review* **LVII** (December 1967), 1131–53.

[2] Colin Wright, "Saving and the Rate of Interest," in *The Taxation of Income from Capital*, A.C. Harberger and M.J. Bailey (eds.) (Washington, D.C.: The Brookings Institution, 1969), pp. 275–99.

[3] Frank deLeeuw and Edward M. Gramlich, "The Channels of Monetary Policy," *Federal Reserve Bulletin* (June 1969), 472–91.

and state and local construction, they found that virtually all increases in these expenditures resulted from a downward movement along the MEI curve. The bulk of the increased expenditure on residential housing was explained by a movement along the MEI curve; the remainder (10–15%) was explained by the increased availability of credit in the housing-mortgage market. In contrast to the neo-Keynesian theory of the transmission mechanism, deLeeuw and Gramlich found that monetary injections directly influenced the household consumption of durable goods. However, contrary to the monetarist theory, they found that only about 20% of the increased expenditure was explained by a downward movement along the MEI curve. The remainder of the increase in expenditures on durable goods was the result of increased household wealth generated by rising stock prices. The increase in stock prices resulted from an open-market purchase made by the central bank, which increased first the price of bonds and then the price of stocks as individual wealth holders readjusted their portfolios.

Using basically the same methodological approach as deLeeuw and Gramlich, Franco Modigliani investigated the direct effect of monetary policy on household consumption.[4] Using Friedman's definition of consumption—the sum of expenditures on nondurable goods and services *plus* the value of the flow services provided by consumer durable goods—Modigliani concluded that consumption was one of the most important channels, perhaps even the most important channel, through which monetary policy can affect aggregate demand. Modigliani showed that approximately one-half of the change in income that results from a change in monetary variables is due to the effect these variables have on wealth. This directly affects consumption expenditures, which in turn directly affects consumer durable expenditures. For example, an open-market purchase increases wealth, and consumption therefore increases; because a portion of this consumption is an increased flow of durable-goods services, expenditures on durable goods must also increase. In addition, Modigliani found that consumer expenditures on durable goods were affected by interest-rate changes but that this channel of the transmission mechanism was less important than the one just described.

In a more recent study, Frederic S. Mishkin examined the role that the illiquidity of consumer durable assets plays in consumer durable expenditures.[5] Mishkin has found that decreased household debt holdings and increased household financial asset holdings result in significantly increased consumer durable expenditures. Specifically, a decrease in consumer debt of $1 at the beginning of the quarter increases durable expenditures by $0.31, and an increase of $1 in gross financial assets held at the beginning of the quarter increases durable expenditures by $0.06. In addition, Mishkin obtained a value of 0.20 for the interest elasticity of demand for consumer durables, and this is the same result obtained by Colin Wright. Because monetary policy affects (1) the interest rate directly, (2) consumer

[4] Franco Modigliani, "Monetary Policy and Consumption: Linkages via Interest Rate and Wealth Effects in the FMP Model," in *Consumer Spending and Monetary Policy: The Linkages* (Boston: Federal Reserve Bank of Boston, 1971), pp. 9–84.

[5] Frederic S. Mishkin, "Illiquidity, Consumer Durable Expenditure, and Monetary Policy," *American Economic Review* **66** (September 1976), 642–54.

debt via changes in the availability and cost of credit to the consumer, and (3) the value of financial assets via stock and bond prices, Mishkin concluded that the composition of the household balance sheet is critical to consumer durable expenditure decisions. This strengthens the monetarist view that monetary policy has a direct and powerful impact on consumer durable expenditures.

Interest Elasticity of the Demand for Money

As we learned in Section 14-5, the effectiveness with which monetary policy is transmitted to the real sector of the economy depends on the extent to which nonmonetary financial assets, such as government bonds, treasury bills, time deposits, and savings and loan shares, are substitutes for money. An open-market purchase of treasury bills by the central bank lowers interest rates, and therefore a fraction of the increase in the quantity of money is absorbed in portfolios as individual wealth holders move down their liquidity preference curves. Portfolio imbalance occurs if the increase in the quantity of money demanded is less than the increase in the quantity of money supplied. Of course, the extent of portfolio imbalance depends on the interest elasticity of the demand for money. Extreme Keynesians argue that there would be no imbalance, because the elasticity of demand is infinite. Extreme monetarists, on the other hand, argue that the interest elasticity of the demand for money is zero and therefore *all* the newly created money would be undesired. The extreme Keynesian position results in the horizontal *LM* curve, whereas the extreme monetarist position is necessary to produce a vertical *LM* curve. Between these two extreme positions lie the Keynesian, neo-Keynesian, and monetarist viewpoints.

By examining the empirical evidence related to the interest elasticity of the demand for money, we can make some determination of which theoretical economic viewpoint is the most valid. Table 14-1 presents a summary of the most important empirical findings to date on the interest elasticity of the demand for money. The authors of these studies have used both the broad and the narrow definitions of money in their analyses. They have also used short-term interest rates, such as the 90-day Treasury bill rate, and long-term interest rates, such as the Aaa corporate bond rate.

The consensus is that there is a significant inverse relationship between the demand for money and interest rates and that the interest elasticity of demand is rather low. As Table 14-1 indicates, the range of results lies between -0.1 and -1.15. This rather wide variation is the result of model specification on the part of the individual investigators. If the broad rather than the narrow definition of money is used, then the estimated interest elasticity will be lower, because the increased fraction of time deposits in portfolios as interest rates increase will not be observed in the regression. If long-term rather than short-term rates are used, the estimated interest elasticity will be higher, because the variation in long-term interest rates is smaller. If quarterly rather than annual data are used, the interest elasticity will be lower, because the time period is probably too short for complete adjustment to occur in financial markets. One particularly interesting result regarding the possibility of a liquidity trap is the study of Gandolfi and Lothian. Using annual cross-

TABLE 14-1   The Interest Elasticity of the Demand for Money: A Summary of Empirical Findings

Author	Data Used	Definition of Money	Interest Rate Used	Interest Elasticity
Bronfenbrenner and Mayer[1]	Annual, U.S., 1919–1956	M_1	Short	-0.33
Chow[2]	Annual, U.S., 1897–1958	M_1	Long	-0.73
Meltzer[3]	Annual, U.S., 1900–1958	M_1	Long	-0.92
	Annual, U.S., 1930–1958	M_2	Long	-0.48
		M_1	Long	-1.15
		M_2	Long	-0.70
Brunner and Meltzer[4]	Annual, U.S., 1930–1959	M_1	Long	-1.09
		M_2	Long	-0.73
Laidler[5]	Annual, U.S., 1919–1960	M_1	Short	-0.21
		M_1	Long	-0.72
	Annual, U.S., 1892–1960	M_2	Short	-0.16
		M_2	Long	-0.25
Lee[6]	Annual, U.S., 1951–1965	M_1	Short	-0.41
		M_2	Short	-0.67
Motley[7]	Annual, U.S., 1920–1965 (households only)	M_2	Short	-0.16
Courchene and Shapiro[8]	Annual, U.S., 1900–1958	M_1	Long	-1.00
		M_2	Long	-0.58
Teigen[9]	Quarterly, U.S., 1946–1959	M_1	Short	-0.07
	Annual, U.S., 1924–1941	M_1	Short	-0.20
Heller[10]	Quarterly, U.S., 1947–1958	M_1	Short	-0.12
		M_2	Short	-0.18
Hamburger[11]	Quarterly, U.S., 1952–1960 (households only)	M_1	Long	-0.16
Kavanagh and Walters[12]	Annual, U.K., 1880–1961	M_1	Stock yield	-0.13
	Annual, U.K., 1926–1961	M_2	Long	-0.31
		M_2	Long	-0.50
Fisher[13]	Quarterly, U.K., 1955–1967	M_1	Short	-0.11
		M_1	Long	-0.3

Laidler and Parkin[14]	Quarterly, U.K., 1953–1967	M_2	Short	-0.26
Bank of England[15]	Quarterly, U.K., 1955–1969	M_1	Long	-1.05
		M_1	Long	-0.80
		M_2	Short	-0.09
		M_2	Long	-0.35
Gandolfi and Lothian[16]	Annual, U.S., 1929–1933	M_2	Long + Short	-0.44
	Annual, U.S., 1934–1938	M_2	Long + Short	-0.13
	Annual, U.S., 1929–1938	M_2	Long + Short	-0.32
	Annual, U.S., 1949–1958	M_2	Long + Short	-0.35
	Annual, U.S., 1949–1968	M_2	Long + Short	-0.34
	Annual, U.S., 1929–1968	M_2	Long + Short	-0.37
Kohn[17]	Quarterly, U.S., 1952–1975	Currency	Short	-0.002

[1] Martin Bronfenbrenner and Thomas Mayer, "Liquidity Functions in the American Economy," *Econometrica* (October 1960), 810–34.

[2] Gregory C. Chow, "On the Long-run and Short-run Demand for Money," *Journal of Political Economy* (April 1966), 111–31.

[3] Allan H. Meltzer, "The Demand for Money: The Evidence from Time Series," *Journal of Political Economy* (June 1963), 219–46.

[4] Karl Brunner and Allan H. Meltzer, "Some Further Investigations of Demand and Supply Functions for Money," *Journal of Finance* (May 1964), 240–83.

[5] David E.W. Laidler, "The Rate of Interest and the Demand for Money—Some Empirical Evidence," *Journal of Political Economy* (December 1966), 543–55.

[6] Tong Hun Lee, "Alternative Interest Rates and the Demand for Money," *American Economic Review* (December 1967), 1168–81.

[7] Brian Motley, "A Demand-for-Money Function for the Household Sector—Some Preliminary Findings," *Journal of Finance* (December 1967), 405–18.

[8] T.J. Courchene and H.T. Shapiro, "The Demand for Money: A Note from the Time Series," *Journal of Political Economy* (October 1964), 498–503.

[9] Ronald L. Teigen, "Demand and Supply Functions for Money in the United States: Some Structural Estimates," *Econometrica* (October 1964), 476–509.

[10] H.R. Heller, "The Demand for Money: The Evidence from the Short-term Data," *Quarterly Journal of Economics* (May 1965), 291–303.

[11] M.J. Hamburger, "The Demand for Money by Households, Money Substitutes, and Monetary Policy, *Journal of Political Economy* (December 1966), 600–623.

[12] N.J. Kavanagh and A. A. Walters, "Demand for Money in the U.K. 1877–1961: Some Preliminary Findings," *Bulletin of the Oxford University Institute of Economics and Statistics* (May 1966), 93–116.

[13] Douglas Fisher, "The Demand for Money in Britain: Quarterly Results 1951–1967," *The Manchester School of Economic and Social Studies* (December 1968), 329–44.

[14] David E.W. Laidler and Michael Parkin, "The Demand for Money in the United Kingdom 1956–1967: Preliminary Estimates," *University of Essex Discussion Paper* (unpublished).

[15] C.A.E. Goodhart and A.D. Crockett, "The Importance of Money," *Bank of England Quarterly Bulletin* (June 1970), Appendix II, 159–98.

[16] Arthur E. Gandolfi and James R. Lothian, "The Demand for Money from the Great Depression to the Present," *American Economic Review* (May 1976), 46–51.

[17] Donald L. Kohn, "Currency Movements in the United States," *Monthly Review of the Federal Reserve Bonds of Kansas City* (April 1976), 3–8.

SOURCE Table 14-1 is a simplified but expanded version of Table A in C.A.E. Goodhart and A.D. Crockett, "The Importance of Money," *Bank of England Quarterly Bulletin* (June 1970), 188, cited above.

sectional state data, they found that during the great depression when interest rates were decreasing, the interest elasticity approached zero. This is precisely opposite to the results that would occur if a liquidity trap existed.

Suppose we limit our attention to the definition of money used in this text—that is, the narrow definition—and use short-term interest rates, since they are on a priori grounds the most relevant to Keynesian liquidity preference theory. In this subset of the results presented in Table 14-1, the average interest elasticity is −0.33.

The results of these studies are sufficiently consistent to indicate several important conclusions. First, it is clear that neither the extreme Keynesian nor the extreme monetarist views are supported by the empirical evidence. The estimated interest elasticities also appear to be far too low to support the Keynesian view of the demand for money.

Interest Elasticity of the Supply of Money

Interest in the nature of the supply of money is fairly recent, and few studies have been conducted in this area to date. Table 14-2 presents a summary of the empirical findings related to the interest elasticity of the supply of money. The results range from a high elasticity of 0.72 to a low elasticity of 0.14; the median elasticity is 0.22.

The results of these studies show conclusively that the extreme Keynesian assumption of a perfectly endogenous money supply is false. They also lay to rest the extreme monetarist view that the supply of money is perfectly exogenous.

Integrating the results of the studies in Table 14-1 and Table 14-2, the emerging picture is a combination of money demand and money supply functions that jointly produce an *LM* curve close to the one hypothesized by the monetarists.

In summary, empirical research has shown conclusively that the extreme Keynesian, Keynesian, and extreme monetarist positions are untenable. Analysis of the transmission mechanism has produced results indicating that monetary policy has a widely diffused, direct influence on all forms of expenditure, and this tends to support the conclusions of the monetarist view of the transmission mechanism. Empirical research on the interest elasticities of the demand for and the supply of money also tends to support the monetarist position. Although this debate is still far from being concluded, its final resolution may well rest close to monetarist views on these issues.

14-7   Concluding Remarks

In this chapter we have examined the theoretical models underlying the phrases "only money matters," "money doesn't matter," and "money matters." We have learned that subtle differences of opinion divide the large group of economists who believe that money matters into the Keynesian, neo-Keynesian, and monetarist camps. Keynesians believe that money matters very little relative to fiscal policy,

TABLE 14-2 The Interest Elasticity of the Supply of Money: A Summary of Empirical Findings

Author	Data Used	Definition of Money	Interest Rate Used	Interest Elasticity
deLeeuw[1]	Quarterly, U.S., 1948–1962	M_1	Short	0.25
deLeeuw and Turek[2]	Quarterly, U.S., 1948–1962	M_1	Short	0.22
Goldfeld[3]	Quarterly, U.S., 1950–1962	M_1	Short	0.22
Goldfeld and Kane[4]	Weekly, U.S., 1953–1963	M_1	Short	0.21
Teigen[5]	Quarterly, U.S., 1946–1959	M_1	Short	0.20
Teigen[6]	Quarterly, U.S., 1953–1964	Demand deposits only	Short	0.14
Brunner and Meltzer[7]	Annual, U.S., 1949–1962	M_1	Short	0.66
		M_2	Short	0.72
Rasche[8]	Quarterly, U.S., 1965–1969	M_1	Short	0.24

[1] Frank deLeeuw, "A Model of Financial Behavior," in *The Brookings Quarterly Econometric Model of the United States*, J. Duesenberry, G. Fromm, L.R. Klein, and E. Kuh (eds.) (Chicago: Rand McNally, 1965).

[2] Frank deLeeuw and J. Turek, "Prediction of Interest Rate Levels and Financial Stocks with Simulation Techniques" (unpublished). Data obtained from David I. Fand, "Some Implications of Money-supply Analysis," *American Economic Review* (May 1967), 380–400.

[3] Stephen M. Goldfeld, *Commercial Bank Behavior and Economic Activity* (Amsterdam: North Holland, 1966).

[4] Stephen M. Goldfeld and Edward J. Kane, "The Determinants of Member-bank Borrowing: An Econometric Study," *Journal of Finance* (September 1966), 499–514.

[5] Ronald L. Teigen, "Demand and Supply Functions for Money in the United States: Some Structural Estimates," *Econometrica* (October 1964), 476–509.

[6] Ronald L. Teigen, "An Aggregated Quarterly Model of the U.S. Monetary Sector, 1953–1964," in *Targets and Indicators of Monetary Policy*, Karl Brunner (ed.) (San Francisco: Chandler Publishing Co., 1969).

[7] Karl Brunner and Allan H. Meltzer, "Some Further Investigations of the Demand and Supply Functions of Money," *Journal of Finance* (May 1964), 240–83.

[8] Robert H. Rasche, "A Review of Empirical Studies of the Money-supply Mechanism," *Review of the Federal Reserve Bank of St. Louis* (July 1972), 11–19.

whereas monetarists believe that it matters very much. The neo-Keynesians adopt an eclectic approach to the problem, taking a position approximately midway between the two extreme camps. Because the correctness of these views has bearing on the appropriate mix of monetary and fiscal policy, the findings of empirical research are extremely important. The empirical results available to date support a view of the relative effectiveness of monetary vs. fiscal policy that is in closest accord with the monetarist view.

15 International Trade and Finance

15-1 Introduction

Thus far, except in Chapter 1, we have assumed that the economy of our model is *closed*—that it does not incorporate international trade. During our study of the closed economy, we have focused our attention on the attainment of full employment and a stable price level; the simultaneous occurrence of these two policy goals is called *internal balance*. In our study of the *open* economy in this chapter, first we examine some fundamental principles of international trade and finance and the concept of *external balance*. Then we construct a model of an open economy that incorporates international trade and finance. Finally, we consider the problem of maintaining equilibrium in an open economy.

15-2 The Open Economy

Nations trade with one another for precisely the same reasons that people, groups, or regions trade within a nation. In the absence of coercion, trade between two individuals occurs because each party in the exchange expects to benefit. Trade increases mutual welfare by permitting parties to concentrate production in the specific area in which they function most efficiently, so that the resulting aggregate output is greater than it would be in the absence of specialization. This additional output is then shared through trading, which thus increases the welfare and the wealth of individuals, groups, regions, and nations.

For example, consider what life would be like if no trade occurred between individuals. Each person would have to provide all of his or her own food, clothing, and shelter. Under these conditions, little or no time could be devoted to such luxuries as medical care or leisure activities, and life would indeed be bleak. In contrast, when individuals trade with one another, each person can do the job for which he or she is best suited. Such a concentration of effort increases production efficiency as labor becomes more and more specialized and specific areas of endeavor develop. This concentration produces a greater aggregate output, which is then shared by trading. This basic argument applies to groups or regions within a nation and is also the premise underlying trade between nations.

In Chapter 8 we argued that the existence of money within a nation is a necessary condition if the concentration of labor just described is to occur. This is equally true of trade between nations, but international trade does present one further problem. The Swedish economist Bertil Ohlin has demonstrated that trade between regions within a nation is equivalent to trade between nations.[1] This premise is theoretically correct, but each nation in the modern world has its own currency, which in general cannot serve as a medium of exchange in other countries. Thus large-scale international trade depends not only on the existence of money (as does interregional trade) but also on an institution that converts foreign currency received from the sale of goods and services to other nations into domestic currency that can be spent at home. The institution that converts currencies is called the *foreign exchange market*.

One additional factor can alter the equivalence between interregional and international trade. A nation is much less likely to create internal barriers to trade between its domestic regions than to impose external barriers to trade with other nations. This is because the gains from interregional trade clearly coincide with the politics of nationalism and less clearly coincide with or even conflict with nationalism. A nation can erect such barriers as tariffs, quotas, and controls over the conversion of foreign exchange. Because barriers to the free international movement of goods, services, and the factors of production reduce the efficiency of the world economy, most economists favor their abolition. In our discussion of the implications of international trade here, we assume that a perfectly *open* world prevails—that no human-made barriers to free trade exist—although this is unfortunately untrue in the real world.

15-3   The Foreign Exchange Market

For simplicity of analysis here, we assume that our world consists of only two countries: the United States and the United Kingdom. A sports car manufacturer in the United Kingdom sells its cars for an export price of £2,000 (read "2,000 pounds sterling," or simply "2,000 pounds"); an importer in the United States is willing to pay $4,000 for one of these cars. Because the exporter cannot spend U.S. dollars

---

[1] Bertil Ohlin, *Interregional and International Trade* (Cambridge, Mass.: Harvard University Press, 1933).

in the United Kingdom, the U.S. importer must convert the $4,000 into £2,000 to purchase a car. This can be accomplished by conducting an offsetting transaction of equal value in the opposite direction. Let us further assume that an importer in the United Kingdom is willing to pay £100 for 20 tape recorders that sell for $200 in the United States. The total value of this transaction would be £2,000, or $4,000. Clearly, the U.S. automobile importer can obtain £2,000 from the U.K. importer of tape recorders who wishes to obtain $4,000. The cost of acquiring one unit of foreign currency is called the *foreign exchange rate*. In this simple example the foreign exchange rate paid by the U.S. importer is $4,000 \div 2,000 = \$2.00$ per pound, and the foreign exchange rate paid by the U.K. importer is $2,000 \div 4,000 = \pounds 0.5$ per dollar.

In a world in which an extremely large number of such international transactions are conducted, it would be extremely time-consuming and inefficient for every U.S. importer to locate a counterpart in the United Kingdom to arrange an offsetting transaction. This situation would be equivalent to a barter economy with all its accompanying disadvantages. The foreign exchange market is designed to eliminate this problem. Members of the foreign exchange market act as intermediaries between buyers and sellers of foreign currencies to depersonalize and greatly increase the efficiency of foreign exchange conversion.

We can obtain additional insight into the nature of the foreign exchange market by considering the behavior of the two importers in our simple example. The American importer is willing to purchase one sports car for $4,000, which the British exporter is willing to sell for £2,000. When the exchange rate is exactly $2.00 per pound, the U.S. importer can purchase the £2,000 in the American foreign exchange market, which is located in New York City. But suppose that the foreign exchange rate decreases to $1.00 per pound, so that the cost of obtaining £2,000 is only $2,000. The U.S. importer views this as a reduction in the price of British goods. However, the U.K. exporter, if manufacturing costs remain constant, is unaffected and continues to sell each car for £2,000. As the price decreases in terms of dollars, the U.S. importer, given a normal, negatively sloped demand curve, will demand a greater quantity of British sports cars. If the American importer wishes to buy two sports cars at a price of $2,000 apiece, then the demand for pounds at a price of $1.00 = £1 would be $2 \times 2,000 = \pounds 4,000$. Should the exchange rate rise, the opposite effect would occur and the quantity of pounds demanded would decrease. If the aggregate demand curve of all U.S. importers of British goods is elastic and negatively sloped when the prices of the imported commodities are given in terms of dollars, then the aggregate demand curve for pounds will also be negatively sloped, as indicated by the $D_\pounds$ curve in Figure 15-1(a).

The counterpart to the American importer in our example is the British importer who wishes to purchase 20 tape recorders. Assuming that the price of each of these tape recorders is fixed in U.S. dollars at $200, we already know that the U.K. importer will purchase the 20 tape recorders when the foreign exchange rate in London is £0.5 per dollar. If the demand for tape recorders is a negatively sloped function of their price in pounds, then as the price of U.S. dollars decreases, a larger quantity of tape recorders will be demanded in the United Kingdom, because their price in terms of pounds will also decrease. In addition, if the absolute value of the price elasticity of demand is greater than unity, then the total amount of pounds spent on these tape recorders will increase as their price decreases. Because these pounds must be converted into U.S. dollars to purchase U.S. exports, this supply of pounds is offered for sale on the New York foreign exchange market. The supply of pounds is a positively sloped function of their price in U.S. dollars, because the New York foreign exchange rate is the reciprocal of the London foreign exchange rate. This means that as the pound price of U.S. dollars declines in London, the U.S. dollar price of pounds rises in New York. If the

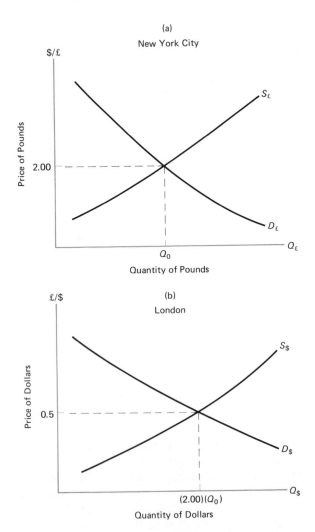

FIGURE 15-1   *The Foreign Exchange Market as Viewed in New York City and in London*

aggregate demand curve of all British importers is negatively sloped and if the absolute value of its price elasticity of demand is greater than 1, then the total supply curve of pounds offered for sale in New York will be positively sloped, as indicated by the $S_£$ curve in Figure 15-1(a). The intersection of the supply of pounds curve $S_£$ and the demand for pounds curve $D_£$ determines the equilibrium foreign exchange rate, which for the purposes of illustration is shown to be $2.00 per pound in Figure 15-1(a).[2]

Using the same line of reasoning, we can develop the aggregate supply and demand curves for dollars in the London foreign exchange market that are shown in Figure 15-1(b). Comparing Figures 15-1(a) and 15-1(b), we can see that the equilibrium exchange rate in New York is the reciprocal of the equilibrium exchange rate in London. This condition exists because a divergence from this reciprocity creates quick and riskless profits for arbitragers, who restore the reciprocal condition of equilibrium in the foreign exchange market by subsequent profit-maximizing operations. Moreover, at this equilibrium exchange rate, the quantity of U.S. dollars that Americans spend on pounds is equivalent to the quantity of U.S. dollars purchased by the British. These conditions follow from the fact that New York and London are the same market, even though they are geographically separated, because they are linked together by telecommunication. In a single market in which competition prevails, only one equilibrium price and quantity can exist. The foreign exchange market probably more closely approximates the economic concept of perfect competition than any other market in existence.

We can now use our simple theory of the foreign exchange rate to determine the effects of various structural changes in either the United States or the United Kingdom on the equilibrium rate of exchange.

Suppose that the tastes of American automobile owners change, and they decide that foreign sports cars are too small. This will cause the demand curve for British sports cars to shift downward to the left and will produce an accompanying shift to the left in the demand curve for pounds, as illustrated in Figure 15-2. Prior to the change in American car buyers' tastes, the supply of pounds curve $S_£$ and the demand for pounds curve $D_£$ intersected at an exchange rate of $2.00 per pound and a quantity of Q_0 pounds were purchased. After the change in tastes, the demand curve has shifted to $D'_£$, the equilibrium exchange rate has decreased to $1.75 per pound, and the quantity of pounds purchased has declined to Q_1. In this free competitive market, disequilibrium cannot prevail at the original exchange rate of $2.00 per pound, and the new equilibrium rate of $1.75 is automatically determined.

In our extremely simplified example at the beginning of this section, we demonstrated that the demand for pounds by an American importer of British goods is a negatively sloped function of the exchange rate when the price of the goods is fixed in terms of pounds. Now suppose that the general price level in the United Kingdom declines and the sports car that sold for £2,000 is selling for £1,500. If the exchange

---

[2] In December 1976, the price of pounds in New York was approximately $1.68.

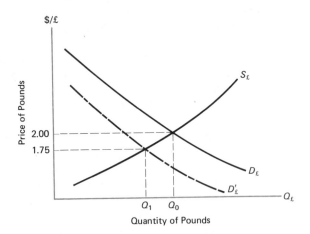

FIGURE 15-2   *The Effect on the Foreign Exchange Market of a Change in Tastes*

rate is $2.00 per pound, then the cost of the sports car in U.S. dollars would decrease from $4,000 to $3,000. It follows from our previous assumption (that the demand for sports cars is a negatively sloped function of their price in dollars) that the quantity of sports cars purchased will therefore increase; if the absolute value of the price elasticity of demand is greater than unity, then the total quantity of dollars spent on sports cars will also increase. This means that the quantity of pounds demanded at the exchange rate of $2.00 per pound will be greater than the quantity of pounds demanded prior to the decline in the U.K. price level. In other words, the demand for pounds increases, shifting from $D_£$ to $D'_£$, as shown in Figure 15-3. Simultaneously, British subjects, finding that domestically produced goods have become relatively cheaper than American goods, begin to purchase British products, instead of American products, causing the demand for dollars in London to decline. This decline in the demand for dollars in London is reflected in New York by a reduction in the supply of pounds on the exchange market. Thus the supply of pounds shifts from $S_£$ to $S'_£$, as shown in Figure 15-3, where the final equilibrium exchange rate rises to $2.75 per pound. In this example the quantity of pounds purchased also increases going Q_0 to Q_1, but this increase is clearly dependent on the leftward shift of the supply of pounds curve. By shifting $S_£$ further to the left, we can obtain a new equilibrium exchange rate in which the quantity of pounds purchased declines. However, it should be noted that the price of pounds will always increase. In general, the same effects graphed in Figure 15-3 will result if an increase in the U.S. price level instead of a decline in the U.K. price level occurs. Thus the critical aspect of this analysis is the direction of change in the *relative* price level, which in the latter example is equivalent to a relative decline in the U.K. price level.

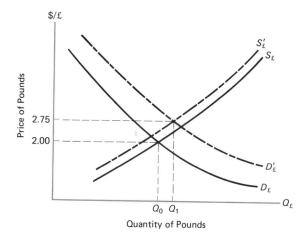

FIGURE 15-3   *The Effect on the Foreign Exchange Market of a Change in the Price Level*

Until this point, our discussion of international trade has been limited to examples in which *goods* are traded across national boundaries, but the international exchange of *services* and *capital* is equally important. A major internationally traded service is tourism. American tourists cannot spend U.S. dollars in the United Kingdom; they must convert their dollars into pounds. The effect of this currency conversion on the foreign exchange market is equivalent to the purchase of a British good, because the conversion also creates a demand for pounds. The cheaper the price of pounds is in dollar terms, the less a given British tour will cost in U.S. dollars. Thus the tourist demand for pounds curve exhibits the same general characteristics as the demand for pounds curve that results from desire to purchase British goods. In addition, the service-derived demand for pounds curve is affected by changes in the relative U.S. and U.K. price levels, just as we demonstrated for the case of the demand for pounds curve for British goods.

Changes in the quantity of foreign exchange demanded for the purchase of goods and services can be shown to depend on the exchange rate and on relative price levels. The international transfer of capital, however, depends on international differences in the rate of return on capital, or, in other words, the rate of interest. Suppose that the rate of return on the marginal increment of capital in the United Kingdom is 10% but that in the United States it is 6%. In this situation an American might prefer to invest in the United Kingdom rather than at home. We say *might*, because it is possible that by the time an American sells a British investment and the accumulated returns for pounds and converts these pounds back into dollars, the exchange rate in New York (dollars per pound) could have decreased to such an extent that a net loss in dollar terms could ensue. But we will disregard this possibility and assume that our American investor is confident that this will not

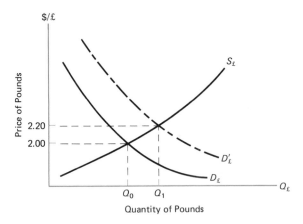

FIGURE 15-4   *The Effect of a Capital Flow from the United States to the United Kingdom on the Foreign Exchange Market*

occur and decides to take advantage of the higher rate of return on investment in the United Kingdom.

One way such a capital transfer can be effected is for an American investor to buy apartment buildings in London.[3] But before purchasing these buildings, the investor must convert U.S. dollars to pounds, which produces the rightward shift in the demand-for-pounds curve shown in Figure 15-4. The price of pounds rises from $2.00, to $2.20, and the quantity of pounds purchased increases from Q_0 to Q_1. The conversion of dollars into pounds to use in purchasing the apartment buildings represents the monetary transfer of capital. The real transfer of capital is actually accomplished after the price of the dollar declines in London. As this happens, American commodities become cheaper and their importation to the United Kingdom increases. The British factors of production that are no longer needed to produce goods now imported from the United States are employed in the production of the capital assets purchased by Americans. The important point of this example, however, is that interest-rate differentials can produce an increase in the quantity of currency offered for sale by residents of the country with the lower interest rate. As a result, the price of the currency in the country with the higher interest rate rises on the foreign exchange market and the price of the currency in the country with the lower interest rate declines. One policy implication to be drawn from this analysis is that it is possible for governments to increase the foreign demand for their currencies by using monetary and fiscal policy to vary the domestic rate of interest.

In the foreign exchange market described in this section we assumed that perfect competition prevails—that the foreign exchange rate is always in equilibrium

---

[3] There are many ways in which capital in various forms is transferred from one country to another. A comprehensive description of these methods is beyond the scope of this book. The interested reader can consult Mordechai E. Kreinin, *International Economics,* Second Edition (New York: Harcourt Brace Jovanovich, Inc., 1975).

because the quantity of foreign exchange demanded is always equal to the quantity of foreign exchange supplied. In this market setting, the foreign exchange rate rises and falls in response to changes in demand or supply. An international monetary system that depends on market forces to determine the exchange rate on a day-to-day basis is usually called a *flexible exchange rate system*. We now consider a monetary system at the opposite end of the spectrum.

15-4   The Fixed Exchange Rate System

In a *fixed exchange rate system* government believes that determining the price of foreign exchange is too important a decision to be left to the "whims" of the market.

The method by which most central banks fix exchange rates today is illustrated in Figure 15-5. Suppose that the governments of the United States and the United Kingdom decide to fix the exchange rate of dollars for pounds at $2.00/£ in New York. We already know this means that the price of dollars in London will then be £0.5/$. Let us further assume initially that at $2/£ the foreign exchange market is in equilibrium, as depicted by the solid supply and demand curves graphed in Figure 15-5. Now suppose that some event (for example, a rise in the general price level in the United Kingdom) upsets foreign exchange equilibrium. This will cause the demand for pounds in New York to decrease and the supply of dollars in London to decrease, as indicated by the dashed curves $D'_£$ and $S'_\$$ in Figures 15-5(a) and 15-5(b). These decreases occur because the price of British goods at the prevailing exchange rate of $2/£ becomes more expensive in terms of dollars, so that a smaller amount of British goods is desired. On the other hand, at an exchange rate of £0.5/$, the price of American goods becomes cheaper relative to the price of British goods. The demand for dollars therefore increases in London as more American goods are imported and the supply of pounds increases in New York, as shown by the dashed curves labeled $D'_\$$ and $S'_£$ in Figures 15-5(a) and 15-5(b).

We have already learned that in a free market the price of pounds will decline to $1/£ in New York and the price of dollars would rise to £1.0/$ in London, given the new demand and supply curves in Figure 15-5. This cannot happen in a system of fixed exchange rates. How the central banks of the United States and the United Kingdom prevent this from happening is also shown in Figure 15-5. At the fixed change rate of $2.0/£ after the demand and supply curves have shifted, in New York there is an excess supply of pounds equal to $Q_{£_2} - Q_{£_1}$, and in London there is an excess demand for dollars equal to $Q_{\$_2} - Q_{\$_1}$. This disequilibrium can be maintained in the foreign exchange market if either the Federal Reserve System purchases all the excess pounds in the New York market or if the Bank of England supplies the excess dollars demanded in London. There is no theoretical limit to the number of dollars the Federal Reserve can print to purchase pounds in New York, but there is a limit to the number of dollars the Bank of England can sell. This limit is determined by the quantity of dollars that the Bank of England has already acquired. These dollar holdings of the Bank of England are called its *international monetary reserves*.

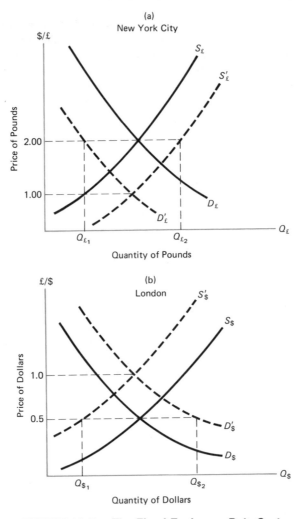

FIGURE 15-5 *The Fixed Exchange Rate System*

Which country actually intervenes in the foreign exchange market to maintain the fixed exchange rate at $2.00/£ depends on whatever arrangements are made between the two central banks, but one *extremely* important point should be noted here. If the Bank of England lacks sufficient dollar reserves to *peg* (fix) the exchange rate at $2.00/£ and if the United States is determined to prevent it from declining—which must be done if the exchange rate is to remain fixed—then the Federal Reserve *must* buy the excess supply of pounds the Bank of England is offering for sale. This action by the Federal Reserve is an open-market operation that increases the quantity of high-powered money in circulation. This action is only a temporary "solution," however, because the foreign exchange market remains in disequilibrium. Because we assume that both governments in this example are dedicated to a fixed exchange rate system, they must subsequently adopt monetary and fiscal policies to return the demand and supply curves to their intersection at the previously fixed rate. Historically, this adjustment process has usually been the primary responsibility of the country whose currency is in excess supply. In our example, this country would be Britain. We will learn shortly how monetary and fiscal policy can be used to establish equilibrium in the foreign exchange market.

15-5　The Balance of Payments

A country's *balance of payments* is the record of all economic transactions between the residents of the reporting country and the residents of foreign countries over a given period of time (usually one year). The balance of payments is based on the principle of double-entry bookkeeping: for every debit entry, there must be a corresponding credit entry. Any transaction that results in a payment from a resident of the reporting country to a foreign resident is treated as a debit; any transaction that results in a payment to a resident of the reporting country by a foreign resident is treated as a credit.

The transactions involved in the balance of payments can be divided into several categories. In this book they are expressed by the following symbols:[4]

ex = Exports of goods and services measured in nominal terms and expressed in absolute value.

im = Imports of goods and services measured in nominal terms and expressed in absolute value.

K = Net capital flow measured in nominal terms (a positive value when the flow on net is outward; a negative value when the flow on net is inward).

IMR = Net change in the stock of international monetary reserves (a positive value when increasing; negative when decreasing).

The balance of payments is the sum of all of a country's international transactions. Because the balance of payments always balances, it must be equal to zero. We can express this statement symbolically as

$$ex - im - K - IMR = 0 \qquad (15\text{-}1)$$

A nation is said to be in *external balance* if

$$IMR = 0 \qquad (15\text{-}2)$$

---

[4] To simplify our subsequent analysis, transactions involving remittances, pensions, and government aid to foreign recipients are not included. For the same reason, capital transactions have not been divided into long- and short-term transactions. For an excellent and more detailed treatment of the balance of payments, see Donald S. Kemp, "Balance-of-Payments Concepts—What Do They Really Mean?," *Review of the Federal Reserve Bank of St. Louis* (July 1975), 14–23.

and thus

$$ex - im - K = 0 = IMR \tag{15-3}$$

In the preceding section we learned that if a system of fixed exchange rates exists and if the foreign exchange market is in equilibrium, then the central bank is not acquiring or losing foreign exchange; in other words, its stock of international monetary reserves remains constant. For a nation to be in external balance, the foreign exchange market must therefore be in equilibrium, because in that situation $IMR = 0$.

We now explain, by example, the sign convention we have adopted in our definition of the balance of payments. Suppose that

$$ex = \$10 \text{ billion}$$
$$im = \$5 \text{ billion}$$
$$IMR = 0$$

Since imports and exports are stated in absolute value, equation (15-3) then becomes

$$\$10 - \$5 - K = 0 \tag{15-4}$$

and it follows from equation (15-4) that

$$K = \$5 \text{ billion} \tag{15-5}$$

In terms of our concept of foreign exchange market equilibrium, this is logically correct, because when a country's exports exceed its imports, there is a net demand for that country's currency. If the country is in external balance, the only other way to obtain the reciprocal supply is to conduct capital transactions, which on net must be outward. We can see that the value given by equation (15-5) satisfies this condition, because it has a positive sign, signifying (according to our convention) a net capital outflow.

Now let us consider an example in which a country has an external *imbalance*, characterized by a net reduction in its international monetary reserves. If

$$ex = \$18 \text{ billion}$$
$$im = \$14 \text{ billion}$$
$$K = +\$10 \text{ billion (a net outflow)}$$

then it follows from our definition of the balance of payments given by equation (15-1) that

$$IMR = ex - im - K$$
$$= 18 - 14 - (+10) = -\$6 \text{ billion} \tag{15-6}$$

Or verbally, it can be stated that the foreign exchange market is in disequilibrium at existing fixed exchange rate values, and to maintain these fixed values with other currencies, the reporting country in this example must purchase its own currency on the foreign exchange market with its international monetary reserves to prevent the value of its currency from declining below the fixed exchange rate. If the country's international monetary reserves are large enough, it can "buy time" in this manner to pursue the policies required to restore external balance. We can now construct an open-economy macroeconomic model and examine various economic policies that can be used to restore and maintain external balance.

15-6 Aggregate Demand with Fixed Exchange Rates

We expand our basic aggregate demand model to include international trade, maintaining the assumption that a fixed exchange rate exists. Recall the definition of national income in an open economy originally derived in Chapter 1

$$Y = C + I + G + (Ex - Im) \tag{15-7}$$

where all terms are measured in *real values*. Since we know that

$$S + C = Y_d = Y - T \tag{15-8}$$

we can write

$$S + C + T = Y \tag{15-9}$$

Substituting equation (15-9) for Y in definition (15-7), we then obtain

$$S + C + T = C + I + G + (Ex - Im) \tag{15-10}$$

which, after canceling the Cs and rearranging terms, gives us

$$S + T + Im = I + G + Ex \tag{15-11}$$

Equation (15-11) is now our condition of equilibrium in the product market in an open economy. It is analogous to the equilibrium condition in a closed economy, or $S + T = I + G$.

To derive the *IS* curve for an open economy, we must first postulate the relationship between the endogenous variables of our model and the level of exports and imports. Because we are assuming throughout this discussion that fixed exchange rates exist, changes in the domestic price level will directly affect the price foreigners pay for exports. Given that the law of demand holds for the products exported and that the price level in other countries remains constant, exports will rise when the domestic price level decreases and decline when the domestic price level increases.

The export function can therefore be expressed

$$Ex = Ex(P) \tag{15-12}$$

where

$$\frac{\Delta Ex}{\Delta P} < 0 \tag{15-13}$$

Graphically, this is illustrated by the negatively sloped export demand curve in Figure 15-6.

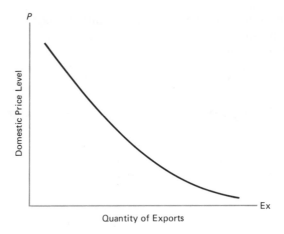

FIGURE 15-6   *The Export Function*

Imports are assumed to be normal goods; thus as income increases, the level of imports rises if all other things remain constant. Imports are also assumed to be a function of the domestic price level. Thus if the domestic price level rises and foreign price levels remain constant, then the price of foreign goods relative to domestic goods becomes cheaper and imports increase. When the price level declines, the opposite effects occur. The import function can therefore be expressed as

$$Im = Im(Y, P) \tag{15-14}$$

where

$$\frac{\Delta Im}{\Delta P} > 0 \tag{15-15}$$

and

$$\frac{\Delta Im}{\Delta Y} > 0 \tag{15-16}$$

Equation (15-14) is graphically illustrated in Figure 15-7. For a given domestic price level, the import function is assumed to be linear and proportional to the level of national income. The slope of this import curve is usually referred to as the *marginal propensity to import* MPI. As the price level rises at a fixed level of income, imports increase and the marginal propensity to import increases.

Given these export and import functions, we can now graphically derive the *IS* curves for an open economy. The derivations of the *IS* curves in Figure 15-8 are simply extentions of our derivations of the *IS* curve for a closed economy. In Figure 15-8(a) the MEI + *G* + Ex curves are obtained by horizontally adding to the

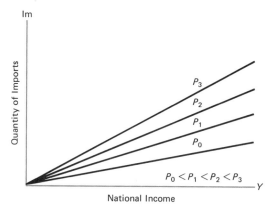

FIGURE 15-7   *The Import Function*

MEI + G curve the level of exports that would exist, for example, at price levels P_1, P_2, and P_3. Thus there is an MEI + G + Ex curve for each price level. Figure 15-8(b) is simply the condition of product-market equilibrium. In Figure 15-8(c) the import function of Figure 15-7 is combined with the savings and taxes diagram that we derived in Chapter 7. The $S + T + $ Im curves are then obtained by vertically adding the import function to the $S + T$ curve; each $S + T + $ Im curve also corresponds to a different price level.[5] Because there are different quantities of exports and imports at each price level, there is an *IS* curve for each price level. The *IS* curves corresponding to price levels P_1, P_2, and P_3 are graphically derived as IS_1, IS_2, and IS_3 in Figure 15-8(d), where the subscripts indicate the relevant price level. The intersections of the *LM* curves (one for each price level for a given nominal money supply) with the *IS* curves in Figure 15-8(d) produce the aggregate demand curve AgD in Figure 15-8(e). The intersection of an *LM* curve at a given price level (say, LM_2 when $P = P_2$) with the *IS* curve for this same price level (in this case, IS_2) gives us a level of aggregate demand (here, Y_2). Carrying out this process at various other price levels produces the aggregate demand curve in Figure 15-8(e). Because imports and exports are sensitive to the domestic price level, the aggregate demand curve for an open economy is more elastic with respect to price than it is for a closed economy.

The open-economy aggregate demand curve we have derived here corresponds to monetary and fiscal changes in the same qualitative manner that our earlier closed-economy aggregate demand curve does. In addition, the open-economy AgD curve will also be affected by factors that influence the level of imports and exports. If the level of exports increases at a given price level due to a change in foreign buyers' tastes, a rise in the foreign price level, decreases in foreign tariffs and quotas, or an increase in government subsidies paid to exporters, then the

[5] To simplify our analysis, we have not included the Pigou effect in this model; therefore the savings function does not shift as the price level varies.

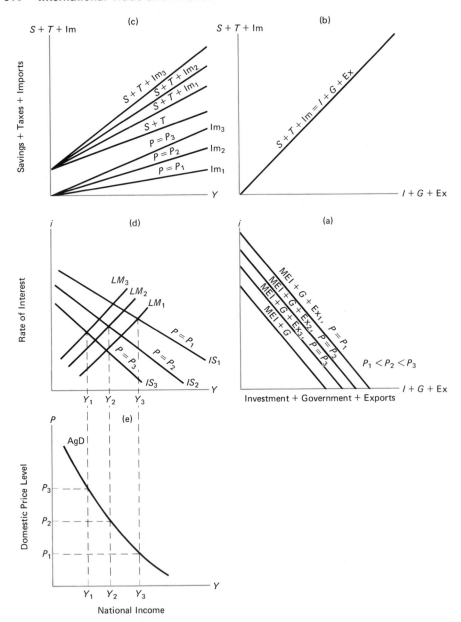

FIGURE 15-8   *Derivation of IS Curves and Aggregate Demand Curve for an Open Economy*

MEI + G + Ex curves will shift outward to the right. This is exactly analogous to an autonomous increase in government expenditure, and the aggregate demand curve will also shift outward to the right. Foreign bias against a country's products, a decline in the foreign price level, increases in foreign tariffs and quotas, or reductions in government subsidies to exporting industries will produce exactly the opposite effects: the level of aggregate demand will decrease, and the aggregate demand curve will shift to the left.

The effect of an increase in imports at a given price level is comparable to an upward shift in the savings function; such an increase produces a decline in aggregate demand with a leftward shift of the aggregate demand curve. An upward shift in the import function can be caused by such factors as a decline in the foreign price level, an increase in the demand for foreign products, or a reduction in tariffs on imported goods. A decrease in the import function at all price levels due to the reverse of any of these factors will increase aggregate demand and shift the aggregate demand curve to the right.

15-7   External Balance

We have previously stated that external balance exists when

$$ex - im - K = 0 = IMR \tag{15-3}$$

or

$$ex - im = K \tag{15-17}$$

The nominal flow of exports and imports responds to price and income changes in the same direction as do the corresponding real flows of exports and imports. Combining the money values of exports and imports, we can express this as

$$\frac{\Delta(ex - im)}{\Delta P} < 0 \tag{15-18}$$

and

$$\frac{\Delta(ex - im)}{\Delta Y} < 0 \tag{15-19}$$

Inequality (15-18) states that as the domestic price level rises, the value of exports decreases and the value of imports increases; thus the numerator will be negative. Inequality (15-19) states that as real income increases, exports remain constant but imports increase; thus the numerator will be negative.

We have also previously assumed that net capital flow is a function of the interest rate; that is

$$K = K(i) \tag{15-20}$$

where

$$\frac{\Delta K}{\Delta i} < 0 \tag{15-21}$$

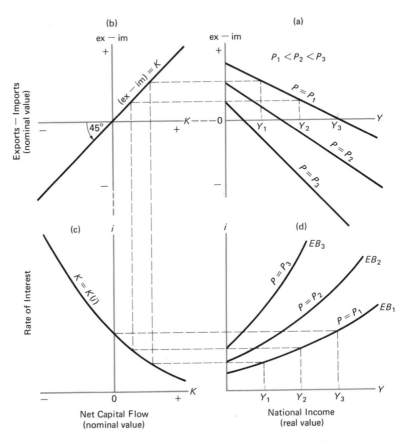

FIGURE 15-9   Derivation of the External Balance Curves

We now have sufficient information to derive the *external balance curve*—a curve indicating all possible combinations of interest rate and national income (for a given price level) that are consistent with ex − im = K. Figure 15-9 illustrates such a derivation. Constant price level curves showing the amount by which nominal exports exceed nominal imports as real national income increases are drawn in Figure 15-9(a). From inequalities (15-18) and (15-19), we know that these curves should be negatively sloped for a given price level and that as the price level rises, these curves must fall for a given level of income. An inspection of Figure 15-9(a) reveals that these conditions are fulfilled. Figure 15-9(b) is simply a graphic expression of the condition of external balance; that is, ex − im = K. Figure 15-9(c) illustrates the net capital flow function K = K(i); its negative slope follows from inequality (15-21). We can now derive the curves in Figure 15-9(d), which show all possible combinations of interest rate and national income (for a given price level) consistent with external balance; these are the external balance curves. To understand how these curves are derived, we choose three levels of real income Y_1, Y_2, and Y_3 in Figure 15-9(a). Then for each of these income levels and for a chosen price level P_1, we determine the corresponding values of (ex − im). For each (ex − im) value, external balance requires that (ex − im) = K, as specified in Figure 15-9(b). In this way we obtain the three values of K required for price level P_1 and income levels Y_1, Y_2, and Y_3 to achieve external balance. Knowing these required values of K and using the net capital flow function in Figure 15-9(c), we can now determine the interest rates required to generate these net capital flows. Finally, by plotting points whose coordinates are national income and the rate of interest that ensures external balance at these income levels and price level, we obtain the external balance curve EB_1 in Figure 15-9(d). By carrying out similar operations on the remaining constant price level curves in Figure 15-9(a), the additional external balance curves EB_2 and EB_3 can be derived in Figure 15-9(d).

15-8   Internal and External Balance with Fixed Exchange Rates

A nation that advocates policy goals of full employment, a stable price level, and fixed exchange rates is committed to achieving joint *internal–external balance*. Of these three policy goals, full employment is probably of primary importance to most governments. In previous chapters we have learned how monetary and fiscal policy can be used to achieve full employment. In the subsequent analysis in this section, we will construct a model in which the level of employment is fixed at Y_{FE}, the full-employment level of income. This has an additional benefit of greatly simplifying our graphic analysis. To construct this model, we derive a variation on the familiar *IS-LM* model.[6]

The first new curve we must derive, the full-employment external balance curve, can be graphed from the data in Figure 15-9(d). Letting $Y_2 = Y_{FE}$, we can see that if we hold income fixed at the full-employment level Y_F, then as the price level rises, the interest rate must also increase if external balance is to be maintained. This functional relationship is illustrated in Figure 15-10, where the curve giving the various combinations of interest rates and price levels required to maintain external balance (or IMR = 0) at full employment is labeled *eb*. Above the *eb* curve the economy will be operating with a balance-of-payments surplus, or IMR > 0; below the *eb* curve, with a balance-of-payments deficit, or IMR < 0.

The second new curve we must develop is a full-employment *LM* curve that indicates all possible combinations of interest rate and price consistent with equilibrium in the money market at FE. To distinguish this curve from our previous *LM* curve, we label it the *lm curve*. The familiar real-money supply curves m_{s_1}, m_{s_2}, m_{s_3}, m_{s_4}, and m_{s_5} for a given nominal money supply are graphed as solid curves in

---

[6] This variation on our basic model was first developed by James P. Quirk and Arvid M. Zarley in "Policies to Attain External and Internal Balance: A Reappraisal," in Quirk and Zarley (eds.), *Papers in Quantitative Economics)* (Lawrence, Kansas: University of Kansas Press, 1968), pp. 433–62.

FIGURE 15-10 *The Full-employment External Balance Curve*

Figure 15-11(a). As before, subscripts refer to the relevant price level. Here this derivation departs from our previous derivation of the *LM* curve: instead of a whole family of money demand curves in Figure 15-11(a), there is only one curve—the money demand curve corresponding to the full-employment level of income.

The intersection of the money supply curves with the full-employment money demand curve gives us the rate of interest necessary for money-market equilibrium $(m_s = m_d)$ for various price levels. These equilibrium quantities of money are plotted against the price level to form the solid curve in Figure 15-11(b). Figure 15-11(c) simply graphs the geometric technique that allows us to transfer the price level from the vertical to the horizontal axis. Finally, by plotting the combinations of interest rate and price level consistent with money-market equilibrium, we obtain the solid *Im* curve in Figure 15-11(d). This curve indicates all possible interest rates and price levels consistent with money-market equilibrium at full employment for a given nominal money supply.

An increase in the nominal money supply will shift the real money supply curves to the right, for example, to m'_{s_1}, m'_{s_2}, m'_{s_3}, m'_{s_4}, and m'_{s_5}, as shown by the dashed curves in Figure 15-11(a). This causes the money-market equilibrium curve to shift to the right in Figure 15-11(b), which in turn produces a rightward shift of the *Im* curve to *Im'*. If the nominal money supply is reduced, then the *Im* curve will shift to the left. Thus it is evident that changing the nominal money supply has exactly the same effect on the *Im* curve as it does on the *LM* curve.

The third and final new curve we must derive is the full-employment *IS* curve, or as we more commonly refer to it, the *is* curve. This curve indicates all possible interest-rate and price-level combinations consistent with equilibrium in the product market at full employment.

Because the level of income is constant at the full-employment level Y_{FE},

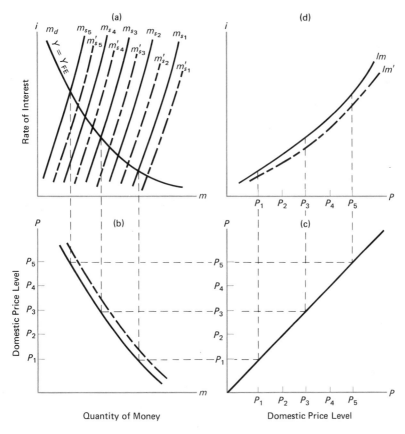

FIGURE 15-11   *Derivation of the Full-employment* **Im** *Curve*

increases in the domestic price level P, if the foreign price level is assumed to be constant, will cause real exports Ex to decline and real imports Im to rise. The effect on (Ex − Im) is indicated by the net export curve in Figure 15-12(a). At low domestic price levels, net exports are positive; at high price levels, net exports become negative.

From the definition of national income we derived in Chapter 1, we know that

$$Y = C + I + G + (\text{Ex} - \text{Im}) \tag{15-7}$$

At full employment with a given level of government expenditure, the following are constant:

$$Y = \bar{Y}_{\text{FE}}$$

$$C = \bar{C}_{\text{FE}} \tag{15-22}$$

$$G = \bar{G}$$

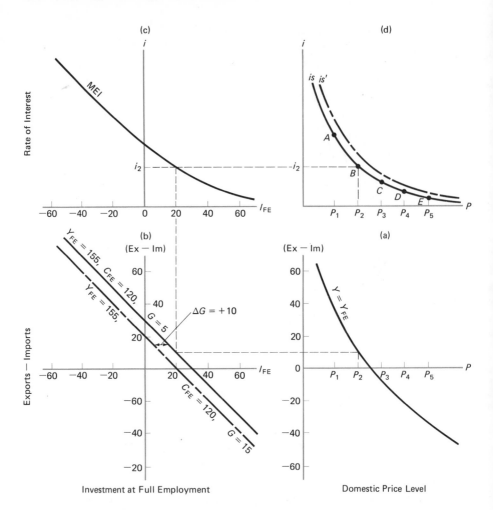

FIGURE 15-12   *Derivation of the Full-employment* is *Curve*

Equation (15-7) can now be rewritten

$$\overline{Y}_{FE} - \overline{C}_{FE} - \overline{G} - I = (Ex - Im) \qquad (15\text{-}23)$$

Now for a given price level we can determine the level of net exports from Figure 15-12(a). Since national income, consumption, and government expenditure are all constant, it follows from equation (15-23) that there can be only one level of net investment consistent with product-market equilibrium at full employment given the level of net exports, Ex − Im. The curve in Figure 15-12(b) gives us that level of net investment. To understand how this curve is obtained, we consider the following numerical example. Suppose that

$$\overline{Y}_{FE} = 155$$

$$\overline{C}_{FE} = 120$$

$$\overline{G} = 5$$

Then equation (15-23) can be written

$$155 - 120 - 5 - I = (Ex - Im)$$

$$30 - I = (Ex - Im)$$

(15-24)

By choosing values for $(Ex - Im)$, we can calculate the required values of I. Some of these values appear in Table 15-1.

Plotting these points gives us the solid curve graphed in Figure 15-11(b), which indicates the required level of net investment for any level of net exports, given the set of conditions hypothesized for this example. We can see that this curve is a negatively sloped straight line.

Figure 15-12(c) is the familiar marginal efficiency of investment (MEI) curve, which graphs the relationship between the rate of interest and the level of net investment. The only addition here is the extension of the MEI curve to include interest rates corresponding to negative net investment rates, that is, reductions in the capital stock.

With the aid of Figures 15-12(a), 15-12(b), and 15-12(c), we can now derive the *is* curve. We choose an arbitrary price level P_2. At this price level, we can determine

TABLE 15-1   Levels of Net Investment Consistent with Product-Market Equilibrium for Various Levels of Net Exports

Ex − Im	I
−30	60
−20	50
−10	40
0	30
10	20
20	10
30	0
40	−10
50	−20

from the net export curve in Figure 15-12(a) that net exports are $10. With this level of net exports, Figure 15-12(b) tells us that net investment must be $20 to maintain product-market equilibrium. For net investment to be $20, the MEI curve in Figure 15-12(c) indicates that the rate of interest must be i_2. Plotting the point whose coordinates are (P_2, i_2) in Figure 15-12(d) gives us point B on the is curve. By selecting price levels P_1, P_3, P_4, and P_5, we obtain the respective points A, C, D, and E plotted in Figure 15-12(d). The curve passing through these points is the full-employment IS curve is.

If autonomous government expenditure increases from $G = \$5$ to $G = \$15$, then the curve in Figure 15-12(b) will shift to the left by $10, which in turn will cause the is curve to shift to the right to is', as shown in Figure 15-12(d). Reducing government expenditure will produce exactly the opposite result, causing the is curve to shift to the left. An increase in taxes will reduce the full-employment level of consumption by reducing disposable income, but it will not affect imports, because they are a function of national income rather than disposable income. This will cause the curve in Figure 15-12(b) to shift to the right and the is curve to shift to the left. Reducing taxes will produce the opposite result. Thus we can see that the is curve in Figure 15-12(d) responds to fiscal policy in the same manner that the IS curve does.

Since the eb, lm, and is curves all have the same axes, we can superimpose these three curves on the same graph. The intersection of the is and lm curves gives the internal balance price level at the internal balance level of income (the full employment level). If the external balance curve passes through the point of internal balance, then joint internal–external balance is achieved. If the external balance curve lies to the left of the point of internal balance, then there will be a net outflow of international monetary reserves; if it lies to the right of this point, then there will be a net inflow.

Suppose that initially we are in internal balance but not in external balance, as illustrated by the solid is, lm, and eb curves in Figure 15-13. The intersection of the is and lm curves at point A determines the price level P_m and the rate of interest i_1 that prevail initially. The eb curve lies to the left and above point A, indicating that the economy is losing international monetary reserves as it maintains a fixed foreign exchange rate. This is only a temporary condition, however, because the supply of international monetary reserves is assumed to be finite.

To achieve external balance, the is and lm curves must be shifted so that they intersect the eb curve and one another simultaneously. At first glance, point B appears to be a possible point of joint intersection. A contraction of the money supply would shift the lm curve to the left until it intersects the is and eb curves at point B. On closer examination, however, we can see that this is impossible, because the price level corresponding to point B, which is P_1, lies below the prevailing price level P_m. Given that wages are downwardly inflexible, the price level P_m is the minimum price level consistent with full employment. In other words, point B cannot be reached. Another possible point of joint intersection seems to be point C. The simultaneous intersection of eb, lm, and is could occur if either government

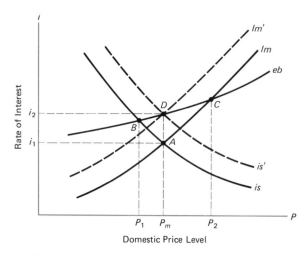

FIGURE 15-13   *The Attainment of Joint Internal–External Balance*

spending is increased or taxes are reduced. Unfortunately, although point *C* is obtainable, it is inconsistent with internal balance, because the price level rises from P_m to P_2 and we have defined internal balance as a condition of full employment *and* stable prices. The only solution consistent with this criterion is point *D*, which can be reached by a combination of contractionary monetary policy and expansionary fiscal policy. Moving from point *A* to point *D* raises the rate of interest from i_1 to i_2, and this in turn produces a net flow of capital into the economy that eliminates the excess demand for foreign exchange. Equilibrium is restored to the foreign exchange market, and the outflow of international monetary reserves is halted.

Until this point in our analysis of joint internal–external balance, we have assumed that all foreign factors that could alter the positions of the *lm, is*, and *eb* curves are constant. We now depart from this assumption to consider the impact of changes in the foreign price level on these three curves.

First, we examine the effect of inflation in foreign countries on the policy goals of external balance at full employment with stable prices. Suppose that prior to the foreign inflation, a condition of joint internal–external balance described by *lm, is,* and *eb* curves in Figure 15-14 prevailed. The price level is P_m, and the rate of interest is i_1. Rising prices abroad tend to increase the demand for exports and to reduce the demand for imports. The net effect is to shift the net export curve in Figure 15-12(a) to the right, which in turn causes the *is* curve to shift to the right. In Figure 15-14, this shift is indicated by the *is* curve *is'*. The external balance curve is also affected by foreign inflation. The *eb* curve in Figure 15-10 shifts to the right, because at a given domestic price level, the interest rate must decline so that a net outflow of capital can occur to offset the increased supply of and the reduced demand for foreign exchange that result from the higher foreign price level.

The new *is* curve *is'* now intersects the *Im* curve at point *A*, and the price level rises from P_m to P_m', the minimum price level that can now occur at the full-employment level of income. At this new condition of full employment, however, external balance is lacking. As before, an infinite number of possible points of joint intersection exist for the three curves. But if we assume that one of the policy goals is to maintain stable prices, or at least to minimize their increase, then the best we can do is to limit the price rise to $(P_m' - P_m)$. To accomplish this, the nominal money supply *must be expanded* to shift the *Im* curve to *Im'* and government expenditure must be contracted or taxes increased to shift the *is* curve from *is'* to *is"*. Joint intersection can now occur at point *B* at an interest rate of i_0 and a price level of P_m'. The important lesson to be learned from this example is that under a fixed exchange rate system, if foreign countries are inflating, it is impossible to maintain full employment with stable prices. Therefore, if one nation embarks on an inflationary expansion of its money supply and if exchange rates remain fixed, then worldwide inflation will result.

Now let us consider the opposite condition: a general decline in foreign price level. Once again we assume that our initial conditions are specified by the *eb, Im,* and *is* curves intersecting at point *A* in Figure 15-15. The initial price level and interest rate are P_m and i_1, respectively. When the foreign price level declines, the *is* curve shifts downward to the left to *is'* and the *eb* curve shifts upward to the left, to *eb'*. If prices and wages were flexible, internal balance would now occur at point *B* in Figure 15-15. But given our assumption of downwardly rigid money wages in the short run, this is impossible, and instead we have a condition of less than full-employment stable disequilibrium. In addition, external balance does not prevail, and there is a net outflow of international monetary reserves. To achieve joint

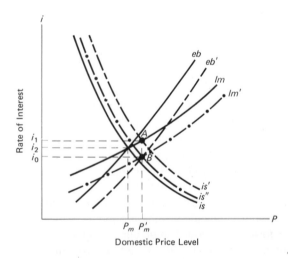

FIGURE 15-14   *The Effect of a Rise in the Foreign Price Level on External and Internal Balance*

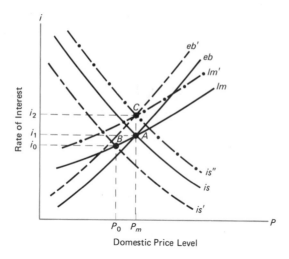

FIGURE 15-15   *The Effect of a Decline in the Foreign Price Level on External and Internal Balance*

internal and external balance, the nominal money supply must be reduced to shift the *Im* curve upward to *Im'* and government expenditure must be increased to shift the *is* curve outward to *is"* from *is'*. Joint internal–external balance can then occur at point *C* at the initial price level P_m but at a new and higher rate of interest i_2.

From our analysis of foreign deflation, it might appear that appropriate monetary and fiscal policy can ensure joint internal–external balance in the face of chronic deflation abroad. This is impossible, however, because according to our analysis in Figure 15-15, the price level remains constant at P_m only if the interest rate is permitted to increase. This eventually presents a problem, partly because the interest elasticity of the external balance curve diminishes as the interest rate increases. This happens because the supply of internationally mobile capital funds is finite and the international capital market is imperfect.

The effect that foreign deflation eventually has on joint balance is illustrated in Figure 15-16. Suppose that the foreign price level has been declining for the past *n* periods and that internal–external balance at the end of the *n*th period is specified by the simultaneous intersection of the *eb*, *Im*, and *is* curves at minimum full-employment price level P_m and at interest rate i_1. When the foreign price level declines in period *n* + 1, the *is* curve shifts downward to *is'*, as it has in previous *n* periods, and the *eb* curve shifts to the left as it also has in previous *n* periods. However, the new *eb* curve *eb'* becomes perfectly interest inelastic at price level P_0, which is less than P_m. Since P_m is the minimum price level consistent with full employment, joint internal–external balance is therefore unobtainable at the prevailing exchange rate. Furthermore, since the *eb* curve lies to the left of the *is–Im* point of intersection, the net flow of international monetary reserves is outward. Thus unless the excess demand for foreign currency is supplied by the foreign

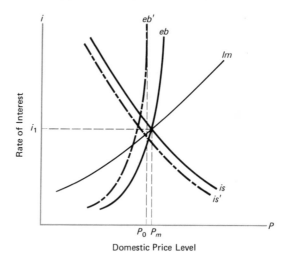

FIGURE 15-16   *Fundamental Disequilibrium Created by Foreign Deflation*

country indefinitely (an extremely unlikely response), the exchange rate cannot be held at its previously fixed value. This condition is referred to as *fundamental disequilibrium,* and the only solution consistent with a policy of free trade is to adjust the exchange rate. In our example, this would mean selecting a new foreign exchange rate at which the price of foreign currency is more expensive in terms of domestic currency. Such a policy change is called *devaluation.* In terms of the curves shown in Figure 15-16, devaluation will shift the *eb* and *is* curves to the right and restore the internal–external balance. This reduces the price that the foreign country, which had the net inflow of IMRs, must pay for a unit of the devalued currency in terms of its own currency; this effect is called *appreciation.* Thus if the currency of one country is depreciated by devaluation, then the currency of the other country will appreciate.

A condition of fundamental disequilibrium similar to the one illustrated in Figure 15-15 can also occur if a nation has abandoned the goal of stable prices to pursue a domestic inflationary policy. The results of this policy are illustrated in Figure 15-17. Prior to the inflation, joint internal–external balance occurs at point *A,* the intersection of the *eb, Im,* and *is* curves in Figure 15-17. Now let us assume that the nominal money supply is increased, causing the *Im* curve to shift to the right to *Im'*. As a result, the price level rises to P_m' and the interest rate decreases from i_1 to i_0 as full employment is maintained. The significant aspect of this inflation, however, is that P_m' now becomes the minimum full-employment price level, and the external balance curve *eb* becomes interest inelastic before this price level is reached. Therefore, full employment and external balance cannot be attained at the established exchange rate. Hence, as in the previous case, a policy of devaluation is required to shift the *eb* curve to the right.

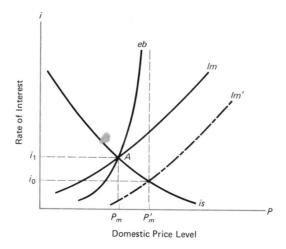

FIGURE 15-17   *Fundamental Disequilibrium Created by Domestic Inflation*

15-9   Fixed vs. Flexible Exchange Rates

Although a thorough examination of the arguments against fixed exchange rates is beyond the scope of this book, a sufficient indictment based on what we have learned at this point is possible.[7]

In our two examples of secular change in the foreign price level, we saw that joint balance was impossible. This dilemma forces a nation to choose whether internal or external balance will be the primary goal of its macroeconomic policy. If a nation chooses a policy of domestic price stability during secular foreign inflation, then it will have an external imbalance characterized by a net increase in its international monetary reserves. What this really means is that the country in question will be exchanging real goods and services for pieces of paper produced by the printing presses of the inflating country. This is a rather poor bargain, and eventually the nation will realize that its own currency must be appreciated (that the foreign currency must be devalued).

In the less likely, but still possible, event that foreign countries experience a secular decline in their price levels, the eventual interest inelasticity of the external balance curve will force the nation pursuing a joint balance policy into fundamental disequilibrium. Moreover, because the prescription for maintaining external–internal balance in this situation is to increase the interest rate steadily, a nation might easily be forced to abandon this policy before the perfect interest inelasticity of the eb curve is reached. This happens because nations also have another goal—

---

[7] For the seminal article on this topic, see Milton Friedman, "The Case for Flexible Exchange Rates," in his book *Essays in Positive Economics* (Chicago: University of Chicago Press, 1953), pp. 157–203.

economic growth.[8] The high interest rates required to maintain external balance will reduce, perhaps even reverse, the growth rate of the nation's capital stock. This means that at some point a country will be forced to choose between economic growth and external balance. Invariably, nations choose the former.

In the absence of trade restrictions, a system of fixed exchange rates is compatible with full employment, stable prices, and external balance only when all member nations of the system maintain stable price levels. Since the establishment of The International Monetary Fund in 1944, there has been an inflationary trend in world prices that appears unlikely to change. This worldwide inflation has led an increasing number of nations to adopt a system of flexible exchange rates.

Politicians have finally concluded that the obvious answer to the dilemma of fixed exchange rates in a world of nations inflating at various rates is the flexible exchange rate system. Given flexible exchange rates, external balance can be automatically maintained by the foreign exchange market. A nation that adopts a system of flexible exchange rates can manage its monetary and fiscal policy to maintain full employment and a stable price level.

15-10 Concluding Remarks

In this chapter we have presented a brief and simple description of why nations trade and how this trade can be financed. Two opposing international monetary systems were discussed. In the first system we examined, the market exchange rate is always the equilibrium exchange rate, because the exchange rate is flexible. In the second system the exchange rate is fixed. We learned that when the foreign exchange market is in disequilibrium under the fixed exchange rate system, the central bank must either buy or sell international monetary reserves. *External balance* was defined to exist when a nation is not gaining or losing international monetary reserves as a result of price-supporting operations in the foreign exchange market. Because a nation does not intervene in the foreign exchange market under a flexible exchange rate system, its level of required international monetary reserves is zero. This level never varies, so that the system is said to always be in external balance.

To analyze joint internal–external balance, we expanded our basic model of aggregate demand to incorporate the economic variables and conditions that prevail in an open economy. Because external balance applies to nominal monetary payments, a model of external balance that is compatible with the models of real aggregate demand and supply was developed. We saw that a stable system of fixed exchange rates is impossible if nations pursue monetary and fiscal policies that lead to varying rates of inflation or deflation. Lastly, given the recent propensity of nations to undergo seciular inflation, it was argued that if a nation chooses to place the goal of internal balance ahead of external balance, the fixed exchange rate should be abandoned and replaced with a flexible exchange rate.

---

[8] The question of economic growth and the policies necessary to obtain it are examined in Chapter 17.

16 Macroeconomic Policy

16-1 Introduction

Every developed economy and virtually all developing economies aspire to certain goals. In the United States, as in most other nations, these goals include high employment, stable prices, and economic growth. To achieve these goals, appropriate macroeconomic policy must be pursued. In this chapter we examine policies designed to attain the first two goals; policies that pertain to the goal of economic growth will be discussed in Chapter 17.

Economists base their policy recommendations on economic theory. Because monetarists and neo-Keynesians disagree about the exact properties of the basic theoretical model, it is not surprising that these two groups advocate dissimilar macroeconomic policies. In this chapter we examine the monetarist and neo-Keynesian approaches to fiscal and monetary policy.

When we refer to fiscal policy here we mean *pure* fiscal policy. A *pure fiscal policy* affects the level of government expenditure or taxation while the nominal money supply remains constant. Similarly, when we refer to monetary policy here we mean a *pure* monetary policy. A *pure monetary policy* increases or decreases the nominal supply of money while the levels of government expenditure and taxation remain constant.

16-2 The Neo-Keynesian Approach

The neo-Keynesian approach to macroeconomic policy is based on the principle that either monetary or fiscal policy can be used to stimulate or to restrain economic activity. Because either policy instrument can increase or decrease aggregate demand, neo-Keynesians determine which policy to emphasize by examining the effect of both monetary and fiscal policy on *secondary* macroeconomic goals.

Monetary Policy

Neo-Keynesian economists believe that monetary policy affects secondary macroeconomic goals more adversely than fiscal policy does. One secondary goal of macroeconomic policy is to have an approximately equal impact on all sectors of the economy. This goal is based on the concept of *equity*—that the cost or benefit of a policy decision should affect all members of society equally.

Neo-Keynesians argue that monetary policy affects economic sectors unevenly and produces distortions in the composition of output. When *monetary restraint* is imposed, interest rates rise and residential and state and local construction are especially hard hit. Small businesses also suffer disproportionately when faced with a monetary restraint in that they find it more difficult than large corporations do to borrow money. *Monetary ease* can also produce the undesirable conditions of excessive speculative construction and business expansion. Hence neo-Keynesians advise against a policy of either excessive monetary restraint or excessive monetary ease, because both extremes have an uneven impact on the composition of output.

Another secondary goal of macroeconomic policy, closely related to the first, is stability of interest rates and of asset values. A tight money policy drives up interest rates and has an inverse effect on the market value of bonds and stocks. Households that hold a major share of their wealth in the form of bonds and stocks suffer a disproportionate disadvantage when the value of their wealth declines. Conversely, these same households enjoy a disproportionate advantage under a policy of monetary ease. Also associated with this secondary goal is the efficient functioning of the financial system, a primary purpose of which is to increase the mobility of money capital within the economy. By *mobility* we mean the ease of impersonal exchange of money for nonmonetary financial assets between lenders and borrowers. Excessive monetary restraint will produce a crisis in the financial system, increasing the level of risk for borrowers and lenders alike. This increase in risk can permanently remove participants from the financial system, thereby impairing the mobility of capital.

Finally, monetary policy can adversely affect economic growth by decreasing the efficiency of capital markets. As we will learn in greater detail in Chapter 17, the rate of economic growth is affected by the rate of capital formation, which in turn is affected by the interest rate. Neo-Keynesians believe that if monetary policy is primarily adopted to restrain the economy and fiscal policy is primarily employed as an economic stimulus, then interest rates will be higher in the long run and a lower economic growth rate will result.

Based on this appraisal of the adverse effects of monetary policy on secondary policy goals, neo-Keynesians recommend that monetary policy remain in the middle of the road, avoiding the extreme cases of ease and restraint. Neo-

Keynesians argue that to determine whether monetary policy is in the middle of the road, long-run concepts of normal interest rates and normal money supply growth rates must be employed. However, because the authorities can initiate monetary policy with a short implementation lag, this recommendation is modified to permit small and prompt deviations from the middle-of-the-road policy. These minor deviations, neo-Keynesians argue, can be used to offset small unexpected changes in aggregate demand. The extent to which monetary policy should be allowed to deviate from the middle of the road is naturally dependent on the importance monetary authorities attach to the effect of their actions on secondary macroeconomic goals.

Fiscal Policy

In light of these recommendations concerning monetary policy, it is logical to assume that neo-Keynesians rely primarily on fiscal policy to stabilize the economy. Conversely, if a middle-of-the-road monetary policy is to be retained, then fiscal policy must be conducted so that an independent monetary authority is not forced to adopt an extreme policy of ease or restraint.

If a middle-of-the-road monetary policy is to be maintained, then fiscal policy must provide the required stimulus or restraint when aggregate demand departs too far in either direction from the full-employment level. According to neo-Keynesians, the appropriate measure of fiscal ease or restraint is the full-employment surplus, which, they argue, should be positive during inflationary periods and negative during recessionary periods. The full-employment surplus can be varied by changing either the level of government expenditure or the rate of taxation. There are certain institutional drawbacks that inhibit the use of each of these approaches as a policy instrument.

It is extremely difficult to vary government expenditure, either in principle or in practice. From the viewpoint of principle, federal expenditure must be considered in terms of compositional constraints. Government operations such as the Bureau of Labor Statistics and the National Weather Service cannot be run efficiently from year to year if their budgets are continually altered to offset changes in private aggregate demand. From the practical point of view, an extensive period of time is usually required to initiate or to phase out a federal program. Hence the lags inherent in a fiscal policy that is based on variations in government expenditure will render it worse than useless as a countercyclical instrument in anything short of a major recession.

Given these severe limitations on expenditure variation, neo-Keynesians consider variations in personal income tax rates the best fiscal policy instrument. In principle, changes in personal income tax rates can be significantly large and frequently exercised. In addition, the effects of these changes can be fairly evenly distributed throughout upper- and middle-income households, overcoming the problem of inequity.

In practice, fiscal policy based on variations in personal income tax rates poses major problems. One source of these problems is the fact that under current laws, any change in personal tax rates must be instituted by the U.S. Congress. As experience with tax-rate variations in 1964 and 1968 indicates, this can be a time-consuming process. To eliminate or to reduce this implementation lag, it has been suggested by neo-Keynesians that Congress:

1. Delegate authority to the President to vary the tax rate within a specified range whenever the rate of unemployment or the rate of inflation reaches a certain amount.
2. Delegate authority to the President to vary tax rates subject to congressional veto.
3. Alter congressional operating rules when tax-rate changes are being considered to facilitate the legislative process.

Thus far, Congress has not approved any of these suggestions, causing neo-Keynesian economists to conclude that greater coordination between the legislative and executive branches of government is needed if countercyclical fiscal policy is to be effectively pursued. The best economic device for furthering this coordination is the concept of the full-employment surplus. The budget request that the President submits to the Congress should be stated in terms of the economic stimulus or restraint that the budget would exert at the full-employment level. The best and easiest way to convey this information is via the estimated level of full-employment surplus. Once understood, this concept will prevent misinterpretation of the actual budget surplus or deficit when the economy is in either a recessionary or an inflationary phase. As we pointed out in Chapter 4, the presence of an income tax automatically throws the actual budget into deficit during a recession and into surplus during inflation. To the uninformed, the actual budget therefore appears to be stimulative when aggregate demand is slack and restrictive when aggregate demand is booming. Although these automatic deficits and surpluses are important, it should be recognized that they are merely shock absorbers—not accelerators or brakes.

The neo-Keynesian view considers a zero full-employment surplus too low in periods of inflation and too high in periods of recession. Hence upward or downward adjustments in the full-employment surplus should be made as conditions warrant. In the long run, however, Arthur Okun believes that a positive full-employment surplus of about 0.5% of the GNP would be sufficient to maintain a high degree of economic stability and to ensure a middle-of-the-road monetary policy.[1]

16-3   The Monetarist Approach

As we have already learned, monetarists believe that there is an extremely stable and close relationship between money and nominal GNP. This relationship is illustrated in Figure 16-1, where the index number of nominal GNP is plotted against

---

[1] Arthur M. Okun, "Rules and Roles for Fiscal and Monetary Policy," in James J. Diamond (ed.), *Issues in Fiscal and Monetary Policy: The Eclectic Economist Views the Controversy* (Chicago: De Paul University, 1971), p. 63.

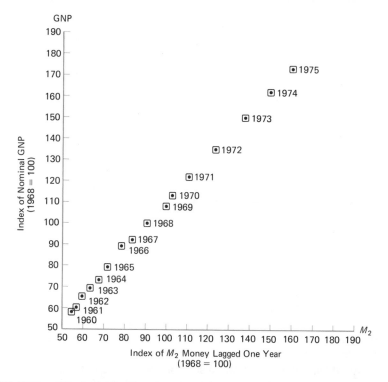

FIGURE 16-1   *The Relationship Between Nominal GNP and the Money Supply: 1960–1975*

the index number of the M_2 definition of the money supply.[2] The close relationship illustrated in this figure implies that if we control the growth rate of M_2, then we can accurately control the growth rate of nominal GNP. This implication critically influences the monetarist approach to monetary and fiscal policy.

Monetarist Fiscal Policy

Monetarists believe that during a major recession, such as the one that occurred in the 1930s, fiscal policy can be used effectively to increase the level of aggregate demand. Very low interest rates accompany major recessions, and the slope of the *LM* curve will be quite shallow at such rates. An expansionary fiscal policy that shifts the *IS* curve to the right will therefore produce an increase in aggregate demand almost equal to the increase that we predicted using the naive multipliers we derived in Chapter 4. This situation is illustrated in Figure 16-2. Prior to the increase in government expenditure, the interest rate is 0.5% and the level of aggregate demand is Y_0, as given by the intersection of the *IS* curve IS_0 with the

[2] I am indebted to David Meiselman for pointing out this particular relationship.

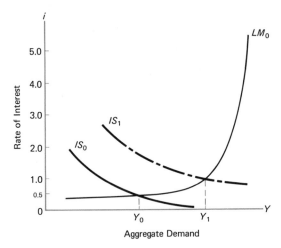

FIGURE 16-2   *The Effect of Expansionary Fiscal Policy During a Major Depression*

LM curve LM_0 in the figure. Now suppose that government expenditure is increased, shifting the *IS* curve to the right, to IS_1. In addition, let us assume that the increase in the price level is so slight that practically no change is produced in the real quantity of money; thus we can also assume that the *LM* curve does not shift. In this case, aggregate demand increases significantly from Y_0 to Y_1 as the interest rate rises from 0.5% to 1.0%.

Faced with any economic situation other than a major recession, monetarists regard fiscal policy as a weak tool at best compared to monetary policy. The essence of the monetarist position is that an increase in government expenditure, financed by increased taxes or by the sale of bonds to the public, will not cause a permanent shift in the aggregate demand curve, even if the economy is at a less than full-employment level. In this situation, increased government demand is matched by a decrease in private demand, and the private sector is said to be "crowded out."

Milton Friedman's explanation (interpreted by Keith M. Carlson and Roger W. Spencer) of how "crowding out" occurs in the context of the *IS–LM* model is illustrated in Figure 16-3.[3] Initially, we are at a less than full-employment, stable disequilibrium income level Y_0 and a price level P_0. The *LM* curve LM_0 intersects the *IS* curve at interest rate i_0. The *LM* curve is steep, and this indicates some, but not much, elasticity with respect to the interest rate. The *IS* curve is shallow, according to Friedman, because "the categories of spending affected by changes in interest rates are far broader than the business capital formation, housing construction, and

---

[3] Keith M. Carlson and Roger W. Spencer, "Crowding Out and Its Critics," *Review of the Federal Reserve Bank of St. Louis* (December 1975), 9–11.

inventory accumulation to which the neo-Keynesians tend to restrict 'investment.'"[4] Now suppose that an increase in government expenditure is financed by the sale of bonds to the public. The IS curve initially shifts to the right to IS', and the aggregate demand curve shifts to the right to AgD'. The shift in aggregate demand is minor due to the steepness of the LM curve and the shallowness of the IS curve. Nonetheless, there is an excess aggregate demand at price level P_0, and the price level rises to P_1, causing the LM curve to shift to the left, to LM_1. The initial change in income is $Y_1 - Y_0$. And according to Friedman, as long as the deficit continues to exist, private expenditures will be reduced as government bonds are substituted for private debt. This will cause the IS curve to shift to the left, reducing—perhaps even eliminating—the increase in national income. Hence from the monetarist point of view, the increase in national income produced by deficit spending is minor and temporary.

Monetarists view pure fiscal policy as an impotent cure not only for unemployment resulting from minor recessions but also for inflation. Suppose that taxes are increased to reduce excess aggregate demand. Of course, the purpose of this policy is to reduce disposable income, thereby decreasing consumption expenditure. But if the government holds expenditure constant, a tax increase will mean that fewer government bonds will be sold to the private sector. This in turn will cause the price of bonds rise and the interest rate to decline. Those institutions and individuals who would have bought these government bonds now hold funds in an amount that is exactly equal to the increase in taxes. If they choose to spend these funds, the reduction in consumer expenditure will be directly offset; if they lend these funds to business firms or to households, the resulting expenditures will indirectly offset the decrease in consumption. Aggregate demand will be significantly reduced only if the decline in interest rates causes an increase in the hoarding of idle cash balances. In other words, the LM curve must *not* be steep. However, even a small reduction in aggregate demand will be temporary, because in successive accounting periods the government debt will be reduced by an amount equal to the increase in taxes, more funds will be available for the private sector to borrow, and the IS curve will shift back to the right, causing aggregate demand to increase and prices to rise.

Monetarists raise another serious objection to fiscal policy based on the fact that often such fiscal policies as tax increases or decreases are legislated to cure temporary deviations from internal balance and are therefore temporary themselves. This allegedly reduces the effectiveness of these tax changes drastically, because as we learned in Chapter 6, consumption is *not* a function of current

[4] Milton Friedman, "Comments on the Critics," in Robert J. Gordon (ed.), *Milton Friedman's Monetary Framework* (Chicago: University of Chicago Press, 1974), p. 140. Friedman actually makes a technical error when he states that only a "minor shift in the IS curve" occurs due to the increase in government expenditure, instead of attributing much of the reduced multiplier effect to the "flatness" of the IS curve. For an elaboration of this point, see T. Norman Van Cott and Gary Santoni, "Friedman vs. Tobin: A Comment," *Journal of Political Economy* **82** (July/August 1974), 883–85.

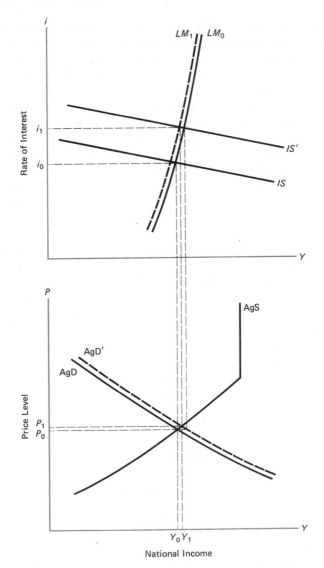

FIGURE 16-3 *A Monetarist Explanation of "Crowding Out"*

disposable income but is a function of expected or permanent income. Hence temporary changes in disposable income for the most part will be ignored by households.

An example of such a fiscal policy is the 1968 addition of a temporary 10% tax surcharge to the federal income tax. If the permanent income hypothesis were valid, then we would expect consumption to be maintained by eductions in savings.

This is actually what occurred in 1968, and the surcharge produced no appreciable effect on consumer expenditures.[5]

In addition to this argument against fiscal policy, monetarists believe that a sizable lag exists between the time when the need for an economic stimulus becomes apparent and the time when it is applied. This means that the increase in aggregate demand that results from the fiscal policy will probably not occur until the economy is well into the expansionary phase of the business cycle. Hence, monetarists argue, this ill-timed stimulus produces excess aggregate demand and inflation, and instead of ensuring increased economic stability, fiscal policy creates greater economic instability.

Monetarist Monetary Policy

Contrary to what their name implies, monetarists generally voice modest claims about the effectiveness of monetary policy. In fact, most monetarist statements on monetary policy are made about the things monetary policy cannot do. The reason for this seeming paradox is implicit in Figure 16-1. This figure illustrates the close relationship between *nominal* GNP and money as hypothesized by the monetarists. It implies that if we know the percentage change in money, we can accurately predict the percentage change in money GNP. But given our present knowledge of the transmission mechanism, we cannot accurately predict in the short run what fraction of the change in nominal GNP will be divided between real-output change and price-level change. Hence monetary policy cannot be relied on for short-run control of either real output or prices—the two primary concerns of macroeconomic policy.

One aspect of this short-run unreliability is the lag in the effectiveness of monetary policy. As in the case of fiscal policy, monetarists believe that expansionary monetary policy in a moderate recession is worse than ineffective, because it increases the cyclical instability of the economy. This increased instability is due to a lag between the time when the monetary stimulus is required and the time when it produces a substantial impact on the economy. Although some economists still debate the precise length of this lag, the consensus seems to be that the lag is about 12–16 months.[6]

The consequence of this lag in the effectiveness of monetary policy, monetarists argue, is that although the monetary authorities may quickly and correctly diagnose the beginning of a recession, expansionary monetary policy may not begin to stimulate the economy until it is well into the recovery phase of the business cycle. This means that there will be excess demand at the full-employment level, and inflation will occur. If the central bank then attempts to counteract the inflation by contracting the money supply, an insufficient supply of money will be available 12–16 months later. This in turn will precipitate another recession, and the business

[5] William L. Springer, "Did the 1968 Surcharge Really Work?" *American Economic Review* **68** (September 1975), 644–59.

[6] Michael J. Hamburger, "The Lag in the Effect of Monetary Policy: A Survey of Recent Literature," *Federal Reserve Bank of New York, Monthly Review* **53** (December 1971), 289–97.

cycle will repeat itself. Monetarists conclude, therefore, that attempts by the monetary authorities to dampen the cyclical behavior of the economy actually increase this behavior. Monetarists not only feel that monetary policy is unreliable in the short run in so-called "fine tuning" the economy but also believe that monetary policy cannot be used to attain certain long-run policy goals.

According to monetarists, monetary policy cannot reduce the rate of unemployment below the so-called "natural rate" of unemployment. Some nonmonetarist economists believe that monetary policy can achieve this goal through the empirically observed short-run relationship between the rate of change in prices and the rate of unemployment—the short-run Phillips curve. Recall that such a relationship for recent U.S. data was illustrated in Figure 12-7. The Phillips curve drawn there suggests that a 5% annual inflation rate will reduce the unemployment level to 3.5%. Because an expansionary monetary policy readily produces this rate of inflation, some economists advocate such a policy because they feel that the social cost of the inflation will be more than offset by the social benefit that will result from the increased output as unemployment declines. Monetarists are opposed to this policy, because as we learned in Chapter 12, the observed decline in unemployment occurs because labor has failed to anticipate the inflation. Once the rate of inflation has been fully and correctly assessed, the unemployment rate rises to the natural rate. The social benefit of increased production is lost at this point, but the social cost of the continuing inflation remains. Hence monetarists are opposed to inflationary monetary policies, because they are of only transitory benefit to society.

Monetarists do not favor monetary policies designed to peg the market rate of interest. Many central bankers have held in an opposite view in the recent past. This opposing view has been motivated by the realization that if the interest rate could be lowered, then the cost of servicing the national debt could be reduced.

The monetary authorities would be successful in their initial attempt to lower the market rate of interest. As the central bank purchases securities on the open market, security prices are driven up and the interest rate is forced down. However, the interest rate will remain at this lower level only if the price level does not rise and reduce the supply of real money. If the economy is at full employment, increasing the nominal money supply will produce a proportionate increase in the price level, and the interest rate will return to the natural rate. Hence this policy will not succeed in reducing the cost of servicing the national debt; instead, it will cause inflation.

To clarify the line of reasoning behind this conclusion, we consider Figure 16-4. Initially, we are in a condition of full-employment equilibrium, where the market rate of interest is equal to the natural rate of interest i_N, the price level is equal to P_0, and the level of aggregate demand is equal to the full-employment level of aggregate supply. This condition is indicated in Figure 16-4(a) by the intersection of IS_0 and LM_0 and in Figure 16-4(b) by the intersection of AgD and AgS. Now suppose that the central bank decides to peg the interest rate below the natural rate at i_0. To accomplish this goal, the monetary authorities increase the nominal money supply, which shifts LM_0 (the LM curve existing at price level P_0) to the right, to LM'_0.

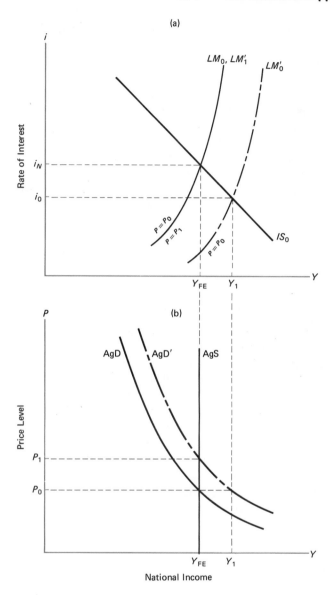

FIGURE 16-4   *The Effects of Attempting to Peg the Interest Rate*

The whole family of *LM* curves associated with LM_0 [which are omitted from Figure 16-4(a) for clarity] also shift to the right, and aggregate demand increases to AgD'. An excess aggregate demand of $Y_1 - Y_{FE}$ now exists at price level P_0, forcing prices to rise. As prices increase, the real money supply decreases, causing the relevant *LM* curve to move to the left of LM_0'. As long as there is any excess demand, prices will continue to rise until the relevant *LM* curve is LM'_1 and aggregate demand equals aggregate supply at the natural rate of interest. Hence the pegging operations of the central bank are doomed to failure in the long run, although they appear to be effective in the short run.

In Chapter 13 we examined the monetarist interpretation of history. There we learned that the monetarists believe that every major recession has been the result of an absolute contraction in the money supply, that minor recessions have probably been the result of declines in the growth rate in the money supply, and that every major inflation has been the result of an excessive expansion of the money supply. According to the monetarist interpretation of history, the obvious means of preventing major economic disturbances is a monetary policy that avoids sharp swings between policies of monetary ease and restraint. The surest way to achieve this goal, monetarists argue, is to remove all discretionary policy from the monetary authorities and replace it with a simple rule that the money supply will grow at a constant annual rate. Milton Friedman has suggested that an annual growth rate in M_2 of 3–5% would be satisfactory.[7] Monetarists contend that such a policy would prevent the recurrence of major economic fluctuations and lessen the impact of minor fluctuations by eliminating discretionary monetary policy—a source of greater economic instability.

A necessary concomitant to the monetary rule is a flexible exchange rate system. In Chapter 15 we learned that under a fixed exchange rate system, a nation cannot pursue a monetary policy that is independent of the policies of the countries with which it maintains fixed exchange rates. If only one of these nations expands its money supply at an inflationary rate, then all the other nations in the system must absorb this money if the exchange rates are to remain fixed. Hence inflation will spread to all nations. Conversely, if one nation experiences a monetary collapse, then the money supply among the nations with which it maintains fixed exchange rates will similarly decline. This decline in the money supply in turn will produce a recession in the initiating country that will spread throughout the other nations in the system. Because monetarists advocate the monetary rule of a fixed growth rate in the money supply, this policy is obviously incompatible with a fixed exchange rate system. Monetarists therefore recommend a flexible exchange rate system.

16-4   Controlling the Money Supply

Although a monetarist monetary policy may seem to be relatively simple to implement, in actual practice several problems may hinder its attainment.

The first problem is one of *political economy*. Although the Federal Reserve is theoretically an independent, nongovernment agency, in practice this is not always true. During periods of recession, for example, strong political pressures are generated to expand government deficit spending. Financing this deficit by selling bonds to the public rather than to the Federal Reserve will generate upward

---

[7] Milton Friedman, "The Role of Monetary Policy," *The American Economic Review* **58** (March 1968), 16.

pressure on the interest rate. A rise in the interest rate will naturally be counterproductive to economic recovery, and consequently politicians will threaten to revoke the Federal Reserve's independent status unless some action is taken to stop the interest rate from rising. This action is the monetization of the newly created debt, which will drive the Federal Reserve off the course of a steady monetary growth policy.

A second problem deals with the mechanism for *controlling the money supply*. Some critics of the monetarists argue that the money supply function is unstable due to the endogenous nature of the money supply and therefore that the quantity of money in circulation cannot be accurately controlled by the central bank. When we derived the money supply relationship in Chapter 8, we reached the general conclusion that

$$M_s = mm \cdot H \tag{16-1}$$

where the money multiplier *mm* is

$$mm = \frac{1}{C_r + R_r - C_r \cdot R_r}$$

and H is the quantity of high-powered money. Because the Federal Reserve can control the quantity of H, it follows from equation (16-1) that if *mm* is a constant, then a constant growth rate in H will produce a constant growth rate in the money supply. Of course, the problem here is that the money multiplier is *not* a constant, for the various reasons outlined in Chapter 8. But from the viewpoint of policy implementation, the question is to what extent variations in *mm* will cause the actual growth rate in the money supply to deviate from the targeted growth rate.

Albert E. Burger[8] has examined how accurately the growth rate in the money supply can be controlled over a 12-month period if the following control techniques are employed:

1. The money multiplier is assumed to be constant, and the Federal Reserve Open-market Committee establishes a growth rate for high-powered money that is equal to the targeted growth rate of M_s.
2. The money multiplier is not assumed to be constant but is predicted by the open-market committee each month, and the growth rate of H is adjusted accordingly to produce the desired growth in M_s.

If the first control technique is used, Burger concludes that the Federal Reserve can be 95% confident that the actual growth rate in the money supply will not deviate more than ±2% from the targeted rate during any 12-month period. For example, if the Federal Reserve chooses a targeted 6% growth rate during a 12-month period, then the actual growth rate will lie within a range of 4–8% with a 95% probability. If the second control technique is used, according to Burger, then the Federal Reserve can be 95% confident that the actual growth rate in the money supply will not deviate more than ±0.8% from the targeted rate during any 12-month period. If the time period is extended to, say, 18 or 24 months, then Burger

---

[8] Albert E. Burger, "The Relationship Between Monetary Base and Money: How Close?" *Review of the Federal Reserve Bank of St. Louis* (October 1975), 3–8.

TABLE 16-1   Actual Annual Percentage Rates of Money Growth

	M_1	M_2
Jan. 1974 to June 1974	8.3	9.2
June 1974 to Jan. 1975	1.0	5.1
Jan. 1975 to June 1975	7.9	11.2
June 1975 to Jan. 1976	2.4	7.5
Jan. 1976 to June 1976	6.6	11.5

SOURCE   Federal Reserve Bank of St. Louis, *Monetary trends*, various issues.

concludes that the deviation of the targeted growth rate from the actual growth rate can be reduced even more. Thus it appears that the money supply can be accurately controlled.

In recent years, the Federal Reserve Open-market Committee has been establishing 12-month objectives for growth rates in the money supply. These objectives (made available to the public by congressional requirement since the spring of 1975) have remained almost constant, with annual growth rates in M_1 of 4.5–7.5% and in M_2 of 7.5–10.5%. If we compare these targeted growth rates with the actual growth rates given in Table 16-1, it becomes apparent that the Federal Reserve has not achieved its objectives. The data in Table 16-1 reveal large and erratic swings in the monetary growth rate.

At first glance Burger's conclusions regarding the ability of the Federal Reserve to control the money supply appear to be in error. However, a closer examination reveals that this is not the case. Milton Friedman points out that the Federal Reserve's poor performance does not indicate inability to hit these monetary targets; rather, according to Friedman, the monetary authorities are using the wrong operating procedures to control the growth rate of the money supply.[9] The error committed by the Federal Reserve Open-market Committee, as Friedman sees it, is the attempt to control the money supply indirectly by controlling the interest rates that commercial banks charge when they borrow funds from one another to meet reserve requirements (the *federal funds rate*). The margin of error in using the federal funds rate to hit monetary targets is much greater than it would be if Burger's suggested techniques were implemented. Even worse, the errors that result from employing the federal funds rate tend to be cumulative and self-reinforcing.

16-5   Economic Policy and Public Choice

The neo-Keynesian reliance on fiscal policy is the result of the so-called "Keynesian revolution." Prior to the 1930s, most economists considered a free-enterprise

[9] Milton Friedman, "What is the Federal Reserve Doing?" *Newsweek* (March 10, 1975), 63, and "How to Hit the Money Target," *Newsweek* (December 8, 1975), 85.

economy to be automatically self-regulating. If the condition of full employment were disrupted in such an economy, then corrective forces would automatically become operative to restore full employment. Government tendency toward profligacy was believed to be a primary source of this disturbance; the maintenance of a balanced budget was considered an effective constraint on this tendency.

When John Maynard Keynes published *The General Theory,* the prevailing economic conditions in the United States, the United Kingdom, and elsewhere seemed to contradict this paradigm. Keynes wrote: . . .

> . . . it is an outstanding characteristic of the economic system in which we live that, whilst it is subject to severe fluctuations in respect of output and employment, it is not violently unstable. Indeed it seems capable of remaining in a chronic condition of subnormal activity for a considerable period, without any marked tendency either toward recovery or toward complete collapse. Moreover, the evidence indicates that full, or even approximately full, employment is of rare and short-lived occurrence.[10]

To solve the problem of unemployed resources, Keynes argued that government intervention—specifically, deficit expenditure—is necessary. Keynes wrote *The General Theory* to gain support for this view from other economists, and in this objective he was most successful. However, it was not until 1961 that politicians and the general voting public in the United States embraced the basic Keynesian concepts and the prescription presented in *The General Theory.*

Table 16-2 lists the annual federal budget surplus and deficit for the United States since World War II. From 1947 through 1960, seven years of surplus were matched by seven years of deficit, resulting in a total deficit of $996 million, or an average annual deficit of $71 million. From 1961 through 1977, however, there were 16 deficit years and only one surplus year. The total deficit during this period amounted to $290,948 million, or an annual average deficit of $17,115 million. Thus the annual deficit for the 1961–1977 period was 241 times greater than the annual deficit for the 1947–1960 period.

The massive increase in the federal debt between 1961 and 1975 was financed by selling approximately two-thirds of the debt to the public and one-third of the debt to the Federal Reserve. The sale of one-third of the debt to the Federal Reserve in turn caused the quantity of high-powered money to increase approximately $60 billion. This increase in high-powered money then produced an increase in the money supply, creating inflation and unemployment (as outlined in Chapter 14).

The question that immediately comes to mind here is, Why did this happen? No inherent concept in Keynesian or neo-Keynesian economic theory advocates a continuous government deficit. In fact, as described in the preceding section, the economic theory underlying neo-Keynesian policy is symmetrical: deficits during periods of unemployment are matched by surpluses during periods of inflation. Hence an appeal to macroeconomic theory does not explain why persistent deficits should have occurred.

---

[10] John Maynard Keynes, *The General Theory of Employment, Interest, and Money,* pp. 249–50.

TABLE 16-2   Federal Surplus or Deficit: Fiscal Years 1947–1977
             (in millions of dollars)

Year	Surplus (+) or Deficit (-)
1947	+ 3,862
1948	+ 12,001
1949	+ 603
1950	- 3,112
1951	+ 6,100
1952	- 1,517
1953	- 6,533
1954	- 1,170
1955	- 3,041
1956	+ 4,087
1957	+ 3,249
1958	- 2,939
1959	- 12,855
1960	+ 269
1961	- 3,406
1962	- 7,137
1963	-4,751
1964	- 5,922
1965	- 1,596
1966	- 3,796
1967	- 8,702
1968	- 25,161
1969	+ 3,236
1970	- 2,845
1971	- 23,033
1972	- 23,227
1973	- 14,301
1974	- 3,460
1975	- 43,604
1976	- 76,001(*)
1977	-47,242(*)

* Estimated by the Council of Economic Advisors.
SOURCE *Economic Report of the President, 1976*, p. 245. The estimate for fiscal year 1977 was obtained by adding the transitional quarter estimate to the fiscal year 1977 estimate and multiplying by 0.8.

Using the *theory of public choice,* James M. Buchanan and Richard E. Wagner do provide an answer to this question.[11] In a democracy, elected politicians determine government expenditures and taxes. Moreover, these politicians are

[11] James M. Buchanan and Richard E. Wagner, *Democracy in Deficit: The Destructive Legacy of Lord Keynes* (New York: Academic Press, *forthcoming*).

returned to office if the benefits their constituency receives from these expenditures exceed the cost of these expenditures. The expenditure of government monies on such projects as day-care centers, highways, and national parks provide benefits; the taxes that pay for these beneficial services represent their cost. Prior to the "Keynesian revolution," politicians and their constituents accepted the balanced-budget rule that benefits should always be matched by their costs. Buchanan and Wagner argue that the Keynesian destruction of the rigid balanced-budget rule has created a political bias in the conduct of economic policy, whereby the perceived benefits of deficit spending exceed their perceived costs and surpluses produce the opposite result.

First let us consider the direct and indirect effects of a budget surplus that is created by raising taxes. The direct effect of such a policy is to impose costs on citizens without providing them with any direct reciprocal benefits. If the surplus is designed to reduce aggregate demand during an inflationary period, then an indirect benefit of such a policy is to stop the inflation. But the amount of information constituents require to evaluate and to comprehend the indirect benefits that they will receive is so large that the overall costs will be perceived to exceed the overall benefits. Hence there will be a strong political bias against surpluses.

In the case of budget deficits in a democracy, the situation is completely reversed. The direct effect of an increase in government expenditure without an increase in taxes is to produce benefits without imposing direct costs. The indirect cost of the inflation produced by the monetization of the debt is only imperfectly perceived. According to Buchanan and Wagner, these budget deficits are permitted in a democracy when the rigid balanced-budget rule is abandoned and may even occur at times when Keynesian theory clearly argues against their use—that is, during periods of full employment or inflation.

The economic result of the net effect of this policy—deficits decidedly dominating surpluses—is secular inflation accompanied by unemployment as resources are drawn into investment projects that cannot be maintained without accelerating inflation. When the rate of inflation is anticipated, these investment projects become unprofitable and unemployment occurs. Thus the application of Keynesian principles in a democratic setting produces the very economic instability that Keynes attempted to avoid.[12]

16-6   The Visible Hand

From earliest recorded history, we know that rulers have been displeased with the distribution of production in market economies and have intervened in and attempted to reorder things in these markets to their own liking. A classic example occurred in ancient Rome during the reign of Diocletian. In A.D. 296, in order to

---

[12] Buchanan and Wagner persuasively argue that Keynes envisaged his theories operating in an elitist, not a democratic, institutional setting.

finance deficit government spending, Diocletian debased Roman coinage (by adding base metals to precious-metal coins). This quickly expanded the quantity of money and increased prices. In response to the complaints of city dwellers who were then forced to pay "unfair" prices for grain, oil, and wine, Diocletian issued an Edict on Maximum Prices in 301. This edict set maximum prices for more than 900 commodities, 130 grades of labor, and various freight rates. The penalty for selling or buying above these established prices was death or deportation for *both* seller and buyer. The enforcement of this edict resulted in numerous deaths and the withdrawal of grain and other necessities of life from the market, until Diocletian was forced to abdicate and the Edict was repealed in 305. Unfortunately, subsequent Roman emperors repeated Diocletian's fiscal and monetary mistakes throughout the fourth century, and these mistakes, coupled with repeated attempts to control wages and prices, caused the collapse of Roman civilization and ushered in the feudal society of the middle ages.[13]

Like these early Roman emperors, some contemporary politicians seem unable to learn the economic lessons of the past. We examine two examples here.

Wage and Price Controls

In response to urgings from the U.S. Congress, business and union leaders, and the news media, President Richard Nixon imposed direct wage and price controls on the entire American economy in August 1971.[14] This authority had been granted to the President in the so-called Economic Stabilization Act of 1970, as amended in 1971. At the time this action was taken, consumer prices had risen only 3.9% during the preceding 12 months, compared to 5.1% from September 1969 to August 1970. The question we attempt to answer here is, What overall effect resulted from these controls? To determine this, first we must construct a model that allows us to predict the behavior of prices in the absence of controls.

Our predictive model is based on the extremely stable relationship (illustrated in Figure 16-1) between nominal GNP and the M_2 definition of money, which has existed for more than 15 years. This stable relationship results from the fact that if the growth rate in M_2 exceeds the growth rate in real gross national product RGNP, then the price level will rise in proportion to the excess growth in M_2. This theory is illustrated in Figure 16-5, where an index of the ratio $M_2/$RGNP and the Consumer Price Index CPI are plotted against time. We can readily see from this graph that the $M_2/$RGNP index is an excellent estimator of the CPI, as the theory predicts.

In Figure 16-6 the curves shown in Figure 16-5 are reconstructed from quarterly, rather than yearly, data for the time period from 1971 I to 1975 IV. If we let $M_2/$RGNP $=$ CPI*, the consumer price estimator, then we can measure the impact of wage and price controls on the American economy.

---

[13] Ludwig von Mises, *Human Action* (Chicago: Henry Regnery, 1966), pp. 767–69.

[14] Some of those who openly opposed the imposition of these wage and price controls included the AFL–CIO, Milton Friedman, *The Wall Street Journal, Barron's,* and First National City Bank (now Citibank).

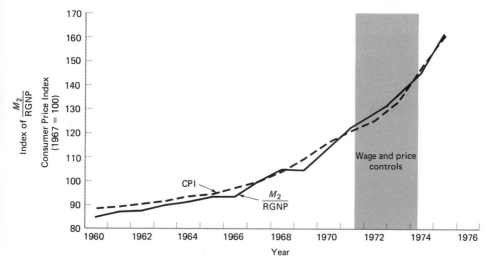

FIGURE 16-5   *The Relationship Between Money (Relative to Output) and the Price Level: 1960–1975*

We mentioned previously that even prior to the imposition of wage and price controls, the rate of price increase was declining due to restrictive monetary policy. It is therefore not surprising that the gap between CPI and CPI* diminished during Phase I (from August 15, 1971 to November 14, 1971), when almost all wages and prices were frozen. Phase II, which lasted from November 14, 1971 to January 11, 1974, restrained wage increases to 6.2% and forced businesses to remain within the upper range of their consolidated profit margins for the three previous years. During this period monetary policy was highly expansionary, and according to CPI* predictions, actual prices would have been much higher in the absence of these controls.

As history would soon reveal, the suppression of prices and wages in Phase II created inevitable shortages and misallocations of resources. In the building industry, for example, such a low price was set on flooring-grade plywood that it was no longer profitable to manufacture, and builders were forced to use higher grades of plywood. This raised home construction costs, which under the guidelines of Phase II could be passed on to home buyers. Literally tens of thousands of such irrational production decisions were made before the controls of Phase II were replaced by the controls of Phase III, which were designed to decontrol the economy gradually. Of course, the gap between CPI and CPI* during Phase II meant that the inflation was only suppressed—not cured. Thus CPI rapidly approached CPI* under Phase III. In fact, CPI approached CPI* so rapidly that a second complete price freeze was initiated on June 13, 1973. This freeze lasted only until August 12, 1973; it was primarily a holding action on the part of the Nixon administration to permit Phase IV to be implemented.

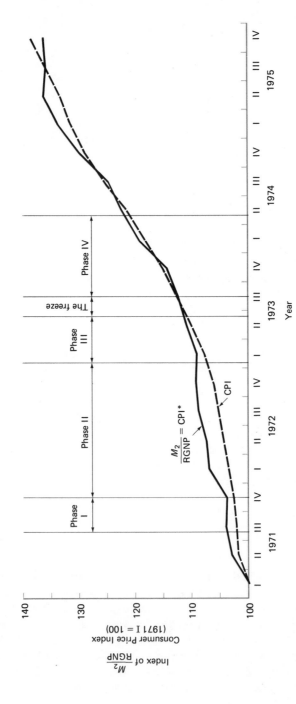

FIGURE 16-6   The Behavior of Estimated and Actual Prices Under Wage and Price Controls

Phase IV lasted from August 12, 1973 to April 30, 1974. Wage and price controls were then removed entirely from all industries. Phase IV, as Figure 16-6 reveals, was simply a continuation of Phase III, until prices returned to a level consistent with the increased quantity of money.

A casual examination of Figure 16-6 could lead to the conclusion that these wage and price controls had no lasting effect on the American economy, but this would be an erroneous assumption. As Michael Wachter points out, the suppression of prices during Phase II permitted the administration to pursue a highly expansionary monetary and fiscal policy whose inflationary implications (unlike its effects on employment) were concealed from the public prior to the presidential election of November 1972.[15] From the end of fiscal year 1971 to the end of fiscal year 1974 the federal budget grew 27%, and from the beginning of Phase I to the end of Phase IV the money supply grew at a rate of more than 11% per year. These facts lead us to the paradoxical conclusion that wage and price controls result in higher, not lower, prices. This is not too surprising, however, when we consider the theory of public choice outlined in the preceding section. Politicians of both political parties in the 1972 presidential campaign were able to tell their constituents that they had played critical roles in the passage and implementation of the policy to control inflation.

Central Economic Planning

The idea that a government can centrally plan an entire economy is relatively new. This concept was first implemented by Lenin in the Soviet Union in the 1920s, but the current *Soviet-style planning system* did not assume its present form until 1929. The primary purpose of this planning system was, and still is, to promote the political goals of Soviet leaders without weakening the totalitarian control they exert over their subjects. In this system economic efficiency is a decidedly secondary goal.

The stated purpose of reviving interest in central planning in the West has been to increase the economic efficiency of the market economy. Western central planning has also been advocated to: . . . reduce unemployment, control inflation, moderate the business cycle, distribute income more justly, make the economy grow faster, make it grow slower, prevent discrimination, eliminate pollution, improve the quality of life, and so on. In other words, planning is frequently hailed as a cure for whatever seems to be the economic ailment of the moment.[16]

The model for Western central planning is usually referred to as *French-style planning,* because it has been employed in France intermittently since 1947. It is also often called *indicative, flexible, soft,* or *voluntary planning.* In actual practice, French planning can vary so radically from year to year that it is impossible to

[15] Michael L. Wachter, "Did Wage–Price Controls Reduce Inflation?" *Wharton Quarterly* (Summer–Fall 1974), 5–9 and 31–32.

[16] G. Warren Nutter, *Central Economic Planning: The Visible Hand* (Washington, D.C.: American Enterprise Institute for Public Policy Research, 1976). The author is greatly indebted to the knowledge and insights of Professor Nutter in much of this section.

describe the system without relating what occurs every year that it is employed.[17] Nevertheless, an idealized concept of central planning has become known as *French-style* or *Western planning*.

A French-style plan is the summed collection of the predicted values of economic aggregates (such as consumption, investment, and government) and specific industries (such as the automobile, electronics, and steel industries) in four to five years. Government economists are largely responsible for determining the aggregate national targets, and the firms in each industry cooperatively prepare an estimate of the final demand and the level of investment required to meet that demand in the industry. These industry estimates are then summed and compared with the aggregate totals, and the planning board makes any necessary adjustments to correct discrepancies. In essence, French-style planning in its idealized form attempts to provide a five-year forecast of a nation's economic activities. We now consider the efficiency of this form of planning in both its idealized and its realized forms.

Western planning in its idealized form is an attempt to construct a more efficient economic order. Such critics of central planning as Ludwig von Mises and Friedrich A. Hayek have argued since the beginning of the Soviet experiment that economic planning would inevitably lessen productive efficiency. This inefficiency, Hayek feels, results from the fact that the necessary knowledge required to plan and to operate an economy is so vast and continually changing that it "never exists in concentrated or integrated form but solely as the dispersed bits of incomplete and frequently contradictory knowledge which all the separate individuals possess."[18] The market economy is more efficient, according to Hayek, because it requires far less information to function. This information is in the form of the market-determined prices of commodities and resources. Precisely how this limited and decentralized information results in an efficient economic system is illustrated in one of Hayek's famous examples, which follows:

> Assume that somewhere in the world a new opportunity for the use of some raw material, say tin, has arisen, or that one of the sources of supply of tin has been eliminated. It does not matter for our purpose—and it is significant that it does not matter—which of these two causes has made tin more scarce. All that the users of tin need to know is that some of the tin they used to consume is more profitably consumed elsewhere and that, in consequence, they must economize tin. There is no need for the great majority of them even to know where the more urgent need has arisen, or in favor of what other needs they ought to husband the supply. If only some of them know directly of the new demand, and switch resources over to it, and if the people who are aware of the new gap thus created in turn fill it from still other resources, the effect will rapidly spread throughout the whole economic system and influence not only all the users of tin but also those of its substitutes and the

---

[17] For an excellent examination of the concept and actual experience with planning in France, see Vera Lutz, *Central Planning for the Market Economy: An Analysis of the French Theory and Experience* (Atlantic-Highlands, N.J.: Humanities Press, 1969).

[18] Friedrich A. Hayek, "The Use of Knowledge in Society," *American Economic Review* **35** (September 1945), 519.

substitutes of these substitutes, the supply of all things made of tin, and their substitutes, and so on; and all this without the great majority of those instrumental in bringing about these substitutions knowing anything at all about the original cause of these changes. The whole acts as one market, not because any of its members surveys the whole field, but because their limited individual fields of vision sufficiently overlap so that through many intermediaries the relevant information is communicated to all.[19]

The reason why a market economy operates more effectively than a centrally planned economy is therefore because a market economy uses information, a scarce and costly resource, more efficiently. The information required for a centrally planned economy to operate as effectively as a market economy is impossible to attain, and hence the planned economy is far less efficient.

Advocates of Western planning do not accept the totality of the Hayekian argument. They point out, quite correctly, that most of the price signals that affect firms are not explicit prices existing in current markets but forecasts of future prices. These future prices can be determined in many ways, ranging from informal "seat-of-the-pants" intuition to sophisticated market-research methods. Advocates of central planning argue that the levels of output and investment that firms choose to undertake on the basis of these anticipated prices may be inconsistent with one another. Such inconsistencies will produce inefficiencies that can be eliminated by harmonizing the various forecasts of firms in individual industries.

Superficially, the harmonization argument in support of central planning seems quite logical, but a closer inspection reveals that its supposed strength is actually its primary weakness. Inconsistencies in marketing forecasts among various firms in a particular industry do not indicate a weakness in the market system; instead these inconsistencies reflect one of the market system's major strengths. Firms make predictions to satisfy future consumer demands. One way in which firms compete for consumer patronage is via prediction. Firms that successfully predict future demands will be relatively profitable and will survive. The central planners who are "merely harmonizing" the inconsistencies in these forecasts are destroying this form of competition. In addition, the central planners have no way to determine which inconsistent company plans should be discarded. The industry forecast that is chosen is just as likely to be wrong by the same margin as any of the rejected forecasts. This results in increased inefficiency if firms try to attain centrally planned goals. When firms are flexible enough to adjust their output as errors in the plan become evident, the central plan will become obsolete. In other words, when firms behave as if there were no central plan, the economy becomes more efficient.

Another inherent danger is that harmonizing industry output forecasts provides the legal and institutional setting for *cartelization*. In industries that have a limited number of firms, collusion to restrict output and to drive up prices is likely to result from central planning.

The practical results of Western or French-style central planning bear out the

[19] Friedrich A. Hayek, *Individualism and Economic Order* (Chicago: University of Chicago Press, 1948), pp. 85–86.

worst fears of its critics. After a study of the French 20-year experience with indicative planning, Vera Lutz concluded:

> The forecasting has not so far achieved the necessary accuracy for there to be effective planning of this kind. Nor have 20 years of French planning shown signs of any continuous improvement in the degree of accuracy, as the planning authorities acknowledge. Indeed their experience with the Fourth Plan inclined them to take the opposite view and to assume that the forecasting was becoming less accurate.[20]

Also as predicted, the central planning authorities in both France and Japan are now favoring greater industrial concentration, thereby reducing competition and innovation.[21]

In the United States there has been a recent curious revival of interest in central economic planning, spearheaded by the Initiative Committee for National Economic Planning, whose members include Wassily Leontief, John Kenneth Galbraith, Robert Heilbroner, and Leonard Woodcock. In addition, in partial collaboration, Senators Hubert Humphrey and Jacob Javits have introduced the *Balanced Growth and Economic Planning Act* in Congress.

The Humphrey–Javits bill describes the organization and staffing of the proposed Economic Planning Board in great detail, but it does not explicitly state what this Board will do or how it will operate. Humphrey and Javits apparently conceptualize a government agency that will make detailed forecasts of economic activity over five-year periods.

The bill's sponsors claim that "there is not a single word or phrase in this bill which could be used to expand the government's control over the economy,"[22] but this seems unlikely. If the Board is to achieve its minimum goal of forecasting economic activity, it must amass detailed data from firms. Thus the government's role in the economic sector will be expanded by the very act of acquiring this information. On the other hand, the Board cannot construct a plan that will "guide the market" without employing coercive powers. Myron Sharpe, speaking for the Initiative Committee for National Economic Planning, suggests the following means of forcing firms and consumers to acquiesce to the inevitably erroneous forecasts of the Economic Planning Board:

> . . . tax incentives and penalties; capital and credit allocation; laws requiring or prohibiting definite actions, such as those specifying how air, water, and land may be used; and the projects within the public sector itself—the space program, for example. Incomes policy [wage and price controls] . . . is also a possible planning instrument.[23]

Advocates of central planning argue correctly that the federal government already exercises these powers. But the government does not presently employ these powers to validate the erroneous forecasts of an Economic Planning Board.

---

[20] Vera Lutz, *Central Planning for the Market Economy*, p. 101.

[21] John Sheahan, "Planning in France," *Challenge* (March–April 1975), 18, and Ryutaro Komiya, "Economic Planning in Japan," *Challenge* (May–June 1975), 19.

[22] Hubert Humphrey, *Notes from the Joint Economic Committee*, Vol. 1, No. 19 (Washington, D.C.: U.S. Government Printing Office, July 1, 1975), p. 19.

[23] Myron Sharpe, "The Planning Bill," *Challenge* (May–June 1975), 7.

In addition, a good case can be made to support the reduction of existing government powers in the economic sector to achieve greater efficiency and a more equal distribution of income.[24] The greatest danger inherent in the concept of central planning, however, is that it will significantly reduce individual freedom. "The guiding principle that a policy of freedom for the individual is the only truly progressive policy remains as true today as it was in the nineteenth century."[25]

16-7   A Policy Recommendation

There is general agreement among economists that the macroeconomic policy goals of high employment and a stable price level are desirable. But there is general disagreement among economists about the roles that various policy instruments should play in achieving these goals. In this section we specify the roles of monetary and fiscal policy given the present state of political economy.

Empirical evidence collected since the late 1950s clearly shows that the demand for money is a highly stable function of a few variables and that the supply of money can be controlled by the central bank within narrow limits over time periods of 12 months or more. This means that the growth rate in nominal GNP can be accurately controlled. In the short run, however, our present knowledge of the monetary transmission mechanism does not permit us to predict accurately how an increase in the money supply will affect the division between increased real output and prices. In the long run an increase in the growth rate in the money supply can be maintained so that growth in nominal GNP will be equal to growth in real GNP, and a stable price level will result. Contractions in the absolute level of the money supply produce major contractions of output and employment, and significant reductions in the growth rate in the money supply over periods of longer than 9–12 months play a major role, if not the major role, in producing minor recessions of economic activity. Hence the adoption of a rule specifying a noninflationary growth rate in the money supply is the best monetary policy that can be implemented now.

To achieve a constant growth rate in the money supply, the monetary authorities must be able to pursue such a policy with no international monetary restrictions. Therefore, a flexible exchange rate system, which permits a nation's money supply to be independent of the money supplies of the other nations with which it trades, must be adopted.

Empirical evidence concerning the effectiveness of fiscal policy supports the view that government expenditure and tax multipliers are minor and temporary policy instruments unless the economy is driven into a severe depression by inept monetary policy. In addition, attempts to "fine-tune" the economy by instituting temporary changes in tax policy have no appreciable impact on the expenditure behavior of the private sector.

Widespread acceptance of the erroneous view that a market economy is

---

[24] For example, see Milton Friedman, *Capitalism and Freedom* (Chicago: University of Chicago Press, 1962).

[25] Friedrich A. Hayek, *The Road to Serfdom* (Chicago: University of Chicago Press, 1944), 240.

inherently unstable and that fiscal policy should be used to maintain full employment has destroyed the orthodox belief in the balanced-budget rule that specified that the govenment budget should be balanced each fiscal year except in unusual circumstances. This in turn has created a public-choice bias toward government deficits, even when the underlying economic theory clearly calls for surpluses. The magnitudes of these deficits are such that it is impossible for the Federal Reserve to maintain a monetary policy that is independent of fiscal policy in the context of the current institutional setting. The result of this interaction between fiscal and monetary policy is an inflationary growth rate in both the money supply *and* unemployment—the very results these policy instruments are designed to prevent. Instead of stabilizing the market economy, government intervention has actually made the economy more unstable. Unfortunately, some individuals do not acknowledge the cause-and-effect relationship between government intervention and increased economic instability. Because they believe that the solution to inflation and unemployment is increased government intervention, these people recommend such policies as wage and price controls and central economic planning. However, history has shown not only that these policies fail to achieve their objectives, but also that they increase economic instability and inevitably contribute to the loss of individual liberty.

To eliminate the deficit bias in fiscal poicy, James Buchanan and Richard E. Wagner advocate the adoption of a fiscal rule requiring that the federal budget be kept in balance.[26] A balanced budget could be maintained by automatically raising (lowering) taxes when the budget goes into deficit (surplus) or reducing (increasing) expenditure when the budget is in deficit (surplus). This rule could be abandoned only during a declared national emergency.

If a combination of monetary and fiscal policy rules are ever to be followed, control over these matters during normal periods should be removed from elected and appointed monetary authorities. This could be accomplished by congressional legislation or, as Buchanan and Wagner suggest, by amending the U.S. Constitution. These proposals undoubtedly seem radical to many present-day economists, but if Buchanan and Wagner's predictions regarding continued deficits, inflation, and unemployment are correct, then public and official opinion will change.

16-8   Concluding Remarks

In this chapter we have learned that both the monetarists and the neo-Keynesians essentially support several major macroeconomic policy recommendations. Specifically, both agree that a middle-of-the-road monetary policy should be maintained and that the government budget should be in balance in the long run. Their major area of disagreement concerns the degree of countercyclical activism that the government should pursue.

Neo-Keynesians argue that an activist countercyclical fiscal policy based on

---

[26] James M. Buchanan and Richard E. Wagner, *Democracy in Deficit: The Destructive Legacy of Lord Keynes* (New York: Academic Press, *forthcoming*).

temporary variations in personal income taxes can be effective in curbing inflation and unemployment and should be pursued. These economic theorists argue that the appropriate fiscal policy indicator, the full-employment surplus, should be increased during periods of inflation and decreased during periods of unemployment. Monetarists, on the other hand, believe that a balanced budget should be maintained in the short run as well as in the long run. Monetarist rejection of fiscal policy is based on the belief that:

1. The impact of the fiscal multiplier is minor and temporary, unless the economy is in a severe depression.
2. Households do not alter their consumption habits in conjunction with temporary changes in their measured disposable income.
3. The implementation lag is too great to enable fiscal policy to create economic stability.

The political adoption of Keynesian fiscal policy has produced a strong deficit bias that is at variance with the theoretical model. The theory of public choice provides an explanation for this behavior.

Federal intervention in the market is not a new phenomenon, but government control of prices and wages by edict is as impossible today as it was during the reign of Diocletian. The objective of complete government control over an entire economy is a phenomenon of the twentieth century. When it is employed, economic efficiency and individual freedom are greatly reduced.

A macroeconomic policy based on rules, not people, has been recommended. This policy prescribes that the growth rate in the money supply in the short run as well as in the long run be fixed at the noninflationary rate. Fiscal policy would be governed by a rule requiring that the government budget be kept in balance except during a national emergency. A necessary concomitant of this policy would be the adoption of a flexible exchange rate system.

17
Economic Growth

17-1   Introduction

Until now, our discussion has been devoted almost entirely to the theory of short-run income determination. To simplify the analysis we have assumed that the state of technology, the size of the labor force, and the stock of capital are all constant. Our assumption of the constancy of both the state of technology and the size of the labor force has not been inconsistent with the theoretical models we subsequently derived. However, our assumption of a constant capital stock is inconsistent, because as long as net investment occurs in all of these models, capital stock and the full-employment level of income *cannot* remain constant. Thus far we have ignored this problem by assuming that additions to the capital stock have been relatively small because we were considering only a short time period. Therefore, for all practical purposes we have been able to treat the capital stock and the full-employment income level as constants.

In this chapter we consider a much longer time period than we have previously, so that the assumption of a constant capital stock is unwarranted. But an even more important reason to abandon this assumption is that we wish to concentrate on the theory of economic growth, and we will learn that the growth of the capital stock is one of the main determinants of economic growth. Technological progress and population growth are as important as capital accumulation in determining economic growth, and their respective roles will also be analyzed in this chapter.

17-2   The Harrod–Domar Model

The first attempts to expand Keynes's basic macroeconomic model to encompass long-run economic growth were made by Roy Harrod and Evsey Domar.[1] Although minor differences do exist between the Harrod and Domar models, they are sufficiently similar in approach to be categorized together as *the Harrod–Domar model.*

A fundamental assumption implicit in the Harrod–Domar model is that national income is proportional to the quantity of capital, that is

$$Y = \sigma K \tag{17-1}$$

where Y = national income
K = the amount of the capital stock employed in the production of Y
σ = the immutable constant of proportionality called the *output–capital ratio*

Our reason for calling σ the output–capital ratio becomes apparent when we rearrange equation (17-1) as

$$\sigma = \frac{Y}{K} \tag{17-2}$$

It follows from equation (17-1) that the growth in income must be proportional to the growth in the physical capital stock employed, because

$$\Delta Y = \sigma \Delta K \tag{17-3}$$

If our initial condition is that the capital stock is fully employed, then the annual growth of income will be limited by the annual growth of the capital stock.

Recalling our discussion of the theory of investment in Chapter 5, we define the annual net change in the physical capital stock to be *net physical investment,* or as it is sometimes called, *net tangible investment.* Hence substituting I for ΔK in equation (17-3), we obtain

$$\Delta Y = \sigma I \tag{17-4}$$

Now let us suppose that the economy saves a constant proportion s of its income each year. Because desired savings must be equal to desired investment, we can write

$$S = I = sY \tag{17-5}$$

where s = the marginal propensity to save. Substituting sY for I in equation (17-4) and dividing both sides by Y, we obtain

$$\frac{\Delta Y}{Y} = \sigma s \tag{17-6}$$

[1] Roy Harrod, "An Essay in Dynamic Theory," *Economic Journal* **XLIX** (March 1939), 14–33, and Evsey D. Domar, "Expansion and Employment," *American Economic Review* **XXXVII** (March 1947), 34–55.

The ratio $\Delta Y/Y$ is the annual rate of growth in income at which the capital stock will be fully employed. At this growth rate, business expectations will be realized, or as Harrod expresses it, "warranted." Therefore, this growth rate is called the *warranted rate of growth*. We can readily see that with a constant output–capital ratio, the warranted rate of growth is simply a function of the fraction of income saved. For example, if $\sigma = \frac{1}{3}$ and $s = 0.10$, then the annual growth in income will be 3.33%. If the marginal propensity to save doubles from 0.10 to 0.20, then the warranted rate of growth will also double.

In the Harrod–Domar model, an economy's warranted rate of growth is not necessarily equal to its actual growth rate. To understand why this is true, first we must consider the type of production function implied by equation (17-1). One possible economic interpretation of the production function implied by an immutably fixed output–capital ratio is that labor is not needed in the production process, or in other words that there is only one input: capital. Because employers do pay wages to labor and because businesses would not purchase an input unless it were productive, this interpretation must be false. The only interpretation of the fixed output–capital ratio that is consistent with the fact that both labor and capital are required factors of production is based on the assumption that capital and labor are *perfectly complementary* and are combined in *fixed proportions*. By this we mean that one and only one combination of labor and capital is required to produce a specific level of income. The isoquants of a production function characterized by perfect complementarity are L-shaped, as shown in Figure 17-1. There we can see that 3 units of capital and 4.5 units of labor are needed to produce a national income of 1 unit. The ratio of capital to labor K/L required for this level of output is $\frac{2}{3}$, which is also the required ratio for any other level of income. If labor remains constant at 4.5 units and if capital is increased, there will be no increase in the level of national income. Similarly, holding capital constant and increasing the amount of labor employed will have no effect on output. However, if all inputs are doubled, then the level of national income will double. Tripling inputs triples output, and so on. Hence this production function exhibits the characteristic known as *constant returns to scale*.

In an economy with an aggregate production function similar to the one illustrated in Figure 17-1, it is obvious that national income can actually grow at the warranted rate specified in equation (17-3) only as long as either a surplus of labor is available or the labor force is growing at the same rate as net tangible investment. If no additional labor is available, then the level of income will *not* grow even if the capital stock is growing. Thus assuming that the output–capital ratio σ is an immutable constant and that the actual growth rate is equal to the warranted rate of growth implies either that there is a surplus of labor or that the labor supply is also growing at a rate equal to the warranted rate. For example, if $\sigma = \frac{1}{3}$ and $s = 0.21$, then the warranted rate of growth σs will be 7% per year and the actual growth rate will also be 7% per year, provided that a surplus of labor is available to combine with the capital in fixed proportions. Once the labor surplus is exhausted, however, a 7% growth rate in income cannot be maintained unless the labor supply is also growing at 7%. If the growth rate of the labor supply is less than 7%, then

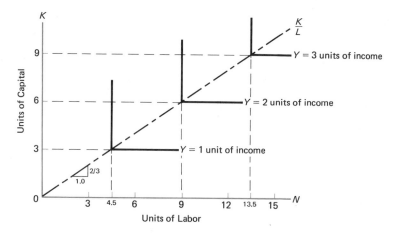

FIGURE 17-1   A Fixed Output–Capital Ratio Production Function

the actual growth rate of the economy is constrained by the growth rate of labor. In other words, if the growth rate of labor were, say, 2% per year, then the maximum rate of change in national income could be no greater than 2% per year. If this were the case, then business expectations would not be realized and unemployment of capital would result.

We can increase the growth rate of income if we recognize *labor-saving technological progress,* so that the same amount of capital will require fewer units of labor for a given quantity of output. The existing labor thus released and the new labor can then be combined with the newly created capital. Hence labor-saving technological progress is equivalent to an increase in the growth rate of labor.

What we mean by labor-saving technological progress is graphically illustrated in Figure 17-2. The production function prior to technological progress is identical with the one depicted in Figure 17-1 and is graphed with solid lines in Figure 17-2. Now if we recognize labor-saving technological progress, then the minimum amount of labor required for a given amount of capital must decrease, and the fixed ratio at which capital combines equally with labor (the *capital–labor ratio*) must therefore increase. This is depicted in Figure 17-2 by the counterclockwise rotation of the capital–labor ratio ray K/L to its new position $(K/L)'$. Because the output–capital ratio σ is assumed to be immutably constant, 3 units of capital will still produce 1 unit of income but will now require fewer units of labor to do so. Instead of 4.5 units of labor, only 3.25 units are now needed. The new production isoquant corresponding to 1 unit of income is drawn with a dashed line in Figure 17-2. The production isoquants for income levels $Y = 2$ and $Y = 3$ are similarly derived and drawn there also. The effective growth rate of the labor force $\Delta L/L$ can be symbolically expressed as

$$\frac{\Delta L}{L} = \frac{\Delta N}{N} + \gamma \qquad (17\text{-}7)$$

where $\Delta N/N$ = the actual growth rate of the labor force
    γ = the growth rate of labor-saving technological progress

In our example of labor-saving technological progress, the increase in the efficiency of the labor supply is approximately 4%. This produces the same effect as a 4% increase in the labor supply. If labor-saving technological progress could be maintained every year at this rate, then the effective growth rate of the labor supply would be 6%, rather than the 2% we assumed would prevail in the absence of technological progress. Given an effective growth rate of 6% in the labor supply, the maximum actual growth rate of national income would be 6%, which is less than the warranted growth rate of 7%. Harrod calls this maximum attainable growth rate the *natural rate of growth* to emphasize that technological progress and population growth, rather than the rate of tangible investment, limit economic growth. Hence, tangible investment plays a subordinate role in the Harrod–Domar model of economic growth.

The *equilibrium rate of growth* is defined to be the growth rate at which full employment of both the labor force and the capital stock is maintained. In the Harrod–Domar model, full employment of the capital stock exists when the growth rate of income is equal to the warranted rate; full employment of the labor force exists when the growth rate of labor is equal to the natural rate. Hence to obtain full employment of capital *and* labor, the warranted rate must equal the natural rate; that is

$$\sigma s = \frac{\Delta N}{N} + \gamma \qquad (17\text{-}8)$$

Because the output–capital ratio, the marginal propensity to save, the growth rate of the labor force, and the rate of labor-saving technological progress are all

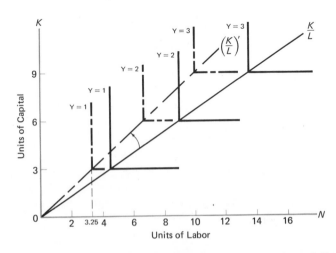

FIGURE 17-2   *Labor-saving Technological Progress in a Harrod–Domar Model Production Function*

arrived at independently of one another, the probability that a Harrod–Domar economy will grow at the equilibrium rate is virtually zero. If the warranted rate is greater than the natural rate, then unemployment of capital will exist; if the natural rate exceeds the warranted rate, then unemployment of labor will exist. For this reason, the Harrod–Domar model is sometimes referred to as a "razor-edge" model, because the slightest change from initial equilibrium in any of the parameters given by equation (17-7) will result in a disequilibrium condition that contains no built-in mechanism to restore the economy to an equilibrium growth path. In other words, if an equilibrium growth rate does prevail, this equilibrium will be unstable.

The Harrod–Domar model is unstable due to the inherent inflexibility of its basic assumptions. For example, the output–capital ratio σ is assumed to be an immutable constant. In our analysis of the neoclassical growth model in Section 17-3, we drop this assumption and adopt a production function that permits substitution between capital and labor.

17-3   The Neoclassical Growth Model

Domar and Harrod's assumption that labor and capital are perfectly complementary factors of production is a radical one that lies outside the mainstream of orthodox economic theory. In the mid-1950s a counterattack on the Harrod–Domar approach was launched by James Tobin, Robert Solow, and Trevor Swan.[2] Their growth models are all based on the assumption that capital and labor can be substituted for one another in the production process. Hence the aggregate production function they chose permits a continuous set of alternative capital–labor ratios and consequent alternative values of the output–capital ratio σ. This approach to economic growth theory has become known as "neoclassical," because it assumes perfect competition, payment of factors equal to their marginal products, and full employment, in addition to a variable output–capital ratio. These basic assumptions are the same as those usually made by such neoclassical economists as Marshall, Wicksell, and Pigou.

The neoclassical growth model also assumes that the production function is characterized by *diminishing marginal productivity* and *constant returns to scale*. By *diminishing marginal productivity* we mean that if the quantities of all production factors except one remain constant, then the marginal output resulting from the application of an additional unit of the variable factor will decrease as the quantity employed increases. For example, let us reconsider Table 2-1 (page 20), where all the production factors except labor are held constant. As we increase the amount of labor employed one unit at a time, the marginal product of each successive unit of labor decreases, and this production function is then characterized by diminishing marginal productivity of labor.

---

[2] James Tobin, "A Dynamic Aggregate Model," *Journal of Political Economy* **63** (April 1955), 103–15; Robert M. Solow, "A Contribution to the Theory of Economic Growth," *Quarterly Journal of Economics* **70** (February 1956), 65–94; and T.W. Swan, "Economic Growth and Capital Accumulation," *Economic Record* **32** (November 1956), 334–61.

By *constant returns to scale* we mean that if all factor inputs increase proportionally, then output will also increase by a proportionate amount. If we double all factor inputs, for example, then output will also double if we have constant returns to scale.

One specific production function widely used in neoclassical growth theory possesses all of these characteristics. This is the so-called *Cobb–Douglas production function,* given by

$$Y = AK^\alpha N^\beta \tag{17-9}$$

where Y = national income
A = a constant
K = the capital stock
N = the quantity of labor
α and β = parameters that sum to unity[3]

Because the parameters in equation (17-9) must sum to unity if the production function is to possess constant returns to scale, $\beta = 1 - \alpha$. Thus we can rewrite equation (17-9)

$$Y = AK^\alpha N^{1-\alpha} \tag{17-10}$$

The neoclassical production function given by (17-10) reduces to the Harrod–Domar production function when $\alpha = 1.0$, and the constant A becomes equivalent to the output–capital ratio σ. Because the neoclassical approach is based on the assumption that labor and capital are substitutable factors of production, it follows that $0 < \alpha < 1.0$.

In the neoclassical production function, the growth rate of national income is a weighted average of the growth rates of capital and labor. This can be shown by solving for the growth rate of income in equation (17-10), which gives us

$$\frac{\Delta Y}{Y} = \alpha \frac{\Delta K}{K} + (1 - \alpha)\frac{\Delta N}{N} \tag{17-11}$$

where $\Delta Y/Y$, $\Delta K/K$, and $\Delta N/N$ are the respective growth rates of income, capital, and labor.[4] Not only are α and $1 - \alpha$ the weights assigned to the contributions of

---

[3] If $\alpha + \beta < 1.0$, then we would have a production function with *decreasing* returns to scale; if $\alpha + \beta > 1.0$, then we would have a production function with *increasing* returns to scale.
[4] Taking the total differential of (17-10), we obtain

$$dY = \alpha AK^{\alpha-1}N^{1-\alpha}dK + (1 - \alpha)AK^\alpha N^{-\alpha}dN \tag{17-10a}$$

Dividing (17-10a) by $Y = AK^\alpha N^{1-\alpha}$ then gives us

$$\frac{dY}{Y} = \frac{\alpha AK^{\alpha-1}N^{1-\alpha}dK}{AK^\alpha N^{1-\alpha}} + \frac{(1 - \alpha)AK^\alpha N^{-\alpha}dN}{AK^\alpha N^{1-\alpha}} \tag{17-10b}$$

and by canceling terms we obtain

$$\frac{dY}{Y} = \alpha \frac{dK}{K} + (1 - \alpha)\frac{dN}{N} \tag{17-10c}$$

Letting $\Delta = d$, as a close approximation to (17-10c), we obtain (17-11).

the growth of the capital and labor stocks to the growth of income, but they are also the relative shares of income that these inputs receive. We can prove this statement in the following manner. At a given level of technology, any change in income must be the result of a change in the quantities of capital or labor utilized. Changes in income are related to changes in capital and labor by the equation

$$\Delta Y = \Delta K \cdot MP_K + \Delta N \cdot MP_N \qquad (17\text{-}12)$$

where MP_K and MP_N are the marginal physical products of capital and labor, respectively. Dividing both sides of equation (17-12) by Y, we obtain

$$\frac{\Delta Y}{Y} = \Delta K \frac{MP_K}{Y} + \Delta N \frac{MP_N}{Y} \qquad (17\text{-}13)$$

Multiplying the first term on the right-hand side of equation (17-13) by K/K and the second term by N/N does not alter the equality. Thus we obtain

$$\frac{\Delta Y}{Y} = \frac{\Delta K}{K}\left(\frac{K \cdot MP_K}{Y}\right) + \frac{\Delta N}{N}\left(\frac{N \cdot MP_N}{Y}\right) \qquad (17\text{-}14)$$

Because the neoclassical model assumes perfect competition and constant returns to scale, each input will be paid its marginal product. The total earnings of the K units of capital and the N units of labor will therefore be $K \cdot MP_K$ and $N \cdot MP_N$, respectively. Labor and capital are the only production inputs, so that they will absorb the entire output. The relative share of income distributed to capital will therefore be $K \cdot MP_K/Y$, and the relative share of income distributed to labor will be $N \cdot MP_N/Y$. Finally, comparing equations (17-14) and (17-11) shows us that

$$\frac{K \cdot MP_K}{Y} = \alpha$$

and

$$\frac{N \cdot MP_N}{Y} = 1 - \alpha$$

Therefore, the weights of equation (17-11) are also the relative income shares of capital and labor.

17-4   The Neoclassical Equilibrium Growth Rate

If we assume that savings are proportional to income in the long run and that the economy is in equilibrium, then

$$S = I = \Delta K = sY \qquad (17\text{-}15)$$

By substituting equation (17-15) into equation (17-11), we then obtain

$$\frac{\Delta Y}{Y} = \alpha s \frac{Y}{K} + (1 - \alpha)\frac{\Delta N}{N} \qquad (17\text{-}16)$$

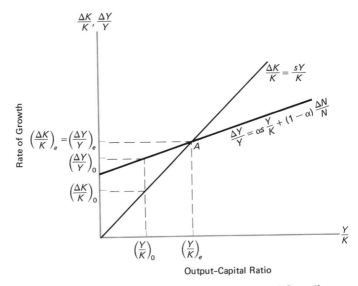

FIGURE 17-3   *The Equilibrium Rate of Growth*

If we further assume that the production function parameters, the marginal propensity to save, and the growth rate of labor all remain constant and greater than zero, then the economy's growth rate will be a function of the output–capital ratio Y/K. But we will show that there can be only one equilibrium output–capital ratio and consequently only one equilibrium growth rate. We can now prove that in a state of equilibrium the growth rate of income must be equal to the growth rate of the capital stock. This proof is illustrated in Figure 17-3, where the output–capital ratio is graphed on the horizontal axis and the growth rates of income and the capital stock are graphed on the vertical axis. There the growth rate of income specified by equation (17-16) is graphed as a function of Y/K, assuming that $\Delta N/N$ is constant and greater than zero. Dividing the last equality in equation (17-15) by K gives us

$$\frac{\Delta K}{K} = s\frac{Y}{K} \qquad (17\text{-}17)$$

which shows that for a given marginal propensity to save, the growth rate of the capital stock is proportional to the output–capital ratio. The curve of equation (17-17) for a given MPS also appears in Figure 17-3.

The equilibrium rate of growth is given by the intersection of the two growth curves in Figure 17-3 (at point A), where the growth rate of income is equal to the growth rate of capital at $(\Delta K/K)_e = (\Delta Y/Y)_e$. To understand why this rate of growth is in equilibrium, we consider what happens if the output–capital ratio is $(Y/K)_0$ instead of $(Y/K)_e$, as shown in Figure 17-3. Because Y is growing faster than K, the output–capital ratio Y/K must increase. The output–capital ratio will continue to increase until we reach point A, where $\Delta Y/Y = \Delta K/K$. Since at point A income and the capital stock are growing at the same rate, the output–capital ratio remains constant; since Y/K is the only variable in equation (17-16), the growth rate is constant and, by definition, equal to the equilibrium rate. If we chose an output–capital ratio greater than $(Y/K)_e$, K would be growing faster than Y and the output–capital ratio would decline until we returned to point A, where Y/K and $\Delta Y/Y$ are constant.

Now suppose that the marginal propensity to save can be increased by appropriate government policy. How will this affect the growth rate of income? Intuitively, it may seem that given higher savings, investment will increase, the capital stock will grow faster, and a higher growth rate of income will result. In the particular growth model we are considering, however, this line of reasoning is invalid, as we will demonstrate here.

We have just proved that to maintain equilibrium the growth rates of income and capital must be equal. Thus $\Delta Y/Y = \Delta K/K$ in equilibrium, and we can express this condition by setting equations (17-16) and (17-17) equal to one another. We then obtain

$$s\frac{Y}{K} = \alpha s\frac{Y}{K} + (1 - \alpha)\frac{\Delta N}{N} \tag{17-18}$$

Solving equation (17-18) for $s(Y/K)$ gives us

$$s\frac{Y}{K} = \frac{1 - \alpha}{1 - \alpha} \cdot \frac{\Delta N}{N}$$

and since $s(Y/K) = \Delta K/K$, we have

$$\left(\frac{\Delta Y}{Y}\right)_e = \left(\frac{\Delta K}{K}\right)_e = s\frac{Y}{K} = \frac{\Delta N}{N} \tag{17-19}$$

From equation (17-19) we can conclude that the equilibrium growth rate of income is independent of the marginal propensity to save and is equal to the growth rate of labor. In other words, increasing the rate of saving will not affect the equilibrium rate of growth, because the MPS and the growth rate of labor are assumed to be independently determined. Should the growth rate of labor become zero, then the equilibrium growth rate of income would also become zero[5] due to the assumption that the marginal product of capital is diminishing. As the stock of capital increases, if the stock of labor is held constant, the marginal product of capital will diminish until it reaches zero. At this point, further addition to the capital stock will not produce any additional increase in income, and therefore, the growth rate of income will become zero.

Dividing equation (17-19) by s gives us

$$\frac{Y}{K} = \frac{1}{s}\left(\frac{\Delta Y}{Y}\right)_e = \frac{1}{s}\left(\frac{\Delta K}{K}\right)_e = \frac{1}{s} \cdot \frac{\Delta N}{N} \tag{17-20}$$

[5] If we recognize technological progress, as we do in Section 17-5, this conclusion is invalid.

which indicates that an increase in s creates a proportionate decrease in the equilibrium output–capital ratio if $\Delta N/N$ is assumed to be constant.

These results concerning the effects of an increase in the marginal propensity to save are summarized graphically in Figure 17-4. Initially, suppose that the marginal propensity to save is s; then the equilibrium output–capital ratio is $(Y/K)_e$ and the equilibrium rate of income growth is $(\Delta Y/Y)_e$, as shown in Figure 17-4. Now assume that the MPS increases from s to s'. This causes the capital growth and income growth curves to rotate counterclockwise; their new positions are represented by the dashed lines in Figure 17-4. Because the value of the MPS cannot affect the equilibrium rate of income growth, these new curves must intersect at the equilibrium growth rate $(\Delta Y/Y)_e$, and the equilibrium output–capital ratio declines from $(Y/K)_e$ to $(Y/K)'_e$.

Although a change in the MPS in this model does not affect the equilibrium rate of growth, this does not mean that such a change produces no lasting economic effects. An increase in the rate of saving will be followed by a period of transition as the economy adjusts to a lower output–capital ratio. During this transitional period the growth rate of the capital stock will exceed the equilibrium growth rate, and the capital stock at the end of this period will be greater than it would have been if the MPS had not increased. This can readily be seen in Figure 17-4, where immediately after the MPS increases from s to s', the growth rate of capital $(\Delta K/K)_1$ exceeds the growth rate of income $(\Delta Y/Y)_1$. Over time, this will decrease the output–capital ratio from $(Y/K)_e$ to $(Y/K)'_e$. During this transitional period, the

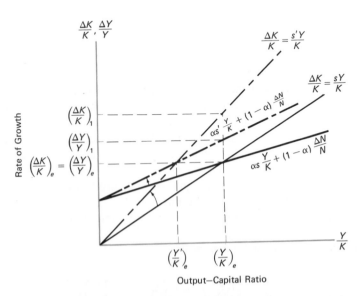

FIGURE 17-4   *The Effect of an Increase in the MPS on the Equilibrium Growth Rate*

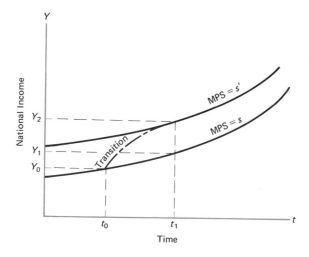

FIGURE 17-5   *Equilibrium and Transitional Growth Paths*

capital stock grows at a faster rate than income grows, so that at the end of the transitional period the capital stock is greater than it would have been if s had not increased to s'. This means that as the growth rate of income returns to the equilibrium rate, the absolute level of income is higher due to the higher-than-equilibrium capital stock growth during the transitional period, and the economy is on a higher growth path. This is illustrated in Figure 17-5. At time t_0, the level of national income is Y_0, as indicated by the equilibrium growth path for MPS $= s$. If the MPS remains at the rate s, then the level of income at time t_1 will be Y_1. However, if the MPS increases to s' at time t_0, then the level of income at the end of the transitional period, $t_1 - t_0$, will be $Y_2 > Y_1$. Once the transitional period has ended, the growth rate of income at any time beyond t_1 becomes the equilibrium growth rate.

17-5   Technological Progress

Thus far in our study of economic growth we have been concerned primarily with the growth rate of national income. However, interest in economic growth is often prompted by a desire to improve human welfare, and the rate of change in the total output is a poor indicator of this. A much better measure would be the growth rate of income per unit of labor (that is, the rate of increase in labor productivity). If output per unit of labor is to increase, it is obvious that the growth rate of income must exceed the growth rate of labor. In our neoclassical model as developed thus far, the growth rate of income can exceed the growth rate of labor only if the growth rate of the capital stock exceeds the growth rate of income. This second conclusion is not as obvious as the first, but it can be easily proved.

Subtracting $\Delta N/N$ from both sides of equation (17-11) and simplifying, we obtain

$$\frac{\Delta Y}{Y} - \frac{\Delta N}{N} = \alpha\left(\frac{\Delta K}{K} - \frac{\Delta N}{N}\right) \tag{17-21}$$

Returning to equation (17-11), we subtract $\Delta K/K$ from both sides of equation (17-11) and multiply both sides by -1 to obtain

$$\frac{\Delta K}{K} - \frac{\Delta Y}{Y} = (1 - \alpha)\left(\frac{\Delta K}{K} - \frac{\Delta N}{N}\right) \tag{17-22}$$

Then solving for $(\Delta K/K - \Delta N/N)$, we obtain

$$\frac{\Delta K}{K} - \frac{\Delta N}{N} = \frac{1}{1 - \alpha}\left(\frac{\Delta K}{K} - \frac{\Delta Y}{Y}\right) \tag{17-23}$$

Substituting the right-hand side of equation (17-23) into (17-21), we finally obtain

$$\frac{\Delta Y}{Y} - \frac{\Delta N}{N} = \frac{\alpha}{1 - \alpha}\left(\frac{\Delta K}{K} - \frac{\Delta Y}{Y}\right) \tag{17-24}$$

Equation (17-24) proves that for labor productivity to increase (that is, for $\Delta Y/Y > \Delta N/N$ to hold), the growth rate of the capital stock must exceed the growth rate of income. Hence the output–capital ratio Y/K must exhibit secular decline.

Historically, however, the productivity per unit of labor has increased as the output–capital ratio has increased! The usefulness of our growth model is challenged, because it cannot predict labor productivity trends given long-run historical data on the output–capital ratio. The reason for this is that our model has thus far ignored the possibility of technological progress. We rectify this shortcoming now.

We can modify the Cobb–Douglas production function to include technological progress if we write it

$$Y = Ae^{rt}K^{\alpha}N^{1-\alpha} \tag{17-25}$$

where e = the Naperian constant 2.71828 . . .
r = the *rate of technological progress compounded continuously*
t = time[6]

By introducing technological progress in this way, we adopt the simplest approach to the problem. The technological progress implicit in equation (17-25) is referred to as *disembodied*, because it increases the efficiency of all existing capital, regardless of its age. In other words, the implementation of disembodied technological progress is not limited to the gross investment of a given period but can be

[6] The Naperian constant enters the Cobb–Douglas production function because time is treated as a continuous variable, rather than as a discrete variable. For a complete discussion of the mathematics involved, see Alpha C. Chiang, *Fundamental Methods of Mathematical Economics* (New York: McGraw-Hill, 1967), pp. 272–80.

applied to the entire capital stock. Technological progress that affects the efficiency of only newly produced capital goods and that does not affect the remaining portion of the capital stock is known as *embodied* technological progress.

To clarify the implications of the concept of disembodied technological progress, we consider the following growth-rate equation derived from equation (17-25):

$$\frac{\Delta Y}{Y} = r + \alpha\frac{\Delta K}{K} + (1 - \alpha)\frac{\Delta N}{N} \qquad (17\text{-}26)$$

where r is once again the growth rate of technological progress.[7] Equation (17-26) reveals that if technology is improving at a rate r per year, then total technological progress can be translated into income growth so that it is independent of the growth rates of labor and capital. This independence is important, because if we solve for the labor productivity growth equation now, we obtain

$$\frac{\Delta Y}{Y} - \frac{\Delta N}{N} = r + \alpha\left(\frac{\Delta K}{K} - \frac{\Delta N}{N}\right) \qquad (17\text{-}27)$$

A comparison of equations (17-21) and (17-27) reveals that an increase in labor productivity no longer requires capital to grow faster than labor. Hence labor productivity growth in this model can result from either technological progress or increased capital per worker, usually called *capital deepening*. An extremely interesting question that we, along with many other economists, can ask is, What fraction of the historically observed growth of output per worker can be attributed to technological change and what fraction can be attributed to capital deepening?

Because the total increase in labor productivity is due to either technological change or capital deepening, we can express the fractions that are attributable to each source if we divide equation (17-27) by $\Delta Y/Y - \Delta N/N$, so that

$$1.0 = \frac{r}{(\Delta Y/Y) - (\Delta N/N)} + \alpha\frac{(\Delta K/K) - (\Delta N/N)}{(\Delta Y/Y) - (\Delta N/N)} \qquad (17\text{-}28)$$

The last term on the right-hand side of equation (17-28) is the fraction of growth in labor productivity due to increased capital per worker. Letting this fraction be symbolized by P, we can then write

$$P = \alpha\frac{(\Delta K/K) - (\Delta N/N)}{(\Delta Y/Y) - (\Delta N/N)} \qquad (17\text{-}29)$$

---

[7] We can justify the result stated in equation (17-26) if we differentiate equation (17-25) with respect to time to obtain

$$\frac{dY}{dt} = rAe^{rt}K^{\alpha}N^{1-\alpha} + \alpha Ae^{rt}K^{\alpha-1}N^{1-\alpha}\frac{dK}{dt} + (1 - \alpha)Ae^{rt}K^{\alpha}N^{-\alpha}\frac{dN}{dt} \qquad (17\text{-}25a)$$

Dividing equation (17-25a) by equation (17-25), we then obtain

$$\frac{dY}{Ydt} = r + \alpha\frac{dK}{Kdt} + (1 - \alpha)\frac{dN}{Ndt} \qquad (17\text{-}25b)$$

Now dY/dt, dK/dt, and dN/dt represent the respective changes in income, capital, and labor when the time period is infinitely small. Letting $\Delta Y = dY/dt$, $\Delta K = dK/dt$, and $\Delta N = dN/dt$, where Δ signifies an annual change in the variables, gives us equation (17-26). Since (17-25b) is stated in terms of instantaneous rates of change whereas (17-26) is stated in terms of annual rates of change, this means that (17-26) is only an approximation of (17-25b). For our purposes, however, it is sufficiently close.

Clearly, if we can determine the value of P, we will be able to determine the contribution of technology to growth in labor productivity.

In Section 17-4 we learned that the parameter in the Cobb–Douglas production function is equal to the marginal productivity of capital. Now if we assume, as neoclassical theorists do, that pure competition prevails in all segments of the economy, then it follows that the capital share of national income will be equal to the marginal productivity of capital. Statistical data concerning the capital share of national income over the last 70 years of American economic history are available. These data reveal that the capital share has averaged about 0.33. Hence, assuming pure competition, we can set $\alpha = 0.33$. Rewriting equation (17-29) with $\alpha = 0.33$ and assuming that $\Delta K/K = \Delta Y/Y$, we then obtain

$$P = 0.33\frac{(\Delta Y/Y) - (\Delta N/N)}{(\Delta Y/Y) - (\Delta N/N)} = 0.33(1.0) = 0.33 \qquad (17\text{-}30)$$

It has already been stated that the growth rate of income has exceeded the growth rate of capital, so that the actual contribution of increased capital per worker is less than one-third according to this model.

Richard Nelson has compiled data, given in Table 17-1,[8] that are suitable for use in equation (17-29). If we assume that $\alpha = 0.33$, then according to equation (17-29) the fraction of increased labor productivity attributable to capital deepening during the 1929–1960 period would be

$$P_{1929\text{-}60} = 0.33\frac{2.0 - 0.7}{3.1 - 0.7} = 0.18 \qquad (17\text{-}31)$$

Calculated values for P are also given in Table 17-1 for various subperiods. Using a slightly different approach to examine the 1909–1949 period in America, Robert Solow concluded that only about 12.5% of the increased productivity per work-hour could be attributed to capital deepening.[9] These results indicate that if technology is treated as disembodied, then the contribution of capital deepening to increased labor productivity has been slight. Thus if we wish to increase household incomes, then the most effective approach would be to encourage research and education (intangible investment), rather than the accumulation of physical capital (tangible investment).

Although this economic concept represented a "new view" of investment in 1956, by 1962 it had become known as the "old view."[10] The old view, as we refer to it hereafter, was criticized on the grounds that technology was actually not disembodied. If technology is to be effective in increasing worker productivity, it must be embodied in gross investment: net *plus* replacement. Hence modernization of the capital stock becomes as important as capital deepening—if not more

---

[8] Richard R. Nelson, "Aggregate Production Functions and Medium-range Growth Projections," *American Economic Review* **LIV** (September 1964), 575–606. The growth rates for GNP and the labor input are estimates of what would have happened if an unemployment rate of 4% had always prevailed.

[9] Robert M. Solow, "Technical Change and the Aggregate Production Function," *Review of Economics and Statistics* **39** (August 1957), 312–20.

[10] Edmund S. Phelps, "The New View of Investment: A Neoclassical Analysis," *Quarterly Journal of Economics* **LXXVI** (November 1962), 548–67.

TABLE 17-1   Annual Growth Rates of the Capital Stock, Full-employment GNP, Full-employment Labor Input, and Estimated Values of P

Years	Full-employment GNP Growth Rate $\frac{\Delta Y}{Y}$	Full-Employment Labor Input Growth $\frac{\Delta N}{N}$	Capital Stock Growth $\frac{\Delta K}{K}$	Fraction of Increased Labor Productivity Due to Capital Deepening P
1929–1960	3.1	0.7	2.0	0.18
1929–1947	2.5	0.5	1.0	0.08
1947–1960	4.0	0.8	3.6	0.28
1947–1954	4.4	0.7	4.0	0.29
1954–1960	3.5	0.8	3.1	0.28

SOURCE FOR $\Delta Y/Y$, $\Delta N/N$, $\Delta K/K$ Richard R. Nelson, "Aggregate Production Functions and Medium-range Growth Projections," *American Economic Review* **LIV** (September 1964), 577.

important. This is the essence of the new "new view," which we refer to as the new view hereafter.

In the new view the capital stock is not considered perfectly homogeneous; it is not like *putty*, which can be formed in any shape and divided into the smallest portion required. Instead, capital is treated like putty in the planning stage, but once it is acquired it becomes like *hardened clay*, which cannot be changed. For this reason, the models employed in the old and new views are sometimes referred to as *putty–putty* and *putty–clay* models, respectively.

According to the new view, the latest technology can be incorporated into the capital stock only when capital is replaced or increased, so that it is fruitful to think of the total capital stock as comprised of different "vintages" of capital. The oldest vintage of capital embodies the oldest technology; the youngest vintage embodies the latest technology. Hence the youngest capital yields the greatest output per unit of labor, and the average productivity of labor therefore depends on the average age of the capital stock. We can reduce the average age of the capital stock if the rate of gross investment is increased, which in turn will increase the growth rate of labor productivity. But this increased growth rate of labor productivity will be short-lived, because increased investment today will result in a larger quantity of older-vintage capital in the future. Edmund Phelps demonstrated that the solution of the equilibrium growth rate of national income in a new-view neoclassical model is independent of the marginal propensity to save. In essence this is the same result we obtained in Section 17-4 using the old-view Cobb–Douglas neoclassical model. This means that if the rate of saving were somehow to increase, then the capital stock would be modernized in the short run. Eventually, however, the average age of the capital stock would approach an equilibrium level equal to the previous equilibrium level, and the growth rate of the economy would return to the equilibrium rate. Hence although a spurt of modernization cannot increase the equilibrium growth rate, it can move the economy onto a higher equilibrium growth path. A graphic illustration of this conclusion would be almost identical to the one shown in Figure 17-5.

Phelps also showed that a permanent decrease in the average age of the capital stock is possible only if the rate of saving continually increases. Clearly, this is an impossibility, and a policy directed toward permanently increasing the economic growth rate would be doomed to failure. But as we can see in Figure 17-5, it is possible to move onto a higher equilibrium growth path if the capital stock can be modernized even temporarily.

The new view of tangible investment is that tangible investment is a more effective instrument in raising the income level than it was according to the old view. Thus increasing the rate of tangible investment might be the most effective way to achieve the policy goal of increasing the level of income per capita. We say "might be" because tangible investment is not the only instrument of economic growth. Nontangible investment in research and education is also an important factor. Before advocating an increase in the rate of tangible investment, it would be worthwhile to examine the net rate of return on tangible investment.

Under conditions of pure competition, if capital never depreciated and technology never progressed, then the net rate of return would be equal to the earnings rate on tangible capital, or

$$NRR = \frac{\pi}{K} \qquad (17\text{-}32)$$

where NRR = net rate of return on capital
π = profits on capital before taxes
K = replacement value of the capital stock

But because capital does depreciate and does become obsolete due to technological progress, the rate at which capital depreciates δ and the rate at which capital becomes obsolete o must be subtracted from equation (17-32) to compute the actual net rate of return on capital. Symbolically, this can be written

$$NRR = \frac{\pi}{K} - \delta - o \qquad (17\text{-}33)$$

Edmund Phelps has estimated the net rate of return on the American capital stock in 1954.[11] Beginning with an estimate by the Council of Economic Advisors of $300 billion for the full-employment business sector output in 1954, Phelps assumed that capital is paid its marginal product, so that the relative share of income distributed to capital in 1954 would be about $\frac{1}{3}$. Hence $\pi = 300/3 = \$100$ billion. The conventionally estimated 1954 dollar replacement cost of the capital stock in 1954 is $650 billion, but this estimate does not take into consideration the variances in quality among different vintages of capital. Assuming that capital becomes obsolete at the rate of $o = 2\%$ per year, Phelps has computed the replacement cost of capital K at only $510 billion. Assuming a standard rate of depreciation δ of 4%, we can compute the net percentage rate of return on tangible investment in 1954 as

$$(100)NRR = 100\left(\frac{100}{510} - 0.04 - 0.02\right) \qquad (17\text{-}34)$$
$$= 100(0.196 - 0.06) = 13.6\%$$

In a study[12] of the rates of return to education (that is, intangible investment), W. Lee Hansen found that the average internal rate of return to total resource investment for males who complete high school is about 12%. Comparing this with Phelps's estimate, we can tentatively conclude that the rate of return on tangible investment is large enough for U.S. policies designed to increase the rate of gross investment to be appropriate.

---

[11] Edmund S. Phelps, "Tangible Investment as an Instrument of Growth," in Edmund S. Phelps (ed.), *The Goal of Economic Growth* (New York: W.W. Norton, 1962), 94–105.

[12] W. Lee Hansen, "Total and Private Rates of Return to Investment in Schooling," *Journal of Political Economy* **81** (April 1963), 128–41.

17-6   Economic Growth Policy

Since 1960, the United States has allocated to gross investment a smaller fraction of its GNP than has any other industrialized Western economy. Total tangible investment, including housing, comprises 17.5% of GNP in the United States, compared to 35% in Japan, 25% in both France and Germany, and 22% in Canada.[13]

Many economists contend that a primary reason for the low rates of capital formation in the United States has been a bias in the federal tax system that creates investment disincentives. This bias against investment takes the form of multiple taxation of saved and invested income. Individuals must pay taxes on all income earned, whether or not they use this income for consumption or investment. Corporations must pay taxes on profits, whether or not these profits are reinvested. In addition, the owners of the corporations—the shareholders—must pay an additional personal income tax on dividends from after-tax corporate profits. To eliminate this bias, David Meiselman recommends that all saving in the private sector:

> . . . should be deductible from the income tax base, whether invested in a savings account, the purchase of machine tools, the education of one's children, or the building of a shopping center. This would mean that businesses could write off 100% of the cost of production facilities in the year that they acquire them, thereby eliminating depreciation and other recovery allowances.[14]

The effect of such a change in the federal tax laws would create strong incentives to reduce consumption and to increase investment.

Another major reason for poor capital formation in the United States has been the recent inflation. Traditionally, corporate profits are determined under the assumption that the replacement cost of plant, equipment, and inventories is equal to the original purchase prices paid. During periods of rapid inflation the prices of the firm's products increase, thereby increasing revenue. If the cost of plant, equipment, and inventories is based on historical rather than replacement costs, then the profits on which corporate taxes are based will be exaggerated. For example, if inflationary effects are ignored, the after-tax earnings of U.S. corporations in 1974 amount to about 5% of GNP. If the true costs of replacing plant, equipment, and inventories are taken into account, however, the real after-tax corporate profits amount to only about 1.5% of GNP.[15] This is the lowest figure for U.S. corporate profits since the 1930s. Thus the accompanying decline in stock prices in 1974 was in no small measure the result of the double-digit inflation that occurred during the year. The drop in stock prices resulting from a reduction in real profit rates reduces the incentive of firms to develop new technology and to acquire additional capital and thus lowers the economic growth rate.

Another factor that has reduced the rate of capital formation in the United States in recent years has been the extremely large deficits of the federal government. As

[13] David I. Meiselman, "Taxing Away Our Economic Growth," *The Alternative* (November 1975), 5–7.
[14] Ibid., p. 6.
[15] Ibid., p. 6.

we have seen, when the federal debt is financed by the sale of bonds to the public, the interest rate is driven up and private investment is crowded out of the market.

In summary the goal of economic growth will be achieved by policies designed to increase the rate of capital formation. These policies should include a reduction in the antisaving bias in federal tax laws and the maintenance of a stable economic environment by eliminating inflation and persistent budget deficits.

17-7   Concluding Remarks

In this chapter we have been briefly introduced to the field of economic growth. Instead of attempting to explore a particular theory of economic growth in great detail, our approach here has been to examine the development of the central models, issues, and controversies that have developed since the publication of *The General Theory.*

The *Harrod–Domar model* is considered to place primary emphasis on the role of investment. After examining the implications of the assumed constant output–capital ratio, we learned that this is true only as long as a labor surplus exists or an effective growth of the labor input is equal to the growth of the capital stock. Without the presence of either of these conditions, investment assumes a subordinate role.

The Harrod–Domar assumption of a constant output–capital ratio and the conclusions that result from this assumption did not appeal to many economists, and by the mid-1950s the so-called *neoclassical* growth theories began to appear. Assuming a variable output–capital ratio and perfect competition, these theories also proved to be unsatisfactory unless technological progress was explicitly included in their formulation. When technology was assumed to be *disembodied*, the historical data indicated that capital deepening accounted for less than one-third of the growth of labor productivity in the American economy. For a brief period this conclusion fostered the belief that tangible investment could play only a minor role in raising the general welfare of an economy and that primary reliance should be placed on research and education. This pessimistic view of the effectiveness of tangible investment lasted for less than half a decade, when new theories began to be developed that treated technological progress as *embodied* rather than disembodied. This "new view" toward investment has reestablished the traditional view of the close relationship between economic welfare and investment in tangible capital.

To foster investment, economic growth policies should be designed to create saving and investment incentives. This can be accomplished by changing the federal tax laws and by implementing the monetary and budgetary rules described in Chapter 16.

Appendix A Estimation of Economic Relationships

A-1   Cross-sectional and Time-series Data

Economic data can be classified into two main categories: cross-sectional data and time-series data. *Cross-sectional data* refers to statistical information derived from several different groups *at the same moment in time.* An example of cross-sectional information appears in Table A-1, where grouping is by income bracket and the statistical data (average measured income and average measured consumption) are for the year 1950.

TABLE A-1   Cross-sectional Data of Income and Consumption by Income Groups in 1950

Income Bracket	Average Income Y	Average Consumption C
$ 0–999	$ 556	$ 2,760
1,000–1,999	1,622	1,930
2,000–2,999	2,664	2,740
3,000–3,999	3,587	3,515
4,000–4,999	4,535	4,350
5,000–5,999	5,538	5,320
6,000–7,499	6,585	6,250
7,500–9,999	8,582	7,460
10,000–	14,033	11,500

SOURCE   F. Modigliani and A. Ando, "The 'Permanent Income' and the 'Life-cycle' Hypothesis of Saving Behavior: Comparisons and Tests," in I. Friend and R. Jones (eds.), *Consumption and Saving*, Vol. II (Philadelphia: University of Pennsylvania Press, 1960), p. 154.

Time-series data refers to statistical information pertaining to a single economic entity, with observations extending *over many time periods.* An example of time-series data appears in Table A-2, where the single entity is the entire population of the United States and the statistical data are disposable income and consumption.

In some studies, time-series and cross-sectional data are combined, and the resulting data are called *pooled data.* For example, if the data presented in Table A-1 are also available for the years 1951–1959, then we would have ten tables similar to A-1 (one table for each year). Combining the data in these tables would then give us the pooled data. Pooling data presents many statistical problems that, unless taken into consideration, can introduce serious errors into the analysis.

A-2   The Scatter Diagram

By plotting the statistical data from such cross-sectional and time-series data tables as Tables A-1 and A-2 on graphs, we can construct what we call *scatter diagrams.* Scatter diagrams are extremely useful in determining whether or not there is a relationship between two variables.

Figures A-1 and A-2 are the respective scatter diagrams for the data given in Tables A-1 and A-2. It is readily apparent that a relationship between income and consumption exists in both of these diagrams. We can also deduce from visual inspection that the relationship is probably linear. How close these data points would lie to an imaginary straight line drawn through them would therefore give us a rough approximation of the strength of the relation.

Using this visual technique in conjunction with the scatter diagram presents one major problem. Visual inspection is a subjective process; what might seem to be a

TABLE A-2   Time-series Data of Disposable Income and Consumption in the United States (billions of 1958 dollars)

Year	Aggregrate Disposable Income Y_d	Aggregrate Consumption C
1950	$249.6	$230.5
1951	255.7	232.8
1952	263.3	239.4
1953	275.4	250.8
1954	278.3	255.7
1955	296.7	274.2
1956	309.3	281.4
1957	315.8	288.2
1958	318.8	290.1
1959	333.0	307.3

SOURCE   *Economic Report of the President, 1970* (Washington, U.S. Government Printing Office, 1970), p.195.

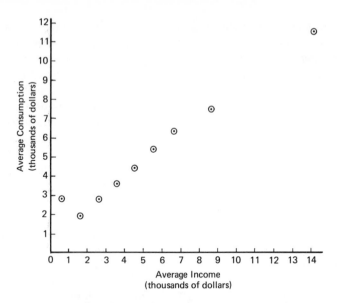

FIGURE A-1   Scatter Diagram Showing the Relationship Between Average Income and Average Consumption for Households Based on Cross-sectional Data for 1950

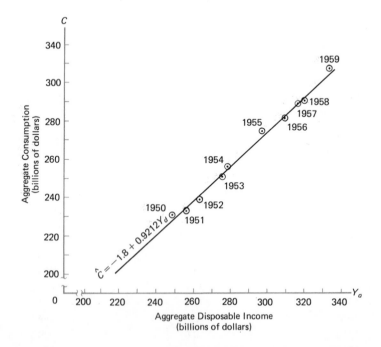

FIGURE A-2   Scatter Diagram Showing the Relationship Between Aggregate Disposable Income and Consumption for the United States, 1950–1959

strong relation to one person might appear to be a weak relation to another person. In addition, if two people each drew a line through the same set of plotted points, the lines would probably be different. For these and other reasons too detailed to mention here, methods have been developed to correct the subjective aspect of the scatter diagram. Despite its margin for misinterpretation, however, the scatter diagram can be an extremely useful tool in preliminary analysis.

A-3   Regression Analysis

Explanation of Least-squares Regression

Regression analysis is a mathematical technique that permits the precise and objective determination of the equation of a line that "best fits" the empirical data. Regression lines can be straight or curved, but they are usually computed for linear relationships due to the relative simplicity of the calculations required. For this reason we will limit our discussion here to the method used to compute linear relationships, which we call *linear regression*.

In linear regression we wish to find the linear equation that best fits the data points. Many criteria can be used, but the criterion used almost exclusively is called the *minimization of the sum of squared deviations,* or in its more popular shortened form, the method of *least squares.*[1] The least-squares method can be best explained by referring to Figure A-3.

Suppose that we have two variables X (an independent variable) and Y (a dependent variable) and that we have four data points $C, E, F,$ and G. Let us further assume that the regression line $\hat{Y} = a + bX$ in Figure A-3 has already been computed according to the criterion of least squares. The meaning of this criterion is:

1. The vertical distance from each data point to the regression line is symbolized by the lower case letter of the point. For example, the vertical distance from point E to the line is e.

2. Squaring each of the vertical distances from the data points to the regression line and summing them, we obtain

$$c^2 + e^2 + f^2 + g^2 = \text{sum of squared deviations}$$

3. The regression line that is defined to fit the data *best* is the line for which the sum of squared deviations is the *least*. An infinite number of lines can be drawn through these four data points, but *only one line* best fits the data in this sense. In other words only one line meets the least-squares criterion. Any other regression line will have a greater sum of squares than that of the best fit regression line.

For the linear regression line $\hat{Y} = a + bX$, a is the vertical intercept on the Y axis and b is the slope of the line. We use $\hat{Y}$ to represent the values of Y that the

[1] Another criterion is minimization of the sum of the absolute differences. For a comparison of "least absolute" and "least squares," see F.R. Glahe and J.G. Hunt, "The Small Sample Properties of Simultaneous Equation Least-absolute Estimators vis-à-vis Least-squares Estimators," *Econometrica* **38** (September 1970), 742–53.

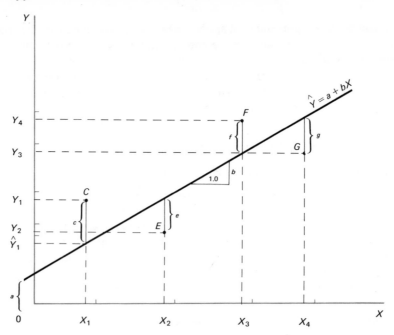

FIGURE A-3   *The Method of Least Squares*

regression equation associates with any particular value of X. For example, if we calculate $\hat{Y}$ when $X = X_1$, then the resulting value of Y is $\hat{Y}_1$, as shown in Figure A-3.

Now note that the deviation between Y_1 and $\hat{Y}_1$ is

$$Y_1 - \hat{Y}_1 = c$$

and that the square of this deviation is

$$(Y_1 - \hat{Y}_1)^2 = c^2$$

Thus the sum of squared deviations can be expressed alternatively as

$$\sum_{i=1}^{n} (Y_i - \hat{Y}_i)^2 = (Y_1 - \hat{Y}_1)^2 + (Y_2 - \hat{Y}_2)^2 + \cdots + (Y_n - \hat{Y}_n)^2 \qquad \text{(A-1)}$$

Derivation of Least-squares Formulas

If we let d_i represent any deviation, then the sum of squared deviations can be expressed as

$$\sum_{i=1}^{n} d_i^2 = \sum_{i=1}^{n} (Y_i - \hat{Y}_i)^2 = (Y_1 - \hat{Y}_1)^2 + (Y_2 - \hat{Y}_2)^2 + \cdots + (Y_n - \hat{Y}_n)^2$$

$$= \sum_{i=1}^{n} (Y_i - a - bX_i)^2 \qquad \text{(A-2)}$$

A necessary condition for minimization of the sum of squared deviations is that the partial derivatives of equation (A-2) with respect to a and b must both be zero. Setting the partial derivative of equation (A-2) with respect to a equal to zero gives us

$$\frac{\partial}{\partial a} \sum_{i=1}^{n} d_i^2 = -2 \sum_{i=1}^{n} (Y_i - a - bX_i) = 0 \qquad \text{(A-3)}$$

Then setting the partial derivative of equation (A-2) with respect to b equal to zero, we obtain

$$\frac{\partial}{\partial b} \sum_{i=1}^{n} d_i^2 = -2 \sum_{i=1}^{n} X_i(Y_i - a - bX_i) = 0 \qquad \text{(A-4)}$$

Now solving equation (A-3) for $\sum_{i=1}^{n} Y_i$, and equation (A-4) for $\sum_{i=1}^{n} X_i Y_i$, we obtain the so-called *normal equations*

$$\sum_{i=1}^{n} Y_i = na + b \sum_{i=1}^{n} X_i \qquad \text{(A-5)}$$

$$\sum_{i=1}^{n} X_i Y_i = a \sum_{i=1}^{n} X_i + b \sum_{i=1}^{n} X_i^2 \qquad \text{(A-6)}$$

Then multiplying (A-5) by $\sum_{i=1}^{n} X_i$ and (A-6) by n gives us

$$\sum_{i=1}^{n} X_i \sum_{i=1}^{n} Y_i = na \sum_{i=1}^{n} X_i + b\left(\sum_{i=1}^{n} X_i\right)^2 \qquad \text{(A-7)}$$

$$n \sum_{i=1}^{n} X_i Y_i = na \sum_{i=1}^{n} X_i + nb \sum_{i=1}^{n} X_i^2 \qquad \text{(A-8)}$$

and subtracting equation (A-8) from equation (A-7) and solving for b gives us

$$b = \frac{n \sum_{i=1}^{n} X_i Y_i - \sum_{i=1}^{n} X_i \sum_{i=1}^{n} Y_i}{n \sum_{i=1}^{n} X_i^2 - \left(\sum_{i=1}^{n} X_i\right)^2} \qquad \text{(A-9)}$$

Now substituting equation (A-9) for b in either equation (A-7) or (A-8), we obtain

$$a = \frac{\sum_{i=1}^{n} X_i^2 \sum_{i=1}^{n} Y_i^2 - \sum_{i=1}^{n} X_i \sum_{i=1}^{n} X_i Y_i}{n \sum_{i=1}^{n} X_i^2 - \left(\sum_{i=1}^{n} X_i\right)^2} \qquad \text{(A-10)}$$

A less unwieldy set of computational equations, easily derived from equations (A-9) and (A-10), is

$$b = \frac{\sum_{i=1}^{n} x_i y_i}{\sum_{i=1}^{n} x_i^2}$$

(A-11)

$$a = \bar{Y} - b\bar{X}$$

(A-12)

where $\bar{X} = (1/n) \sum_{i=1}^{n} X_i$
$\bar{Y} = (1/n) \sum_{i=1}^{n} Y_i$
$x_i = X_i - \bar{X}_i$
$y_i = Y_i - \bar{Y}_i$

In addition to providing us with a simple formula for the computation of a, equation (A-12) also shows that the regression line must pass through the average values of the dependent and independent variables $\bar{X}$ and $\bar{Y}$.

For a numerical example using the computational forms of equations (A-11) and (A-12), we compute the regression line

$$\hat{C} = a + bY_d$$

(A-13)

using the data from Table A-2. The detailed computations are given in Table A-3. In this problem C_i is equivalent to Y_i and Y_{d_i} is equivalent to X_i in the preceding derivations.

From Table A-3 we can see that

$$\bar{X} = 289.6$$

$$\bar{Y} = 265.0$$

$$\sum_{i=1}^{n} x_i^2 = 7,631.3$$

$$\sum_{i=1}^{n} x_i y_i = 7,030.3$$

Then using the formulas we have derived, we obtain

$$b = \frac{\sum_{i=1}^{n} x_i y_i}{\sum_{i=1}^{n} x_i^2} = \frac{7,030.3}{7,631.3} = 0.9212$$

and

$$a = \bar{Y} - b\bar{X} = 265.0 - (0.9212)(289.6)$$

$$= -1.8$$

Therefore

$$\hat{C} = -1.8 + 0.9212 Y_d$$

(A-14)

TABLE A-3   Computation of $\hat{C} = a + bY_d$ Using Data from Table A-2

$X_i = Y_{d_i}$	x_i	x_i^2	$Y_i = C_i$	y_i	Y_i^2	$x_i y_i$
249.6	− 40.0	1,600.0	230.5	− 34.5	1,190.3	1,380.0
255.7	− 33.9	1,149.2	232.8	− 32.2	1,036.8	1,091.6
263.3	− 26.3	691.7	239.4	− 25.6	655.4	665.4
275.4	− 14.2	201.6	250.8	− 14.2	201.6	201.6
278.3	− 11.3	127.7	255.7	− 9.3	86.5	105.1
296.7	7.1	50.4	274.2	9.2	84.6	65.3
309.3	19.7	388.1	281.4	16.4	269.0	323.1
315.8	26.2	686.4	288.2	23.2	538.2	607.8
318.8	29.2	852.6	290.1	25.1	630.0	732.9
333.0	43.4	1,883.6	307.3	42.8	1,831.8	1,857.5

$$\Sigma x_i^2 = 7{,}631.3$$

$$\Sigma X = 2{,}895.9$$

$$\Sigma y_i^2 = 6{,}524.2$$

$$\bar{X} = 289.6$$

$$\Sigma x_i y_i = 7{,}030.3$$

$$\Sigma Y = 2{,}650.4$$

$$\bar{Y} = 265.0$$

$$a = \bar{Y} - b\bar{X} = 265.0 - (0.9212)289.6$$

$$\Sigma x_i^2 \, \Sigma y_i^2 = 49{,}788{,}127.5$$

$$= 265.0 - 266.8 = -1.8$$

$$(\Sigma x_i y_i)^2 = 49{,}425{,}118.1$$

$$b = \frac{\Sigma x_i y_i}{\Sigma x_i^2} = \frac{7{,}030.3}{7{,}631.3} = 0.9212$$

$$R^2 = \frac{(\Sigma x_i y_i)^2}{\Sigma x_i^2 \, \Sigma y_i^2} = \frac{49{,}425{,}118.1}{49{,}788{,}127.5}$$

$$= 0.9927$$

This is the regression line drawn earlier in Figure A-2.

The Correlation Coefficient

Lastly, we must establish a technique for measuring the *strength* of the relationship specified by the regression line. To do this, we use what we call the *correlation coefficient.*

In Figure A-4 the XY quadrant is divided by $\bar{X}$ and $\bar{Y}$ into four quadrants. The coordinates of the modified data points, x_i, y_i, are either positive or negative values in each quadrant, as specified in Figure A-4. In quadrant I the product $x_i y_i$ will be positive; in quadrant II it will be negative; in quadrant III, positive; and in quadrant IV, negative.

If most of the points lie in quadrants I and III (as they do in Figure A-4), then the quantity $\sum_{i=1}^{n} x_i y_i$ will be positive, indicating that the association or *correlation* between X and Y is positive. If most of the points lie in quadrants II and IV, then $\sum_{i=1}^{n} x_i y_i$ will be negative, indicating negative correlation. If there is no relationship

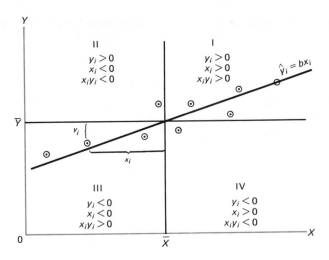

FIGURE A-4   *The Correlation Coefficient*

between X and Y, then the points will be evenly distributed throughout all four quadrants and $\sum_{i=1}^{n} x_i y_i \cong 0$, indicating zero correlation.

Using $\sum_{i=1}^{n} x_i y_i$ as a measure of correlation presents one problem: we can make this quantity arbitrarily large (or small), as we please, either by increasing the sample size or by changing the scale of the units with which we measure the two variables. For example, if we increase our sample size from 50 to 100 observations, then $\sum_{i=1}^{n} x_i y_i$ will become larger. Let us further suppose that we are trying to correlate the length of a person's arm with his or her height. If we originally record both of these measurements in units of feet and then change our measurements to units of inches, then $\sum_{i=1}^{n} x_i y_i$ will increase. This problem is eliminated if we define the correlation coefficient R_{xy} as

$$R_{xy} = \frac{\sum_{i=1}^{n} x_i y_i}{\sqrt{\sum_{i=1}^{n} x_i^2} \sqrt{\sum_{i=1}^{n} y_i^2}} \tag{A-15}$$

where $-1.0 \leq R_{xy} \leq 1.0$

For our purposes here, it is more useful to use the *square* of the correlation coefficient, called the *coefficient of determination*. Squaring equation (A-15) gives us

$$R_{xy}^2 = \frac{\left(\sum_{i=1}^{n} x_i y_i\right)^2}{\sum_{i=1}^{n} x_i^2 \sum_{i=1}^{n} y_i^2} \tag{A-16}$$

where $0 \leq R_{xy}^2 \leq 1.0$

The coefficient of determination is an extremely useful analytical tool in that it measures the fraction of the variation in the dependent variable Y that is explained by the variation in the independent variable X. For example, if $R_{xy} = \pm 1.0$, then $R_{xy}^2 = 1.0$. This indicates that 100% of the movement in Y can be explained by the movement in X, so that if we know the value of X, then we can predict the value of Y with certainty. If $R_{xy} = 0$, then $R_{xy}^2 = 0$, and we can conclude that movements in X tell us absolutely nothing about movements in Y; thus knowing the value of X is of no help in predicting the value of Y.

In actual regression analysis we seldom, if ever, obtain a coefficient of determination that is equal to zero or unity. Instead, our computed values of R_{xy}^2 lie between these two extremes. When R_{xy}^2 is quite low (say, in the neighborhood of 0.01–0.20), we have little confidence that knowledge of the independent variable will be helpful in predicting the dependent variable. When R_{xy}^2 is high (say, in the neighborhood of 0.80–0.99), we can be confident that knowledge of X will allow us to predict Y accurately. As R_{xy}^2 approaches 1.0, our confidence increases.

A high correlation between two variables does not necessarily mean that movement in one variable *causes* the movement observed in the other variable. For example, both variables could be responding to a third variable. However, if one variable is the primary causal factor in determining the value of the other variable, then a high correlation *must* be observed. For example, a *high* correlation between income and consumption would *not* prove causality, but a *low* correlation would prove *lack* of causality. In other words, a high correlation between two variables is a necessary, but insufficient, condition to prove causality. Hence we can use regression analysis to reject theories, but not to prove them.

Returning to our numerical example we have

$$R_{xy}^2 = \frac{\left(\sum_{i=1}^{n} x_i y_i \right)^2}{\sum_{i=1}^{n} x_i^2 \sum_{i=1}^{n} y_i^2} = \frac{49,425,118.1}{49,788,127.5} = 0.9927$$

This equation tells us that 99.27% of the variation in aggregate consumption is explained by the variation in disposable income when the relationship is assumed to be linear. This relationship does not prove that rising income causes rising consumption, but it would support this hypothesis vs. the alternative hypothesis that no relationship exists between income and consumption.

Appendix B The Concept of Slope and Its Application to Graphic Analysis

B-1 Slope at a Point on a Straight Line

The *slope of a straight line* is defined as the tangent of the angle formed by the line and the horizontal measured counterclockwise from the horizontal. For example, the slope of line *aa* at point *C* in Figure B-1 is the tangent of the angle θ. At any other point on line *aa* (say, point *D*), the angle ω must be equal to θ. Therefore, the slope at any point on a straight line must be a constant.

If a straight line slopes upward to the right, as line *aa* does, we say that the line has *positive slope*, because any tangent will have a positive value. The slope at any point on line *bb* in Figure B-2 is, by definition, equal to the tangent of the angle α. Because the angle α is greater than 90°, we cannot easily measure the slope of *bb* directly. However, we do know from trigonometry that $\tan \alpha = -\tan \beta$, where the

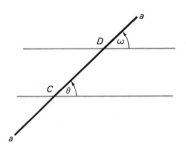

FIGURE B-1

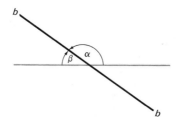

FIGURE B-2

angle β is measured clockwise from the horizontal. It necessarily follows from the definition of slope that the slope at any point on line *bb* is equal to $-\tan \beta$ and has a negative value. Because the slope at any point on a line that slopes downward to the right will also have a negative value, we say that lines with this property have *negative slope*.

B-2   Slope at a Point on a Curved Line

The *slope* at a point *on a curved line* is defined as the tangent of the angle formed with the horizontal by a straight line drawn tangent to the curve at that point.[1] This is illustrated in Figure B-3, where we are concerned with the slope of curve *cc* at point *X*. The slope at point *X* is determined by drawing a straight line tangent to curve *cc* at point *X* and then measuring the tangent of the angle thus formed with the horizontal. In this example, the slope at point *X* will be equal to the tangent of the angle θ. Because the numerical value of $\tan \theta$ will be greater than zero, Figure B-3 illustrates a case of positive slope. Figure B-4, on the other hand, illustrates a case of negative slope because the slope at point *Y* on curve *dd* will have a negative value.

Our use of the concept of slope will be primarily qualitative rather than quantitative. It is common practice to treat the slopes at various points on a curve in absolute, rather than algebraic, terms, because we can easily associate the steepness of the tangent with qualitative differences in absolute slope. For exam-

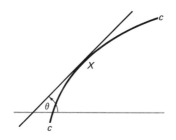

FIGURE B-3

[1] Note that the word "tangent" has two meanings in this sentence.

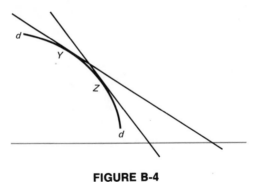

FIGURE B-4

ple, we may say that the absolute value of the slope at point Z in Figure B-4 is greater than the absolute value of the slope at point Y; this is a *qualitative* statement. On the other hand, if we say that the absolute value of the slope at point Z is 2.0 and the absolute value of the slope at point Y is 1.5, then this is a *quantitative* statement.

B-3 Economic Applications

Let us suppose that a behavioral relationship between consumption C and disposable income Y_d is graphed as a straight line in Figure B-5. The equation of this line can be generally expressed as

$$C = a + bY_d \qquad\qquad \text{(B-1)}$$

If $Y_d = 0$, then $C = a$, and the graph of the consumption function in Figure B-5 intersects the vertical axis at $C = a$. For this reason a is usually referred to as the *vertical intercept*. For any marginal change in disposable income ΔY_d, the marginal change in consumption ΔC will clearly be $b\Delta Y_d$. For this reason b is called the *marginal propensity to consume* MPC. If $\Delta Y_d = 1.0$ in equation (B-1), then $\Delta C = b\Delta Y_d = b(1.0) = b$, as shown in Figure B-5. Because the slope of the con-

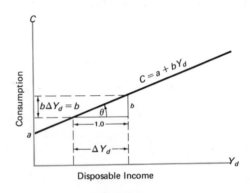

Disposable Income

FIGURE B-5

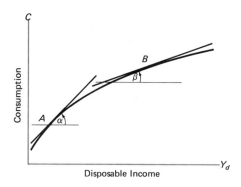

FIGURE B-6

sumption function is equal to the tangent of the angle θ and $\tan \theta = b \div 1.0 = b$, it is obvious that the marginal propensity to consume is equal to the slope of the consumption function.

If the consumption function is nonlinear, as it is in Figure B-6, then the marginal propensity to consume will not be a constant but will vary, because the slope of the consumption function will decrease as disposable income increases. For example, the MPC at point A is equal to $\tan \alpha$, which is greater than $\tan \beta$, the MPC at point B.

B-4 The Relationship Between Slope and Differential Calculus

If we have a curved line such as *bb* in Figure B-7, then we say that a *functional relationship* exists between X and Y; that is, for any value of X between X_0 and X_1, there is a corresponding and unique value of Y. We usually say that Y *is a function of X*. Often we do not know the exact relationship between X and Y (this is the case

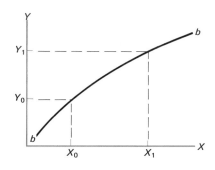

FIGURE B-7

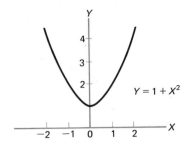

FIGURE B-8

in Figure B-7), and we signify that a functional relationship exists by using the symbolic notation

$$Y = f(X) \quad \text{or} \quad Y = Y(X) \tag{B-2}$$

read "Y is a function of X."

When the functional relationship is known exactly, it can be stated in the form of an equation. For example, the function described by the equation

$$Y = 1 + X^2 \tag{B-3}$$

is graphed in Figure B-8.

Differential calculus permits us to compute the rate of change of Y per unit change in X. For example, if our function were the straight line *aa* in Figure B-9 and we wanted to know the rate of change in Y per unit change in X when X has the value X_1, differential calculus would supply us with the answer. But this is exactly equivalent to wanting to know the slope of the line at point S when X has the value X_1 and the corresponding point on the line *aa* is S. The slope of the line at point S is the rate of change in Y per unit change in X. Thus differential calculus is simply a technique that allows us to compute the slope of the function at point S.

We can express the rate of change in Y per unit change in X symbolically. Let ΔX represent a small change in X and ΔY a small change in Y; our convention is that

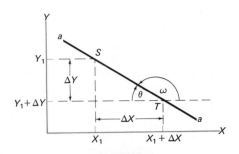

FIGURE B-9

small additions have positive values and small subtractions have negative values. If we increase X_1 by ΔX in Figure B-9, then we will be at a new value of $X = X_1 + \Delta X$. The new value of Y corresponding to $X_1 + \Delta X$ is $Y_1 + \Delta Y$, where ΔY has a negative value according to our convention. The rate of change in Y per unit change in X is expressed algebraically as $\Delta Y/\Delta X$, and since $\Delta X > 0$ and $\Delta Y < 0$, this ratio will be less than zero. By definition, this ratio is

$$\frac{\Delta Y}{\Delta X} = \tan \omega = -\tan \theta \qquad \text{(B-4)}$$

As we have already demonstrated, this is the slope of the line aa at point S as well as at any other point on the line aa, because aa is a straight line.

In differential calculus instead of considering small changes in X and Y about the point (X, Y), we consider the limit of $\Delta Y/\Delta X$ as $\Delta X \to 0$. To signify this limit, we refer to the change in X as dX, instead of ΔX, and to the resulting change in Y as dY, instead of ΔY. Thus in differential calculus the rate of change, or slope, at a point on either a straight line or a curve is represented symbolically as

$$\frac{dY}{dX} \qquad \text{(B-5)}$$

This is referred to as the *derivative of the function.* Of course, the use of the letters X and Y is simply a generalization. For the specific function illustrated in Figure B-6, for example, we would express the slope of the function at any point as

$$\frac{dC}{dY_d} \qquad \text{(B-6)}$$

From our earlier discussion it follows that because the slope of a straight line is the same at any point on the line, the derivative of a linear function is a constant. However, the slope of a curved line continually varies, so that its derivative cannot be a constant but must be some function of the independent variable.

The general form of the equation for a straight line is

$$y = a + bx \qquad \text{(B-7)}$$

where $a = $ the vertical intercept
$b = $ the slope of the line

If b is positive, then the line slopes upward to the right (positive slope); if b is negative, then the line slopes downward to the right (negative slope). This is illustrated in Figure B-10 for the case where $b > 0$ and $a < 0$. As previously stated, b is referred to as the slope of the line, because

$$\frac{b}{1.0} = b = \tan \theta \qquad \text{(B-8)}$$

Moreover, and more importantly, because we are considering a straight line

$$b = \frac{\Delta Y}{\Delta X} = \frac{dY}{dX} \qquad \text{(B-9)}$$

so b is the derivative of the function.

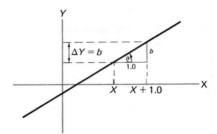

FIGURE B-10

Now we can determine the derivative of any linear function. For example, if

$$Y = 10 - 0.5X \tag{B-10}$$

then

$$\frac{dY}{dX} = -0.5 \tag{B-11}$$

In calculus you compute the derivatives of many different functions. For example, the derivative of the function

$$Y = 1 + X^2 \tag{B-12}$$

which is illustrated in Figure B-8, is

$$\frac{dY}{dX} = 2X \tag{B-13}$$

This substantiates our earlier statement that the derivative of a curved line cannot be a constant but must be a function of the independent variable. When X is 1.0, the slope of the curve at the point corresponding to this value of X is

$$\frac{dY}{dX} = \tan \theta = 2(1.0) = 2.0 \tag{B-14}$$

as shown in Figure B-11.

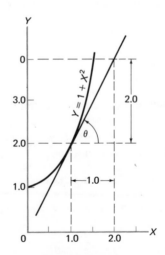

FIGURE B-11

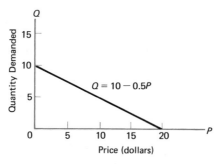

FIGURE B-12

B-5 Economic Application of the Derivative

Suppose that the demand function for some commodity is specified by the equation

$$Q = 10 - 0.5P \tag{B-15}$$

where Q = quantity demanded
      P = price in dollars

Equation (B-15) is graphed in Figure B-12.

Now suppose that we wish to compute the price elasticity of demand at various prices, ranging from $P = 0$ to $P = \$20$.

We already know from principles of economics that the formula for the arc price elasticity of demand is

$$\eta_{arc} = \frac{(\Delta Q/Q)}{(\Delta P/P)} = \frac{\% \text{ change in quantity}}{\% \text{ change in price}} \tag{B-16}$$

or equivalently

$$\eta_{arc} = \frac{P}{Q} \cdot \frac{\Delta Q}{\Delta P} \tag{B-17}$$

If we wish to know the elasticity of a given price, rather than a range of prices, the arc elasticity formula is insufficient, and we must use the formula for the point price elasticity of demand. To obtain the point elasticity, we simply substitute the derivative of the function, dQ/dP, for $\Delta Q/\Delta P$ to obtain

$$\eta_{pt} = \frac{P}{Q} \cdot \frac{dQ}{dP} \tag{B-18}$$

From the example given in equation (B-15), we know that

$$\frac{dQ}{dP} = -0.5 \tag{B-19}$$

Substituting equation (B-19) into equation (B-18), we obtain

$$\eta_{pt} = -0.5\frac{P}{Q} \tag{B-20}$$

Given equation (B-20), we can now calculate the price elasticity of demand at any point on the curve.

If $P = 0$, then $Q = 10$, so that

$$\eta_{pt} = -0.5\frac{0}{10} = 0 \tag{B-21}$$

An elasticity of zero corresponds to the condition called *perfect inelasticity.*

On the other hand, if $P = \$20$, then $Q = 0$, so that

$$\eta_{pt} = -0.5\frac{20}{0} \tag{B-22}$$

This case is not defined, because division by zero is not allowed. However, we can say what will happen to η_{pt} in the limit as P approaches $20. Mathematically, this can be stated

$$\lim_{P \to 20} \eta_{pt} = -\infty \tag{B-23}$$

which is read "the limit of η_{pt} as P approaches $20 is minus infinity." When the price elasticity of demand is infinite, the demand function is said to be *perfectly elastic.* For any value of price between these two limits of zero and $20, in our example, the point price elasticity of demand will lie between zero and minus infinity.

Now note that Figure B-12 is not drawn according to the usual economic practice, showing price on the vertical axis and quantity on the horizontal axis. We broke this precedent so that the slope of the demand curve would be equal to dQ/dP. Now suppose that our demand curve, drawn in the conventional manner in Figure B-13, is perfectly horizontal. If we reversed the axes, then the curve would become perfectly vertical, and in the limit as a demand curve drawn in this fashion approaches the vertical, its slope dQ/dP approaches infinity. Hence the price elasticity of the demand curve shown in Figure B-13 is infinitely elastic, or as we say, *perfectly elastic.* If the demand curve in Figure B-13 were vertical rather than horizontal ($dQ/dP = 0$), then the elasticity of demand would be zero and the demand curve would be *perfectly inelastic.* These concepts and their graphic representations appear throughout this book.

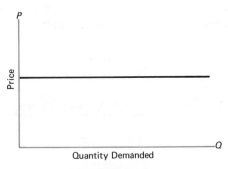

FIGURE B-13

Index